Company Law in China

To Liling and Yuguo

Company Law in China

Regulation of Business Organizations in a Socialist Market Economy

Jiang Yu Wang

Associate Professor, Faculty of Law, National University of Singapore

Edward Elgar

Cheltenham, UK • Northampton, MA, USA

Published by
Edward Elgar Publishing Limited
The Lypiatts
15 Lansdown Road
Cheltenham
Glos GL50 2JA
UK

Edward Elgar Publishing, Inc.
William Pratt House
9 Dewey Court
Northampton
Massachusetts 01060
USA

A catalogue record for this book
is available from the British Library

Library of Congress Control Number: 2013957759

This book is available electronically in the ElgarOnline.com Law Subject Collection, E-ISBN 978 1 84980 573 5

FSC www.fsc.org MIX Paper from responsible sources FSC® C013056

ISBN 978 1 84980 572 8 (cased)

Typeset by Columns Design XML Ltd, Reading
Printed and bound in Great Britain by T.J. International Ltd, Padstow

Contents

Foreword

Tan Cheng Han

With the rise of China as a major economic power, this book is a welcome addition to the scholarly literature on Chinese law as the corporation is the dominant business vehicle in China. Though China is a socialist state, it is one that is heavily leavened with commercial sensibilities and China has therefore seen fit to allow companies to be incorporated through registration under a national law relating to companies, the present law being the 2005 Company Law. The dominance of the corporate vehicle as a business enterprise is a far cry from the early decades of the People's Republic of China when the corporation did not exist. Instead, all economic activities in China were then held by the state or collectives as part of the country's planned economy. This changed after the reforms of the former paramount leader of China, the late Mr Deng Xiaoping. Given that corporations are now an integral part of a dynamic Chinese economy, the manner in which the corporate vehicle is regulated and/or facilitated will have an impact on the evolution of China's socialist market economy, and in turn, the world economy. In particular, there is a need for the law to continue to emphasize issues of governance, as well as minority shareholder and creditor protection.

As the corporation is the most widely used business organization worldwide, it is not surprising that there are many aspects of Chinese Company Law that will be readily recognizable to corporate scholars and practitioners outside China. Thus Chinese Company Law recognizes the separate personality of the company and from this the limited liability of shareholders. It also recognizes that there will be occasions where the corporate veil should be pierced, notably when a shareholder abuses his or her rights to harm the interests of the company or those of other shareholders. The *ultra vires* doctrine is also a part of Chinese Company Law even as many developed economies have retreated from this. It is also noteworthy that aspects of company law recognized by other jurisdictions but not explicitly a part of China's Company Law, such as the 'business judgment rule', are considered by many Chinese academics and jurists to be part of Chinese Law. Yet because of China's position as a socialist state, there are provisions in its Company Law that are unusual such as Article 5, which states inter alia that a company must 'observe social morals and commercial ethics, act in an honest and trustworthy manner, subject itself to the supervision of the government and the public and assume social responsibility'. It is somewhat unclear how every aspect of such a statutory obligation will or can be meaningfully enforced.

An issue of interest is the extent to which Chinese corporate law sufficiently protects minority shareholders and creditors against rent-seeking behaviour by corporate controllers. In particular, there is the problem of the dominance of state-owned enterprises in the context of a lack of independence on the part of the judiciary in China together with perceptions of widespread corruption. To this end it is not surprising that Professor Wang devotes a substantial part of the book to such issues. He points out, for instance, that unlike the fairly clear distinction between ownership and management in companies incorporated in common law jurisdictions, such a distinction is blurred in China. This is because the general meeting is in charge of determining the company's business and investment plans while the board has the power to decide on the company's business operation plans and investment proposals. It is not clear what the line is between the two.

While some may welcome the existence of stronger shareholder rights in this context, the explanation by Professor Wang is less positive. He submits that the purpose behind these powers is to favour the majority shareholder, which, in the Chinese context, is often the state. As the powers of the general meeting can only be exercised collectively through voting by the shareholders, this means that the state as the largest shareholder in the SOEs is given some key decisional powers that can potentially undermine the independence of the board so as to prevent the latter from making decisions that are not in the interests of the state. Accordingly, the general meeting's possession of such comprehensive powers does not necessarily entail better protection of the minority shareholders. In fact, the interests of minority shareholders are often overlooked in such a system.

This book provides a comprehensive account of Chinese Company Law that will be useful to all those with an interest in this area. Not only is the treatment of the doctrinal aspects of the law impressive, Professor Wang has injected into the book many of the policy issues and other realities that underlie the law, something that non-native observers will sometimes find difficult. For example, he points out that there is a large gap in the public expectation of independent directors and the performance of such directors (though this is not unknown in many other countries as well). The main problems are the manner in which independent directors are nominated and the 'guanxi' based cultural environment of 'giving face' and not wanting to undermine personal relationships.

With this work, Professor Wang has made a valuable contribution to Company Law scholarship. His work will undoubtedly be useful to practitioners in and outside China who require an understanding of Chinese corporate law. It also deserves careful study by the academic community as it contains valuable insights not only about Chinese corporate law but also on the malleable nature of corporate law as it takes root in a socialist market economy. I welcome this learned work and commend it to all who are interested in this area.

Professor and Chairman
Centre for Law and Business, Faculty of Law,
National University of Singapore

Preface and acknowledgements

This book is based on the materials for a course called 'Chinese Corporate and Securities Law', which I started to teach at the Faculty of Law of the National University of Singapore in 2005. The materials were also used for the courses 'Chinese Company Law' and 'Chinese Securities Regulation', which I offered at the Chinese University of Hong Kong from 2006 to 2009. It was always a challenge to teach Chinese law, in English, to international students. Very soon, both my students and I figured out the need to have a text, in English, that not only offers a critical introduction to the fundamental principles and rules of China's corporate law regime, but also put the rules in the contexts of China's own legal, political, and economic systems. With this aim, I started to write this book in 2008, and finally completed it in November 2013. Most chapters of this book have already been used in my teaching, and I have been tremendously encouraged by the positive and constructive feedback from my students over the years. Indeed, my students have always been the major driving force behind the writing of this book.

This work would not have been possible without the generous support and encouragement of a lot of academic friends and institutions. Professor Tan Cheng Han, an internationally distinguished corporate law scholar who was also the former Dean of the Faculty of Law of the National University of Singapore, must be mentioned first as he was the person who strongly encouraged me to continue when I almost decided to give up this project in the belief that there was no international market for such a book. Professor David C. Donald of the Faculty of Law of the Chinese University of Hong Kong read most of the chapters of the book and provided invaluable comments that significantly improved both the language and analyses in this work.

I have also benefited from the collegial environments of the Faculties of Law of the National University of Singapore, the University of Hong Kong, the Chinese University of Hong Kong, and Tsinghua University. Especially, as the book has evolved over more than six years, I have benefited from discussions with many colleagues, including, among others, Ling Bing, Xi Chao, Zhang Xianchu, Yu Guanghua, Huang Hui, Lu Haitian, Zhu Ciyun, Shi Tiantao, Liu Junhai, Randall Peerenboom,

Jacques deLisle, James Li Zhaojie, Lim Chin Leng, Leng Jing, Guo Li, Peng Bing, Meng Fanpeng, Zhang Yihong, Tan Fugui, Bryan Mercurio, Lu Xiaojie, Julia Qin Ya, Chen Jianfu, Zheng Yongnian, M. Sornarajah, Tan Cheng Han, Tjio Hans, Lan Luh Luh, Alexander Loke, Victor Ramraj, Wee Meng Seng, Dan W. Puchniak, Chen Weitseng, and Umakanth Varottil.

Finally, I am grateful for the financial support from a research grant in Singapore, the Academic Research Fund (R-241-000-086-112), provided through the Faculty of Law of the National University of Singapore, which made it possible for me to hire research assistants and travel to different places of the world to present several chapters of the book.

Abbreviations

AIC	Administration of Industry and Commerce
AML	Anti-Monopoly Law
CJV	Contractual joint venture; cooperative joint venture
COE	Collectively-owned enterprise
CSRC	China Securities Regulatory Commission
EJV	Equity joint venture
FDI	Foreign direct investment
FIE	Foreign-invested enterprise
FSC	Farmers' special cooperative
GP	General partnership
GPCL	General Principles of Civil Law of the People's Republic of China
JSLC	Joint-stock limited company
LLC	Limited liability company
LP	Limited partnership
M&A	Mergers and acquisitions
MOFCOM	Ministry of Commerce
NDRC	National Development and Reform Commission
NPC	National People's Congress
OECD	Organisation for Economic Co-operation and Development
PEL	Partnership Enterprise Law
PRC	People's Republic of China (China)
SAIC	State Administration of Industry and Commerce
SASAC	State-owned Assets Supervision and Administration Commission
SGP	Special General Partnership
SOE	State-owned enterprise

SPC	Supreme People's Court
SSE	Shanghai Stock Exchange
SZSE	Shenzhen Stock Exchange
WFOE	Wholly foreign-owned enterprises
WSOC	Wholly state-owned companies

1. Overview of the company law regime in China

1.1 WHY STUDY CHINESE COMPANY LAW?

The development of company law in China is increasingly catching the eye of international investors, practitioners, and academics and government officials who are China observers. The study of Chinese company law is moving towards the forefront of international scrutiny for a number of reasons. First, companies (or 'corporations')[1] are the dominant players in China's rapidly growing economy. Business entities with the nature of modern companies did not exist in China during the first few decades of the Peoples' Republic ('PRC'), as it then practiced a planned economy in which all economic entities were run directly either by the state or collectives.[2] However, after years of economic reform, the company limited by shares is now the dominant form of business organization. According to official statistics, by the first half of 2005, there were about 1.2 million enterprises in the People's Republic of China ('China' or the 'PRC')[3] registered in the form of companies legally established under the national Company Law.[4] Companies are overwhelmingly predominant in China's major economic sectors. The enterprise companies, themselves a result of an economic revolution that is

---

[1] 'Company' and 'corporation' are used interchangeably in this book. Company law, when referring not specifically to the national Company Law, is also used interchangeably with corporate law.

[2] Naughton (2007) (noting in the command economic system in China between 1949 and 1978 the government owned all large factories and other enterprises, and, in rural areas, agricultural collectives owned farming lands). It should, however, be pointed out that Western-style companies existed in the first decade of the PRC until they were all eliminated by 1957. See Dong (2001), pp. 174–97.

[3] Depending on the context, China is also frequently used to refer to the pre-PRC Chinese nation in this book.

[4] An Jian (2005), p. 1. The currently enforceable company law in China is the Company Law of the People's Republic of China amended in 2005 (hereinafter the PRC Company Law, or Company Law 2005, or the 'new

ongoing in China, are making the most significant contribution to the dynamism of the Chinese economy. It is not exaggerated to say that the fate of enterprise reform will determine the future of the Chinese economy, namely whether China will successfully complete its transformation from a planned to a market-based economy, and in this process, improve the long-term competitiveness of its industries. In this cause, China's companies and securities laws will play the central role of defining enterprises as legally independent and responsible market participants, encouraging corporatization of state-owned enterprises, and providing a national legal basis for the establishment, governance, and transaction activities of business enterprises registered as companies.[5]

Chinese company law finds further importance through its expanding coverage of foreign-invested enterprises (FIEs). As discussed in more detail in section 1.3 below, China is phasing out its dualist regime, which subjected domestic business organizations and FIEs to different regulatory frameworks. Subject to certain exceptions, FIEs are now governed by the Company Law under the doctrine of general law–special law relationship, which connotes that the FIE laws, as long as they concern registered companies, are special laws in relation to the Company Law. Indeed, the Organisation for Economic Co-operation and Development (OECD) has suggested that, '[t]he Chinese government may wish to consider a possible evolution towards the integration of FDI law into domestic company law so that FIEs are eventually treated on a par with domestic enterprises'.[6]

As Chinese companies are rapidly expanding overseas and seeking listing in foreign stock exchanges, even those persons who have never set foot in China could be affected by (the positive and negative aspects of) Chinese company law if they purchase shares of a Chinese company. Thus, the Vice Chairman of the U.S.–China Economic and Security Review Commission (USCC) remarked, quite negatively, about the impact of Chinese companies going overseas:

Company Law'). The evolution of the PRC Company Law will be discussed in later sections.

[5] See e.g. OECD (2000), p. 433 (stating 'The current Company Law [1993] constitutes the legal basis for the drive to establish SOEs as separate legal entities through corporatisation. For China, corporatisation was a continuation of past gradual reforms and a new means to increase SOE autonomy while maintaining oversight by the State. The assumption is that corporatised SOEs would behave like privately-owned corporates in an advanced market economy, even though they constitute to be owned by the State'.

[6] OECD (2003), p. 59.

> The vast majority of U.S.-listed Chinese enterprises – 92 percent – are owned and operated by the Chinese state. Questionable corporate governance, accounting practices, and minority shareholder rights make this a subject of particular concern to Congress. These issues have significant implications for U.S. investors looking to purchase stock in Chinese firms, as well as financial analysts tasked with unraveling Chinese companies' complex web of relationships and finances. These facts raise questions abut the suitability of Chinese debt and equity listings in the U.S. markets, and so-called 'China funds' – mutual funds focused on investing in China securities. I am concerned that U.S. investors may not have sufficient information to make informed decisions about the risk of these investments ... [7]

From a theoretical perspective, Chinese company law is also worthy of study because it poses conceptual challenges to the conventional wisdom of corporate law; this will be further discussed in section 1.3.

1.2 A SHORT HISTORY OF CHINA'S COMPANY LAW[8]

Company Law, in the form of a national code, existed before the People's Republic of China was established. The Qing Dynasty enacted China's first Company Law (*Gongsilü*) in 1904. As noted by commentators, '[t]he 1904 Company Law, which drew broadly upon both English and Japanese company law models, established a number of different types of companies, created them as juristic persons and introduced the idea of the limited liability company limited by shares'.[9] Enacted in the wake of the Dynasty's demise, the law was barely implemented when,[10] seven years later, the Qing monarchy was abolished.

---

[7] USCC (2004), p. 8 (Prepared Statement of Vice Chairman C. Richard D'Amato).

[8] This section presents a very brief, summarized history of China's corporate law. It is not intended to provide a complete analysis of this historical development, and must completely neglect the interesting social and human factors that this development entailed. A more detailed explanation will be offered in later chapters of this book as opportunity and need for discussion of the historical background of corporate law arises.

[9] Tomasic and Fu (1999), p. 136. See also Kirby (1995), pp. 47–8 (noting that this Company Law ran up to 131 articles and established four types of companies, with its central contribution lying in introducing 'the company limited by shares, wherein the liability of shareholders and directors was limited to the value of their shares').

[10] Kirby (1995, p. 48) observes that there were 227 companies registered in 1908, but only 22 of them were of significance size.

In the Republican period, several company laws were promulgated at different times. A Company Ordinance (*Gongsi Tiaoli*) replaced the 1904 Qing Company Law in 1914. As William Kirby observes, '[t]he law was much clearer than its predecessor in its basic regulations … and would serve as the foundation of future revisions of the law', although, 'as in 1904, its effect on the structure of Chinese enterprises would be small'.[11]

The Nationalist Government of the Republic of China, the first Republican Government that had more effective control of the almost dismantled country, enacted a new Company Law in 1929. Kirby (1995) notes that the law was given an instrumental task by the government to serve as 'one vehicle in promoting state ascendancy over all private enterprise, Chinese and foreign'.[12] This was, however, in line with the policy and spirit of that government: an important principle of the government's national development policy framework, originally crafted by the new republic's 'State Father' (*Guofu*), Dr. Sun Yat-Sen, was one of 'restricting private capital' (*jiezhi ziben*) and promoting state control of the economy. For example, the law significantly suppressed the power of large shareholders by limiting the voting power of any shareholder to less than one-fifth of the votes of all shares, regardless of the percentage of their ownership in the company.[13] Interestingly enough, the law does not govern state enterprises, which were left to special regulations promulgated later.[14]

The 1929 Company Law was eventually replaced by the New Company Law of 1946. The new law aimed to achieve a compromise between the Chinese government's enthusiasm to develop state capitalism and foreign corporations' desire for a Delaware-like, liberal company code.[15] The background of the revision was the total abolition of extraterritoriality enjoyed by foreign business then as a reward for China's alliance with the Allied Powers during World War II. The foreign firms, which were

---

[11] Kirby (1995), p. 49.

[12] See Kirby (1995), p. 51 (also noting 'the abolition of extraterritoriality and the regulation of private enterprises were part of a larger agenda of state-building' for the Nationalist regime).

[13] Kirby (1995), p. 52. It is interesting to note that the European Court of Justice recently chastised a German state for exactly this kind of restriction in its attempt to keep control of Volkswagen AG, so as to protect its local labor force. See *Commission of the European Communities v Federal Republic of Germany* [2007] C 112/05.

[14] Kirby (1995), p. 52. See also Fang 2002, p. 283.

[15] Kirby (1995, p. 55) notes that during the making of the 1946 law the U.S. government advised the Chinese government in vain to take Delaware as its model for company law.

then required to register in China, were not willing to operate under the very restrictive 1929 law, and sought amendment. To this end, a section for 'foreign corporations' was created in the 1946 law for the first time in China's corporate law history. As a result, foreign firms would be treated as Chinese companies once they obtained 'recognition and permission' (*renxu*) from the Chinese government.[16] Unlike the 1926 law, this law applied also to state enterprises. After losing the civil war, the Nationalist Government carried this law to Taiwan, where it remains in force today, albeit substantially revised in 1966.

After the People's Republic of China was established in 1949, one of the first decisions of the Communist Government was to abolish the Six Codes (*liufa quanshu*), which represented the legal system of the Nationalist Government.[17] Starting from 1950, new regulations were introduced to nationalize and collectivize the economy. As a result, companies, upon their nationalization, directly and immediately lost their corporate nature, becoming non-independent economic units, or *danwei*, either state- or collectively-owned.

After Chairman Mao's death in 1976, Deng Xiaoping steered the country toward pursuing economic growth rather than promoting class struggle, and this model for growth welcomed foreign investment. A Sino-foreign joint venture law was enacted in 1979 to legalize the establishment of foreign-invested limited liability companies. This law was among the first efforts of the post-Mao government to reintroduce independent business organizations with limited liability, and was followed by a series of laws on foreign investment enterprises.

On the domestic front, localities preceded the central government in making laws to create procedures for the restructuring of traditional enterprises into modern corporations. Shenzhen, one of the Special Economic Zones established in 1980 to try out capitalist policies on socialist soil, was the first local government to enact regulations for a corporatization experiment in 1986.[18] In the same year, the National People's Congress passed the General Principle of Civil Law, which since then has served the PRC as a mini 'civil code', setting forth conditions for establishing enterprises with legal personality that possess property and are able to bear civil liability independently. This 'civil

---

[16] Wen (2005), p. 125.

[17] The Six Codes originally referred to the Constitution, the Civil Code, the Commercial Code, the Civil Procedure Code, the Criminal Code, and the Criminal Procedure Code. Later, it was general usage to refer to these texts as the collective body of statutes of the Republic of China.

[18] Walter and Howie (2003), p. 91.

code' was followed by the extremely controversial 1988 Law on Industrial Enterprises owned by the Whole People (the '1988 Enterprise Law').[19] A key principle of this last law was that, at least in theory, it made all state-owned enterprises ('SOEs') 'legal persons with civil responsibility for the property left by the state to their management and with independent budgets'.[20] Obviously, limited liability re-penetrated into the Chinese legal system.

A nationally unified company law was not promulgated until 1993. However, three sets of regulations released in the prior year deserve special attention, as they laid a foundation for the national law. On 15 May 1992, the State Commission for the Restructuring of the Economic System ('SCRES'), in association with other interested central ministries, issued the Share Enterprise Trial Measures.[21] Pursuant to the Measures, the SCRES released the Standard Opinion on Companies Limited by Shares (hereinafter the 'CLS Standard Opinion')[22] and the Standard Opinion on Limited Liability Companies (hereafter the 'LLC Standard Opinion').[23] These two ministerial level decrees, soon to be replaced by a national company law, already set up the general corporate framework in China.

The most significant development in China's system of corporate law, however, remains the National People's Congress 1993 promulgation of the national Company Law (hereinafter the '1993 Company Law'), which took effect on 1 July 1994.[24] As Article 1 of that Act states, it was intended to 'meet the needs of establishing a modern enterprise system, to standardize the organization and activities of companies, to protect the legitimate rights and interests of companies, shareholders and creditors, to maintain the socio-economic order and to promote the development of the socialist market economy'. Consolidating the rules of the two standard opinions, the 1993 Company Law stipulates two types of companies, prescribes their corporate finance and corporate governance

---

19 *Quanmin Suoyouzhi Gongye Qiyefa.*

20 Walter and Howie (2003), p. 92.

21 Gufenzhi Qiye Shidian Banfa, SCRES Document No. 30 (1992).

22 Gufen Youxian Gongsi Guifan Yijian, SCRES Document No. 31 (1992). The Chinese *gufen youxian gongsi* has been translated as 'company limited by shares' or 'joint-stock company' in the English language literature on Chinese law.

23 Youxian Zeren Gongsi Guifan Yijian, SCRES Document No. 31.

24 Zhonghua Renmin Gongheguo Gongsifa, adopted at the Fifth Meeting of the Standing Committee of the Eighth National People's Congress on 29 December 1993.

structures, and articulates the responsibilities, rights, and liabilities of shareholders, directors, supervisors, and corporate managers. Although it has been subjected to strong criticism,[25] one must admit that the 1993 Company Law has, for the first time, established an effective and comprehensive corporate law framework for the PRC and facilitated the development of the Chinese securities market.

The 1993 Company Law has been revised three times since its adoption. The first two revisions occurred in December 1999 and August 2004 and touched only a very few technical aspects of the law.[26] The third revision, made by the Standing Committee of the National People's Congress on 27 October 2005, almost completely rewrote CL 1993, as only about 24 articles of the 1993 law were left untouched.[27] For this reason, the revised text is customarily referred to as the new 2005 Company Law (or the 'Company Law') rather than a revision of the 1993 Company Law, as if it is entirely new legislation. The 2005 Law brought many changes and relaxed many restrictions on business incorporation and operation in China, including a reduction of the capital requirement, increases in shareholder and creditor protection, and other improvements in corporate governance, such as an increase in information disclosed, and greater power for shareholders to file lawsuits against directors. These 2005 revisions will be discussed at length in the following chapters.

---

[25] See e.g. Howson (1997), p. 128 (noting, 'In many cases, the Company Law was privately termed a "disaster," a keen expression of conservative compromises or the wholesale avoidance of difficult issues implicit in China's transition from state ownership and the mandated allocation of capital to a "socialist market economy."').

[26] The 1999 revision changed only two articles, including one new paragraph under Article 67 requiring the installation of a supervisory board in companies 100 percent owned by the state and another paragraph added to Article 292 authorizing the government to approve a 'second board' to support advanced and high-tech companies. The 2004 revision only deleted a paragraph from Article 131 to remove the approval requirement by the securities regulatory authorities for issuance of company shares at a premium.

[27] One commentator, who was also a member of the NPC's company law revision group, remarked that he would call the 2005 revised law the 'New Company Law'. See Wang Yong (2005), p. 166.

1.3 STRUCTURE AND SCOPE OF APPLICATION OF THE COMPANY LAW, INCLUDING ITS RELATIONSHIP WITH THE FOREIGN INVESTMENT LAWS

The Company Law, comprising 13 chapters and 219 articles, does not govern all types of business organization. Rather, it provides rules only for limited liability companies ('LLCs') and joint-stock limited companies (JSLCs), also known as 'companies limited by shares'. The Law does not prohibit other business organizations authorized under other laws from being designated as 'companies' (*gongsi*). For the two types of registered companies, the Law regulates incorporation and registration, finance, transfer of equity interests, shareholder's rights, qualifications, and duties of corporate directors and officers, mergers, and acquisitions, as well as the operation of foreign corporations in China.

A first look at the business law system in China will lead to the impression that domestically-invested companies and foreign-invested enterprises (FIEs) are subject to different regulatory regimes and rules. Apparently, various laws have been created especially for FIEs, including, but not limited to, Chinese–foreign joint ventures, cooperative projects, and wholly foreign-owned enterprises. What is then the impact of the Company Law on FIEs? It depends on what interest a foreign investor is allowed to acquire in China. Today's legislative scheme offers a broad range of options:

1. equity ownership in a joint venture with limited liability;
2. equity ownership in a wholly foreign-owned limited liability company;
3. equity ownership in a foreign-invested joint-stock company;
4. partnership in a Chinese–foreign cooperative project;
5. Ownership of 'B' shares in a listed joint-stock company;
6. ownership of 'H' shares of Chinese companies traded on a foreign stock exchange;[28]
7. ownership of a holding company for all subsidiary companies in China;

---

[28] H shares originally referred to shares of PRC incorporated companies traded on the Hong Kong Stock Exchange. It is now a generic term referring to all the PRC corporate shares traded on overseas stock exchanges, including those in Hong Kong, New York, London, and Singapore.

8. equity ownership in joint venture or wholly foreign-owned financial institution (with limited liability); and
9. mergers with and acquisitions of all types of PRC companies.

Although various special regulations have been issued on the most common regulatory issues facing foreign investment, it is impossible for those discrete regulations to provide self-contained solutions to all the problems. In this sense, the Company Law supplements the FIE laws and regulations. This is made clear by Article 218 of the new Company Law, which reads:

> This law shall apply to foreign-invested limited liability companies and joint-stock companies. Where laws on foreign investment provide otherwise, such provisions shall apply.[29]

Evidently, the national Company Law applies to foreign investors and FIEs only when the special legislation on foreign investment is silent on a particular issue. Furthermore, in cases where the FIEs laws differ from provisions of the Company Law, the former prevail.[30]

China appears to be moving toward granting national treatment to FIEs and foreign investors, which would likely close the difference between the Company Law and the FIE laws. In 2007, the National People's Congress passed the Corporate Income Tax Law, unifying the different tax treatments for domestic and foreign-invested companies. Under this Law, FIEs soon will lose the preferential tax treatment they currently receive from the Chinese government.

---

[29] Article 18 of the 1993 Company Law is similar to Article 218 of the 2005 Company Law. For a judicial decision on the applicability of the Company Law to FIEs see *infra*, Chapter 3, §3.12.1.

[30] CCH (2005), ¶26-110. It is worth noting that the Chinese securities regulation is also a dualist regulatory system, as noted in Wang Jiangyu (2004, p. 18):

> [A]lthough it is not explicitly established in the relevant laws, the dualist nature of the Chinese securities regulatory framework shall be understood as such, namely that regulations on foreign investment in China's stock market serve as 'special' laws to the general framework, whose provisions shall take precedent to relevant provisions of the general laws in cases in which there is overlap or conflict. For matters not stipulated in foreign investment-specific laws, the provisions of general laws (such as the Securities Law or the Takeover Measures) shall be followed.

1.4 SOURCES AND APPLICATION OF CHINA'S COMPANY LAW

1.4.1 The Primacy of Legislation in China

As Keller notes, '[a] person cannot live in China long without becoming aware of the complex, interwoven web of social rules which governs every aspect of Chinese life'.[31] This also applies to the regulation of companies in China. Needless to say, in China there is always a disparity between the law on paper and the law in practice. This interesting topic, however, is beyond the scope of this book. Here I seek to clarify the 'hierarchy of legal norms and the delineation of law-making powers'[32] with respect to companies in China.

It is increasingly difficult to characterize China's evolving legal system as belonging to either the civil law or common law family,[33] simply because the contemporary Chinese legal system has been tremendously influenced by Anglo-American law. It is submitted that, although China has extensively borrowed legal concepts, principles, terminologies, institutions, and procedures from Anglo-American jurisdictions (most significantly the United States), it remains a civilian jurisdiction, at least insofar as sources of law are concerned. As in countries in the Romantic and Germanic families, 'enacted law or legislation … is apparently the primary, almost exclusive, source of law today'[34] in China. Case law has never gained legitimacy in China, although more and more court decisions are being published and studied by law students as persuasive legal materials. It is important to remember, moreover, that the so-called 'Chinese characteristics' should always be borne in mind: courts in China often act like legislative bodies, making China distinguishable from other civil law countries at least with respect to law-making.[35]

1.4.2 Legislative Bodies

State organs at different levels are authorized by the PRC Constitution and the Legislation Law[36] to enact laws, regulations, or other normative

[31] Keller (1994), p. 711.
[32] Chen A.H.Y. (2004), p. 111.
[33] See generally Chen A.H.Y. (2000).
[34] David and Brierley (1985), p. 102.
[35] See generally Peerenboom (2006).
[36] Zhonghua Renmin Gongheguo Lifafa, adopted on 29 April 2000 by the National People's Congress.

documents. As this section will show, different legislative bodies have different powers, while the enactments they have made, generally called 'laws', actually have different designations and degrees of binding force. Under the Chinese constitutional rules, the following organs have power to make laws or normal documents:

- The National People's Congress or NPC (*Quanguo Renmin Daibiao Dahui*), and its Standing Committee (*Changwu Weiyuanhui*)
- The State Council (*Guowuyuan*), which is China's central government
- People's congresses at the provincial level
- Ministries and commissions under the State Council
- Provincial governments
- Self-regulatory organizations

1.4.3 *Falü* (Laws) Made by the NPC and its Standing Committee

Under the Chinese constitutional principles, the NPC is the country's highest state organ and the source of power for all other state organs. According to Article 7 of the PRC Legislation Law, the NPC and its Standing Committee, being the national legislature, 'exercise the legislative power of the State'. As a matter of legislative principle, only the legislation enacted by the NPC or its Standing Committee can be designated as 'laws' (*falü*). Further, only the NPC has the power to make and amend 'basic laws' (*jiben falü*), a term that is not clearly defined in China's Constitution.[37] In the economic arena, the Legislation Law stipulates that 'laws' must be enacted to govern the country's basic civil and economic systems.[38] The Company Law, Securities Law, General Principle of Civil Law (GPCL), Partnership Law, Property Law, Enterprise Bankruptcy Law, etc., are all such basic laws that either directly or indirectly govern.

1.4.4 *Xingzheng Fagui* (Administrative Regulations) Made by the State Council

The State Council, which is the top authority in the executive branch, is also a legislative body in China, with law-making authority immediately

---

[37] Legislation Law, Article 7.
[38] Legislation Law, Article 8.

below the NPC and its Standing Committee. Only the legislative enactments of the State Council may be designated as 'administrative regulations' (*xingzheng fagui*), or simply 'regulations'. Under the Legislation Law, the central government may formulate administrative regulations in the following situations: (a) when it is necessary to enact regulations to implement provisions of law; (b) when it is necessary to enact regulations to govern matters within the administrative functions and powers of the State Council as stipulated in the PRC Constitution; and (c) when the State Council is delegated the law-making power by the NPC or its Standing Committee to enact regulations for matters originally within the national legislature's exclusive legislative jurisdiction.[39] In fact, from 1983 to 1985, the NPC and its Standing Committee delegated their law-making power three times to the State Council, for matters mainly relating to economic affairs.[40] In reality, the State Council and its departments form, de facto, the most powerful law-making body in China.

Enactments of the State Council may be entitled 'regulations' (*tiaoli*), 'provisions' (*guiding*), or 'measures' (*banfa*), depending on the scope of subject matter. When the State Council exercises delegated law-making power, its enactment will be called a 'provisional' (*zanxing*),[41] implying that formal statutes will eventually be enacted by the NPC or its Standing Committee in due course.[42] In the area of corporate and securities law, the most important set of administrative regulations is the Company Registration Regulations.

1.4.5 *Bumen Guizhang* Made by the Ministries under the State Council

The various ministries, commissions, and bureaus and the People's Bank of China (which is China's central bank) are authorized to promulgate departmental rules (*bumen guizhang*) within the limits of their respective power. The rules, promulgated by either one ministry alone or by several ministries jointly, should be made only pursuant to and for the purpose of enforcing laws or administrative regulations.[43] As a matter of fact,

---

[39] Legislative Law, Article 56.

[40] Chen A.H.Y. (2004), p. 104.

[41] *Zanxing* may also be translated as 'interim' or 'tentative'.

[42] The scope of matters governed by 'regulations' is the widest, that of 'measures' the narrowest, and that of 'provisions' finds its place in between the latter two. See Chen A.H.Y. (2004), p. 105.

[43] Legislation Law, Article 71.

departmental rules, forming the largest group of normative legal documents, constitute the most relevant and practical body of law for the daily life of ordinary citizens and businesses.

Of the State Council's 28 ministries and commissions, several of them could legislate in the area of corporate and securities law. The State Administration of Industry and Commerce (SAIC), in charge of the registration of enterprises, certainly make rules in this area. Shareholders in China are probably most familiar with the China Securities Regulatory Commission (CSRC), which, as the state regulator of China's securities markets, issues the most corporate and securities rules, covering, inter alia, corporate articles of association, corporate governance, corporate finance, information disclosure, mergers and acquisitions, shares transfer, and the listing and delisting of companies. The Ministry of Commerce, empowered with the authority to regulate all types of foreign investment in China, make rules in relation to foreign participation in China-incorporated companies. The Ministry of Finance promulgates rules relating to companies' accounting practices, as well as related-party transactions. The State-owned Assets Supervision and Administration Commission (SASAC) enacts rules concerning the administration of state assets in enterprises. The National Development and Reform Commission (NDRC), believed to be the most powerful ministry under the State Council, is in charge of formulating the country's macroeconomic development policies and strategies, and it occasionally makes rules that concern the regulation and operation of companies. Other ministries could also be involved in making rules governing business enterprises.

A set of departmental rules may have the generic designation of 'provisions' (*guiding*) or 'measures' (*banfa*). Apart from *guizhang*, the State Council and its ministries promulgate from time to time other forms of official documents, including 'orders' (*mingling*), 'decisions' (*jueding*), 'notices' (*tongzhi*), 'communications' (*tongbao*), 'replies' (*pifu*), 'opinions' (*yijian*), and 'guidelines' (*zhiyin*, or *zhidao yijian*), many of which are used as normal documents to regulate business organizations.[44]

1.4.6 *Difang Falu Fagui* (Local Enactments)

Governments at the provincial level, including provinces, autonomous regional municipalities directly under the central government, and large

---

[44] Chen A.H.Y. (2004), pp. 106–7 (noting these documents 'are authoritative to various degrees, and insofar as some of them provide for rules of general application, they may also be regarded as a source of legal norms'.

cities, are granted law-making power. According to the Legislation Law, two kinds of 'local laws' may be enacted. The first category is 'local regulations' (*defang fagui*) made by local people's congresses and their standing committees (the 'local legislature'). They may enact local regulations 'in light of the specific conditions and actual needs of their respective administrative areas, provided that such regulations do not contradict the Constitution, as well as, the laws and the administrative regulations made under the Constitution'.[45] In the spirit of local law regulating local affairs, the Legislation Law empowers the local legislature to enact local regulations on any matters not yet governed by any national laws or administrative regulations. As Professor Albert Chen has noted, this created 'room for innovation in local regulations which can pave the way for the enactment of national laws on particular subjects'.[46]

Another kind of 'local law' is local rules (*defang guizhang*), made by governments at the level of provinces, autonomous regions, municipalities, and large cities, for matters concerning the implementation of national laws, administrative regulations, or local regulations.[47]

As previously noted, in the area of corporate law, local regulations, especially those made by governments in Shenzhen and Shanghai, preceded national legislation. For example, long before the 1993 Company Law, and even the two standard opinions, the Shenzhen municipality had enacted rules to regulate the restructuring of its SOEs.[48] In these days, although national laws, regulations, and rules are becoming increasingly pervasive and cover almost all areas of corporate and securities matters, the existence of many local corporate rules demonstrates that local law could still play a significant role in creating innovative legal institutions as well as filling the gaps left by national law.

1.4.7 *Sifa jieshi* (Judicial Interpretations): Case Law's Equivalent?

China's legal system is officially a civil law system, in which the decisions of courts constitute guidance, but not law, with respect to the subject matter. As Peerenboom (2006) observes, unlike their counterpart in common law jurisdictions, Chinese courts theoretically do not possess the power to 'make law'. 'Their role is to apply law to the facts. If the laws or regulations are unclear, the courts are supposed to seek

45 Legislation Law, Article 63.
46 Chen A.H.Y. (2004), p. 109.
47 Legislation Law, Article 73.
48 See *supra* note 21 and the accompanying texts.

guidance and clarification from the entities that promulgated the laws or regulations.'[49] Given that statutes cannot possibly be applied without proper interpretation, especially in the context of adjudication, a legal system must provide either rules of statutory interpretation or authoritative precedent or both, to guide interpretation.[50] In China, in addition to the law interpretation system, which places the power of interpreting laws in the hands of the NPC Standing Committee, 'a rudimentary system has evolved which might be interpreted as the functional equivalent of case law in other jurisdictions'.[51] This essentially refers to the power of the Supreme Court to make the so-called 'judicial interpretations' (*sifa jieshi*). As Peerenboom (2006) remarks,

> What is distinctive about China's legal system is that the Supreme People's Court (SPC) makes law in a much more direct and visible way. Every year the SPC issues a variety of interpretations, regulations, notices, replies, opinions and policy statements (collectively, 'interpretations'). Most are binding upon the courts; others are highly persuasive and likely to be followed by the courts. Sometimes they are rather general; other times they are very specific and issued in response to an inquiry from [a] lower court in regard to a particular case pending before the court.[52]

A 1981 NPC Standing Committee decision began to permit the SPC to promulgate judicial interpretations in the reform era.[53] The SPC has issued a series of provisions to elaborate on its law interpretation work, the most recent being the 2007 SPC Provisions on Judicial Interpretation Work.[54] In essence, judicial interpretations, having the binding force of law, could only be promulgated by the SPC. They may take the forms of 'interpretations' (*jieshi*), 'provisions' (*guiding*), 'replies' (*pifu*), and 'decisions' (*jueding*). Interpretations deal with the application of a specific law or a type of case or problem; provisions are used to create norms or opinions relating to adjudication; replies are answers to inquiries from

---

49 Peerenboom (2006), p. 2.

50 In addition, 'the courts are often required to expound the meaning of a statutory provision by … deciding whether or not it applies to a particular set of facts'. See Mayson, French and Ryan (2006), p. 23.

51 Chen A.H.Y. (2004), p. 118.

52 Peerenboom (2006), p. 2.

53 Resolution of the NPC Standing Committee on Strengthening the Work of Interpretation of Law. See Chen A.H.Y. (2004), p. 119.

54 Zuigao Renmin Fayuan Guanyu Sifa Jieshi Gongzuo De Guiding, Fafa (2007) Di 12 Hao, promulgated on 23 March 2007.

the provincial courts regarding issues concerning concrete application of law; and decisions are used to revise or abolish judicial interpretations.[55]

The three judicial interpretations on the application of the Company Law (Company Law Interpretation (I), Company Law Interpretation (II), and Company Law Interpretation (III)) are the three most important *sifa jieshi* ever issued for corporate and securities disputes by the SPC. In addition, the SPC has promulgated several interpretations on disputes involving foreign-invested enterprises, SOE restructuring, and securities misrepresentation in recent years.

Given the increasing convergence of the Chinese legal system with the Anglo-American legal tradition, many would wonder whether decided cases also play a role in the courts' adjudication of corporate and securities disputes. But even accepting that China is still a civilian jurisdiction, the rather simplistic view that civil law excludes judicial precedent as a source of legal authority is no longer accepted. As David and Brierley (1985) note, in countries such as France or Germany, 'cases have been of primary importance in the evolution of some branches of the law'.[56] Certainly, judicial decisions do not constitute law in China.[57] However, it is correct to observe that court decisions 'do generate legal norms and have persuasive or even binding force in practice'.[58] The most noticed cases are those judgments or summary of judgments selected and published by the SPC in the *Gazette of the Supreme People's Court*, which are considered 'authoritative and an important means through which the Supreme People's Court provides guidance to lower courts with regard to their adjudicative work'.[59] Many published cases, some of which will be discussed in the following chapters, are about corporate and securities disputes.

1.4.8 Rules Made by Self-regulatory Organizations

The Securities Association of China (SAC) and the two securities exchanges, namely the Shanghai Stock Exchange (SSE) and the Shenzhen Stock Exchange (SZSE), are officially considered 'self-regulatory organizations' (SROs) in China's securities markets. They are hence empowered to make self-regulatory rules. The binding nature of these

[55] Id, Article 6.
[56] p. 133.
[57] Chen A.H.Y. (2004), p. 128.
[58] Chen A.H.Y. (2004), p. 128.
[59] Chen A.H.Y. (2004), pp. 128–9.

rules is augmented because the so-called SROs are under tight governmental control, which lends the rules they issue the weight of state endorsement. At this stage in the development of the PRC legal system, the SROs, which enjoy almost no independence from the government, are themselves de facto state organs.

Under the PRC Securities Law, the SAC, established in 1991, is an SRO with legal personality.[60] According to the SAC's own articles of association, it is also a non-profit organization under the supervision of the CSRC and the Ministry of Civil Affairs.[61] All securities companies (Chinese brokers, dealers, and investment banks) must join the SAC.[62] The law also authorizes the SAC to formulate membership rules, mediate disputes between members and between members and their clients, oversee the conduct of members, and initiate disciplinary action 'in the event of members' violation of laws, administrative regulations or the articles of association of the SAC'.[63] In addition, the CSRC has authorized the SAC to facilitate innovation in the securities industry, manage the professional qualification system, supervise the disclosure of members' information, promote standardization, communication, and training with respect to securities information technology, facilitate compliance with applicable regulations, and supervise and manage the Share Transfer System.[64]

Much related to the operation of companies is, in fact, the Share Transfer Agent System (STAS).[65] The STAS is managed by the SAC and serves a function similar to an over-the-counter market both for companies that have been recently delisted from one of the two stock exchanges and those originally listed on STAQ and NET, two electronic trading systems dismantled by the government in 1998 for unknown reasons. Since June 2001, the SAC has issued a host of rules concerning share trading on STAS.

---

60 Securities Law, Article 174.

61 The Articles of Association of the Securities Association of China, Articles 1 and 3 (available at http://www.sac.net.cn).

62 Securities Law, Article 175.

63 Securities Law, Article 176, paras. (4), (5), and (7).

64 CSRC (2006), p. 33.

65 Daiban Gufen Zhuanrang Xitong.

The Securities Law and the 2001 CSRC Measures for the Administration of Securities Exchange[66] define a securities exchange as a 'self-regulatory legal person which provides the venue and facilities for centralized trading of securities and which is responsible for organizing and supervising of securities trading'.[67] A stock exchange is, however, not necessarily a non-profit organization under the new Securities Law.

Securities exchanges are authorized to enact rules for the following purposes:

1. Formulating exchange listing rules, share trading rules, exchange membership rules, and other rules in accordance with securities laws and administrative regulations, subject to the approval of the CSRC;
2. Safeguarding the security and fairness of centralized exchange trading;
3. Monitoring securities trading at all times and supervising information disclosure of listed companies and relevant persons; and
4. Taking disciplinary actions against violators of securities laws and regulations.

The two securities exchanges have promulgated hundreds of rules to govern listing, trading, information disclosure, corporate finance, corporate governance, mergers and acquisitions, and even corporate social responsibility. From a commercial perspective, for listed companies, securities firms, and investors, complying with these trading and listing rules can be just as important as meeting the requirements of law. Needless to say, exchange rules are 'soft law' in nature, and are treated as contractual arrangements by the courts.

1.4.9 Custom

As observed in David and Brierley (1985), '[a]ccording to a sociological concept of the sources of law, custom plays a preponderant role in all legal systems; and in developing or applying the law, legislators, judges and authors are, as a matter of fact, more or less consciously guided by the opinion and custom of the community'.[68] Custom as a source of law

[66] Zhengquan Jiaoyisuo Guanli Banfa, promulgated by the State Council Securities Commission in 1997; revised and re-promulgated by the CSRC on 12 December 2001.

[67] Securities Law, Article 102.

[68] David and Brierley (1985), p. 130.

is recognized in China's legal system, especially with respect to civil and commercial disputes.[69]

1.4.10 Legal Writings

Just as in many other countries, works of legal scholarship play an eminent role in the legal system, although they are not formally recognized as a source of law. This is largely because legal writings shape legal 'doctrine', which is of fundamental importance to the formation and application of written laws in civil law countries and the creation of common law in common law countries. The importance of legal writing in the civil law tradition is beautifully summarized in David and Brierley (1985) in the following passage, which to some degree also sheds light on China's situation:

> One may, of course, define law as only enacted rules. Nevertheless, for the person who takes a realistic approach and has a more comprehensive – and to our mind, more exact – view, *doctrine* is now, as in the past, a very important, living source of law. This is shown by the fact that it creates the legal vocabulary and ideas which legislators subsequently use; it is even more evident from the fact that doctrinal writing establishes the methods by which law will be understood and statutes interpreted. There is, further, the influence that legal scholarship can exercise on the legislators themselves; often the latter merely give expression and effect to tendencies that have developed doctrinally, or enact laws which have been conceived by legal writers … [Legal writing] also plays a role in the application of enacted law.[70]

Scholarly writing is not a formal source of law in China. It may never be admitted that there is not one 'enacted writing' and that there will always be different scholarly views about the same things. Yet the role of legal scholars in China should not be underestimated. They were heavily involved in the legislative process of major laws, including inter alia, the Company Law, and the Securities Law. To some extent, it is not incorrect to say that the scholars were themselves the lawmakers, as the drafts of law made by them were largely accepted by the NPC and other legislative bodies. Furthermore, some courts, especially the SPC and some provincial high courts, have developed the tendency to consult

---

[69] Liang (2004), p. 28.
[70] David and Brierley (1985), p. 135.

prominent scholars in their adjudication of legal disputes. One commentator hence suggests that this indicates that legal writing may be regarded as an 'indirect source of law' (*jianjie fayuan*) in China.[71]

1.4.11 Understanding the Complex Hierarchical Structure of the Chinese Legal Order

It is essentially important to understand the hierarchy of law in China. As discussed above, the multiple legislative bodies have made numerous laws and regulations, often on the same subject. Conflicts and inconsistencies have also inevitably arisen between laws made by different legislative bodies. For instance, with respect to the registration of a company, there are provisions in the national Company Law, a special administration regulation enacted by the State Council, as well as departmental rules released by the State Administration of Industry and Commerce. Two interrelated questions therefore arise: (1) which level of laws has higher legal effects? and (2) which law should a court apply if there are conflicts between different laws?

Under the Constitution and the Legislation Law, law enforcement organs should observe the following principles on the hierarchy of legal order:

- The PRC Constitution has the highest legal authority, and no other laws, administrative or local regulations or rules may contradict it.[72]
- The legal effect of laws (made by the NPC and/or its Standing Committee) is higher than that of administrative regulations, local regulations, and rules.[73]
- The legal effect of administrative regulations is higher than that of local regulations and rules.[74]
- The legal effect of local regulations is higher than that of local rules made by governments of the same and lower levels.[75]
- The legal effect of the departmental rules made by different central departments is equal between those departments, and the effect of departmental rules and local rules is equal between the departments

---

71 Liang (2004), p. 27.
72 Legislation Law, Article 78.
73 Legislation Law, Article 79.
74 Legislation Law, Article 79.
75 Legislation Law, Article 80.

and local governments; their application should be confined to their respective limits of authority.[76]

Having identified that departmental rules and local regulations have the same legal status, the Legislation Law, however, does not solve a key problem: the conflict of authority between the central and provincial departments. As remarked in Cohen and Lange (1997), '[t]he conflict between central and local authorities will continue to handicap the development of the Chinese legal system, and to heighten the risks for foreign investors, at least until China evolves and enforces a reasonably clear and rational allocation of authority between the central and provincial governments'.[77] Further, '[o]ften investors are caught in the middle, between the more investor-friendly local authorities and the more macro-oriented central authorities, each offering their own – often sharply divergent – visions of the applicable regulatory framework and the proper way to proceed. In addition, the vastness of China and the existence of entrenched local power bases often makes it difficult for the central government to enforce laws it adopts for the benefits of investors'.[78]

Although the legal status of administrative regulations is higher than local law according to the Legislation Law, many rules – probably those most relevant to the corporate world – are promulgated by central ministries such as the SAIC, the CSRC, and the SASAC. Many localities have also adopted regulations and rules to regulate corporate activities in their own districts. Article 86 attempts to provide a solution for conflict of laws in this situation, and stipulates that, where there is inconsistency between local regulations and departmental rules on the same matter, and the governing rules cannot otherwise be decided, the State Council can make a decision that local regulations should prevail. But if the State Council determines that departmental rules shall apply instead, the case should be submitted to the NPC Standing Committee for a ruling.[79] As an NPC procedure is time-consuming, this provision probably does not offer much practical solace to the courts, which are faced with disputes on a daily basis.

The Legislation Law does not address the place of judicial interpretations in the hierarchy of legal order. In theory, an 'interpretation' should not contradict the original enactment it aims to interpret. In practice, judicial interpretations have gone far beyond that, making the SPC a de

---

76 Legislation Law, Article 82.

77 p. 349.

78 Id.

79 Legislation Law, Article 86, para. 2.

facto legislative body, a status not recognized by the Legislation Law. Given the tight control of the SPC over the lower courts, its judicial interpretations are more faithfully enforced by courts than many laws, as the interpretations provide timely, practical, and specific responses to concrete issues.

On the courts' choice of law, an SPC document released in 2004 is very illustrative. Entitled 'SPC Meeting Minutes on the Application of Law Issues in the Trial of Administrative Cases',[80] it is not itself a judicial interpretation, but would definitely guide the adjudication practice of courts at all levels. The Minutes stipulate the following principles with regard to courts' choice of law:

- In trying administrative cases, the people's court shall apply laws, administrative regulations and local regulations, and make reference to rules.
- Interpretations of laws, decisions, orders or other official normative documents issued by the State Council departments and local governments are not binding upon courts; they will be applied in trial only after the court has reviewed the legality of those documents under laws or administrative regulations.
- The court will apply a higher-level law if there is inconsistency between laws.
- If there is inconsistency between departmental rules and local regulations, the court will make choices according to the following principles: (1) departmental rules authorized to implement the laws or administrative regulations should take priority; (2) departmental rules concerning matters which require national actions or concerning foreign trade or foreign investment shall take priority; (3) local regulations concerning purely local matters shall take priority.

Although the Minutes concern, as a matter of law, only court adjudication of administrative cases, they provide significant guidance for the trial of civil and commercial disputes. Furthermore, one has to bear in mind that most official normative documents are administrative in nature. It is also worth noting that the Minutes establish a formal mechanism of judicial review of legality of laws. According to the Minutes, although Chinese courts do not have the power to invalidate any written laws,

---

[80] Zuigao Renmin Fayuan Guanyu Shenli Xingzheng Anjian Shiyong Falv Guifan Wenti de Zuotanhui Jiyao, Fafa (2004) No. 96, promulgated by the SPC on 18 May 2004.

regulations, or rules, they seem to have great discretion to choose the law they wish to apply.

1.5 THE CONCEPT, PURPOSES, AND PRINCIPLES OF COMPANIES AND COMPANY LAW IN CHINA

1.5.1 Development of Corporate Law Driven by Legal Transplantation and Local Needs

As noted above, the corporate law regime, as it currently stands and possibly evolves, could pose a theoretical challenge to the conventional wisdom on the law of business corporations. First, does the evolution of corporate law in China show convergence or divergence in the structure and practice of corporate law globally? One stream of the corporate law literature, represented in Hansmann and Kraakman (2001), has famously declared 'the end of history for corporate law'. The development of Chinese corporate law, in the sense that it has extensively borrowed institutions from both Anglo-American and European Continental jurisdictions, has provided evidence of the power of one of the world's largest markets, once an entirely socialist, plan-based economy, to induce convergence. If a definition needs to be given to the company, it is firstly understood as a creature of law, or a legal artifice, offering limited liability to its owners.[81] In the wake of China's marching toward the 'socialist market economy', the companies incorporated in China are, at least in theory, expected to have the typical attributes of modern corporations. Those include, most well known, '(1) full legal personality, including well-defined authority to bind the firm to contracts and to bond those contracts with assets that are the property of the firm, as distinct from the firm's owners; (2) limited liability for owners and managers; (3) shared ownership by investors of capital; (4) delegated management

[81] From a theoretical perspective, the origin of the company can be explained by two conflicting theories, namely the concession theory and the contract theory. The concession theory claims that the corporation is a creation of the state and that its legal power is derived from the state. In contrast, the contract theory maintains that the corporation is an association formed by the shareholders through agreement, namely it is a nexus of contracts rather than a creation of the state. As we shall see from provisions of the PRC Company Law, there is no doubt that the company is viewed as a legal creature rather than a contractual product.

under a board structure; and (5) transferable shares'.[82] As Hansmann and Kraakman (2004) point out, these attributes are to some extent universal in nature:[83]

> These characteristics are ... included by the economic exigencies of the large modern business enterprises. Thus, corporate law everywhere must, of necessity, provide for them. To be sure, there other forms of business enterprise that lack one or more of these characteristics. But the remarkable fact – and the fact we wish to stress – is that, in market economies, almost all large-scale business firms adopt a legal form that possess[es] all five of the basic characteristics of the business corporation. Indeed, most small joint-owned firms adopt this corporate form as well, although sometimes with deviations from one or more of the five basic characteristics to fit the special needs of closely held firms ... Self-evidently, a principal function of corporate law is to provide business enterprises with a legal form that possesses these five core attributes.

Hansmann and Kraakman (2004) further remark that '[b]usiness corporations have a fundamentally similar set of legal characteristics – and face a fundamentally similar set of legal problems – in all jurisdictions'.[84]

Indeed, the laws of corporations around the world, when they were first enacted, were very similar[85] largely because of the inherent nature of Western commerce and capitalism. The transplantation of corporate law from leading origin countries of the civil law and common law families, mainly England, France, Germany, and the United States, to countries in other regions has led to tremendous similarities in the basic legal framework of corporations across the globe. However, as the corporate world grew, divergence began to emerge among the origin countries, as they had to provide legal and institutional solutions to indigenous problems that occurred in different national settings that bore – sometimes slightly and other times extremely – different legal culture and philosophy from others. As a result, in terms of corporate law, the origin countries differ 'in how they responded to the challenges of the rapid growth of the enterprise and financial sectors and to the booms and busts

---

[82] Hansmann and Kraakman (2001), p. 440. Clark (1986, p. 2) identifies four characteristics of the corporation: '(1) limited liability for investors; (2) free transferability of investor interests; (3) legal personality (entity-attributable powers, life span, and purpose); and (4) centralized management'. See also Monks and Minow (2004), p. 11.

[83] pp. 1–2.

[84] p. 1.

[85] Pistor *et al.* (2003), p. 89 (noting '[w]hen the first corporate statutes were enacted, there were remarkably few differences among countries and legal families').

of financial markets that accompanies it'.[86] In spite of the differences, the corporate laws in the origin countries have been, in various degrees, successful. Time is to be credited for this: the development of capitalism and credit culture in Western Europe and North America has lasted for over two centuries, a time span wide enough for those countries to adjust and rationalize their regulatory and market institutions of corporations through learning from experiment and falsification, or trial and error.

In the successful origin countries, a central task of corporate governance is to control the 'controller', which is normally the management of the corporations. But countries differ in the tools used for corporate governance; and '[m]ost important are differences, particularly between the common law and civil law families, in the allocation of control rights'.[87] With few exceptions, the board of directors is the primary governance organ in the Western corporations. Over the years, two types of board structures have evolved, namely the unitary board and the two-tier board. The unitary system, adopted in Anglo-American countries, allows for only one board, or the board of directors, which 'directs' and oversees the company, including proving strategic guidance for company, and appointing and monitoring the performance of the executives. In the Anglo-American systems, independence of the board of directors is supposed to be ensured by its composition, namely the board is composed of mainly independent directors. In the two-tier board structure, most notably adopted by Germany, the governing body of the corporation comprises two separate boards, including the management board (also called board of directors), and the supervisory board. The supervisory board chooses the directors of the management board and monitors their performance.

In the area of corporate law, developing and transition countries have their legal system transplanted from the one or two of the origin countries mentioned above. Pistor *et al.* (2003) survey the transplant effect of six representative countries that adopted foreign law[88] and concludes that

> [c]ountries that adopt foreign law are frequently unprepared for it or the changes it brings. It is therefore not surprising that the new law does not

---

86 Pistor *et al.* (2003), p. 94.

87 Pistor *et al.* (2003), p. 94.

88 The countries in this survey have transplanted their corporate law from the following origins: Chile, Colombia, and Spain (from French law); Israel and Malaysia (from English common law); and Japan (from German law and U.S. law).

> become well incorporated into the institutional landscape or contributes to an ongoing process or institutional change.[89]

The conclusion's overgeneralization is apparent.[90] After all, companies in quite a number of countries that have transplanted legal systems from abroad are running well: although the corporate law of New York State preceded Britain's 1848 Joint Stock Company Act by over 30 years, the U.S. legal system indisputably finds its origin in England. Further, a country's adoption of foreign corporate institutions might respond to an internal need to rationalize its enterprise sectors. Despite this weakness, the survey correctly suggests that 'legal transplantation is not an easy (and certainly not a short-term) solution for countries with less developed legal systems'.[91]

China adopted its corporate law through a 'transplant'. As its Company Law (or 'Corporation Law' as it is translated by some) shows, China has imported the organizational structures of Western capitalist business into its own enterprise sectors.[92] However, as some commentators observe:

> Difference from Western models bracket this general similarity at both the broad level, in ideology and over objective, and the technical level, in details and specific rules. [*sic*] The melding of Western forms with the goal of promoting a 'socialist market economy' has produced a Corporation Law with distinctly Chinese characteristics.[93]

Further, although China's corporate law embraces a significant amount of institutions imported from foreign sources, it is difficult to identify the single most significant 'origin' country. Broadly speaking, the Chinese system is a hybrid one, containing institutions borrowed from both the common law family, mainly the United States, and continental civil law family, i.e. Germany. This is most visible in the board structure of China's listed companies, which have both a supervisory board and independent directors in the management board. Even with these two 'safety nets', corporate governance in China's listed companies still remains very unsatisfactory.[94] In fact, both empirical studies and analysis

---

89 Pistor *et al.* (2003), p. 98.

90 The authors of this survey admit this by saying 'the small size of the sample cautions us against overgeneralization'. See Pistor *et al.* (2003), p. 109.

91 Pistor *et al.* (2003), p. 109.

92 Art and Gu (1995), p. 275.

93 Art and Gu (1995), p. 275.

94 Wang (2004a), pp. 40–42 (discussing the poor corporate governance of China's listed companies).

of the legal framework show that the supervisory board and the independent directors, the 'strange partners' in China's listed companies, have not significantly improved the overall corporate governance of those companies.

Indeed, although business corporations in China possess the same fundamental legal characteristics as seen in all jurisdictions, and are plagued with some similar legal problems, the corporate law system in China demonstrates strong Chinese characteristics. Among the problems that have been alleged to cause most, if not all, the scandals in corporatized enterprises, the most salient are conflict of interests between the shareholders (owners) and managers and between the majority shareholders and minority shareholders, the two classic agency problems of company law. In SOEs the state is normally the majority shareholder. There are also many other companies, including some listed companies, which are controlled by private owners. In essence, the agency problems in Chinese companies are not fundamentally different from those in other market economies.

Therefore, subject to some universal and indigenous exceptions,[95] there must be many Chinese companies that have the core characteristics of modern corporations. These characteristics are required by the nature of a market economy, as they, individually or in combination, 'offer important efficiencies in organizing the large firms with multiple owners that have come to dominate developed market economies'.[96] Anyone who has noticed the sheer number of shareholders and the growing shareholder activism in many listed companies in China would understand the need for Chinese companies to perform the same functions as their foreign counterparts. However, in a country that is still in the process of transitioning from plan to market, its enterprises often are either striving to learn how to behave like corporate citizens, or just happy to act as units that, under the disguise of independent corporate structure, are actually not independent of other entities or individuals.

In this view, principles of Chinese company law should be understood in their unique economic, political, and culture contexts. Article 1 of the PRC Company Law is a telling presentation of this need, as it states: 'This Law is formulated in order to standardize the organization and activities of companies, protect the lawful rights and interests of companies, shareholders and creditors, safeguard the social and economic

---

[95] Such as restrictions on the transfer of shares in limited liability companies, or the doctrine of piercing the corporate veil, which will be discussed in later chapters.

[96] Hansmann and Kraakman (2004), p. 440.

order and promote the development of the socialist market economy'. Indeed, the multiple objectives of the law demonstrate strong Chinese characteristics. For example, an important social fact in China is that the state sector, albeit diminishing, still dominates the country's economy, at least in terms of its leading role in shaping and implementing central and local industry policies. This is, however, accompanied by another phenomenon: China is also experiencing the largest privatization of assets in world history. As a result, the state business sector has withdrawn significantly from many forefronts of the economy, while the private sector has been growing so rapidly that it has already become the country's 'major driver of growth in productivity and new jobs'.[97] Nevertheless, the vast majority of companies listed on China's two stock exchanges are still state controlled.[98]

In this light, the regulation and governance of companies in China demonstrate some distinctive Chinese characteristics, in addition to the universal characteristics. Those characteristics will be explored at appropriate points in later chapters.

1.5.2 The Concept of Companies in China

Discussing the concept of company under Chinese law cannot really attempt precisely to define the concept 'company', as 'the word company has no strictly legal meaning'.[99] Scholarly writings define the company as a kind of social organization legal person (*Shetuan faren*), which means an association of persons organized for certain purposes, as opposed to a property-based legal person (*Caituan faren*), which normally refers to a foundation or trust constituted as a legal person.[100] Article 2 of CL 2005 simply states that 'For the purposes of this Law, the term "companies" shall mean limited liability companies and companies limited by shares established pursuant to this Law in China'. Obviously, this provision does not provide a workable definition of companies.

---

97 OECD (2005), p. 80.

98 Id.

99 Davies (2003), p. 3 (citing Buckley J in *Re Stanley* [1906] 1 Ch. 131 at 134). Soderquist *et al.* (1999, §1:2.3) define a U.S. corporation as 'an entity that consists of an intangible structure for the conduct of the entity's affairs and operations, the essence of which is created by the state, and that possesses the rights and obligations given or allowed it by the state, which rights and obligations more or less parallel those of natural persons'.

100 Shi Tiantao (2006), p. 6; Zhao Xudong (2006), pp. 6–7.

Nonetheless, under the PRC Company Law, or at least according to the law on the books, a Chinese company features the core structural characteristics of the modern business corporation, including legal personality, limited liability, centralized management, shareholder's ownership and residual claims, and free transferability of shares.

Legal personality and limited liability

Article 3 of CL 2005 provides:

> A company is an enterprise legal person which has independent legal person property and enjoys legal person property rights. A company shall be liable for its debts to the extent of all its property.
>
> A shareholder of a limited liability company shall be liable to the company to the extent of the capital contribution it subscribes. A shareholder of a company limited by shares shall be liable to the company to the extent of the shares it subscribes.

Article 3 encompasses two of the core characteristics of modern business corporations, namely legal personality and limited liability. The operation of these two principles under China's corporate law regime will be discussed in detail in Chapter 5 of this book. A few general points should nevertheless be outlined at this point.

A company is, firstly, an enterprise legal person. As Clark (1986) observes, 'one of the law's most economically significant contributions to business life, and one often ignored by lawyers because it generates less litigation than many other contributions, has been the creation of fictional but legally recognized entities or "persons" that are treated as having some of the attributes of natural persons'.[101] A legal person is one of the key institutions in the civil law system of China, defined in the PRC General Principles of Civil Law (GPCL) as 'an organization which possesses both the capacity for civil rights and the capacity for civil acts and which enjoys civil rights and assumes civil obligations independently according to law'.[102] The legal criteria determining the valid establishment of a legal person include (a) establishment strictly in accordance with the law; (b) possession of the necessary property of capital; (c) possession of a name, organizational structure, and premises; and (d) ability to bear civil liability independently.[103]

The legal person doctrine suggests that PRC Company Law treats the company as a legal creature, which could not exist without the law

101 Clark (1986), p. 15.
102 GPCL, Article 36.
103 GPCL, Article 37.

creating it. In other words, the firm must be established by law according to the required procedures (the so-called incorporation process). By incorporation, the firm acquires the status of a legal person and becomes the holder of legal rights and duties. This gives it the ability to 'own assets that are distinct from the property of other persons, such as the firm's investors, and that the firm is free not only to use and sell but – most importantly – pledge to creditors'.[104] Specifically, corporate personhood allows the company to have its own name, to make by-laws for self-governance, to enter into legal transactions, to sue and be sued, and to be held accountable for its debts. Shareholders of the company share collective ownership in the company, and own equity interest in the company individually. They are, however, never owners of the assets of the company, either collectively or individually.

With respect to corporate ownership, a strong Chinese characteristic is that the Company Law does not explicate whether the company has ownership of its own assets. The use of the term 'ownership' was intentionally avoided and replaced with 'enterprise legal person property rights', although some commentators have argued that these two are functionally equivalent terminologies.[105] Significantly, as corporate assets include the capital contributions made by the shareholders, capital contributions cannot be withdrawn by the shareholders once they are made; otherwise, it would be an infringement of corporate property rights. In this spirit, CL 2005 abandons a provision of CL 1993, which provided that 'the ownership of state assets in a company belong[s] to the state'.[106]

Acquiring legal personality may result in perpetual existence, although, again, the language of the law is not clear. The GPCL grants a legal person full capacity with respect to having rights and obligations during its whole life, namely from its establishment to its termination.[107] Presumably, the absence of explicit provisions means that, according to the Company Law, there is no prohibition on companies stipulating in their articles of association perpetual existence. Indeed, the Guidelines for Articles of Association of Listed Companies issued by the China Securities Regulatory Commission (CSRC) (hereinafter 'CSRC Model Articles') states that a joint-stock company can elect to have a fixed term

---

104 Kraakman *et al.* (2004), p. 7.
105 Zhao Xudong (2006), pp. 4–5.
106 CL 1993, Article 4, para. 3.
107 GPCL, Article 36, para. 2.

of duration or simply provide for 'perpetual existence' in its articles.[108] This privilege, however, cannot be taken for granted by every type of company. For instance, most foreign-invested companies would need to stipulate in their contracts and articles of association a fixed term of operation, and apply to the authorities if an extension of the business were desired.[109]

Article 3 also indicates that the concept of legal personality is closely tied to the concept of limited liability. Shareholders are liable to the extent of their capital contributions. This means that, by default, a shareholder's financial liability to the creditors of the company is limited to his/her investment in the company. The creditors of the company 'are limited to making claims against the assets that are the property of the firm itself, and have to further claim against the personal assets of the firm's shareholders'.[110]

In the context of Chinese company law, a shareholder's liability to the company is fully satisfied when his/her capital contribution is paid up. The shareholder is liable to the company to the extent of the capital contribution or shares he or she subscribes, not the amount of capital he or she has actually made. That is to say, a shareholder who has entered into an agreement to buy equity interest in a company will always be under the obligation to make up the difference if he or she did not pay the full value of the consideration.

Limited liability has lost its function as an undefeatable protective shield under the current corporate law regime in China. Amending CL 1993, CL 2005 has added a brand new provision, now Article 20 of CL 2005, which requires investors not to abuse their position as shareholders; otherwise, the court will apply the doctrine of 'piercing the corporate veil' and hold them accountable for corporate debts.

Investor ownership and centralized management

As under the company law of every other major jurisdiction, shareholders are owners of the company, but not of the assets of the company. Ownership in the firm encompasses two elements: 'the right to control the firm, and the right to receive the firms' net earnings'.[111] Article 4 of

---

[108] Guidelines for Articles of Association of Listed Companies, issued by the CSRC, Zhengjian Gongsi Zi [2006] 38 Hao, 16 March 2006.

[109] See e.g. Article 13 of the PRC Law on Sino-foreign equity joint ventures (stating that whether a fixed term of operation is needed depends on the nature of the industries concerned).

[110] Kraakman *et al.* (2004), p. 8.

[111] Kraakman *et al.* (2004), p. 13.

CL 2005 embodies the two elements, and states that 'Shareholders of a company shall enjoy such rights as earnings on assets, participation in major decision-making and selection of management personnel according to law'.

In terms of the right to control, the PRC Company Law gives most of the powers to determine the company's overall direction and to manage the company's day-to-day operations to the company's managers, board of directors, and supervisory board. Shareholders as owners are required to give up the powers to make decisions on all but the most fundamental issues facing the company, and to delegate the powers to the directors and managers. In this regard, China is not different from other jurisdictions, although shareholders in China ostensibly have more power than their Western counterparts under the written laws. As Kraakman *et al.* (2004) observe, '[d]elegated management is an attribute of nearly all large firms with numerous fractional owners. Delegation permits the centralization of management necessary to coordinate productively. Equally important, delegation of decision-making power to specific individuals notifies third parties as to who in the firm has the authority to make binding agreements'.[112] Proper functioning of delegated management depends on a sound corporate governance structure, which is further discussed below.

Free transferability of investor interests

For investors, one of the biggest advantages associated with the corporate form is that they are legally guaranteed the right to transfer equity interests in the firm to others, and thereby exit the firm. In China, as in most civil law countries, a limited liability company does not issue share certificates, so that the equity stake of a shareholder is stipulated in the company's incorporation agreement as well as in the articles of associations, in the form of a figure percentage. Transfer of the equity interest takes place in a purely dematerialized fashion, on the books of the company. Equity interest transferability is subject to legal restrictions under certain circumstances. For example, the right of a shareholder to transfer his equity interest to an outsider is subject to the 'right of first refusal' of other shareholders.[113]

Transferability shares in a company limited by shares is a right by default under the Company Law, meaning the investors automatically have the right unless the law imposes restrictions on transferability for

---

[112] Kraakman *et al.* (2004), p. 11.
[113] CL 2005, Article 72.

special reasons or the transferability is constrained by the investor's contractual obligations, e.g. commitments to other shareholders or to the stock exchange on which the shares are listed. In a company limited by shares, the promoters may not transfer their shares within one year from the date of incorporation. The directors, supervisors, and senior corporate officers may not transfer more than 25 percent of their total shareholding in the joint-stock company during their term of office. Their shares will be barred from transfer for one year from the date the company goes public. More such restrictions are discussed in later chapters.

1.5.3 2005 Revision of the Company Law: Marching Toward Rule of Law in the Corporate World?

The 2005 revision of the Company Law is a breakthrough in the development of China's corporate law. This is not to say that the new Company Law has established a regime that is totally different from the former one; instead, the new law represents an accelerated movement in an ongoing trend toward developing a rule-based, investor protection oriented, transparent legal system for modern business companies in China. During the past two decades, there were several separate but interrelated developments in the corporate law regime, all of which can be explained by the changes brought by the 2005 Company Law.

General applicability: from a law for state-owned enterprise to a general law for all types of companies

The first law for domestic enterprises promulgated in the reform era was the 1988 Law of the PRC on Industrial Enterprises Owned by the Whole People[114] (hereinafter the '1988 SOE Law'), which is still valid and governs purely state-owned enterprises. Although the 1993 Company Law posed as a law for all kinds of companies regardless of ownership, it was designed primarily for SOEs. 'The enterprise envisaged by the Company Law is not one formed by a group of private entrepreneurs; it is a corporatized traditional SOE.'[115]

The 2005 law becomes a more general corporate statute by deleting the many provisions of the 1993 law that gave special privileges or protection to SOEs. As Wang Baoshu (2007) observes, about 14 Articles in the old law specially designed for SOEs were abrogated by the new law, although the special section on wholly state-owned companies

---

114 See *supra*, §1.4.3.

115 Clarke (2003), p. 30.

remains.[116] For example, CL 1993 only permitted CLS or state-owned LLC to issue corporate bonds.[117] In so doing, the new law does away with the decades-long practice of discriminating against privately-owned companies.

Deregulation: from government control of enterprise to freedom of enterprise

The most significant change in the new law is that it represents a movement from restrictive to enabling statute, thus shifting the regulatory philosophy from tight government control to deregulation. Under the new law, the freedom of enterprise, which means the enterprise and the entrepreneurs are free to operate the business and dispose of corporate resources, has gained considerably larger room. This shift is demonstrated in the following aspects:

> *Relaxed incorporation requirements*: In the regulation of business incorporation, the new law has largely completed the process of moving from an approval system to a registration system. Under the new system, as long as the application for incorporation meets the conditions specified in the law, the companies registrar (which is normally the central and local bureaus for industry and commerce) is required to register the company.[118] The number of promoters has been reduced to two from five for establishing a CLS. In addition, the new law permits an LLC to be incorporated by a single natural or legal person.
>
> *Relaxed registered capital requirements*: CL 1993 required a minimum registered capital between RMB100,000 and RMB500,000 for setting up domestic LLCs, making incorporation unaffordable for many. The new law replaces this capital spread with a standard minimum capital of RMB30,000 and makes the corporate form available to more investors.[119] In addition, for the first time, Chinese law allows registered capital to be partially paid, with the remainder in installments, as long as the initial contribution is not

---

[116] Wang Baoshu (2007), p. 13.

[117] CL 1993, Article 159.

[118] In contrast, the application for establishing a CLS must be approved by a central ministry or provincial government on a case-by-case basis.

[119] The minimum registered capital for CLS is reduced from RMB10 million to RMB5 million.

less than 20 percent of the total registered capital. Most significantly, the new law expands the means of capital contribution, bringing in more varieties of non-cash assets that can be used as investment, as long as the non-cash assets are transferable and can be monetarily valued.

More discretionary and enabling rules, and expanded corporate power: CL 1993 is often described as a restrictive statute that tended to impose heavier regulation on companies.[120] It was full of restrictive phrases 'should', 'must', and 'must not', which compelled companies to do or not do specified things. Under CL 1993, the articles of association, a company's constitution, were not treated as a living document, as they had to copy the mandatory provisions of Company Law. In a stark contrast, CL 2005 grants tremendous power to the articles of association and allows shareholders to stipulate rules of conduct in the articles by changing the discretionary provisions of the Company Law. For example, under the old law, corporate profits had to be distributed strictly in proportion to the shareholders percentage of capital contribution in the company. The new law now allows shareholders to specify in their articles any manner of profit distribution agreed to by the shareholders. Indeed, '[t]here are virtually no provisions related to management that cannot be altered or expanded in a manner determined by the shareholders in their articles of association'.[121] Further, under CL 1993, a company's external investment in other companies could not exceed 50 percent of the company's net assets. The new law eliminates this restriction by allowing companies to freely invest in other enterprises, provided it does not act as a contributor that assumes joint and several liability for the debts of the investee.

Corporate governance and minority shareholder protection: from indifference to activism

Revolutionary changes were brought by CL 2005 to strengthen corporate governance and shareholders' protection. The most significant and interesting change is the introduction of a framework of management duties resembling common law fiduciary duties,[122] under which corporate

---

[120] Jiang Ping (2006).
[121] Dickinson (2007), p. 2.
[122] Anderson and Guo (2006a), p. 19.

directors, supervisors, and senior management personnel owe the company a duty of care and a duty of loyalty. A violation of the fiduciary duty might make the aforesaid persons personally liable.

In a stark contrast with the old law, CL 2005 explicitly grants shareholders a great deal of new rights, thus shareholders now have the statutory rights to inspect the company's books and records, to convene a shareholders' meeting themselves if the company's governing institutions fail or are unable to call such a meeting, and to petition the court to revoke an illegal resolution passed by the company's board or shareholders' meeting. Shareholders are also given the option to adopt a cumulative voting system. They are entitled to sell their shares back to the company under certain circumstances, and to invite judicial intervention to liquidate the company if the company has serious operational difficulties.

The most significant development is probably the addition of the statutory right to file derivative lawsuits to defend their and the company's interests. Civil litigation, known as private enforcement by the shareholders, enables the shareholders to sue the wrongdoer before a court of law to seek damages. Private enforcement seems apparently to be a form of legal remedy that is more consistent with the concept of distributive justice as it helps the shareholders whose interests are harmed to recover their losses. More importantly, private enforcement provides a more effective deterrent to violations of minority shareholders' rights. Minority shareholders suffering damage, with the assistance of lawyers, are more motivated and effective than anyone else to enforce their rights that cannot be enforced through ordinary corporate law mechanisms, such as removing management.

The legal provisions concerning private enforcement contained in the 1993 Company Law (the Old Company Law) were vague and rudimentary, and for all intents and purposes unenforceable. The shift of the focus of shareholder protection from public enforcement to private enforcement represents arguably the single most important rule of law development in China's corporate law system. Judicial protection would enable minority shareholders to monitor the management in a more efficient way and ensure more careful and faithful corporate decisions. Compared with the old law, the new rules are clearer, more practical, and more enforceable, and thus more likely to bring about effective and just settlement of corporate legal disputes.

Creditor protection: from absolute limited liability to 'piercing the corporate veil'

Under the old Company Law shareholders are always sheltered by the statutory limited liability, leaving creditors virtually no legal recourse if the shareholders use the company as a sham to defraud them. CL 2005 introduces new doctrines of 'abuse of shareholder rights' and 'piercing the corporate veil'. Shareholders are prohibited from abusing the independent legal person status of the company or their own limited liability privilege; otherwise, the creditors may catch the personal assets of the shareholders for the repayment of company debts.

1.6 COMPANY LAW IN THE CONTEXT OF CHINA'S POLITICAL, SOCIAL, AND LEGAL CULTURE

In understanding China's Company Law one must also understand the unique political–legal environment in China. In China's one-party political system, the ruling party has the basic instinct to put everything, including business corporations, under its political control, although in the reform era the party has long realized that independent commercial enterprises are the key to achieving economic growth and for this it has returned autonomy to enterprises through the implementation of a variety of civil and commercial laws. Furthermore, the socialist nature of the political–legal system also requires business firms to sacrifice a certain degree of freedom of enterprise to cope with the state's official ideology and the regulators' policy agendas. In summary, as one commentator advises, '[f]oreign investors who wish to set up enterprises in China should take note of [the uniquely Chinese definition of the business corporation as a hybrid economic-political-sociocultural institution] and be prepared to interact closely with the CCP and other government-affiliated organizations, and to provide their willingness to comply with the official interpretation of corporate social responsibility'.[123]

1.6.1 Organization of the Chinese Communist Party in Companies

An often-ignored provision in the Company Law is Article 19, which states, 'an organization of the Communist Party of China (CPC) shall be established in a company to carry out party activities according to the Charter of the Communist Party of China' and mandates the company to

[123] Hawes (2007), p. 823.

'provide necessary conditions for the activities of the [CPC organization]'. An annotation of the Company Law published by the Legislative Affairs Commission of the National People's Congress interprets Article 19 as follows:[124]

> According to our country's Constitution, the basic task of the nation is to concentrate its effort on socialist modernization along the road of building socialism with Chinese characteristics. The Chinese people of all ethnic groups will continue to be under the leadership of the Communist Party of China to construct our country and turn it into a socialist country that is prosperous, powerful, democratic and culturally advanced. The provision of the constitution explicitly points out the leadership position of the CPC in our country's political life and economic construction. In order to better strengthen the role of the CPC grassroots organizations and CPC members in the company's development and economic construction, this Law makes specific provisions in regards to the activities of CPC grassroots organizations according to the Constitution. The provision has a two-prong meaning. First, the CPC Charter should be obeyed to establish the CPC organization and carry out Party activities in a company. Under the CPC Charter, a grassroots Party organization should be established in an enterprise, village, governmental agency, school, science research institution, residential district, military company or other grassroots unit if the aforesaid unit has more than three official members of the Party. The CPC's grassroots organization should carry out its activities according to the CPC Charter. Secondly, the company should give support, such as providing the necessary venue, to the CPC organization's activities.

Article 19 begs the question about what the party organizations do in business firms. According to the CPC Charter,[125]

> In a state-owned or collective enterprise, the primary Party organization acts as the political nucleus and works for the operation of the enterprise. The primary Party organization guarantees and supervises the implementation of the principles and policies of the Party and the state in its own enterprise and backs the meeting of shareholders, board of directors, board of supervisors and managers (or factory director) in the exercise of their functions and powers according to law. It relies wholeheartedly on the workers and office staff, supports the work of the congresses of representatives of workers and office staff and participates in making final decisions on major questions in the enterprise. It works to improve its own organization, provides leadership over trade unions, the Communist Youth League organization and other mass

---

124 An Jian (2005), p. 41.

125 Charter of the Communist Party of China, Article 32, quoted in Hawes (2007), p. 818.

> organizations, and carries out ideological and political work, and cultural and ethical improvement programs.
>
> In a non-public economic institution, the primary Party organization carries out the Party's principles and policies, provides guidance to and supervises the enterprise in observing the laws and regulations of the state, exercises leadership over the trade union, the Communist Youth League organization and other mass organizations, rallies the workers and office staff around it, safeguards the legitimate rights and interests of all stakeholders, and stimulates the healthy development of the enterprise.

At this stage, there are no fundamental contradictions between the CPC's disciplines and the companies' business objectives, as the party–state's self-imposed task is to achieve economic development. In fact, party members in business enterprises are required to help the firms grow their revenue and profit.[126] However, since CPC members are obligated under the CPC Charter to implement party policies and put 'the interests of the Party and the people above everything',[127] uncertainty remains as to what will happen if party policies and interests change. Further, notwithstanding the NPC Legislative Commission's enthusiastic 'justification' above, the constitutionality of Article 19 is questionable from the perspective of legal positivism. In essence, there might be no constitutional basis for granting such a privileged position to the CPC. Under the PRC Constitution, no individual or organization, including any political party and its members, is above the law. The Constitution does not offer such special rights to CPC organizations and members that they can enjoy such free 'tribute' offered by any enterprise more than three of whose employees are CCP members. As such, Article 18, if enforced, effectively constitutes an unconstitutional expropriation of (private) corporate property without fair compensation. If the company is privately owned, Article 18 provides a basis for the CPC's unconstitutional infringement of private property; if the company is an SOE, Article 18 is accordingly an infringement of the SOE's 'corporate property rights' and also undermines its autonomy as an independent legal person.

1.6.2 Trade Union, Labor Rights, and 'Democratic Management'

The protection of company employees' rights traditionally does not fall within the jurisdiction of corporate law, and hence it will not be

---

[126] Hawes (2007), p. 819 (quoting a party member working at Wal-Mart as saying that 'one of the criteria for evaluating Party members' progress is *whether we have helped to increase sales* at the Wal-Mart stores where we work').

[127] Charter of the Communist Party of China, Article 3.

discussed in detail in this book. It is, however, worth noting that the PRC Company Law has two very interesting provisions, namely Articles 17 and 18, which govern labor rights and labor organizations in companies. Article 17 mandates that a company should protect the lawful rights of its staff and workers, sign labor contracts with them, and provide social security insurance and labor protection. Article 18, a provision for trade union and workers' 'democratic management', reads:

> The employees of companies may organize trade union[s] and carry out union activities in accordance with the Trade Union Law of the People's Republic of China to protect the lawful rights and interests of the employees. The company should provide the requisite conditions for the activities of the trade union. The trade union shall sign collective contracts on behalf of the employees with the company on matters such as wages, working hours, welfare, insurance, work safety and health etc according to law.

Under China's 1992 Trade Union Law (amended in 2001), there is only one trade union lawfully allowed in China, which is the All-China Federation of Trade Unions (ACFTU).[128] Under the ACFTU are different levels of trade union organizations. It further requires that a basic-level trade union organization be set up in an enterprise, an institution or a government agency with a membership of 25 or more.[129] However, a trade union organization is not permitted to be established on the initiative of the workers. The Trade Union Law mandates that the establishment of a union at a particular level should be submitted to the union organization at the next higher level – and ultimately the ACFTU – for approval. Obviously enough, the trade union is a tool to strengthen the CPC's political control of workers' activities in Chinese enterprises. It is, however, important to note that this kind of control is not necessarily for interfering with the enterprise's business management. It is more of a tool for social control, in order to prevent workers from being organized by forces outside the Chinese government.[130]

---

128 Article 2, para. 2 of the PRC Trade Union Law states: 'The All-China Federation of Trade Unions and all trade union organizations under it represent the interests of the workers and staff members and safeguard the legitimate rights and interests of the workers and staff members according to law'.

129 PRC Trade Union Law, Article 10.

130 On 29 July 2006, Wal-Mart, which was infamous for its anti-union stance, witnessed the first trade union established by its China workers at its store in Quanzhou City, Fujian Province of China. In about two weeks, 19 Wal-Mart stores in China established trade unions. Outside China, Wal-Mart permitted the operation of unions in only one of its stores, in Canada. However, the pressure to

1.6.3 Corporate Social Responsibility

Corporate social responsibility (CSR) has emerged as an issue of increasing social and business importance in corporate China. The concept of CSR was invented in the West long before China arose as a central part of the global production network.[131] In recent years, CSR has caught considerable attention in China, leading to an emerging normative framework. The Company Law has a specific provision on CSR. Article 5 of the law stipulates: 'When engaging in business activities, a company must abide by laws and administrative regulations, observe social morals and business ethics, act in good faith, accept supervision by the government and the public, and bear social responsibilities'. On 27 September 2006, the Shenzhen Stock Exchange issued the 'Social Responsibility Instructions to Listed Companies', which defines CSR as 'the obligations listed companies should assume for the comprehensive development of the nation and the society, for natural environment and resources, and for stakeholders including the shareholders, creditors, employees, customers, consumers, suppliers and communities'.[132]

A more recent initiative by the government is the promulgation of the Guiding Opinions on Practicing Social Responsibility by Central Enterprises by the SASAC (hereinafter the 'CSR Opinions'),[133] in which the SASAC ordered China's centrally administered SOEs to play a leading role in CSR. It provides a broad definition of CSR that covers environmental protection, energy and resources conservation, work safety, labor protection, consumer rights, maintaining market order, upholding business ethics and philanthropy, shareholder value, and job creation. Apparently, these are often mutually conflicting objectives that are difficult to implement by one enterprise.

---

approve the establishment of trade unions was not from the desire of workers. Instead, Wal-Mart received direct state influence through the ACFTU, which has launched an aggressive campaign to set up branches in all foreign-invested companies. The decision to allow China trade unions was a result of direct negations between Wal-Mart and the ACFTU. See BBC, 'Chinese "create Wal-Mart union"', 31 July 2006, available at http://news.bbc.co.uk/2/hi/business/5230378.stm (accessed 13 March 2012).

131 Jensen (2006).

132 Shenzhen Zhengquan Jiaoyisuo Shangshi Gongsi Shehui Zeren Zhiyin [Shenzhen Stock Exchange Social Responsibility Instructions to Listed Companies], promulgated on 25 September 2006, available at http://www.szse.cn (accessed 2 August 2007) (hereinafter the SZSE CSR Instructions).

133 Guanyu Zhongyang Qiye Luxing Shehui Zeren De Zhidao Yijian, SASAC Doc. No. 1 of 2008, 4 January 2008.

At the industry level, the China National Textile and Apparel Council (CNTAC) was the first among industry associations to launch a programme pushing for CSR. It held the first industry-wide annual conference for CSR in December 2006 and issued the first Annual CSR Report for China's Textile and Apparel Industry.[134] In May 2007, CNTAC, joined by the International Labour Organization (ILO) and United Nations Industry Development Organization (UNIDO), launched the Joint Project on Corporate Social Responsibility in the Chinese Textile Industry.[135] It purports to develop training programmes and toolkits based on the ILO's Factory Improvement Programme (FIP), UNIDO's Cleaner Production Programme (CP) and Responsible Entrepreneurs Achievement Programme (REAP), as well as the CNTAC's CSC9000T. Sinochem, one of the largest SOEs in China, was one of the first Chinese companies to release a CSR report on 13 April 2007.[136] Foreign-invested enterprises (FIEs) moved even faster: on 27 March 2006, 69 FIEs, with the endorsement of the PRC Ministry of Commerce, signed a Corporate Social Responsibility Beijing Declaration.[137]

The CSR movement in China appears to be a top-down process at this stage. At first, it was a response of the business community to a call from the central leadership, in particular President Hu Jintao, to adopt a new approach to the project called the 'scientific development concept', and to build a 'harmonious society' in China.[138] In fact, all the above CSR

---

[134] 'To Build a Responsible Supply Chain by Putting CSR Management into Practice – Annual Conference on CSR for China's Textile and Apparel Industry and Its Annual CSR Report Release', 12 December 2006, available at http://www.csc9000.org.cn (accessed 2 August 2007).

[135] 'Opening Ceremony of the Joint Project (ILO/UNIDO/CNTAC) on Corporate Social Responsibility in the Chinese Textile Industry', available at http://www.csc9000.org.cn (accessed 2 August 2007).

[136] 'Sinochem Releases Its First CSR Report', Xinhua News Agency, 18 April 2007, available at http://news.xinhuanet.com/fortune/2007-04/18/centent_5992203.htm (accessed 2 August 2007).

[137] 'Promoting CSR for a Harmonious Society – Press Conference for the Beijing Declaration on CSR' 28 March 2007, available at http://caefi.mofcom.gov.cn/article/cz/huiyuan/200603/20060301767990.html (accessed 2 August 2007).

[138] Fewsmith (2004), and Miller (2006). The concept of 'Socialist Harmonious Society' is seen as an effort of President Hu Jintao to install a new type of ideology, emphasizing harmonious relationships among social players, into Chinese society, presumably as a replacement for the traditional 'class struggle' theory of the CCP. Although a definition of 'harmonious society' has not yet been given, it seems to ask for social tolerance and caring for the interests of others.

initiatives refer to the concept of 'harmonious society' as a justification for their 'good deeds'.[139] It is also a response of China's export industries, especially the textile and apparel industry, to 'sharp foreign criticism about conditions in [China's] factories amid claims that its cheap exports come at the expense of the environment and workers' safety and pay'.[140]

In spite of Article 5 of the PRC Company Law, it is still an open question whether CSR should be a concern for company law. As Henry Manne remarks, '[t]he illusion of great and threatening power, the superficial attractiveness of the notion, and the frequent repetition of the mantra of corporate social responsibility have made this fallacy a part of the modern corporate zeitgeist'.[141] Even though CSR should be pursued by companies, it imposes moral rather than legal obligations on corporate behavior. In brief, it is submitted that Chinese company laws should not even consider codifying and enforcing CSR.

139 For instance, Article 1 of the SZSE CSR Instructions: 'These Instructions have been formulated in accordance with the Company Law, the Securities Law and other laws, administrative regulations and the rules of competent authorities for the purpose of implementing the scientific development concept, building a harmonious society, accelerating sustainable economic and social development and promoting commitment to social responsibilities'. SZSE CSR Instructions, *supra* note 118.

140 Richard McGregor, 'China's good corporate citizens find their voice', *Financial Times*, 27 February 2007, at http://www.ft.com.

141 Manne (2006).

2. Types of companies in the diverse world of business organizations in China

2.1 WORLD OF BUSINESS ORGANIZATIONS IN CHINA

2.1.1 Diverse World of Business Organizations in China

A commentator has noted that 'One of the most perplexing aspects of Chinese enterprise law concerns the conditions under which state institutions will acknowledge and give effect to the existence of a business organization distinct from the natural or legal persons that participate in its operations'.[1] During China's reform period (from 1978 to present), it recognized the following business organizations:

- State-owned enterprises (SOEs) [*Guoyou Qiye*]
  - Industrial enterprises owned by the whole people [*Quanmin Suoyouzhi Qiye*]
- Collectively-owned enterprises (COEs) [*Jiti Suoyouzhi Qiye*]
  - Township and village enterprises (TVEs) [*Xiangzhen Qiye*]
- Foreign-invested enterprises (FIEs) [*Waishang Touzi Qiye*]
  - Sino-foreign equity joint ventures (EJVs) [*Zhongwai Hezi Jingying Qiye*]
  - Sino-foreign cooperative joint ventures (CJVs)[*Zhongwai Hezuo Jingying Qiye*]
  - Wholly foreign-owned enterprises (WFOEs) [*Waishang Duzi Qiye*]
- Companies
  - Limited liability companies (LLCs) [*Youxian Zeren Gongsi*]
    - One-person limited liability company [*Yiren Youxian Zeren Gongsi*]

[1] Clarke (2005), p. 51.

        - Wholly state-owned companies (WSOCs) [*Guoyou Duzi Gongsi*]
    - Joint-stock limited companies (JSLCs) [*Guyou Youxian Gongsi*]
        - Foreign-invested joint-stock limited companies (FI-JSLCs) [*Waishang Touzi Gufen Youxian Gongsi*]
- Farmers' special cooperatives (FSCs) [*Nongmin Zhuanye Hezuoshe*]
- Shareholding cooperative enterprises (SCEs) [*Gufen Hezuozhi Qiye*]
- Partnerships [*Hehuo*]
    - General partnerships (GPs) [*Yiban Hehuo*]
    - Special general partnerships (SGPs) [*Youxian Zeren Hehuo*]
    - Limited partnerships (LPs) [*Youxian Hehuo*]
- Wholly individually-owned enterprises (WIOEs) [*Geren Duzi Qiye*]
- Individual industrial and commercial households (IICH) [*Geti Gongshanghu*]

Students and practitioners face two crucial questions. One, using the question posed by Clarke (2006), how do we know when a business organization exists? Two, what are the relationships between the business entities mentioned above? In the following sections, we attempt to address these questions.

The evolution of China's SOE reform and the emergence of the private economy are the topic of another chapter of this book. For the time being, it is useful to note that, before the reform era, there were only two types of business entities in China, namely state-owned enterprises (once officially called state-run enterprises) and collectively-owned enterprises. With the rise of the private economy since 1978, state-owned business organizations have undergone a corporatization process, which inevitably involves the participation of private owners. New forms of business entities have begun to be used widely in China, although their numerous names have brought tremendous confusion to investors.

2.1.2 No Enterprise Without a Law Providing for It?

Jiang (2006) points out that China has established an incomplete system of *qiye fading zhuyi*, which, drawing an analogy between company law's principle of incorporation and the criminal law principle of *nullem crimen sine lege*, means 'no enterprise without a law providing for it'.[2]

---

[2] Clarke (2005), p. 52.

Under this doctrine, a business enterprise cannot be established and operated in China without legal basis in Chinese law. However, Clarke notes that 'there simply does not exist any consistent rule of recognition guiding the decisions of various governmental agencies in China when they face the question of whether or not to acknowledge a claim that a particular business entity "exists" and that particular consequences should follow from the existence'.[3] Further, 'while such a consistent rule might be a good idea, there is nothing in the Chinese legal system that will operate to produce one'.[4]

It is definitely true that the world of business organizations is confusing. In fact, for a long time, although China promulgated numerous laws and regulations providing for the establishment of various business organizations, many other business entities, although their numbers are diminishing, exist without a 'solid legal basis'. Clarke points out that 'Chinese courts and government agencies do not consider a statute to be necessary for the recognition of an organization's existence'.[5] It is doubtful whether this statement is still true today. It is, however, clear that *nullem crimen sine lege*, although not formally established by the law possibly exists as a de facto legal practice.[6]

Most types of business organizations in China have already been given legal basis under national laws (made by the NPC or its Standing Committee) or administrative regulations (made by the State Council). As discussed in Chapter 1, laws and administrative regulations, in the sense that they both apply to the whole territories of the PRC, have the same legal force, provided that the regulations do not contradict national laws, which are the source of the regulations. There are no other rules on a par with the regulations. As a matter of fact, in terms of law-making, the State Council is no less important than the NPC and its Standing Committee. As such, we could consider a business organization to have a solid legal basis if it is provided for in either a national law or administrative regulation.

As noted in Chapter 1, major laws and regulations that concern the establishment of business organizations have been promulgated over the years; they have covered SOEs, collective enterprises, private enterprises, TVEs, companies, FIEs, partnerships, and sole proprietorships. However, a few types of business vehicles are not prescribed in national laws or regulations. Using Clarke's words, they are without a 'solid statutory

---

3 Clarke (2005), p. 64.
4 Clarke (2005), p. 64.
5 Clarke (2005), p. 52.
6 Jiang Ping (2006).

basis', which is defined as 'a basis in law that can, consistent with China's constitutional order, explain why certain legal consequences follow from an acknowledgement of the organization's existence'.[7] But, as explained above, this statement ignores the importance of the State Council's administrative regulations. Laws or administrative regulations should have the same force to give a 'solid legal basis' to business vehicles.

There are still a few types of business organizations that are created neither by national laws nor by administrative regulations. Instead, they have to find a legal basis from ministerial rules. One example concerns the shareholding cooperative enterprises (SCEs). As Clarke observes, the regulation of SCEs began at the municipal and provincial level. In time, three central ministries issued three sets of rules regulating SCEs in the urban and rural areas.[8] In the end, neither the NPC or its Standing Committee nor the State Council has made any rules concerning SCEs. As a former member of the NPC Standing Committee remarked, SCEs were not a form of business that can have a valuable long-term existence in China.[9] However, even though eye-catching business vehicles such as foreign-invested joint-stock limited companies (FI-JSLC) and foreign-invested securities companies (FISC) have no statutory basis, that fact does not affect their use as popular business vehicles for foreign investors and their recognition as legal entities.

2.1.3 Classifying Business Organizations in China

Business enterprises can be classified according to whether they are registered companies or legal persons shielded by limited liability. An alternative, simpler way is to classify them as business individuals, business partnerships, and business legal persons. Business individuals comprise individual industrial and commercial business/household businesses and sole proprietorships. Business partnerships encompass general partnerships, limited partnerships, and special general partnerships (limited liability partnerships). Business legal persons include companies, state-owned enterprises, collectively-owned enterprises, and some foreign-invested enterprises.[10]

---

7 Clarke (2005), p. 55.
8 Clarke (2005), p. 58.
9 Jiang Ping (2006).
10 Some foreign investment projects, for example, Sino-foreign cooperative enterprises, can form partnerships.

To be called a company, an enterprise must be duly registered under the national Company Law, follow the prescribed registration procedures, and pay the registered capital. We may say that some SOEs and FIEs are companies, provided that they are so registered. Broadly speaking, all companies not owned by the state are privately-owned companies. However, 'solely individually-owned enterprises', 'enterprises owned by the whole people', and 'collectively-owned enterprises', each having their own laws (adopted by the NPC) and legal structures as will be examined in the later parts of this chapter, are not companies.

Business enterprises could also be classified according to whether they enjoy limited liability. In Chinese law, this depends on whether the enterprise is a legal person. The concept of a legal person will be discussed in Chapter 4. Suffice to say here that the General Principles of Chinese Law (GPCL) of 1986 define a legal person as an 'organization' that has the rights and capacity to independently enjoy civil rights and assume civil obligations.[11] To become a legal person, an enterprise must establish itself in accordance with legal procedures, possess necessary property or funds, and have a name, organizational structure, and premises.[12] Chinese law recognizes that only legal persons have limited liability.[13]

2.2 THE CONCEPT OF COMPANIES UNDER THE COMPANY LAW

Under the doctrine of *qiye fading zhuyi,* enterprises recognized as companies must register themselves and/or receive recognition from the national Company Law. The Company Law governs organizations with the following characteristics:

- The organizations are business companies, not non-profit, government, or public[14] entities. Many of these non-business companies

[11] GPCL, Article 36.
[12] GPCL, Article 37.
[13] GPCL, Article 37.
[14] A public corporation is a corporation that functions as a government. In the U.S., many cities, towns, and villages are incorporated. Airport authorities are also public corporations. In China, government agencies, including townships, municipal governments, and central ministries are granted independent legal person status for the purpose of bearing civil liabilities.

are treated as *shiye danwei*, or public services units (PSUs), under a variety of separate regulations.[15]

- Companies governed by the Company Law all have limited liability, and hence unlimited companies are not allowed in China, although partnership enterprises under the PRC Partnership Enterprise Law are the functional equivalent of unlimited companies.[16]
- Companies under the Company Law must all have share capital. China does not allow companies limited by guarantee.[17]

The Company Law recognizes two types of business companies; they are limited liability companies (*youxian zeren gongsi*), or LLCs, and joint-stock limited companies limited by shares (*gufen youxian gongsi*), or JSLCs, also called companies limited by shares (CLSs) in other contexts (see section 2.3.1 below). The Company Law recognizes one-person companies and wholly state-owned companies as special types of LLCs. It is important to recall that the Company Law does not apply to other business organizations, regardless of whether they have limited or unlimited liability.

From the perspective of incorporation and registration, a company can only register as an LLC or JSLC. However, companies are also classified according to other criteria.

---

[15] See World Bank (2005a).

[16] An unlimited company in English common law jurisdictions is a company in which the members are personally liable for all the company's debts. See Stott (2005), p. 5. This form is attractive to some investors because it requires no share capital and offers privacy and flexibility. In practice, it is rarely used. See Davies (2003), p. 16.

[17] In English common law jurisdictions, shareholders of a company by guarantee do not need to pay capital contributions initially and throughout the company's life. Instead, the company retains the right to receive from shareholders 'the amount which they have undertaken to contribute in the event of the company being wound up'. See CCH (2006), ¶2-160. A company limited by guarantee 'is appropriate when there is no intention to distribute the company's profits to its members and does not therefore need to have shares; it is typical of charities and quasi-charitable organisations such as schools and hospitals, but is only suitable if the company does not need an initial share capital'. Stott (2005), p. 5.

2.3 LIMITED LIABILITY COMPANIES (LLCS) AND JOINT-STOCK LIMITED COMPANIES (JSLCS)

2.3.1 Standardized LLC and JSLC

Article 2 of the Company Law provides: 'Companies referred to in this Law shall mean limited liability companies and joint-stock limited companies established in China in accordance with provisions of this law'. As noted, JSLCs are also called companies limited by shares (CLSs) in many writings.[18] Although LLCs do not divide their capital into equal units or shares, investors in both types of companies are still called 'shareholders' (*gudong*) under the Company Law. In essence, a shareholder in an LLC can limit his liability to his capital contribution; for a shareholder of a JSLC, his liability is limited to the shares he has subscribed.[19]

LLCs are intended for corporations with a limited numbers of shareholders. Although they are most attractive to small- and medium-sized enterprises, LLCs are not theirs exclusively.[20] According to official statistics, among China's 1.2 million registered companies, only about

---

[18] Although joint-stock companies or companies limited by shares are popular translations of *gufen youxian gongsi* in writings on Chinese law in the English-speaking world, we use in this book the term 'joint-stock limited company' or JSLC because it is the standard translation used in the English version of the corporate charter (articles of association) of PRC companies listed in foreign stock exchanges. It is useful to note that the concept of joint-stock company (JSC) in the U.S. is substantially different from what is customarily understood in China. In the U.S., the JSC is a variant of the partnership form, defined as '[a]n unincorporated association of individuals possessing common capital, the capital being contributed by the members and divided into shares, of which each member possesses a number of shares proportionate to the member's investment', or '[a] partnership in which the capital is divided into shares that are transferable without the express consent of the partners'. See *Black's Law Dictionary* (8th edition), 'joint-stock company'. Cox and Hazen (2003, p. 19) note that 'the principle disadvantage the joint stock company has in common with a common law partnership, even where the joint stock company has been recognized by statute, is that the members do not enjoy limited liability'.

[19] Company Law, Article 3. The 2005 Company Law revision brought a change to the limited liability requirement. Under the 1993 Company Law, the liability of a shareholder is confined to the capital contribution he has actually paid or shares he holds. This leads to disputes when capital is paid in installments.

[20] See Art and Gu (1995), p. 292 (noting 'the Limited Liability Company form is generally for smaller corporations').

10,000 were joint-stock companies, while the rest were LLCs. Moreover, a number of giant companies and corporate groups are still utilizing the LLC model.

A JSLC is the functional equivalent of a publicly held corporation in the United States and a public company under English law. The key difference between a JSLC and an LLC lies in their degrees of openness. The detailed characteristics are more appropriately discussed later. At this stage, a brief comparison is all that is necessary.

First, the number of LLC shareholders is limited to 50. JSLCs have no such limits; however, the number of promoters when it incorporates should be between two and 200. Second, a JSLC, as its name '*gufen youxian gongsi*' implies, has 'share capital', meaning its capital is divided into equal shares and members take the shares issued to them by the company. Each share is assigned a 'par value' and is always issued at a premium. On the other hand, an LLC does not divide its capital into equal shares and issue them. Instead, the shareholders agree to determine the equity interest of each of them in terms of a percentage holding, e.g. 49 percent. Third, the regulatory requirements for the establishment of an LLC are less stringent than for a JSLC. For example, the minimum registered capital of an LLC is RMB30,000, while that for a JSLC is RMB5 million. With certain exceptions (especially foreign-invested LLCs), the incorporation of an LLC is very simple; it is subject mainly to the registration requirements of the state or local Administration of Industry and Commerce. The documentation requirements are also easier to satisfy. Depending on the way of incorporation, to establish a JSLC the incorporators might need approval from a variety of agencies, from local governments to central ministries. Moreover, they must solicit expensive services from intermediaries (e.g. underwriters, sponsors), and meet very burdensome documentation requirements such as having to publish a prospectus. Fourth, while the shares of JSLCs are almost always freely transferable (through securities exchanges or OTC markets, or by private agreements), the law imposes draconian restrictions on the transfer of LLC ownership interests. JSLCs can list their shares on the securities exchanges while a transfer by a shareholder of his equity stake in an LLC to an outsider needs approval from a majority of shareholders. Further, while the other shareholders have a right of first refusal, there are no such restrictions on the transfer of JSLC shares. Fifth, the articles of association of a JSLC are approved by a simple majority of the subscribers of corporate shares at the company's inaugural meeting, while the articles of association of an LLC must receive approval from each and every shareholder, reflecting the fact that the LLC is treated very similarly to a partnership. Finally, a JSLC should have a corporate governance structure that includes general shareholders' meetings, a board of directors, and a supervisory board. However, an LLC could omit both board of directors and supervisors, substituting an executive director and one or two supervisors for the two boards.

From a comparative law perspective, the LLC is similar in concept to – and is in fact a functional equivalent of – the closely held corporation under ordinary American corporate laws.[21] For example, the Delaware General Corporation Law defines close corporation as having the following attributes: '(1) all of the corporation's issued shares must be held by not more than 30 persons; (2) all of the issued shares must be subject to one or more authorized restrictions on transfer; and (3) the corporation cannot make any public offering of its shares within the meaning of the Securities Act of 1933'.[22] The similarities between Chinese LLCs and American close corporations are obvious.

The LLC is also the functional equivalent of the 'private company' in English common law jurisdictions.[23] To compare a Chinese LLC with an English private company, the starting point should be the recognition of

---

[21] Choper, Coffee, and Gilson (2004, p. 738) note that the close corporation under American law has six attributes. 'First, a close corporation is "owned by a small number of persons … " Second, there is often a high overlap between the shareholders and the managers and employees of the business, as many, if not most, shareholders are actively involved in the business. Third, it is desirable to customize the management structure and corporate governance rules whether because the business is too small to support the cost of formalities or because the overlap of management and ownership make the standard corporate governance structure inappropriate. Fourth, shareholders have little investment liquidity. Fifth, the value of an ownership interest in a close corporation has no readily observable market price, so that the difficulty of valuation adds to the illiquidity problem. Sixth, deadlocks may arise because of the relatively small number of shareholders and because shareholders may have required a higher than majority vote to resolve contested issues'.

[22] Delaware General Corporation Law §342 (1998), cited in Choper, Coffee, and Gilson (2004), p. 740.

[23] Under §29 of the Companies Ordinance of Hong Kong, 'the expression "private company" (私人公司) means a company which by its articles

(a) restrict the right to transfer its shares; and
(b) limit the number of its members to 50, not including persons who are in the employment of the company and persons who, having been formerly in the employment of the company, were while in that employment, and have continued after the determination of that employment to be, members of the company; and
(c) prohibit any invitation to the public to subscribe for any shares or debentures of the company'.

one of the major differences between them: Chinese LLCs do not issue shares. They do not divide their capital into equal units for subscription by members, although members are still called 'shareholders'. Instead, a shareholder's stake in an LLC is defined by the amount of capital invested. Apart from that, the two share common characteristics, including inter alia, more stringent restrictions on the right to transfer shares, the prohibition of offering shares to the public, and the restriction on the number of members. Further, they are subject to less demanding reporting regimes in several areas, and no reporting requirements in most other areas. In fact, except for the annual inspection of companies conducted by the State Administration of Industry and Commerce and its local agencies, an LLC has no reporting obligations. For the annual inspection, the authority is merely interested in regulatory compliance concerning the proper use of the company's name and business license, the updating of registration information regarding changes in management personnel, amendments to the company's articles of association, maintenance of registered capital, etc.[24]

One has to be mindful of an often-occurring misunderstanding when comparing a Chinese limited liability company with the limited liability company in the United States because they are very different animals. In 1977, the State of Wyoming promulgated the first corporate statute authorizing LLCs. By the end of the 1990s, it became a legalized business form in all 50 American states of the U.S. The American LLC is more than a traditional type of corporation with limited liability. As noted in Choper, Coffee and Gilson (2004),

> The [American] LLC was intended as a hybrid – a combination of two distinct entities each of which had distinct desirable characteristics. An LLC is like a corporation in that it provides limited liability to investors and the opportunity for centralized management through an operating agreement. It is also like partnership in that it is accorded pass through taxation, and is not subject to the same rigidities as a traditional corporation.[25]

The Company Law permits an LLC to be converted into a JSLC, and vice versa. According to Article 9 of the Company Law, '[i]f a limited liability company is to be converted into a joint stock limited company, it shall meets the conditions for joint stock limited companies stipulated in this law; if a joint stock limited company is to be converted into a limited

---

[24] Qiye Niandu Jianyan Banfa (Measures for the Annual Inspection of Enterprises), promulgated by the State Administration of Industry and Commerce, 24 February 2006.

[25] p. 839.

liability company, it shall meet the conditions for limited liability companies stipulated in this law'. This is a liberal improvement from the 1993 Company Law, which did not provide mechanisms for joint-stock limited companies to be converted into limited liability companies.[26]

2.3.2 One-person LLC

The new Company Law for the first time allows the establishment of one-person limited liability companies (*yiren youxian zeren gongsi*). The shareholder is either a natural or legal person. This is a special type of LLC; to date, Chinese law does not recognize one-person JSLCs.

Prior to the 2005 revision of the Company Law, Chinese law disfavored one-person companies in the sense that Chinese natural persons were not allowed to establish such companies.[27] However, the government did permit the establishment of wholly state-owned companies; moreover, under the Wholly Foreign-Owned Enterprise Law a foreign investor could establish a solely-owned limited liability company. The hostility towards one-person companies was not easily comprehended, although academically, this type of company is inconsistent with the orthodox theory of corporate law, which asserts that a company is a 'social group legal person' (*shetuan faren*). In the legislative debates that occurred during the drafting of the 1993 Company Law, there was concern for creditor protection.[28] In practice, it is very difficult to prevent the establishment of one-person companies, as it is rather easy to find a mere nominee to serve as another shareholder who takes no part in the company's affairs. Further, as Clarke (2005) correctly points out, if there is a concern that a single shareholder will falsify the value of capital contribution, '[i]t is hard to see how requiring more than one promoter would solve this problem, since the promoters could easily collude to overstate the value of their capital contributions by the same multiple'.[29] In the end, one-person companies were inserted into the Company Law in the 2005 revision, with certain strings attached. Significantly, Article 64 of the Company Law mandates a 'presumption of guilt' with respect to the liability of the shareholder: if he is unable to prove that the

---

[26] CCH (2005), §14-170.

[27] Clarke (2005), p. 55.

[28] Clarke (2005), p. 56 (citing Jiang Ping's comment that 'legislators were concerned that company promoters might falsify the value of the capital contributions, thus giving a company a high initial value').

[29] p. 56, n. 14.

company's assets are independent of his personal assets, he shall bear joint and several liability for the company's debt.

2.3.3 State-owned Enterprises and Privately-owned Enterprises as Companies

'State-owned enterprise' (SOE) is not a legal term. It is difficult to define SOE, but the Company Law does describe wholly state-owned companies (WSOCs) as 'a limited liability company wholly funded by the State', in which the central or local authority in charge of the administration of state assets is authorized to serve as the investor/shareholder.[30] Literally, a WSOC is a one-person company in which the state is the only shareholder, represented by the central State-owned Assets Supervision and Administration Commission (SASAC) and local SASACs. The Company Law has a special section for the WSOC, indicating that it is a special type of LLC and one that is also different from the typical one-person company. Significantly, there is no 'presumption of guilt' and the state will probably never have to bear unlimited liability despite the participation of the state and its agents in the management of WSOCs. In addition, the WSOC's board of directors and supervisory board must have employee representatives.

SOE as a generic form of business organization will be examined in section 2.8.

2.3.4 Foreign-invested LLC and Foreign-invested JSLC

Since the early days of the reform period, China has allowed foreign investors to establish Sino-foreign equity joint ventures (EJVs), Sino-foreign contractual joint ventures (CJVs), wholly foreign-owned enterprises (WFOEs), foreign-invested joint-stock limited companies (FI-JSLCs), foreign-invested holding companies (FIHCs), foreign-invested securities companies (FISCs), foreign-invested assets management companies (FIAMCs), and Chinese subsidiaries of foreign banks and financial institutions. They have participated in PRC domestic firms (including both industrial firms and financial institutions) by purchasing equity interests.

Both EJVs and WFOEs are LLCs.[31] An EJV is a company in which foreign partners contribute not less than 25 percent of the investment

---

[30] Company Law, Article 65.

[31] A WFOE might assume other forms of business. It is, however, not clear whether foreigners can establish partnership enterprises in China.

with the net profits and risks shared proportionately by all the partners. A WFOE does not require a local partner. If approved, foreign investors must establish it exclusively with their own capital.

A CJV is more complex. It is a relatively loose contractual arrangement under which the Chinese and foreign parties are relatively free to stipulate in their CJV contract the terms of investment, cooperation, earning and product distribution, sharing of risks and losses, models of management, and the ownership of property if the CJV ceases to exist. There are two types of CJVs: CJVs with legal person status and CJVs without legal person status. A legal person CJV is always an LLC. The status of the non-legal person CJV is not entirely clear; however, in practice it is treated as a partnership, although it is not clear whether foreigners may establish partnerships in China.

In 2004, the Ministry of Commerce began to allow foreign investors to establish holding companies (called 'investment companies', or *touzi xing gongsi*) under which they could consolidate all their Chinese projects under one corporate umbrella. The foreign holding company, FIHC, is an LLC in the form of an EJV or WFOE. Also, foreign-invested securities firms, asset management companies, and subsidiaries of foreign financial institutions are LLCs.

Since 1995, China has permitted foreign investors to establish joint-stock limited companies. If foreign shareholders own at least 25 percent of the company's shares it is a JSLC. Such a company may offer its shares to the public and list its shares on a stock exchange.[32]

2.3.5 Listed Companies and Non-listed Companies

A JSLC – and only a JSLC – may offer, list, and trade shares on a stock exchange. Although Chinese processes combine share offerings and listings, the law regards them as two separate things. To offer shares for public subscription, a company must obtain approval from the China Securities Regulatory Commission (CSRC). In the 2005 revision of the PRC Securities Law the CSRC returned the power to approve company listing to the stock exchanges. Both the Shanghai Stock Exchange (SSE) and the Shenzhen Stock Exchange (SZSE) examine applications from JSLCs according to their Listing Rules. A company that lists its shares on a stock change is called a 'listed company' (*shangshi gongsi*). A listed company can obtain large amounts of low-cost capital through initial and subsequent public offerings of shares, which means the supply of capital from an almost unlimited number of investors. JSLCs, however, are not

---

[32] The first FI-JSLC by a major foreign company was the Kodak (China) Joint-Stock Liability Company incorporated in 1998. See EIU (2007), p. 46.

necessarily listed companies. There are currently about 2000 companies listed on China's two stock exchanges,[33] but that is a small number compared with the total number of JSLCs incorporated in China.

All companies not listed on stock exchanges are called 'unlisted companies', which include LLCs. In practice, unlisted companies customarily refer to JSLCs whose shares are not listed and traded on any exchange.

2.3.6 Parent Company, Branch, and Subsidiaries

Under Article 14 of the Company Law, a company may incorporate subsidiaries and register branch companies. Although the law calls a company a 'branch company' (*fengongsi*), it is not a new company; it is merely one that manages part of a company's business or the local business of the company in a region not its domicile. Branch companies need to get business licenses from local administrations of industry and commerce, but they do not possess legal person status, and any legal liability arising out of their activities is eventually borne by the company.[34] However, in practice the creditor to whom the branch company owes debts should seek repayment from branch assets before he resorts to recourse from the company.

Companies invest in subsidiaries, but the latter are separate and independent legal entities. They possess legal person status and bear their own civil liabilities.[35] Companies must form the subsidiary and become its controlling shareholder. The controlling company is called a 'parent' company. Two interesting legal questions flow from parent–subsidiary relationships under Chinese law.

First, what is the legal nature of this relationship? How does the parent company control the subsidiary? Given that the subsidiary is an independent legal person, the parent cannot give it direct orders. The parent's control derives from the shares it controls, and so it has to behave as a shareholder, respecting the subsidiary's internal governance rules and procedures. Like any other shareholder, the parent also faces typical agency problems inherent in corporate governance.

Second, what is the legal form of the subsidiary? If the parent is just one of several shareholders, then the subsidiary could be either a standard LLC or a JSLC. Under the 1993 Company Law, because one-person

---

[33] The data is updated as of December 2010. The statistics are available at http://www.csrc.gov.cn.

[34] CL 2005, Article 14.

[35] CL 2005, Article 14.

companies were not allowed, it was viewed that there was an inconsistency in the law and, as such, wholly owned subsidiaries could not possibly be established. As Howson (1997) critiques the 1994 Company Law,[36]

> Although the Company Law states that companies may set up independent legal person subsidiaries, it also mandates that 'a limited liability company is established by capital contributions made together by at least two and no more than 50 shareholders'. Thus, any corporate entity intent on forming its own wholly-owned subsidiary (as limited liability company) is effectively blocked, unless it finds at least one co-investor and thus takes only a partial interest in the subsidiary entity. This limitation is at odds with practice as it has developed throughout China since the mid-1980s and throws into serious doubt the true limited liability nature of such entities already established under pre-existing PRC companies. In a clear concession to the powerful remnants of the state-run economy, it is only state-authorized investment institutions or departments which may act as the sole investor in 'wholly state-owned companies' (a special class of limited liability company).

According to a commentary published by the NPC Legislative Affairs Commission (which is in charge of drafting laws), it is clear enough that, under the new Company Law, 'a company 100 percent owned by another company is both a subsidiary and a one-person company, and as such must comply with the provisions of [the Company Law] concerning a one-person company'.[37] To the extent wholly owned subsidiaries are legal, they are also subject to the 'presumption of guilt' in terms of limited liability, unless of course they are wholly state-owned enterprises. It appears that there is a hidden discrimination against privately-owned companies.

2.3.7 Chinese Branches of Foreign Companies

Chapter 11 of the Company Law regulates branches of foreign companies in China. A 'foreign company' is defined as 'a company established outside China in accordance with foreign laws'.[38] The legal status of foreign companies under Chinese law is unclear as, unlike many other jurisdictions, Chinese Company Law has rules especially for branches of

---

36 Howson (1997), p. 145.
37 An (2005), p. 33.
38 Company Law, Article 192.

foreign companies establishing themselves in China.[39] In principle, to establish a branch in China, a foreign company must submit a written application together with its articles of association and certification of incorporation issued by the country of origin. Upon approval, the company can then complete the registration formalities and obtain a business license.[40] The branch is part of the foreign company, does not possess legal person status, and its foreign headquarters bear all legal liabilities arising from its Chinese activities.[41]

A foreign company, however, does not establish its branch in China by simply adhering to the Company Law, as that law authorizes the State Council to enact regulations for the examination and approval of foreign companies applying to set up branches in China.[42] Except in regard to foreign financial institutions, the State Council has not promulgated rules for foreign companies.

Despite the provisions of Chapter 11, the legal status of foreign companies in China is unclear. Does Chapter 11 mandate that foreign companies establish a branch in order to transact business in China? It seems no provision in Chapter 11 explicitly prohibits foreign companies from doing business in China. However, by stipulating the requirements for the establishment of branches, the legislature intends that foreign companies set up branches in China before they carry out business activities.

2.4 SOLE PROPRIETORSHIPS

The sole proprietorship takes a few forms in China. It can be an 'individual industrial and commercial household' (IICH), a 'rural contracting household' (RCH), or a 'wholly individually-owned enterprise'

---

[39] Under the Delaware General Corporation Law, foreign corporations can do business if they pay a franchise fee, file a certificate of incorporation from their home jurisdiction, and file statements setting forth the name and address of their registered local agent, the assets and liabilities of the corporation, and the business it proposes to do in Delaware. In addition, the corporation must also submit a statement regarding the scope of its authorized business in its home jurisdiction.

[40] Company Law, Article 193.

[41] Company Law, Article 196.

[42] Company Law, Article 193, para. 2.

(WIOE). Under the GPCL, a Chinese citizen[43] can establish, upon registration, an IICH with a business name, and engage in any business not prohibited in mandatory laws.[44] A member of a collective rural economic organization, such as a village, can sign a contract with the collective (which is the owner of rural lands) and lease land for an agricultural production business.[45] The PRC Constitution and the GPCL protect the rights and interests of households. The liability of households depends on who operates the business. If an individual conducts the household's business, then that individual is personally responsible for all business losses and must bear them to the full extent of his personal assets. Where a family conducts the business, the family's communal property may be attached to satisfy the household's liability.[46] Although the formalities for forming sole proprietorships are simple, they still require formal state endorsement, in the form of a business license (for a household) or a land use contract (between the collective organization and the household).

The PRC Law on Wholly Individually-owned Enterprises allows individuals to establish more formal sole proprietorships in the form of

---

[43] Initially only Chinese citizens from Mainland China were allowed to establish IICHs. Under the Mainland and Hong Kong Closer Economic Partnership Arrangement (2003) and its supplements, Hong Kong residents with PRC nationality may now incorporate IICHs across China. From 1 December 2007, Taiwan farmers could register IICHs in China's Fujian Province to engage in agriculture-related production, processing, research, and distribution. See Taiwan Nongmin Zai Haixia Liang'an Nongye Hezuo Shiyanqu He Taiwan Nongmin Chuangyeyuan Shenban Geti Gongshanghu Dengji Guanli Gongzuo De Ruogan Yijian [Several Opinions of the State Administration of Industry and Commerce on the Administration of Taiwan Farmers' Applications to Establish Individually-owned Industrial and Commercial Households in the Experimental Cross-Strait Agricultural Cooperative Zone and Taiwan Farmers' Development Parks], promulgated on 26 November 2007.

[44] GPCL, Article 16; See also Article 4 of the Administrative Regulations on Individual Industrial and Commercial Households, adopted by the State Council on 30 March 2011 and took effect on 1 November 2011. The new regulations have replaced State Council Provisional Regulations on the Administration of Individual Industrial and Commercial Households promulgated in 1987. Under the latter, an IICH could only engage in manufacturing, craft, retail, services, construction, transportation, restaurants, processing, and other trades as permitted by the law.

[45] GPCL, Article 27. See also PRC Rural Land Contracting Law, adopted by the National People's Congress Standing Committee on 29 August 2002.

[46] GPCL, Article 29.

an enterprise.[47] A WIOE is ‘a business entity … that is invested by a single natural person, the property of which is owned by the investor personally, and for the debts of which the investor assumes unlimited liability with his personal property’.[48] Although the business identifies with its individual investor, it has a distinct legal personality as a business and it can conduct business under a name different from its owner, open a business banking account, sign contracts, take loans, and acquire land use rights. The owner has full control over assets and operations, although the WIOE can hire others to manage the firm. However, the unlimited liability of the WIOE is a serious disadvantage to the investor. If the WIOE’s assets are not enough, all personal assets must be made available to satisfy business liabilities, even after the termination of the WIOE. If the investor declares in the registration documents that he wishes to use family assets as capital contribution to the enterprise, then the unlimited liability extends to family assets.[49] However, creditors must make claims within five years of the enterprise’s termination, otherwise the debts will perish.[50] On the other hand, the owner has absolute control over the extent of the enterprise’s liabilities. A further advantage is that the WIOE does not pay corporate tax – the investor needs only to pay personal income tax.

The formation of a WIOE requires registration with the state. If conditions are met, the registration authority (normally the local Administration for Industry and Commerce) will register the company and grant a business license. If rejected, then the registrar must give a written explanation. The relatively simple registration procedures make WIOEs a popular choice for many individuals, in addition to the IICH.[51] However, the line between IICHs and WIOEs is becoming increasingly obscure, especially from the incorporators’ perspective.[52]

---

47 Zhonghua Renmin Gongheguo Geren Duzi Qiye Fa, promulgated by the NPC Standing Committee on 30 August 1999 and effective as of 1 January 2000 (hereinafter the WIOE Law).

48 WIOE Law, Article 2.

49 WIOE Law, Article 18. However, the law does not address what happens if the investor makes a declaration without the knowledge and/or permission of other family members.

50 WIOE Law, Article 28.

51 NBSC (2009). According to the National Bureau of Statistics of China, at the end of 2008, there were 28.737 million licensed IICHs in China, employing 81.95 million people.

52 In the 1980s and early 1990s, the dividing line between IICHs and WIOEs was clear because the laws were rather ideologically based. Thus, IICHs were normally allowed to hire up to five employees but WIOEs were allowed to

A WIOE is not registered under the Company Law, which distinguishes it from one-person LLCs and WFOEs (which could also be a single-person LLC). As noted in Chapter 2, there are further differences with respect to liability: the investor in a one-person LLC is protected by limited liability provided he can prove he has not co-mingled his personal and company assets. A WIOE owner always has to bear unlimited liability. However, a sole foreign investor in a WFOE enjoys limited liability, as the WFOE receives super-national treatment because under Company and WFOE Laws, the foreign company is regarded as a standardized LLC in which there is the protection of limited liability.

2.5 PARTNERSHIPS

2.5.1 Partnerships in Civil Law and Commercial Law

China governs partnerships through two major statutes, namely the GPCL and the PRC Partnership Enterprise Law (PEL). To some extent, this resembles the distinction between civil law and commercial law partnerships in German law.[53] Under the GPCL, a partnership is a contractual arrangement in which two individuals contribute cash, property, or technology and conduct business together on negotiated terms.[54] The formation of the civil law partnership is fairly simple: in most cases a written agreement between the partners suffices.[55] In the absence of a written agreement or official registration, a Chinese court will still 'confirm the relationship of a partnership' if 'two uninterested witnesses attest to the existence of an oral partnership agreement'.[56] The civil law partnership may adopt a business name through registering with the state, but this is not compulsory. The partners are jointly liable under the GPCL.[57]

employ more than eight persons. See Zhao Xudong (2006), p. 25. In that case, the WIOE owner was considered to belong to the 'exploiting class'.

53 See Liu Kaixiang (2003), pp. 113–14. For partnerships in German law see Horn, Kotz and Leser (1982), Chapter 14.

54 GPCL, Article 30.

55 GPCL, Article 31.

56 Zuigao Renmin Fayuan Guanyu Guanche Zhixing <Zhonghua Renmin Gongheguo Minfa Tongze> Ruogan Wenti de Yijian [Supreme People's Court Opinions on Questions Concerning the Implementation of the General Principles of Civil Law], promulgated on 2 April 1988, Article 50.

57 GPCL, Article 35.

The PEL, as its name suggests, is the law intended for commercial partnerships registered as enterprises. It governs partnerships established by natural persons, legal persons, or other organizations.[58] To establish a partnership enterprise, the state obliges parties to enter written agreements and register with the state. The PRC Partnership Enterprise Law was first promulgated in 1997 (hereinafter the PEL 1997). It purported to establish a comprehensive legal framework for commercial partnerships, covering partnership registration, ownership, management, partnership rights and obligations, relations with third parties, admittance and retirement of partners, and termination. The PEL was amended in August 2006 (PEL 2006). The amendments brought three significant changes to the regime. The first was the introduction of the limited partnership. PEL 1997 only allowed general partnerships. The second was the introduction of the limited liability partnership, officially known as a 'special general partnership' in China. The third concerned the identity of partners. PEL 1997 only permitted natural persons to be partners but with PEL 2006, now legal persons and other organizations can be partners.

2.5.2 General Partnership Enterprises

The general partnership enterprise (GPE) is the classic form of commercial partnership under the PEL 2006. A general partnership comprises general partners who assume unlimited liability for the debts of the partnership.[59] General partnerships in China have the following characteristics:

Qualifications of investors. The Company Law does not impose any restriction on the qualifications of shareholders. That is to say, any person can be a corporate shareholder. Under the PEL 2006, although all 'persons' (including natural persons, legal persons, and other organizations) may in principle assume the role of partner, it prohibits SOEs, listed companies, and charitable institutions from being general partners.[60]

Investor's liability. The principle of limited liability protects corporate shareholders in the sense that their liability is confined to their initial capital contribution. General partners in China undertake unlimited *liandai zeren* liability, which refers to joint and several liability. According to Articles 38 and 39, a partnership enterprise shall first use its own

[58] PEL 2006, Article 2.
[59] PEL 2006, Article 2.
[60] PEL 2006, Article 3.

property to repay its debts. Partners' personal and unlimited liability arises only when the partnership is unable to repay its debts. The creditor must pursue the partnership first.

Management and representation. Companies practice centralized and delegated management. Under the Company Law, shareholders delegate managerial power to the board of directors and eventually the managers. Shareholders have little say in corporate management except in the few circumstances under which the law entitles them to vote.[61] In a partnership, there is a horizontal management structure, which means all general partners have equal rights in the management and conduct of the business.[62] Partners resolve all relevant matters by vote pursuant to the manner prescribed in the partnership agreement. If the agreement fails to provide a clear voting method, the one-partner-one-vote basis prevails.[63] Partners may also elect one or several executive partners as their representatives to conduct partnership affairs, but the executives have no powers except those stipulated in the partnership agreement, and they can expect scrutiny from their partners.

A company's board and management represent it in accordance with the authorization given in the company's articles of association or the Company Law. In a general partnership, all partners represent the partnership. If the partners elect executive partners to conduct their affairs, the non-executive partners will cease to represent the partnership except in cases that would otherwise prejudice bona fide third parties.[64]

Investor's ability to transfer interest. One of the fundamental attributes of companies is that shareholders may freely transfer their equity interest. Thus, shareholders of a JSLC can sell their shares in the highly organized stock market (which usually can be done in seconds), and shareholders of an LLC may transfer their equity interests through agreement (subject to other shareholders' preemptive rights). In addition, once the equity interest is transferred out, the investor will have nothing to do with the company because the transfer takes away the investor's rights and liabilities. Partnerships do not enjoy that liquidity because their interests are not so readily transferable. A partner can transfer his share in the partnership property to other partners by notifying them. However, he must obtain the unanimous consent of all other partners if he wants to

---

[61] As will be discussed in later chapters, China's Company Law gives shareholders relatively more powers than other jurisdictions.

[62] PEL 2006, Article 26.

[63] PEL 2006, Article 30.

[64] PEL 2006, Articles 26 and 37.

transfer to an outsider.[65] In addition, there are transferable and non-transferable interests. A partner can transfer his financial interest (e.g. shares in partnership property) as well as voting rights, but not liability. Thus, a partner who has withdrawn from the partnership shall bear unlimited liability joint and severally for any debts the partnership incurred prior to his withdrawal.[66]

Taxation of income. A company is subject to 'double taxation' in that the company must pay corporate income tax, and the shareholders must pay personal income tax on their dividends. A partnership pays no income tax in China. Instead, each partner must pay income tax individually.[67]

Legal personality. As a separate legal personality, an enterprise has a name of its own, the ability to sign contracts and own property in its own name, and it can sue and be sued.[68] But whether partnerships have separate legal personality is debatable. Comparatively, a partnership is treated 'either as an aggregation of the individual partners or as an entity separate from its partners'.[69] English law has adopted the aggregate approach, while Scottish law has an entity approach that recognizes partnerships as separate legal entities.[70] In China, although the law does not explain whether a partnership has separate legal personality, it can be clearly inferred from the rules that partnership enterprises have separate personality,[71] while civil law partnerships probably do not.

2.5.3 Special General Partnership Enterprises

As the name suggests, a special general partnership (SGP) is a special form of general partnership in China, known as limited liability partnership in some other jurisdictions.[72] In essence, although general partners presumably bear joint and several liability for the debts of the partnership, a partner is not responsible or liable for another partner's misconduct or negligence. According to Article 57 of the PEL 2006, 'where debts of the partnership enterprise were incurred as a result of one or

---

65 PEL 2006, Article 22.
66 PEL 2006, Article 53.
67 PEL 2006, Article 6.
68 Kraakman *et al.* (2009), p. 9.
69 Law Commission UK (2003), p. 45.
70 Law Commission UK (2003), p. 45.
71 For example, under the PEL 2006 a partnership can acquire a business name and business license through registration with the state. In addition, it can own property, sign contracts, and litigate, all in its own name.
72 Such as the U.S., UK, Canada, India, Singapore, Germany, etc.

more partners having acted intentionally or negligently in the course of providing professional services, the responsible partner(s) shall bear unlimited liability or unlimited liability jointly and severally, while the other partners shall be liable to the extent of their respective share of assets in the partnership enterprise'. Further, the responsible partner(s) must indemnify the partnership according to the partnership agreement. In other respects, the rules for general partnerships apply.[73]

The SGP is designed for professional service providers such as law firms, accounting firms, or consulting firms, although most of those firms in China have not yet adopted this form of business. The business name of an SGP must include the words 'special general partnership'.[74] The PEL also requires SGPs to purchase professional liability insurance and have a practice risk fund.[75]

2.5.4 Limited Partnership Enterprises

Limited partnership enterprises (LPEs) are significant new additions to the family of partnerships in China under PEL 2006.[76] LPEs must have both general and limited partners, but the total number of partners may not exceed 50.[77] Further, LPEs must have at least one general partner who faces the same responsibilities as a partner in a general partnership. The most important difference between LPEs and conventional general partnerships is the existence of limited partners, who, like shareholders in limited liability companies, assume the partnership's business liability to the extent of his subscribed capital contribution.[78]

The rights and duties of LPE general partners are the same as those in conventional general partnerships. All management and control vest with the general partners. Limited partners, as a matter of law, should not conduct partnership affairs and/or represent LPEs in external dealings.[79] However, they may participate in matters concerning the admission and withdrawal of partners, advise the general partners, obtain an accounting report of the partnership, bring a derivative action on behalf of the partnership, etc.[80]

---

73 PEL 2006, Article 55, para. 2.
74 PEL 2006, Article 56.
75 PEL 2006, Article 59.
76 PEL 2006, Chapter III.
77 PEL 2006, Article 61.
78 PEL 2006, Article 2.
79 PEL 2006, Article 68.
80 PEL 2006, Article 68.

Limited partnerships are increasingly used by private equity and venture capital firms in China.[81] LPEs can work around the requirement that they have one general partner who bears unlimited liability by forming a limited liability company to serve as the general partner, thus effectively making every investor a limited partner. In practice, many LPEs in the private equity and venture capital industries use an asset management limited liability company as both the general and managing partners.

2.5.5 Foreigners as Partners

For a long time, it was debatable whether foreigners could be partners in partnerships in China. Article 108 of the PEL provides that 'administrative measures for establishing partnership enterprises in China by foreign enterprises or individuals shall be formulated by the State Council'. That article implied that no foreign-invested PEL would be established before the State Council issued appropriate regulations. However, partnerships with foreign partners have existed in China for a long time. First, it is impossible to prevent foreigners from being partners in civil law partnerships in China because people may establish partnerships themselves through oral or written agreements without registering with the government. Second, the PRC Law on Cooperative Joint Ventures, adopted in 1988, permits foreigners to establish non-legal person, cooperative joint ventures (CJVs) in China. According to the Legislative Affairs Commission of the National People's Congress Standing Committee, the rules concerning general partnerships in the GPCL have regulated the non-legal person CJVs.[82]

On 25 December 2009, the State Council promulgated the Administrative Measures on the Establishment of Partnership Enterprises in China by Foreign Enterprises and Individuals.[83] Foreign investors are now permitted to set up general or limited partnership enterprises in China independently or with local partners. Potential partnerships must file applications for registration with the Administration of Industry and Commerce (AIC) at the local level and obtain a business certificate. They do not have to seek approval from the central authorities.

---

[81] CVCRI (2009), p. 252 (noting more than half of the venture capital firms established in 2008 were organized as LPEs).

[82] NPCLCA (2006), pp. 171–2.

[83] Waiguo Qiye Huozhe Geren Zai Zhongguo Jingnei Sheli Hehuo Qiye Guanli Banfa, adopted by the State Council on 18 August 2009 and effective as of 1 March 2010 (hereinafter the Foreign-Invested Partnership Measures).

2.6 COLLECTIVELY-OWNED ENTERPRISES (COEs)

Collectivized ownership exists in many jurisdictions[84] but probably nowhere other than China has it achieved such a prominent position in the economy, both ideologically and economically. Ideologically, insofar as China is still a self-proclaimed socialist state,[85] the basis of its socialist economic system is 'the socialist public ownership of the means of production, namely ownership by the whole people and collective ownership by the working people'.[86] Economically, collective ownership was once the pillar of China's economy. In recent years, corporatization and privatization of the Chinese economy have led to a significant decline in the collective economy. That said, collectively-owned enterprises (COEs) continue to play an important role.[87] In fact, many of China's best-known enterprises, including some multinational corporations, such as Haier, TCL, Royalstar, etc., were founded as collective enterprises.

Collective ownership comes in the form of urban collective enterprises (UCE) and rural collective enterprises (RCE). UCEs are established according to the PRC Regulations on Urban Collective Enterprises.[88] A UCE is owned either by all its employees or all the members of the collective economic organization (such as an urban resident community). It is a legal person that assumes civil liabilities with its own assets. Although members of the UCEs have limited liability, they are not regarded as shareholders because they may not dispose of their interests. UCEs practice 'democratic management' under which a workers' congress serves as the highest authority to elect or remove management personnel and decide major operational and management matters. Similarly, a rural collective organization (such as a village) can establish

---

[84] For example, cooperatives are very much the counterparts of collectively-owned entities. As a legal entity owned and democratically controlled by its members, they are widely adopted in many societies. These collectivized entities can trace their roots back to the socialist philosophy initially developed by Robert Owen (1771–1858).

[85] PRC Constitution, Article 1.

[86] PRC Constitution, Article 6.

[87] By the end of 2008, there were about 192,000 registered collectively-owned enterprises in China's non-agricultural sectors, owning only 2.1 percent of China's total enterprise assets but hiring millions of employees. These statistics do not include the assets owned and employees hired by COEs in the rural areas. See NBSC (2009).

[88] Zhonghua Renmin Gongheguo Chengzhen Jiti Suoyouzhi Qiye Tiaoli, promulgated by the State Council on 9 September 1991.

RCEs under the PRC Regulations on Rural Collective Enterprises.[89] The decision-making authority for RCEs is the farmers' representative meeting or the rural collective organization representing the farmers. They decide major issues concerning the operation and management of RCEs, including the appointment and removal of managerial personnel. As a legal person with limited liability, the RCE is collectively owned by all the farmers in the rural collective organization. The farmers, however, are not shareholders because they cannot individually dispose of their interest.

2.7 FARMERS' SPECIAL COOPERATIVES (FSCs)

The NPC Standing Committee adopted the PRC Farmers' Special Cooperatives Law in 2006.[90] The FSC is a business vehicle specially designed for producers and operators of agricultural products, or providers of agricultural services and their users. Once registered with the local administration for industry and commerce, it is recognized as a legal person. An FSC should have at least five members, and at least 80 percent must be farmers. Business enterprises, public service institutions, and social organizations can make up the rest. FSCs practice democratic management; they have members' meetings, a council, and a supervisory board. The members' meeting is the highest authority and it makes decisions by a one-member, one-vote rule – except that, if the FSC charter provides otherwise, those members who have contributed significantly more capital or have a much greater volume of transactions may have additional votes. In essence, the FSC is a hybrid business organization that combines different features of companies and collective enterprises. It is not clear whether foreign investment is allowed in the FSC, although nothing in the law prohibits FIEs from being the FSC's enterprise members.

2.8 STATE-OWNED ENTERPRISES (SOEs)

Although Chinese SOEs are mentioned everywhere, they are not legally defined. That is to say, SOEs are not a registered form of business;

---

89 Zhonghua Renmin Gongheguo Xiangcun Jiti Suoyouzhi Qiye Tiaoli, promulgated by the State Council on 11 May 1990.

90 Zhonghua Renmin Gongheguo Nongmin Zhuanye Hezuoshe Fa, adopted on 31 August 2006, effective as of 1 July 2007 (hereinafter the FSC Law).

whether an enterprise is an SOE is rather an empirical question. Ownership alone cannot be the determinative factor. An enterprise in which the government owns more than 50 percent of the equity interest is apparently an SOE, but the fact that the government owns less than half of the ownership does not necessarily mean it is not an SOE. In many cases, a minority shareholder holding 20 or 30 percent of the total shares of a company could be an effective controller if the firm's ownership is dispersed. Multiple layers of ownership further complicate the situation. If several private companies hold shares of an SOE rather than the state directly, it looks like a privately-owned firm. However, the state might directly own or control its major shareholders.

The law only defines wholly state-owned enterprises. There are two kinds: SOEs owned by the 'whole people' and wholly state-owned companies (registered under the Company Law). The 1988 PRC Law on Industrial Enterprise Owned by the Whole People governs traditional SOEs.[91] Traditional SOEs have the following features: (i) the 'whole people' (represented by the state) owns the firm; (ii) they have legal person status to ensure they have limited liability; (iii) they have limited enterprise autonomy, meaning that the SOE Law prevents the government from interfering with the daily operation of the firms. Traditional SOEs are, however, not independent of the government in the sense that the government appoints the heads of the SOEs to implement state plans. Practically, it is not totally wrong to view traditional SOEs as part of the state.

Very few traditional SOEs exist today. Most have been converted into modern business organizations (LLCs, JSLCs, or partnerships) through the enterprise corporatization and privatization efforts in the past decades. However, the Company Law preserves a special place for wholly state-owned companies (WSOCs) as previously mentioned.

---

[91] Zhonghua Renmin Gongheguo Quanmin Suoyouzhi Gongye Qiyefa, adopted by the NPC on 13 April 1988 (hereinafter the SOE Law).

3. Corporate legal personality and limited liability

3.1 THE CONCEPTS OF LEGAL PERSONALITY AND LIMITED LIABILITY

The incorporation of a company brings two most important consequences. First, the separate legal personality for the company, and second, limited liability for the shareholders of the company. The two consequences form the two most fundamental concepts of corporate law as embodied in Article 3 of the Company Law, which provides:

> A Company is an enterprise legal person which owns independent legal person properties and enjoys legal person property rights. A company shall be liable for its debts to the extent of all of its property.
>
> The liability of a shareholder of a limited liability company shall be limited to the capital contribution it subscribes. The liability of a shareholder of a joint-stock limited company shall be limited to the shares it subscribes.

Although theorists have long debated about the nature of a corporation, namely whether it is a legal creation, a real entity, or a nexus of contracts,[1] Chinese law apparently follows the legal creation approach. As noted in the previous chapter, a Chinese company must be established in accordance with the law, following strictly the required formalities. In particular, the establishment of a company must be registered with the relevant Administration for Industry and Commerce (AIC) to take effect,[2] and a company is viewed as being legally established only when the AIC grants a business license to it. Since the company is only a legal creature, it might be cancelled – namely de-registered or its business license revoked – by the AIC.

---

1 Zhou Yousu (2006), pp. 43–6; Shi Tiantao (2006), pp. 14–24.
2 Company Law, Article 6.

3.1.1 Separate Corporate Legal Personality

The main function of the separate personality of a company is thus to ensure the company's independent identity – separate from its members – in legal relationships, namely confining the rights and obligations of a company's legal relationships to the company as a separate person, not the persons who established the company. This protects the company's property rights, ensures the company's autonomy, and prevents other persons, including, among others, the shareholders, directors, supervisors, and managers, from interfering with the operation of the company's business.

According to the Company Law and corporate law scholarship in China, separate corporate legal personality entails the following characteristics:

1. In general, a company as an entity with legal personality means it can have a separate name, can own property and enter into contracts in its own name, can sue and be sued, and can have a lifespan (including perpetual existence).
2. A company is always a legal person. The concept of legal person will be examined in the following section.
3. The separate legal personality of a company could only be granted by the state (through the AICs or other authorities) upon fulfillment of the registration formalities by the incorporators. In other words, corporate legal personality in China cannot be acquired through private arrangement. Chinese law currently does not recognize de facto corporations.
4. A company's property is its own property. Although the Company Law purposely uses 'property rights' rather than 'ownership' of the companies to avoid the then existing ideological controversies, in practice there are no longer any contemporary political or legal obstacles to view a company as the owner of its property.
5. Most importantly, the separate legal personality brings about the separation of equity ownership of the shareholders, namely a company's business is its own business, not the shareholders' business.

3.1.2 Limited Liability

There is a vital connection between the separate personality of a company and the limited liability enjoyed by its shareholders. These two concepts together separate the company legally from the people who created it, and vice versa.

If, as Cox and Hazen (2003) argue, 'limited shareholder liability is not simply a principle of corporate law, but a cornerstone of capitalism',[3] this doctrine is well received in China, a country steadily marching towards a capitalism-based market economy. Under Article 3 of the Company Law, a shareholder's liability in either the LLC or JSLC is limited to a fixed sum, which is the share of capital contributions the shareholder has subscribed. If the shareholder hasn't met his or her promise to pay in full the subscribed capital contributions, his or her liability is confined to making up for the differences. Even in the case of the company's bankruptcy, the liability of the company, in principle, cannot be transferred to the shareholders to enable the company's creditors to reach the shareholders' own assets.

Limited liability is, however, not an absolute and unconditional protection for shareholders. As will be examined in other parts of this chapter, the separate legal entity of the company can be disregarded by courts in China, under certain circumstances, to transfer the liability to the shareholders. In addition, in the case of the one-person LLC, limited liability is not presumed – namely, the shareholder bears the burden of proving that he did not abuse this privilege.

3.2 THE CENTRAL CONCEPT OF 'LEGAL PERSON'

3.2.1 The Legal Person and its 'Capacities'

The legal basis of legal personality and limited liability of companies in China is based on a central concept in China's civil law, namely the institution of 'legal personality'. In the highly abstract conceptual framework of Chinese civil law, legal personality is used to recognize the quality of a natural or legal person being a 'person' under the law. While a natural person may naturally have their 'capacity for civil rights' from birth to death, a legal person is, however, a creature of the law. Article 36 of the GPCL thus reads:

> A legal person shall be an organization that has the capacity for civil rights and capacity for civil acts and independently enjoys civil rights and assumes civil obligations in accordance with the law.

---

[3] Cox and Hazen (2003), p. 100.

> A legal person's capacity for civil rights and capacity for civil acts shall begin when the legal person is established and shall end when the legal person terminates.

Not surprisingly, a few terms in this definition beg explanation. Conceptually, Chinese civil law distinguishes between a person's capacity to have civil rights and the capacity to perform civil acts. Put simply, 'rights are powers over certain and specific things or powers to enter into certain specific transactions, while capacity is a general qualification or possibility to acquire or exercise rights, and the capacity for acts defines a person's capacities and is a legal prerequisite for actually enjoying rights and assuming liabilities'.[4]

More significant is the phrase 'independently enjoys civil rights and assumes civil obligations in accordance with the law'. This, in the whole Chinese civil and commercial law system, is the ultimate legal basis for limited liability and separation of ownership and control. A Chinese enterprise is an independent business entity with the attribute of limited liability primarily because it is a legal person in the civil law. We know a company is such an entity also because it is defined as an 'enterprise legal person' by the Company Law.[5]

Logically, a company, which is by definition a legal person,[6] begins to have both its 'rights' and 'acts' capacities when it is granted a business license by the company registration authorities.[7] It ceases to have these when it is dissolved.[8] However, unlike natural persons, this legal person's civil rights are placed under some legal limits in the Company Law.

First, generally speaking, a legal person does not possess certain rights that are exclusive to natural persons, such as right to life or right to image, although it is still entitled to the right of reputation and the right of honor.[9] It is unclear whether a legal person is protected by the PRC Constitution's 'bill of rights', such as freedom of (commercial) speech, as the Constitution apparently indicates that those rights are for 'citizens' that are understood as natural persons.[10]

---

4 Chen Jianfu (2008).

5 Company Law, Article 3.

6 Company Law, Article 3.

7 Company Law, Article 7.

8 Under Article 189 of the Company Law, in case of liquidation, a company finally terminates after the liquidation group makes a public announcement of the termination of the company.

9 GPCL, Articles 101 and 102.

10 See PRC Constitution, Chapter 2.

Second, a company's reinvesting capacity is explicitly restricted to the effect that it cannot be exposed to unlimited liabilities. Article 15 of the Company Law thus stipulates that, although a company may invest in other enterprises, it 'shall not become an investor with joint and several liability' in that enterprise, 'unless otherwise provided by the law'. The 1993 Company Law, in its Article 12, once provided that the total accumulative amount of a company's investment in other enterprises should not exceed 50 percent of the company's net assets. Although the existing Company Law abolishes this quantitative restriction, it still does not allow a company to (1) invest in any unlimited company;[11] or (2) become a general partner in a partnership enterprise. However, the restriction with respect to partnership seems to have been compromised by the 2006 amended Partnership Enterprise Law, Article 2 of which defines a partnership enterprise as one 'that is established by a natural person, legal person or any other organization in China pursuant to this law'. It has been suggested that this is exactly what the phrase 'unless otherwise provided by the law' means in Article 15 of the Company Law.[12] Namely, irrespective of the aforesaid Article 15, a company could now legally serve as a general partner, subject to Article 3 of the Partnership Enterprise Law, which prevents only wholly state-owned companies, state-owned enterprises, listed companies, charitable institutions, and social organizations from becoming a general partner.

Third, in a company's operation, what it can do is theoretically limited to the scope of business prescribed in its articles of association; otherwise, it might be regarded as acting *ultra vires*. However, as will be discussed below, the *ultra vires* doctrine, if not entirely abolished, has been largely set aside by the judiciary.

3.2.2 The Legal Representative

Closely associated with legal person is the highly unique institution of the legal representative in Chinese civil and commercial law, which is a concept that possibly has no counterpart in common law countries. A legal representative is defined as 'a person who, in accordance with the law or the articles of association of the legal person, is responsible for

---

[11] Unlimited Companies do not exist in China, but this prohibition still applies to Chinese companies' investment in foreign unlimited companies.

[12] See Liu (2011), pp. 108–9. Hao (2008), p. 654.

representing the legal person in the exercise of its duties and functions'.[13] On this basis, a legal representative has the following characteristics:[14]

1. All legal persons established in China must have a legal representative. The legal representative must be a natural person.
2. A legal person has only one legal representative, whose name is mandatorily provided for both in the legal person's articles of association (which are filed with the enterprise registration authorities) and in its business license. A change of the legal representative involves an amendment of the legal person's articles of association, as well as the need for a renewed business license.
3. The legal representative has a priori authority to represent the company insofar as the exercise of the legal person's rights, duties, and functions are concerned. In particular, the signature of the legal representative is required for a contract signed in the name of the company to be valid. Any other person, in order to sign a contract to hold the company bound, must have a power of attorney or an equivalent document signed and issued by the legal representative.
4. The legal representative is the final controller of the company's finances, as a company's application for loans, its negotiable instruments, as well as any other financial dealings with outsiders, must be signed by the legal representative.
5. The legal representative must represent the legal person in a lawsuit; otherwise, the suit would not have been activated in the first place.
6. Overall, the power of the legal representative is so extensive that it covers all aspects of the legal person's activities. He or she can perform all acts regarding general administration of the company and in accordance with the purpose of the entity. In this sense, the legal representative is the 'king' in the enterprise.

A company might have a chairperson of the board, a CEO, and/or leaders of any other title, but who is the single most powerful leader depends only on who assumes the title of the legal representative. The 1993 Company Law provided mandatorily that a company's legal representative would be the chairperson of the board of the directors.[15] This provision has been replaced by Article 13 of the existing 2005 Company Law, which states that either the chairperson of the board, the executive

[13] GPCL, Article 38.
[14] Fang (1999).
[15] Company Law 1993, Articles 45 and 113.

director (in the case of an LLC, which does not have a board), or the manager (referring to the general manager or chief executive) can be appointed as the company's legal representative by the corporate charter. This makes it easier for a company to change its legal representative, but still does not completely resolve the dilemmas associated with this position, especially when the company faces an uncooperative legal representative.

3.3 THE DOCTRINE OF *ULTRA VIRES* IN CHINA

Traditionally, the commercial purpose of a business enterprise is to be prescribed by the law. In the framework of Chinese civil law, the company's objects (*mudi*), which essentially means its powers and purpose, are subject to the legal limits set in the law.[16] A company's object is embodied in the scope of authorized business (*jingying fanwei*) clause in its articles of association. If a company engages in conduct not authorized by the law or its articles, the conduct would be deemed as *yuequan xingwei,* or *ultra vires*, using the borrowed Latin phrase.

Like early common law, Chinese law before the 1990s was very restrictive about a company's object limiting its scope of business. The 1986 GPCL provides that 'an enterprise legal person shall operate within its approved and registered scope of business'[17] and that the legal person and its legal representative shall be liable if the legal person 'carries out illegal business activities beyond the scope of business approved and registered by the registration authorities'.[18] Early courts applied this with vigor and construed the scope of business clause narrowly. They invalidated most corporate transactions beyond the powers stated in the company's articles of association, which were otherwise valid in the years after the GPCL was adopted, resulting in both injustice and inefficiency.[19]

Why was the law so harsh to *ultra vires* acts? One explanation is that, in the 1980s and 1990s when contracts were held void on a massive scale, industrial and commercial activities were still dominated by SOEs.

---

16 Zhao Xudong (2006), pp. 197–8.

17 GPCL, Article 42.

18 GPCL, Article 49(1).

19 Zhao Xudong (2006), p. 198 (citing a rule in an 1987 judicial interpretation of the PRC Supreme People's Court which provided that 'contracts beyond the scope of business or methods of business operation shall be regarded as void'). See also Ling (2002), p. 137.

The Chinese version of *ultra vires* was thus used to limit the capacities of SOEs to conclude and perform contracts not authorized by the state. Consequently, it also limited the counterparties' legal ability to enforce contracts against SOEs in case the latter acted *ultra vires*. With the emergence of non-state sectors in China, the downfall of the *ultra vires* doctrine became inevitable. Since the late 1990s, several legislative and judicial efforts have been made to alleviate the negative impact of the doctrine.

First, the Company Law now allows a broader power clause in the Company's articles. Article 12 of the Company Law provides that the 'scope of business of a company shall be specified in its articles of association and registered according to the law'. The company may revise its articles but this should be followed by a matching change of the registration information.[20] This implies that the company has the freedom to specify its own business scope, which must be registered with – rather than approved by – the registration authority. Only those items in the business scope under which the relevant laws or administrative regulations must be approved shall be approved.[21] Essentially, this refers to businesses such as banking, insurance, the manufacturing of special products, etc., for which special licenses are required under the law.

Article 12 begs the question of whether a company could provide in its articles a broad power clause such as 'this company shall be engaged in any lawful business'. It is submitted that literally Article 12 does not prohibit such a clause. But in practice, no Chinese companies have been seen to have attempted to do this. Instead, they provide in their articles a very lengthy power clause that contains a long list of things they are doing or plan to do in the future.

Second, the uniform Contract Law of 1999, which was adopted by the NPC to unify the rules governing contracts dispersed in several different laws, has revised a principle of agency law with respect to the legal representatives. Previously, even the contracts signed by the legal representatives, if going beyond the representatives' power of representation, would be voided by the courts.[22] Article 50 of the Contract Law now states, 'If the legal representative or a person in charge of a legal person or an organization acts *ultra vires* when concluding a contract, the act of representation is valid unless the other party knew or ought to have known that the contract was concluded *ultra vires*'. As such, a contract

---

[20] Company Law, Article 12, para. 1.
[21] Company Law, Article 12, para. 2.
[22] Ling (2002), p. 150.

signed by the legal representative in violation of the legal person's scope of business is not necessarily void, and its validity depends on whether the counterparty has actual or constructive notice of the violation.[23]

Thirdly, since 1993 the judiciary has been increasingly taking a liberal approach to *ultra vires* contracts, which peaked with the adoption of an SPC judicial interpretation on the Contract Law in 1999.[24] Article 10 of the interpretation provides, 'The People's Court shall not declare a contract invalid because a party exceeded its scope of business in concluding the said contract, unless such party has violated provisions whereby the state restricts or requires special permission of a business activity or whereby laws or administrative regulations prohibit a business activity'. By this rule, the Supreme Peoples' Court, as the leading authority of the judiciary, simply disallows all courts from using *ultra vires* as a ground to invalidate contracts.

Obviously, the aforesaid Article 10 almost amounts to the abolition of the *ultra vires* doctrine, but this judicial abolition is binding upon only the judiciary. The object/power clause still has remaining relevance in other areas. For example, acting beyond the scope of authorized business may still constitute an administrative offence. Article 73 of the Administrative Regulations on Registration of Companies provides that if there is a change in the registered items of the company's business scope and the company fails to register it with the company registrar as requested by the registrar, it will be fined an amount between RMB10,000 and RMB100,000. That is to say, it is still important to define carefully the business scope of the company.

3.4 PIERCING THE CORPORATE VEIL

3.4.1 Development of the Veil-piercing Doctrine

Piercing the corporate veil, also known as disregarding the corporate personality, occurs when the court takes away the legal shelter of limited liability from the shareholders and allow the company's creditors to pursue all reasonable avenues to reach the personal assets of the shareholders, on the grounds that the company is not truly a separate

---

23 Ling (2002), p. 150.

24 *Zuigao Renmin Fayuan Guanyu Shiyong <Zhonghua Renmin Gongheguo Hetongfa> Ruogan Wenti de Jieshi* (1) [Interpretation I of the Supreme People's Court on the Application of the PRC Contract Law], Fashi (1999) 19 Hao, adopted 1 December 1999. See also, Ling (2002), p. 138.

entity, which is the prerequisite for limited liability. This doctrine was formally introduced into China's corporate law regime by Article 20 of the 2005 Company Law.

Although the 1993 Company Law contained no mention of the veil-piercing doctrine, the Chinese judiciary cautiously applied it even without a clear statutory basis before its codification in 2005. In response to a question presented by the Higher People's Court of Guangdong Province, the SPC replied that, in the case in which one company has established a subsidiary and the subsidiary has been closed down or gone out of business, 'if the assets of the [subsidiary] company are not great enough to satisfy its debts, then the enterprise that established the [subsidiary] will assume civil liability to the extent that the amount of registered capital of that company exceeds the actual capital contribution made to it'.[25] Under a different circumstance, 'if no capital was actually contributed to the terminated company, or the amount was not sufficient according to the law, then the company will be determined not to be a legal person and its full civil liability will be assumed by the enterprise that established the company'.[26] In a similar vein, the SPC, in a 2003 judicial interpretation, mandates that, in merger and acquisition transactions whereby controlling shareholding is achieved by acquisition, 'if the controlled enterprise is unable to repay its debts due to the withdrawal of funds or evasion of debts by the controlling enterprise, the debts of the controlled enterprise shall be borne by the controlling enterprise'.[27]

3.4.2 Veil Piercing under the Company Law

The codification of the doctrine of piercing the corporate veil in the 2005 Company Law is something quite extraordinary among corporate law statutes in the world. Even in those jurisdictions where this doctrine was developed and applied long ago, the legal basis of the doctrine still remains solely in case law. Article 20 of the Company Law, after stating the general principle that the shareholders of a company should not abuse shareholders' rights, the company's legal person status or shareholders' limited liability, provides:

---

25 Albert (2002), p. 883.

26 Id.

27 *Guanyu Shenli yu Qiye Gaizhi Xiangguan de Minshi Jiufen Anjian Ruogan Wenti de Guiding* (*Provisions on Several Issues Concerning the Trial of Civil Disputes Relating to Enterprise Restructuring*), promulgated by the Supreme People's Court of China on 3 January 2003, Article 35.

> Any of the shareholders of a company who abuses the independent legal person status of the company and the limited liability of the shareholders to evade the payment of the company's debts, thus seriously damaging the interests of the company's creditors, shall bear joint liabilities for the debts of the company.[28]

Article 20 establishes a three-pronged legal test for judicial application of the doctrine. Firstly, it has to be proved that the shareholder concerned has abused the company's legal person status and their own limited liability in the form of evading debts. The abuse of the company's legal personality and that of the shareholder's limited liability are not separate actions. 'Indeed, abusing the independent legal person status would mean abusing the limited liability at the same time, and abusing the limited liability would amount to abusing the independent legal person status.'[29] However, the text of Article 20 suggests that the abuse should take the form of 'evading' the payment of debts.

Secondly, the interests of the creditors must be 'seriously' (*yanzhong*) damaged. Needless to say, 'seriously' is a word not defined in the Company Law, and will have to be interpreted by the courts on a case-by-case basis. Zhou (2006) suggests that the court should consider three factors when determining whether the damage is serious enough to activate veil piercing: (1) the actual damage to the creditors; (2) the debt-paying ability of the company; and (3) the subject intent of the shareholder concerned.[30]

Thirdly, there must be a causal link between the shareholder's abusing behavior and the damage/losses suffered by the creditors.

Although the law does not specify the situations in which the doctrine will be invoked, scholarly writing in China, borrowing from both comparative law and China's judicial practice, has suggested that the following circumstances might trigger the doctrine's application:[31]

1. Undercapitalization. It could be either that the shareholder did not make adequate contributions to the company's registered capital or that the capital, including corporate cash and assets, was drained out of the company by the shareholder.
2. Company used as a device to evade contractual obligations. This

---

28 Company Law, Article 20, para. 3.

29 Liu Junhai (2011), p. 546.

30 Zhou Yousu (2006), p. 105.

31 Zhu Ciyun (1998), pp. 140–63. Zhao Xudong (2006), pp. 12–13; Liu Junhai (2011), pp. 547–52; Zhou Yousu (2006), p. 103; Li Hua (2008).

occurs when the shareholder, who has to refrain from doing something under a non-competition agreement or confidentiality agreement, incorporates a company to evade his obligations. Another example is when the shareholder of a heavily indebted company incorporates another company, which takes away the first company's valuable assets. It could also happen when the shareholder uses the company as a sham to defraud the creditors.

3. Company used as device to evade statutory restrictions, involving illegal activities such as tax evasion or money laundering.
4. Lack of formality and confusion of affairs. The shareholder himself disregards the separate legal personality of the company and makes the company an alter ego of the shareholder. This could include the control of the company so that the decision-making of the company is entirely dominated by the shareholder, or the confusion or intermingling of assets, business, affairs, and even management personnel.

3.4.3 Veil Piercing in a One-person Company

Under the Company Law veil piercing is automatically triggered in disputes involving one-person LLCs in which there is only one natural person or legal person shareholder.[32] Article 64 of the Company Law provides that, 'the shareholder of a one-person limited liability company who is unable to prove that the company's assets are independent of the shareholder's personal assets shall bear joint liability for the company's debt'. To borrow a phrase from criminology, the 'presumption of guilt' applies to the shareholder of such company, and the shareholder is under the burden to prove that the company is an independent entity whose assets are separately owned and managed.

Two carve-outs should be pointed out here. One is for those wholly state-owned enterprises (WSOEs) established under Section 4, Chapter II of the Company Law. As WSOEs are solely owned by the Chinese state, they are literally one-person companies. However, insofar as limited liability is concerned, a WSOE is treated as a normal LLC, in which the state is automatically protected by limited liability. The same can be said of the single shareholder, if that is the case, in a wholly foreign-owned enterprise (WFOE).[33]

---

32 Company Law, Article. 58.

33 Implementing Regulations of the PRC Law on wholly foreign-owned enterprises, approved by the State Council in October 1990 and revised in April 2001, Article 18 (providing that a WFOE shall take the form of an LLC unless

3.4.4 Limits of the Chinese Veil-piercing Law

As Article 20 of the Company Law is vague and ambiguous, the legal framework for piercing the corporate veil seems to have a number of limits, which are more like legislative loopholes at this stage.

A major problem is the absence of clear-cut rules to determine the standard for invoking the veil-piercing doctrine. In particular, it is unclear what factors the court will consider to determine whether the corporate personality and shareholders' limited liability have been abused. U.S. courts have produced a long list of factors that point toward veil piercing in a series of cases.[34] It is far from being clear what are the critical factors the court considers in any veil-piercing case, as the law has almost no mention of the factors.

A pressing issue is whether the shareholder's subjective intent is a precondition for lifting the veil. There is no doubt that the courts will ignore the separate personality of a company that is formed or used merely to carry out a dishonest scheme. Article 20 is equivocal about whether evidence of dishonest or fraudulent intent needs to be shown to establish a veil-piercing case, although textual reading suggests it at least does not explicitly require proof of subjective intent. One concern then is that this equivocal provision might be interpreted by some judges as requiring subjective intent, or even fraud, as a precondition for lifting the corporate veil. It is, however, agreeable to some Chinese scholars and judges that the display of abusing acts would suffice to eliminate the need for showing subject intent in veil-piercing cases.[35]

Another problem is that the condition of 'evading debts' seems to confine the plaintiffs to debt creditors, e.g. those to whom the company owes money through contractual transactions.[36] This narrow interpretation, which will certainly be followed by courts in most cases, would exclude victims in environmental protection, product liability, or other types of tort cases.[37] It is, however, submitted that an alternative interpretation under the Chinese civil law is probably more plausible.

---

otherwise approved and that the foreign investor's liability is limited to its investment).

[34] See Bainbridge (2009), pp. 58–61.

[35] Zhao Xudong (2006), p. 12; Zhou Yousu (2006), p. 104; Li Hua (2008); Ma Baihua (2009).

[36] Zhou Yousu (2006), p. 106 (suggesting that the veil-piercing doctrine in Chinese Company Law does not cover torts, competition, and environment protection related cases).

[37] Wu (2007–2008), pp. 334–5.

Under the GPCL, debt is defined as 'a specific relationship of rights and obligations established between the parties concerned, either according to the agreed terms of a contract or provisions in the law'.[38] On this basis, a debt could arise by virtue of any the following reasons: (1) the signing of a contract; (2) management of affairs without mandate; (3) unjust enrichment; or (4) torts.[39] Such a broad definition of debts would certainly allow the courts to expand the coverage of the veil-piercing doctrine to environmental, consumer protection, or any other type of cases that may involve a debt as defined in the GPCL. It is, however, yet to be known whether the judiciary is willing to adopt such a broad interpretation in veil-piercing cases.

---

38 GPCL, Article 84, para. 1.

39 Wang Liming (2004), pp. 504–18.

4. Formation of companies and the rules of capital maintenance

4.1 CHANGING PHILOSOPHY OF BUSINESS ENTRY REGULATION IN CHINA

4.1.1 Movement from Approval to Registration

The purpose of incorporation is to create a corporate entity – with legal personality – distinct from its members. *Doing Business in 2004*, the first issue in the World Bank's annual reports investigating the regulations that affect business activities, points out that incorporation has four advantages. 'First, legal entities can outlive their founders. Second, resources are pulled together, as shareholders join forces in establishing the company's capital. Third, the formal introduction of limited liability ... reduces the risks of doing business ... Fourth, registered businesses have access to services – provided by public courts or private commercial banks – that are not available to unregistered firms.'[1]

Djankov, La Porta, Lopez-de-Silanes, and Shleifer (2002) examined regulation of entry for start-up firms in 85 countries. The authors focused on procedures, and the time and cost that a start-up must spend before it could operate legally. They observed that:

> Countries differ significantly in the way in which they regulate the entry of new businesses. To meet government requirements for starting to operate a business in Mozambique, an entrepreneur must complete 19 procedures taking at least 149 business days and pay US$256 in fees. To do the same, an entrepreneur in Italy needs to follow 16 different procedures, pay US$3946 in fees, and wait at least 62 business days acquire the necessary permits. In contrast, an entrepreneur in Canada can finish the process in two days by paying US$280 in fees and completing only two procedures.[2]

1 World Bank (2004), p. 17.
2 Djankov, La Porta, Lopez-de-Silanes, and Shleifer (2002), pp. 1–2.

Some of the figures mentioned above are already outdated, as many countries have undertaken regulatory reform in recent years. For example, in 2008 it took 10 procedures over 29 days to start a business in Mozambique; in Italy it took nine procedures and 13 days to incorporate.[3] France, the world's top reformer in 2003, went from nine procedures to seven and reduced the time from 48 days to eight.[4] Given that the ease of establishing business varies so significantly among different countries, one might ask why national governments, including China, regulate the incorporation of new business and, if they should, how much regulation is appropriate?

China is said to be a leading reformer in improving business climates.[5] It takes 14 procedures and 38 days to incorporate in China, with the cost being 4.9 percent of and the paid-in minimum capital 130.9 percent of the country's general national income (GNI) per capita, respectively.[6] This does not compare with advanced Western countries such as Australia and Canada, or even Hong Kong and Singapore, two self-governing predominantly Chinese societies. However, when looking at China, an observer should pay sufficient attention to its trends and directions: in 2003, businesses needed 12 procedures and 46 days to establish a business in China, costing 14.3 percent of and 3,855.9 percent of China's GNI per capita.[7]

According to mainstream Chinese corporate law scholars, human history has seen four regulatory approaches to business incorporation, including *ziyou sheli zhuyi*, *texu shelizhuyi*, *hezhun sheli zhuyi*, and *zhuize sheli zhuyi*.[8] 'The legislative history of corporate law worldwide suggests that [the legal policy governing business incorporation] moved from *ziyou sheli zhuyi* to *texu sheli zhuyi*, and further to *hezhun sheli zhuyi*, and eventually to *zhunze sheli zhuyi*.'[9]

---

[3] World Bank, 'Doing Business,' at http://www.doingbusiness.org (accessed 27 June 2008).

[4] World Bank (2005), p. 17.

[5] World Bank news release, 'Doing Business 2008: East Asia Drops in Ranking on Pace of Reform; China is a Top Reformer, Singapore Ranks 1st Again,' available at http://www.doingbusiness.org (accessed 27 June 2008).

[6] World Bank, Doing Business in 2010, available at www.doingbusiness.org (accessed 1 September 2010).

[7] World Bank (2004), p. 141.

[8] Zhao Xudong (2006), pp. 112–14; Shi Tiantao (2006), pp. 83–4; and Zhou Yousu (2006), pp. 110–11.

[9] Shi Tiantao (2006), p. 83.

Ziyou sheli zhuyi literally means *laissez-faire* incorporation. In spite of the fact that corporation statutes did not exist until the nineteenth century, Chinese company law textbooks argue that it began in the 'free trade era' in medieval Europe.[10] Further, they say that business organizations could freely establish themselves from the Roman period to the Middle Ages, during those times the law did not recognize business entities as legal persons nor did it interfere with their establishment.[11]

Texu sheli zhuyi, meaning incorporation with special approval, apparently refers to the period, roughly from the late eighteenth century to the first half of the nineteenth century. During those times, the establishment of a company required a state charter or a concession from the state (usually in the form of a special act of state legislature). The British East India Company was an example of such a special chartered company.[12]

Hezhun sheli zhuyi entails that any incorporation must meet legal conditions (e.g. capital, members, etc.) and receive approval from the designated state agency. While many jurisdictions (and all advanced economies except that of the European Union pursuant to the second Company Law Directive) have abandoned this doctrine, Chinese law still adheres to it as a general principle. For instance, under Article 41 of the General Principles of Civil Law, an SOE or collective enterprise, in order to obtain the legal person status granted by the law, must receive approval from and register with the authority in charge. However, companies no longer have to meet this requirement.

Zhunze sheli zhuyi, known as the registration-based system, refers to incorporation according to prescribed threshold conditions. Under this system, as long as the applicant meets the required conditions, the state is obliged to register the company; there is no special, case-by-case government approval. This system prevails in most jurisdictions.

The evolution of China's incorporation system saw it move from the approval to the registration system or from *hezhun sheli zhuyi* to *zhunze*

---

[10] Shi Tiantao (2006), p. 83; Zhao Xudong (2006), p. 112.

[11] Zhao Xudong (2006), p. 112.

[12] Through a Royal Charter issued in 1600, Queen Elizabeth granted the East India Company a monopoly on all trade in the East Indies.

sheli zhuyi. Since the early 1980s, the following historical stages have marked the reform of China's business entry system:[13]

- Prior to the reform era (1979): There were only state-owned enterprises, which were not independent legal persons; rather, they were deemed part of the state/government.
- 1979: The Sino-Foreign Joint Venture Law was adopted to allow foreign investors and their Chinese partners to establish limited liability companies subject to case-by-case approval from the Chinese authorities.
- 1980s: The government established an administrative approval system for domestic enterprises in 1982. Under that system, new businesses were subject to careful regulatory review with approvals granted on a case-by-case basis. In 1988, the Qiye Faren Dengji Guanli Tiaoli (State Council Administrative Regulations on Registration of Enterprises Legal Persons) formalized the registration process. The new regulations classified enterprises by their ownership, e.g. wholly state-owned enterprises, collective enterprises, joint-operation enterprises, foreign-invested enterprises, private enterprises. Presumably, approval was on a case-by-case pre-approval for each type of enterprise.
- 1993: The Company Law was passed. It granted limited liability to registered companies irrespective of their ownership. With the exception of joint-stock limited companies (JSLC), prior administrative approval was no longer needed for other types of companies.
- 2004: The Xingzheng Xuke Fa (Administrative Licensing Law) deprived administrative authorities of the regulatory power to approve establishment of enterprises.
- 2005: The Company Law was rewritten to delete the provision concerning state approval for establishing JSLCs. It marked a complete shift by China with respect to the registration system. In addition, it provides that a business will be registered as long as application documents meet the express conditions prescribed by law. The refusal by registration authorities to register a company may subject it to administrative discipline or even litigation.

---

[13] See World Bank (2008a), p. 9. There are a few factual errors in the World Bank's (2008a) understandings regarding the history of business registration in China.

4.1.2 The Significance of Registration

Although academic writings[14] in China offer introductions to the fiction theory,[15] the real entity theory,[16] the contractarian theory,[17] and even discuss liberal approaches embedded in the latter two theories,[18] Chinese corporate law endorses the fiction theory. Article 6 of the Company Law states:

> To establish a company, an application for establishment and registration shall be filed with the company registration authority. If the application meets the incorporation requirements stipulated in this Law, the authority shall register the company as a limited liability company or joint-stock limited company. If the application fails to meet the requirements, it shall not be registered as a limited liability company or joint-stock limited company.

Article 7 of the Company Law provides that, 'A company established in accordance with law shall be issued a business license by the company registration authority. The date of issue of the company business license shall be the date of establishment of the company'. Moreover, Article 3 of the PRC Administrative Regulations on Company Registration[19] makes clear that a duly registered company will receive an Enterprise Legal Person Business License and shall qualify as a legal person with

---

[14] See e.g. Zhou Yousu (2006),pp. 42–6, and Shi Tiantao (2006), pp. 14–22.

[15] The fiction theory maintains that through incorporation, the law gives business a legal personality existing only in law. See Foster (2000), pp. 581–2. As Chief Justice Marshall of the United States Supreme Court famously remarked, 'A corporation is an artificial being, invisible, intangible, and existing only in contemplation of law.' *Trustees of Dartmouth College v Woodward*, 17 U.S. (4 Wheat.) 518, 636 (1819).

[16] The real entity theory argues that corporations are, in fact, living things with their own legal personality. The associations of individuals that make up corporations give them distinct personality with their own will and sphere of existence, as 'real' as the individuals that make them up. The law 'should recognize this "reality" by granting it the same rights as a natural person'. Foster (2000), p. 584.

[17] The contractarian theory, popularly known as the 'corporation as a nexus of contracts' theory, views the corporation not as a person or entity, 'but rather a nexus of explicit and implicit contracts establishing rights and obligations among the various inputs making up the firm'. Bainbridge (2008), p. 28.

[18] Shi Tiantao (2006), p. 24.

[19] Zhonghua Renmin Gongheguo Gongsi Dengji Guanli Tiaoli (Administrative Regulations on the Registration of Companies), adopted by the State Council in December 2005; hereinafter the Registration Regulations.

limited liability, and that entities that do not complete the registration formalities shall not engage in business with the name of 'company'.

In short, the law suggests that, to incorporate, a company must meet statutory formalities and obtain a business license; otherwise, the 'company' does not exist. In other words, Chinese corporate law does not recognize 'de facto corporations'.[20] Without an Enterprise Legal Person Business License obtained through the registration process, an entity shall not hold itself out as a 'company'.[21] In practice, if self-proclamation occurs, the court normally treats the entity as a partnership or an individual business, requiring that the persons directly responsible bear personally liability.[22] In one case, two individuals registered their jointly owned oil manufacturing factory as an Individual Industrial and Commercial Business (IICB) and obtained a business license. In 1995, they changed the name of the IICB to 'Changyuan Oil Joint Stock Limited Company' and began to engage in business activities on a larger scale in the name of a company. In a lawsuit regarding the sale of goods, the court ruled that the 'company' did not exist because it was never lawfully registered. The court treated the entity as a partnership, and the two 'shareholders' had to bear joint and several liability.[23]

---

[20] The 'de facto' doctrine in the U.S. treats a defectively incorporated entity as a 'de facto corporation' if a 'colorable' attempt to incorporate was made. See Cox and Hazen (2003), p. 92.

[21] Please note that non-legal person business organizations may also obtain business licenses other than the Enterprise Legal Person Business License.

[22] A Judicial Interpretation issued by China's Supreme People's Court has stated, in regard to Article 4, that '[i]f a person or organization which is not duly registered with the authorities conducts civil activities in the name of, impersonates the name of, or continues to act in the name of a registered legal person or organization after it has legally ceased to exist, the court shall add the person or organization as a party to the lawsuit and make it directly responsible for liabilities arising out of the dispute'. See Zuigao Renmin Fayuan Guanyu Shiyong Zhonghua Renmin Gongheguo Minshi Susong Fa Ruogan Wenti de Yijian (Opinions of the SPC Several Questions Concerning the Application of the PRC Civil Procedure Law), promulgated 14 July 1992.

[23] 'A Case on Self-proclaimed Company,' in Zhao Xudong (2005), p. 6. Professor David C. Donald of the Faculty of Law of The Chinese University of Hong Kong argued, in commenting on this chapter, that a Delaware court could do the same on those facts as 'de facto comes up when there is some sort of clerical error in a good faith effort to incorporate'.

4.2 PRACTICAL STEPS FOR CORPORATE ESTABLISHMENT IN CHINA

In China it takes four 'factors of production' to make a company. They are: people (the promoters), money (registered capital), paper (corporate charter/articles of association), and the official act (registration and license). Although incorporation procedures vary depending on the type of company, there is a general pattern for corporate formation in China. It entails the following steps:

1. Concluding the promoters' incorporation agreement;
2. Reserving a desired corporate name through an application to the company registration authority;
3. Drafting and signing articles of association;
4. Subscribing and paying according to capital contributions;
5. Opening a preliminary bank account, depositing initial capital contributions, and obtaining a certificate of deposit;
6. Obtaining a capital verification report from auditors;
7. For LLCs, submitting the application to the company registration authority; if approved, obtaining the Enterprise Legal Person Business License;
8. For JSLC, holding the company's inaugural meeting and afterwards submitting an application to the company registration authority; if approved, obtaining the Enterprise Legal Person Business License.

After establishment, companies must go through further steps before they can legally engage in business activities. These could include: police approval for a company seal, a code certificate from the quality and technology supervision authority, registration with the statistics authority, registration with the central and local tax authorities, an official bank account, authorization to print or purchase financial invoices/receipts, registration with the government-sponsored career center, and registration with the social welfare insurance center.[24]

As can be seen from above, LLCs and JSLCs have different incorporation requirements under the Company Law. Understandably, there are differences owing to their different natures. For example, during incorporation, a JSLC might offer shares to the public and hence securities regulation might be involved.

---

[24] For details of these steps see 'Starting a Business in China' at the World Bank's Doing Business website (http://www.doingbusiness.org).

4.3 COMPANY REGISTRATION AUTHORITIES

The chief 'company registration authority' referred to in the Company Law is the Administration for Industry and Commerce (AIC) at the central and local levels. The State Administration for Industry and Commerce (SAIC) registers (i) companies to which the State-owned Assets Supervision and Administration Commission (SASAC) is the capital contributor; (ii) foreign-invested companies; and (iii) companies for which national laws, administrative regulations, State Council decisions, or SAIC decisions so provide.[25] Similarly, AICs at the provincial and district level are in charge of certain state-owned companies and companies invested in by natural persons, as well as companies that delegate registration power with the upper levels of AICs.[26]

To establish, a company needs to register the following items with the authority:[27]

- Company name
- Company domicile
- Name of the company's legal representative
- Registered capital
- Paid-up capital
- Type of the company
- Scope of business
- Duration of the company
- Names of shareholders (for LLCs) or promoters (for JSLCs)
- The amount of capital contribution subscribed or paid up and the time and method of delivery.

Registration is also necessary for any subsequent changes to the company's particulars, termination of the company, and the establishment of a branch. The Registration Regulations provide that applicants may register in person, by mail, or by electronic means including telegraph, telex, facsimile, electronic data exchange, or email.[28] In any case, the AIC must act within five days and decide whether to accept an application and

---

25 Registration Regulations, *supra* note 20, Article 6.

26 Registration Regulations, *supra* note 20, Article 7.

27 Registration Regulations, *supra* note 20, Article 9.

28 Registration Regulations, *supra* note 20, Article 51. Under this mandate, various levels of AICs at established Internet portals deal with company registration. For example, the portal for accessing the registration services offered by the SAIC is at http://www.saic.gov.cn.

thereafter it has 15 days to approve the registration.[29] Rejecting an application may subject AICs to administrative reconsideration or litigation.[30]

4.4 LEGAL CONDITIONS FOR CORPORATE ESTABLISHMENT

According to Article 23 and other relevant provisions in the Company Law, an LLC must satisfy the following legal conditions to incorporate:

1. The number of shareholders meets the statutory number, between two and 50 for a standard LLC, and one for a one-person LLC.
2. The capital contributions of shareholders meet the minimum statutory capital requirement, RMB30,000.
3. The shareholders have jointly written the company's articles of association.
4. The company has a name and the organizational structure required by law.
5. The company has a domicile. While the Company Law does not define domicile, Article 38 of the General Principles of Civil Law (GPCL) provides that a legal person's domicile is its main place of business.

To incorporate a joint-stock limited company (JSLC), the applicant must follow the legal conditions listed in Article 77 and other related provisions of the Company Law:

1. The number of promoters is between two and 200. In addition, more than half of the promoters must have a domicile in China. However, the law does not define 'domicile'.
2. The share capital subscribed for and raised by the promoters must reach the minimum statutory capital requirement, RMB5 million.
3. A JSLC may form by means of promotion or share offer. In either case, share issuance and other preparatory matters must conform with securities law.
4. The promoters have formed the company's articles of association and/or adopted them at the inaugural meeting (in case of establishment by means of share offer).

---

[29] Registration Regulations, *supra* note 20, Articles 52 and 54.

[30] The Registration Regulations mandate that the AIC inform the rejected applicants that they may apply for administrative reconsideration and litigation. See Registration Regulation, Articles 53 and 55.

5. The company has a name and an organizational structure required by law.
6. The company has a domicile, which is its main place of business.

This chapter examines some of common and special issues concerning company incorporation in detail below.

4.5 TWO METHODS FOR INCORPORATING JSLCS

Although LLCs and JSLCs share some similar incorporation procedures, there are significant differences in the procedural and substantive requirements. One of the key differences is that Company Law has special provisions for the establishment of JSLCs, and through those, a JSLC: by promotion, or share offer.[31]

Establishment by promotion means that promoters subscribe the entire share capital to meet the capital requirements.[32] The company's registered capital is the total share capital subscribed by the registered promoters. That is to say, the promoters shall subscribe, in writing, to the total shares stipulated in the articles, pay at least 20 percent of the subscription, and pay the remaining balance over the next two years (or five years if an investment company). Company Law prohibits such companies from issuing shares to others if the promoters have not paid their committed share capital.[33] Further, only after promoters have made their first capital contribution can they elect a board of directors and supervisory board. The board of directors shall then submit to the AIC the company's articles of association, certificate of capital verification, and other requisite documents, and apply for registration of incorporation.[34]

Alternatively, a company could establish itself through a share offer, under which the promoters subscribe a certain portion of the total shares and offer the balance to the public.[35] According to the Company Law, after the promoters subscribe 35 percent or more of the total number of shares, they may offer the remaining shares to either the general public through a public offering or a private placement to 'specified targets,' or qualified investors. Either way, the Company Law and the China Securities and Regulatory Commission (CSRC) regulate the offering. In the case of a public offering,

---

31 Company Law, Article 78, para. 1.
32 Company Law, Article 78, para. 2.
33 Company Law, Article 81.
34 Company Law, Article 84, para. 3.
35 Company Law, Article 78, para. 3.

the company must prepare and deliver share offer prospectuses and subscription forms.[36] A legally established securities company must underwrite the public offering.[37] Within 30 days after the company's stipulated share capital is fully paid up and verified, the promoters shall convene an inaugural meeting comprised of its promoters and subscribers. The attendees have power to adopt the company's articles of association, elect members of the board of directors and supervisory board, examine and approve the incorporating activities of the promoters, and decide not to incorporate in case there is a significant change of circumstances.[38] Moreover, if the members have not fully subscribed the share capital, or if the promoters fail to hold the founding meeting in time, then the subscribers may demand a refund of their payment plus interest.[39] If things work well, the newly elected board of directors shall submit the documents specified in Article 93 of the Company Law to the relevant AIC for registration of incorporation.

In essence, establishment of a JSLC by share offer is both an incorporation and 'going public' process because the company incorporates and makes its initial public offering (IPO) at the same time (in the case of incorporation by public share offer). Despite detailed provisions in the Company Law, establishment of a JSLC by share offer is practically impossible thanks to the rules issued by the CSRC. Under China's securities regulation, the CSRC must approve any public offering of securities. In its Administrative Measures for Initial Public Offering and Listing of Shares[40] promulgated in May 2006, the CSRC indicated that the issuer of an IPO must not only be an existing JSLC[41] but also have been in operation for three years, unless otherwise approved by the State Council.[42] The CSRC only allows the establishment of a JSLC by share offer when it is the conversion of an LLC into a JSLC. As the Company Law does not have such a restriction, it remains an open question whether the relevant CSRC rules, as ministerial rules in the legislative hierarchy, violate a basic national law enacted by the National Peoples' Congress.[43]

---

36 Company Law, Articles 86 and 87.

37 Company Law, Article 88.

38 Company Law, Article 91.

39 Company Law, Article 92.

40 Shouci Gongkai Faxing Gupiao Bing Shangshi Guanli Banfa, promulgated by the CSRC on 17 May 2006 and effective as of 18 May 2006 (hereinafter the CSRC Measures for IPO).

41 CSRC Measures for IPO, Article 8, para. 1.

42 CSRC Measures for IPO, Article 9, para. 1.

43 See the discussion in *supra*, Chapter 1 on sources of corporate law in China.

4.6 COMPANY NAMES

A company shall adopt only one name, and once registered, the law protects its use. The Administrative Provisions on the Registration of Enterprise Names[44] and its Implementing Measures restrict the incorporators' freedom to formulate a corporate name.[45]

A company name, such as *Beijing Haohua Gongcheng Youxian Gongsi* (literally the Beijing Haohua Engineering Limited Company), comprises four components, namely the administrative region (e.g. Beijing), trade name with the distinctive element (e.g. *Haohua*), type of business (e.g. *Gongcheng,* which means 'engineering'), and a legal ending indicating the type of the company (e.g. *Youxian Gongsi*). There are, however, a few exemptions. First, companies approved to use 'China', 'Chinese', or 'international', historically famous trade names, and foreign-invested companies do not need to include an administrative region in the name. Second, enterprise legal persons approved by the State Council, registered with the SAIC, or with a registered capital of RMB50 million do not need to indicate the administrative region in their names. Third, certain enterprises, including holding companies of enterprise groups or those with registered capital of RMB100 million or more, do not need to indicate the type of business in their names.

The words *Zhongguo* ('China'), *Zhonghua* ('Chinese'), *Quanguo* ('national'), *Guojia* ('state'), and *Guoji* ('international') are exclusively reserved for enterprises set up by the State Council. However, foreign-invested enterprises that use foreign trade names or in which the foreign investors are controlling shareholders may include 'China' in their names.[46]

Trade names may not contain expressions that are: (i) detrimental to state and public interests; (ii) likely to mislead the public; (iii) names of foreign countries or international organizations; (iv) names of political parties, party, government, or military organs, mass organizations, social organizations, or military unit organizations; (v) Chinese Pinxin or numeric characters; and (vi) names prohibited by other laws.

For many years, enterprises had to register their foreign names together with Chinese names. In 1999, the SAIC decided to ignore the foreign

---

[44] Qiye Mingcheng Dengji Guanli Guiding, promulgated by the SAIC in May 1991.

[45] Qiye Mingcheng Dengji Guanli Shishi Banfa, promulgated by the SAIC in June 2004.

[46] For example, the registered name of Microsoft's China subsidiary is Weiruan (Zhongguo) Youxian Gongsi Microsoft (China) Ltd.

names or the foreign translation of China-incorporated enterprises. Enterprises now have freedom to choose the foreign translation of their names.[47]

Application for pre-approval of the company name is a compulsory step in the incorporation process.[48] A key purpose of this mechanism is to prevent using a name already on the AIC's index of names. An equally important purpose is to allow the AIC to pre-examine the legality of proposed names. A pre-approved name may be kept for six months, during which it may not be used for business activities or transferred.

4.7 CORPORATE CHARTER (ARTICLES OF ASSOCIATION)

Gongsi Zhangcheng, literally translated as the corporate charter and popularly known as the articles of association, is the most important corporate document.[49] It is actually a single document and serves as the company's constitution. The charter is the only document dealing with the company's internal governance and it must be filed for registration with the registrar. As such, it gives notice to third parties and, to some extent, protects the company and its insiders from liabilities accrued to third parties.

4.7.1 Contents of the Charter

Corporate law literature in China classifies charter items into three types: mandatory provisions, recommended provisions, and discretionary provisions.[50] Under the Company Law, the charter of an LLC or JSLC must include the following mandatory items:

---

[47] Guanyu Qiye Mingcheng Buzai Heding Waiwen Mingcheng de Tongzhi (Notice of the SAIC on Stopping the Practice of Registering Foreign Names of Enterprises), promulgated on 19 January 1999.

[48] Registration Regulations, *supra* note 20, Article 17.

[49] For the purpose of this book, corporate charter and articles of association will be used interchangeably, although the former will be used in most cases to refer to the *gongsi zhangcheng*.

[50] See Liu Junhai (2008), p. 88; Shi Tiantao (2006), p. 121; and Zhou Yousu (2006), p. 202.

LLC[51]	*JSLC*[52]
1. Name and domicile	1. Name and domicile
2. Scope of business	2. Scope of business
	3. Method of establishment
3. Registered capital	4. Total number of shares, par value of each share, and registered capital
4. Names of shareholders 5. Methods, amount and time of capital contribution by shareholders	5. Names of promoters and number of shares subscribed for by promoters, and methods and time of their capital contribution
6. Organization of the company and its methods of establishment, functions and powers, and rules of procedure	6. Composition, functions and powers, and rules of procedure of the board of directors 7. Composition, functions and powers, and rules of procedure of the supervisory board
7. Legal representative	8. Legal representative
	9. Method of profit distribution 10. Reasons for dissolution of the company and method of liquidation 11. Methods of notices and announcements of the company

The common mandatory items are: (1) corporate name and domicile; (2) scope of corporate business; (3) registered capital; (4) names of shareholders or promoters; (5) methods, amount, and time of capital contribution; and (6) legal representative.[53] However, the charter of a JSLC must also include its method of establishment, total shares and par value of

---

[51] Company Law, Article 25.
[52] Company Law, Article 82.
[53] Zhou Yousu (2006), p. 203.

each share, profit distribution methods, dissolution and liquidation, and its methods for serving notices and announcements to shareholders.

4.7.2 CSRC Model Charter

Model sets of articles enacted by the regulators of China's securities markets further limit the freedom of JSLCs to create their own corporate charter. One set of model articles is the Guidance for Corporate Charter of Listed Companies issued by the China Securities Regulatory Commission (hereinafter the Model Charter). The first Model Charter was released in 1997, which has been replaced by a new version promulgated in 2006.[54] These guiding articles apply not only to listed companies but also to those companies that will or have offered shares to the public, including non-listed JSLCs.

The main question is to what extent the articles in the Model Charter are compulsory. In the Circular promulgating the Guiding Articles, the CSRC states that listed companies 'should' include the Guiding Articles in their own articles of association, if they issue domestic shares (A shares) and/or domestically list shares denominated in a foreign currency (B shares). The Circular further provides that listed companies may make minor changes to the Guiding Articles in light of actual circumstances. However, if the listed company wishes to alter the mandatory provisions stipulated in the Guiding Articles, it must highlight the changes in a public announcement after amending its articles.[55] The CSRC's approach is 'comply or disclose' with respect to the binding nature of the Guiding Articles.

Chinese companies that wish to list their shares in overseas stock exchanges must comply with another set of model articles, ones tailored especially for them, namely the 1994 Mandatory Provisions in the Corporate Charter of Companies Listed Overseas (hereinafter the '1994 Mandatory Provisions').[56] As its name suggests, the 1994 Mandatory

---

[54] Zhongguo Zhengjianhui Guanyu Yinfa 'Shangshi Gongsi Zhangcheng Zhiyin (2006 Nian Xiuding)' de Tongzhi (Circular of China Securities Regulatory Commission on Printing and Distributing the Guidance for the Articles of Listed Companies (Revised 2006)), 16 March 2006 (hereinafter the Circular on Guiding Articles).

[55] Id.

[56] Guanyu Zhixing 'Dao Jingwai Shangshi Gongsi Zhangcheng Bibei Tiaokuan' de Tongzhi (Circular on Implementing the Mandatory Provisions of Articles of Association of Companies Listed Overseas), jointly issued by the State Council Securities Committee and the State Commission for Restructuring

Provisions are legally binding. The Circular promulgating the provisions' Essential Clauses mandates that 'companies seeking to list shares overseas shall include the contents of the Essential Clauses in their articles of association and must not alter or delete the contents of the Essential Clauses without authorization'.[57]

4.7.3 Adoption and Amendment of the Corporate Charter

According to the Company Law, incorporating shareholders of an LLC draft the company's articles and file them with the AIC for registration.[58] The law does not specify the percentage of votes required for adoption but presumably, the shareholders must reach a consensus with respect to the articles.[59] For a JSLCs established by promotion, the promoters shall draft the articles and summit them at the company's inaugural meeting for adoption.[60]

The Company Law does not restrict companies from amending their articles, but it does provide that that the power to amend remains in the hands of the shareholders. The CSRC Guiding Articles provide that the shareholders may amend the articles under the following circumstances: (i) the articles conflict with new laws or regulations; (ii) the company's situation no longer conforms with its original articles; or (iii) the shareholders' decide to amend the articles at their meeting.[61]

A question remains as to who may propose amendments at the shareholders' meeting. The Company Law is silent on this but presumably, the board of directors, the supervisory board, and the shareholders can all propose amendments at the shareholders' meeting. In any event, amendments require a two-thirds majority vote of the shareholders for passage.[62]

---

the Economic System in 27 August 1994 (hereinafter the Circular on Essential Clauses).

57 Id.

58 Company Law, Article 23(3).

59 A legislative annotation suggests that 'The Articles of Association should be made collectively by all the shareholders, representing the will of all the shareholders.' See An Jian (2005), p. 50.

60 Company Law, Article 77(4).

61 Model Charter, Article 188.

62 Company Law, Articles 44 and 104.

4.7.4 Charter and Corporate Autonomy

Corporate literature in China views the articles as the most important self-governing tool the company has to safeguard its autonomy against arbitrary state intervention and regulatory abuse.[63] The 2005 Company Law is the embodiment of a shift from a restrictive to an enabling regime, which has significantly increased corporate autonomy by giving more weight to the corporate charter. Compared with the 1993 law, the new legislation contains more empowering provisions and allows the charter to regulate certain corporate affairs. For example, Article 12 permits the company to stipulate its scope of business in its charter. Article 13 allows the Company to decide whether the chairman of the board or company manager should serve as the company's legal representative. Article 16 authorizes the company to stipulate whether the board of directors or the shareholders (at their annual meeting) have the competence to decide the company's capacity to make external investment and provide guarantees to third parties. In addition, the new Company Law adds numerous provisions that grant companies the exclusive power to regulate their own corporate affairs, including profit distribution, shareholder participation, powers and duties of the corporate organs, transferability of shareholders' equity interests, and more.

4.7.5 Binding Force of a Company's Charter

Academics have long debated the legal nature of the articles. Whatever the nature of the document, it has the binding force of law. Article 11 of the Company Law mandates that '[t]he articles of association of the company shall be binding upon the company, shareholders, directors, supervisors, and senior management personnel'.[64] Article 10 of the Model Charter also provides:

> The Articles of Association shall, as of the date of its entry into force, become a legally binding document governing the organization and conduct of the company and the relations between the company and its shareholders as well as that between the shareholders. It has legally binding force on the company and its shareholders, directors, supervisors, and senior management personnel.

---

[63] See Liu Junhai (2008), p. 85; Gan Peizhong (2007), pp. 256–8; Shi Tiantao (2006), p. 117.

[64] According to Article 217 of the Company Law, senior management personnel refers to the company's manager, deputy manager, senior corporate finance officers, the secretary to the board of directors, and other personnel stipulated in the articles.

> In accordance with the Articles, a shareholder may sue other shareholders, the company's directors, supervisors, manager and other senior management personnel, as well as the company. In addition, the company may sue its shareholders, directors, supervisors, manager, and other senior management personnel.

Once the corporate charter takes effect, its provisions override all earlier agreements between the shareholders, including the incorporators' agreement. In *Wanjia Jingdian v Xinhua Bookstore*,[65] three parties, including the defendant, signed the incorporators' agreement to establish a limited liability bookselling business named Qiusuo Qiuzhi Ltd. The three incorporators, including the defendant Xinhua, pledged 40 percent (RMB2 million), 35 percent (RMB1.75 million), and 25 percent (RMB1.25 million) of the share capital, respectively. In December 2004, Qiusuo Qiuzhi registered and its articles listed the aforementioned contributions. In January 2005, one of the company's corporate shareholders, Siyi Jiaye, transferred its capital contribution to the plaintiff. The plaintiff then signed a new incorporators' agreement with the other two shareholders. Their agreement provided that the other two shareholders, including the plaintiff, would undertake to jointly contribute RMB0.75 million on behalf of Xinhua in consideration of Xinhua's reputation as a nationally famous brand name. As result, Xinhua's actual contribution was worth (in kind) only RMB1.25 million. After the plaintiff became a shareholder, it sued Xinhua for not making the capital contribution stipulated in the corporate charter.[66]

In its ruling, the first instance court emphasized the incorporators' 'true manifestation of intention'. The court reasoned that the amount and means of capital contribution stipulated in the charter did not reflect the parties' true intention because the parties agreed in the incorporators' agreement to different amounts and means of capital contribution. As such, the other two shareholders' promise to contribute RMB0.75 million for Xinhua was a legally binding contractual commitment and Xinhua had fully satisfied its capital contribution obligations by transferring RMB1.25 million in kind.[67]

Overruling the first instance court, the Beijing First Intermediate Court held that, in spite of the incorporators' agreement, the corporate charter, once filed with the AIC, was legally binding. The court ruled that the

---

[65] The facts and decisions of the case are summarized and discussed in Liu Lanfang (2009), pp. 50–58.

[66] Liu Lanfang (2009), pp. 51–3.

[67] Liu Lanfang (2009), pp. 53–4.

obligations in the charter were both contractual and mandatory obligations under the law; they could override prior contractual promises. Since the charter stipulated that Xinhua should make a capital contribution of RMB2 million and in fact it only made an in kind investment of RMB1.25 million, it was still under legal obligations to make up the difference.

The implication of the case is that a duly filed and registered corporate charter takes the highest place in the hierarchy of agreements concluded among shareholders. However, the appellate ruling runs directly against certain legally recognized principles in Chinese law, such as the sanctity of contract and promissory estoppel. Further, it might be unfair and unreasonable not to allow the shareholders to change, by side agreement, the contents of the charter. In fact, a judge who adjudicated the case wrote that it was lawful for LLC shareholders to make collateral agreements to stipulate the means, methods, and amount of their capital contributions. However, unless they also amended the corporate charter accordingly, those contractual commitments are unenforceable.[68]

4.8 REGISTERED CAPITAL

4.8.1 Principles of Legal Capital

Like many other civil law jurisdictions (and the common law jurisdictions in the European Union), China maintains legal capital requirements that are sometimes onerous for small businesses. All capital requirements in Chinese corporate law derive from the famous academic doctrine of the 'Three Principles of Corporate Capital'. That maxim mandates capital determination, capital maintenance, and unchanging capital for a registered company.[69] The principle of capital determination (*ziben queding yuanze*) requires the total amount of a company's capital to be stipulated in its articles and fully paid or subscribed. Otherwise, the company may not have a valid existence. The principle of capital maintenance mandates that the company must maintain a level of assets equivalent or above its legal capital. Once the company's net assets fall below that of its legal capital, it must take measures to restore the adequacy of its legal capital. Lastly, the principle of unchanging capital

[68] Liu Lanfang (2009), p. 58 (case commentary written by Judge Du Weihong of the Beijing First Intermediate Court).

[69] Zhou Yousu (2006), pp. 176–7; Shi Tiantao (2006), pp. 162–4; Liu Junhai (2008), pp. 124–9; and Zhao Xudong (2006), pp. 224–8.

entails strict procedures for the increase or reduction of capital. It makes it difficult to lawfully change the amount of capital.[70]

The 'Three Principles' mentioned above are, however, purely a scholarly invention. Their specific meaning was never articulated in the corporate law literature in Chinese. Chinese writings never point to original comparative law authorities; rather, they firmly believe that company laws around the world universally embody such principles.[71] Even so, it is also believed that the 'Three Principles' have profoundly influenced modern corporate legislation in China, and that the rules concerning capital requirements are entirely based on the principle of capital determination.[72]

4.8.2 Statutory Minimum Registered Capital Requirements

The 2005 Company Law mandates a minimum requirement of RMB30,000 to incorporate an LLC and RMB5 million for a JLSC. On average, the capital requirement to establish an LLC is about 130 percent of China's per capita income.

Compared with many developed economies, many of which require no specific legal capital, China's current capital requirements are very high. However, the current threshold is already a significant reduction from earlier, recent law. The capital requirements in the 1993 Company Law were draconian. For example, under Article 23 the minimum capital requirements for LLCs were: '(i) RMB500,000 for a manufacturing company; (ii) RMB500,000 for a commercial wholesale company; (iii) RMB300,000 for a commercial retailing company; and (iv) RMB100,000 for a high technology or consultancy company'. As remarked by the World Bank, 'Prior to [the 2005] reform, China had the 8th highest minimum capital requirement in the world, equivalent to 947% of the country's average annual income per capital, $1,290'.[73] The capital

---

[70] Id.

[71] See e.g. Zhao Xudong (2006), p. 225 (stating that 'Although different countries have different legal capital principles, after long-term development, a set of capital principles have been commonly recognized and implemented in the company laws of nations of the world, of which the most important are the so-called "Three Principles of Capital".'

[72] Zhou Yousu (2006), pp. 176–7; Zhao Xudong (2006), pp. 225–6.

[73] 'China's a top reformer in Asia, improving its business environment tremendously since 2005', World Bank press release, 7 December 2005, available at http://www.worldbank.org (accessed 7 July 2007).

requirements in the new law significantly lowered the amount of minimum capital. The same requirements now apply to all companies regardless of the type of business in which they engage. It represents a substantial liberalization in the efforts of lawmakers to make doing business easier in China.

4.8.3 Capital Contribution by Installment

A further liberalization measure provided in the new law is that now stakeholders can pay the registered capital of an LLC in installments over two years, provided that shareholders' initial contribution is not less than 20 percent of the total registered capital.[74] For investment companies – or companies whose major business is investment, not manufacturing or services – the payment period may extend to five years.[75] Article 81 of the Company Law prescribes the same formula for JSLCs established by promotion.

It is worth noting that, to establish an LLC, the first installment of capital contribution must exceed the statutory minimum registered capital. This is a bit confusing and it indeed confused the World Bank, which once praised China for reducing the minimum registered capital from 947 percent of average annual income per capita to '56% of income per capital, similar to the amount required in Germany and lower than the requirement in Japan or Korea', shortly after the 2005 Company Law was promulgated.[76] In making such a statement, the World Bank must have mistakenly believed that shareholders need only make an initial capital contribution of 20 percent of the statutory minimum registered capital but in actuality the Bank did not correctly consider that the first installment cannot be less than the statutory minimum registered capital.

However, it can be inferred from the Company Law that, for incorporating a JSLC, stakeholders can pay the RMB5 million minimum capital in installments, provided that the promoters pay the balance within two years (or five years for an investment company) from the date of incorporation.[77] That is to say, it suffices for the promoters to pay RMB1 million when they incorporate the company.

---

[74] Company Law, Article 26.
[75] Company Law, Article 26.
[76] World Bank press release, *supra* note 59.
[77] Company Law, Article 81.

4.8.4 Means of Capital Contribution

The 2005 Company Law greatly expands the various means of capital contribution. Under the 1993 Company Law, shareholders could only pay their share in the form of (1) cash; (2) in kind; (3) industrial property rights; (4) non-patented technology; and (5) land use rights.[78] Further, the cap for using intangible assets such as industrial property rights and non-patented technology was set at no more than 20 percent of the total registered capital.[79] As this was an exhaustive list, it effectively excluded all other means of capital contribution such as copyright, equity interest, or receivables.

In contrast, the 2005 Company Law, in addition to making the stipulations in the 1993 version, contains a catch-all provision that states that the contribution can be made with any 'non-cash assets that can be appraised in the form of currency and transferrable according to law'.[80] That is to say, the Company Law adopts a negative-listing approach under which promoters may contribute as capital anything that has a market value, unless laws and administrative regulations prohibit its use as a capital contribution. However, certain things, including labor/services, credit, names of natural persons, business reputation, franchises, or pledged property have been explicitly carved out from the list of contributable assets.[81]

In addition, the new Company Law lifts the ceiling for non-cash contribution to 70 percent of the total registered capital by stipulating that 'the amount of cash contribution to the capital by all the shareholders shall not be less than 30 per cent of its registered capital'.[82] Presumably, a stakeholder can pay the remaining 70 percent of the legal capital with non-cash consideration, including tangible or even intangible assets. In any event, 'non-cash assets used for capital contribution shall be valued and verified, and shall not be overvalued or undervalued'.[83] The law, however, does not require professional agencies to do the valuation, although it does provide that a professional capital verification agency shall verify the total registered capital.[84]

---

78 Company Law 1993, Article 24 (for LLC) and Article 80 (for JSLC).

79 Id.

80 Company Law, Article 27, para. 1. Article 27 applies to JSLCs by way of Article 83.

81 Registration Regulations, Article 14, para. 2.

82 Company Law, Article 27, para. 3.

83 Company Law, Article 27, para. 2.

84 Company Law, Article 29.

4.8.5 Equity Interest as a Means of Capital Contribution

In theory, the new Company Law makes it possible for applicants to use almost any marketable asset for capital contribution. However, the State Council has made it clear that, beyond cash, in kind assets, intellectual property rights, and land use rights, the AICs will register assets for capital contribution purposes only when the SAIC (together with other central agencies if needed) adopts administrative measures for registering such assets.[85] In January 2009, the SAIC promulgated the Administrative Measures for the Registration of Capital Contributions Made with Equities. Those measures make it possible for investors to use their equity interests in LLCs or JSLCs as capital contributions in exchange for equity stakes in new companies.[86] In essence, investments with equity interests are no different from transferring equity held by an investor to a new company. The only restriction attached to this form of capital contribution is that the equity interest should have no strings attached. There should be no dispute with respect to the ownership interest, and the interest must not be under pledge or frozen according to law. In addition, there should be no contractual or legal hurdles in the buyer's articles or in the general law that would prohibit such transfers.[87]

4.8.6 Liabilities for Failing to Make Adequate Capital Contribution

Shareholders must contribute the capital they have subscribed in the articles on time and in full. For LLCs, shareholders shall deposit their cash contributions into the LLC's bank account and transfer the ownership of any non-cash contributed asset to the company according to law.[88] For JSCs established by promotion, the promoters shall subscribe in writing all shares to be issued according to the articles, and pay either in full or in installments for all the shares they have subscribed.[89] Making adequate capital contributions is a contractual obligation and a very

---

[85] Registration Regulations, Article 14, para. 1.

[86] Guquan Chuzi Dengji Guanli Banfa, promulgated by the SAIC on 14 January 2009, and effective as of 1 March 2009 (hereinafter the Equities Contribution Measures).

[87] Equities Contribution Measures, Article 3.

[88] Company Law, Article 28.

[89] Company Law, Article 84.

serious statutory obligation.[90] Violations can lead to civil, administrative, and even severe criminal liabilities under the PRC laws.

Civil liability

A shareholder who fails to make the promised capital contribution has the statutory obligation of *bujiao*, meaning he is one that the company shall call upon to make a full contribution.[91] After the establishment of the company, if the actual value of non-cash contributions made by shareholders is markedly lower than the value specified in the corporate charter, then the shareholder concerned must make up the differences.

The Company Law clearly establishes two civil liabilities. First, shareholders may enforce the incorporators' agreement and a shareholder who fails to make the promised capital contribution is liable in contract to the other shareholders according to the incorporators' agreement. Interestingly, the relevant wording in the Company Law applies a bit differently to LLCs and JSLCs. For LLCs, the Law mandates that shareholders 'shall be liable for breach of contract to the shareholders that have made their capital contributions on time and in full'.[92] However, for JSLCs, the Law simply states that promoters that fail to pay adequately are liable in contract 'according to the promoters' agreement'. Apparently, the Law gives promoters more freedom to deal with this issue through private contract.[93]

---

[90] In *Fujian Xiongtong v Fujian Motor Factory* (Fujian Provincial High Court, 2002), one shareholder sued another for failing to make adequate capital contributions. The former sued and requested termination of the contractual co-investing relationship. The Fujian High Court ruled that, because the defendant seriously breached the incorporators' agreement, it would terminate the incorporators' agreement and hold the defendant liable in contract and award liquidated damages. However, the Supreme People's Court (SPC) criticized the decision in an edited volume of case commentaries. The SPC suggested that the Fujian court ignored the fact that making adequate capital contribution is both a contractual and legal obligation under compulsory provisions in the Company Law. It reasoned that by permitting the termination of the agreement, the court both deprived the defendant of its capacity as a shareholder and relieved it of the legal obligation to contribute capital. In addition, the SPC explained that the lower court failed to address the question of the company's capital adequacy and left open the question: who would replace the defendant and make sure the company would not be under-capitalized? See SPC Civil and Commercial Division II (2006), pp. 139–43.

[91] Company Law, Articles 28 and 94.

[92] Company Law, Article 28, para. 2.

[93] Company Law, Article 84, para. 2.

A second liability is the joint and several liability shareholders/promoters have in case there is an insufficient capital contribution. As noted above, if the actual value of the non-cash assets contributed by a shareholder is markedly below the value stipulated in the company's articles, the contributor shall make up the difference at the time of the company's establishment or bear joint and several liability.[94] The Company Law does not specify whether other shareholders are jointly and severally liable when one shareholder fails to make a capital contribution (e.g. cash contribution) on time and in full.[95] In stark contrast, the Law explicitly provides that the promoters are jointly and severally liable for one promoter's obligations to make a full capital contribution as stipulated in the company's articles. They must make up for the difference between the actual value of the non-cash consideration and its stated value in the articles.[96] However, the Beijing Higher People's Court (binding upon all the courts in the Beijing Municipality) ruled that, if shareholders fail to or only partially contribute to the LLC's registered capital, the Beijing courts should support the claims of the LLC or the creditors and request the responsible shareholders to bear joint and several liability.[97]

Administrative liability

The regulators will also step in and impose administrative penalties against both the company in question and the shareholders/promoters if there is inadequate capital contribution. If the company reports a false amount of registered capital, the AIC may impose a fine ranging from 5 percent to 15 percent of the false amount. In serious cases, the AIC may revoke the company's registration or business license.[98] The promoters/shareholders making false capital contributions will likely receive a fine ranging from 5 percent to 15 percent of the declared amount of false contribution.[99]

---

[94] Company Law, Article 31.

[95] Some scholars in China argue that by analogy to the joint liability of LLC, promoters of JSLCs should have joint liability; moreover, the joint and several liability of shareholders/promoters for non-cash asset contribution should also apply to cash contributions. See Zhao Xudong (2006), p. 265.

[96] Company Law, Article 94.

[97] The Second Guiding Opinions of the Beijing Higher People's Court on Several Questions Concerning Trial of Corporate Disputes (北京市高级人民法院《关于审理公司纠纷案件若干问题的指导意见之二》), Article 2, promulgated by the Beijing Higher People's Court on 21 April 2010, document Jing Gao Fa Fa (2008) No. 127 (hereinafter Beijing HPC Judicial Opinions II (2008).

[98] Company Law, Article 199.

[99] Company Law, Article 200.

Criminal liability

Under the PRC Criminal Law, any incorporator who has registered a company by making a false declaration of registered capital through submitting falsified documents to deceive the AIC is criminally liable if the declared false amount of registered capital is very substantial. If the falsity caused serious consequences, then if the person is an individual, he may face three years' imprisonment and have to pay a fine ranging between 1 percent and 5 percent of the falsely declared registered capital.[100] If such person is a 'unit', namely a business organization such as a company, it must pay a fine and its officers who are directly in charge or responsible may receive three years' imprisonment or criminal detention.[101]

Company promoters or shareholders who make false capital contributions by failing to deliver the promised cash or non-cash assets or who have withdrawn the contributed capital are also liable to receive up to five years' imprisonment and/or a fine ranging from 2 percent to 10 percent of the false contribution or withdrawn contribution.[102] If the promoter or shareholder is a 'unit,' it may receive a fine and its responsible officers are liable for up to five years' imprisonment.[103]

4.8.7 Reconsidering the Functions of Minimum Registered Capital in the Chinese Context

Although the 2005 Company Law significantly lowered the minimum amount of registered capital for LLCs from RMB500,000 to RMB30,000, the new threshold is still not a small number and it is '3 times greater than annual per capita income in central China'.[104] Since the lawmakers made a 94 percent reduction of the statutory minimum registered capital, why do they not simply abolish it?

To answer this question one must trace back to the original legislative purpose of the statutory minimum capital. The minimum capital requirement certainly functions to prevent frivolous incorporation and furnish a material basis for the company's business operation.[105] But as one

100 PRC Criminal Law, Article 158, para. 1.
101 PRC Criminal Law, Article 158, para. 2.
102 PRC Criminal Law, Article 159, para. 1.
103 PRC Criminal Law, Article 159, para. 2.
104 World Bank (2008a), p. 11.
105 Chan (2009), p. 307.

Chinese commentator remarks, the main purpose of the minimum capital rule is to protect the creditors:[106]

> The legislative rationale for the minimum registered capital rule is grounded in the limited liability system [in corporate law]. The limited liability system confines the liability of shareholders to their capital contributions and thus limits the investment risk they face. Simultaneously, it poses potential risks for other parties transacting with the company. To balance the benefits and liabilities faced by the shareholders and creditors, the law requires the contribution of minimum registered capital as a precondition for shareholders enjoying the protection of limited liability in order to set up a necessary threshold for the market access of corporate entities and to offer a minimum protection for the company's creditors.

Chan (2009) points out that the 'unreasonably high threshold' of the minimum capital rule gave rise to two major problems, and they eventually led to the rule's revision. First, 'the old law impeded people's ability to gain access to limited liability and hindered the development of entrepreneurship'.[107] Second, 'the old law had led to wastage of resources' in the sense that it required new companies to keep in their accounts funds that far exceeded their first business commitments.[108] In addition, the high requirement encouraged people to get around the legal rule using illicit tactics, such as falsifying capital contribution documents or secretly withdrawing (borrowed) capital from the company after registration.[109]

Despite the problems, in his surveys, Chan (2009) finds support from Chinese corporate legal scholars for the retention of the minimum capital rule. First, it is argued that RMB30,000 is a rather modest level sufficient to restore efficiency especially when one considers the rapid rise of China's GDP per capita. Second, many Chinese scholars believe that the authorized capital system prevalent in the United States is not suitable for China because the latter is at the infant stage of the market economy. The scholars contend that an authorized capital system will only encourage speculative and fraudulent activities targeted at the creditors. Third, if there is strengthened supervision and enforcement within the traditional legal capital system, it could better protect creditors, especially those involuntary creditors such as tort victims. Fourth, the minimum registered

106 Zhao Xudong (2006), p. 234.
107 Chan (2009), p. 307.
108 Chan (2009), pp. 307–8.
109 Chan (2009), p. 308.

capital system is the most effective tool to prevent frivolous incorporation (by the so-called 'empty-shell' companies) in China.[110]

That the minimum capital requirements can provide meaningful protection for creditors is, however, a delusion in the contemporary Chinese context because of two facts. First, if adjusted for inflation, the figure of RMB30,000 is hardly enough to satisfy most claims. Second, in most cases, a company would spend its minimum registered capital – receiving other, less liquid assets in return – in the first few weeks of its operation. In practice, almost no trade creditor is so naïve as to believe that a company's registered capital could meaningfully represent the company's creditworthiness. In significant transactions, creditors would request a review by an independent third party (such as an auditing firm) to review the company's solvency. Creditors can protect their interests in a number of ways: mortgage, pledge, guarantee, charge, lien, standby letters of credit, and performance bonds, among others. If private contracts are not good enough, then they might either ask a court to 'pierce the corporate veil' or turn to the functioning insolvency law.

Indeed, alongside the significant reduction of minimum capital, the 2005 Company Law also introduces the doctrine of 'piercing the corporate veil', a doctrine which, as discussed in Chapter 3, allows third parties to seek recourse directly from individual shareholders who employ limited liability protection to abuse the company's separate legal person status.[111] In addition, the 2007 Enterprise Bankruptcy Law, which brings China's corporate insolvency system closer to international practices, gives creditors more control over the bankruptcy process through creditors' meetings. With these contractual and statutory tools in place, it becomes increasingly less desirable to have a mandatory capital regime in Chinese corporate law.

4.9 DEFECTIVE INCORPORATION

Defective incorporation is a failure to comply with minor or substantial formalities set by the law as conditions of incorporation. It occurs often in China. It is important to point out that, in considering the corporation as a legal creature, Chinese corporate law recognizes neither the doctrine of de facto company nor the doctrine of company by estoppel. An entity is either a legal company or another form of business, but never anything in between.

---

110 Chan (2009), pp. 308–10.

111 Company Law, Article 20, para. 3.

The 1993 Company Law required that incorporation of LLCs or JSLCs 'must' [*bixu*] comply with the statutory 'conditions', including, of course, both substantive and procedural requirements.[112] Courts have followed a rather rigid approach in interpreting this rule. Thus in *Ye Yanli et al. v Zhejiang Lishui Lock Ltd*,[113] the plaintiff falsified a certificate of deposit, with which the plaintiff and other promoters registered the Qingtian Mineral Ltd (Mineral). None of the shareholders made any actual capital contribution, although the company later admitted another shareholder who contributed a large amount of cash capital. In October 1996, Mineral's shareholders signed a share transfer agreement with the defendant to transfer their equity interests in Mineral to the defendant for RMB1 million. They executed the transfer in the sense that both Mineral's articles and the registration with AIC were amended. However, the defendant subsequently refused to pay the consideration on the ground that the plaintiffs made false capital contributions and therefore, Mineral was not a legal corporation. In its ruling, the first instance court treated Mineral as an entity with some elements of a de facto company. The court ruled that, although the plaintiffs paid no capital to Mineral during incorporation, their subsequent investment in the company reached the statutory minimum for registered capital. Further, since the defendant treated Mineral as a company during their initial dealings, it could enforce the share transfer agreement and the defendant should pay the consideration. The Zhejiang Provincial High Court reversed and ruled that the plaintiffs' false capital contribution was a plain violation of the substantive requirements for company registration in China. The court reasoned that, since Mineral did not have the requisite legal person status to stand as a company, the shareholder transfer agreement was invalid.

It seems, however, that the first instance judgment in the above case is more in line with the spirit of the 2005 Company Law, which takes a rather liberal approach in recognizing the status of companies. Softening the tone, the new law provides that companies 'should' submit applications for registration of incorporation to the registration authority. In the case of undercapitalization during the incorporation stage, the Law only requires that the responsible shareholders make actual adequate contributions, which the law can enforce as contractual and statutory

---

[112] Company Law 1993, Article 8.

[113] The Intermediate Court of Lishui Prefecture, Zhejiang Province rendered the first instance judgment, case no: (1998) Li Zhong Jing Chu Zi No. 123. The Zhejiang Provincial High Court rendered the second instance judgment, case no: (2000) Zhe Jing Zhong Zi No. 339. Zhang, Xuebing (2004) reported and analyzed the case, pp. 34–41.

obligations.[114] However, undercapitalization will not necessarily make the company's legal person status invalid, especially when the company obtained a business license from the relevant AIC. That said it is still true that Chinese law will never view an entity as a company unless it obtains a business license through registration.[115]

4.10 COMPANY PROMOTERS

4.10.1 Notion and Qualifications of Promoters

The Company Law does not define promoters but Article 80 provides that '[t]he promoters of a joint stock limited company shall undertake matters concerning the preparation of the company'. There is no mention of the concept of promoters in the rules concerning LLCs in the Company Law. Whenever it concerns the incorporation of the LLCs, the law unhesitatingly uses the word 'shareholders', as if there could be shareholders even before the company is established. This is probably the first indication, as alleged in scholarly writings, of the birth defects of Company Law provisions that concern promoters.[116] One should treat the founding 'shareholders' used in the Law concerning LLC incorporation as 'promoters' because they are legally responsible to contribute capital and ensure compliance with the legal formalities of incorporation. As one commentator remarked, 'although Chapter II, Section 2 of the [2005] Company Law uses the concept of "shareholders", there are however no shareholders at the incorporation stage. As such, the term "shareholders" used by the lawmakers here is obviously an imprecise concept. From the perspective of legislative intent, "shareholders" used here could only be understood as "promoters".'[117] It is, however, reasonable to opine that probably not all the shareholders of an LLC are in fact shareholder-promoters.

Although anybody, be it a natural or legal person, can be a company shareholder, there are certain restrictions on promoters' capacity. Under the General Principle of Civil Law, a promoter shall have the capacity for civil acts. Therefore, minors, mentally challenged people, and others for

---

[114] Company Law, Articles 28, 31, 84, and 94.

[115] See *supra*, §3.1.2.

[116] Chan (2009a), p. 233.

[117] Liu Junhai (2008), p. 70. Chan (2009a, p. 226) also notes that 'all the founding shareholders of LLCs will assume the function of promoter' in spite of the fact that they are addressed by the Company Law as 'shareholders'.

whom the law limits their civil capacity cannot be promoters. Moreover, the Law requires more than half of the promoters of a JSLC to reside in China. However, there are no similar strings attached to the founding shareholders of an LLC. Further, Chinese corporate law does not have any limitation on the nationality of promoters, and so both Chinese citizens and foreigners can all be promoters for companies incorporated in China. In addition to natural persons, legal persons and other organizations with legal personality can be promoters.

4.10.2 Promoters' Responsibilities

The main job of promoters is to organize the formation of a legal company. For this purpose, their responsibilities fall under two categories: incorporation preparatory work and capital contribution.[118] Promoters have different tasks and they depend on the type of the company. In most cases, they must sign promoters' agreements, draft articles of association, seek pre-approval of the corporate name, and establish the company's domicile. Moreover, they have to convene the founding meeting, establish an organizational structure for the company, prepare share offering documents, seek regulatory approval for share offerings, hire professional verifiers to verify the capital contributed, and make sure to file the applications for registration with the relevant AIC. In addition to these preparatory matters, promoters must make adequate capital contributions, which in fact constitutes their main duty. They must subscribe to the total share capital and pay at least the first installment, in case they establish (an LLC or JSLC) by promotion. For a JSLC established by share offer, promoters must make significant purchases (35 percent) of the shares that the company will issue. As noted previously, civil, administrative, and even criminal liabilities follow if there is undercapitalization of a company.[119]

4.10.3 Promoters' Liabilities and Legal Remedies

Along with the great power given promoters to form companies, the law assigns them serious responsibilities. Promoters are, of course, liable for their own criminal acts and those committed by their agents, and administrative authorities (such as the AIC or the CSRC) may punish them for administrative violations, especially in cases of false capital contribution. The 2005 Company Law, however, has shifted the focus –

---

[118] Chan (2009a), p. 230.
[119] See *supra*, §3.8.6.

without prejudice to the criminal and administrative liabilities – to civil liability, in which case the promoters have to pay monetary damages. The circumstances under which the Company Law imposes civil liability are:

Contractual liability between promoters *inter se*

In both LLCs and JSLCs, the founding shareholders/promoters assume contractual obligations between themselves under the incorporation agreement.[120] LLC founding shareholders who fail to make adequate capital contribution are liable for breach of contract to the other shareholders.[121] It is not clear whether promoters of JSLCs have similar liabilities.

Statutory duty to make adequate capital contribution

Founding shareholders/promoters who fail to contribute adequate capital shall make it up to the company in full.[122] If non-cash assets are greatly overvalued, then the responsible shareholders are under obligation to make up the difference.[123] It is, however, not clear from reading the Company Law whether the company at that stage has legal standing to sue. Of course, the company has standing if the company's articles constitute a contract between a company and its shareholders. This is, however, not yet an established rule in China as the nature of the articles is quite controversial. Some courts, such as those in Beijing, interpret non-contribution of capital as a tort against the company, thus granting it a cause of action in tort.[124] In either case, the shareholders/promoters are jointly and severally liable for their obligations to make adequate capital contributions.

Tort liability to the company

Article 95(3) of the Company Law provides that the company has a cause of action in tort against the promoters. It requires JSLC promoters to

---

[120] Company Law, Articles 28 and 84.

[121] Company Law, Article 28, para. 2.

[122] Company Law, Article 28, para. 2.

[123] Company Law, Articles 31 and 94.

[124] Beijingshi Gaoji Renmin Fayuan Guanyu <Shenli Gongsi Jiufen Anjian Ruogan Wenti de Zhidao Yijian (Guiding Opinions of the Beijing Higher People's Court on Several Questions Concerning Trial of Corporate Disputes), Article 16, promulgated by the Beijing Higher People's Court on 24 January 2004, document Jing Gao Fa Fa (2004) No. 50 (hereinafter Beijing HPC Judicial Opinions 2004).

'compensate the company for damage incurred by the company in the course of incorporation due to the fault of the promoters'. The company, as plaintiff, has the burden to prove that a tortious act has been committed during incorporation and caused damage to the company, for which the promoter is at fault. Although this provision applies to JSLC promoters, one commentator has remarked, '[t]here is no persuasive reason why it should not be made applicable also to the promoters of LLCs'.[125]

It is, however, unclear whether promoters' tort liability directly relates to the fiduciary duties imposed on directors, supervisors, and senior managers of the company by Article 148 of the Company Law. There is no mention of such duties for promoters. The fact that plaintiffs need to prove fault indicates that the lawmakers probably had no intention to impose fiduciary duties on promoters, as fiduciary duties attach irrespective of fault.[126] In this sense, the tort liability in Article 95(3) only covers the 'secret profit' issue. Making 'secret profits' is one of the most common forms of promoter misbehavior. Promoters make secret profits when they personally profit from side transactions they make with the company, either by overvaluing an asset they sell to the company or by taking a commission or kickback from the vendor. Although this is a common phenomenon in incorporation, the Company Law is largely silent on this problem. However, it does require that the promoter make up for the difference in case there is a significant gap between the stated and market value of non-cash contributions. Without invoking fiduciary duties, Article 95(3) covers the secret profit problem to a limited extent. In cases where promoters receive commissions from vendors, 'the promoter may not have to compensate the company unless it can be proved that his commission forms part of the purchase price, and the company thereby suffers "a loss" because it has not received the best possible bargain'.[127] In cases where promoters sell the company their own property for a profit, it might be very difficult for Article 95(3) to come to play unless the property is significantly overpriced.[128]

Statutory liability to third parties with respect to pre-incorporation transactions

Company Law Article 95(1) provides briefly that promoters of JSLCs 'shall bear joint and several liability for the debts and expenses incurred

---

[125] Chan (2009a), p. 236.
[126] Chan (2009a), p. 237.
[127] Chan (2009a), p. 238.
[128] Chan (2009a), p. 238.

for the incorporation in the event the company cannot be established'. Although there is no explicit mention of this liability for LLC founding shareholders, scholarly writings in China suggest that there is no reason not to apply Article 95(1).[129]

Article 95(1) seemingly covers pre-incorporation transactions in cases of unsuccessful incorporation, thus making it possible for promoters to be personally liable on their pre-incorporation contracts even though they made the contracts on behalf of a company not yet formed. The text of this legal provision is, however, frustratingly vague. Of course, an unformed company, since it is never an entity with legal personality (and hence without necessary capacity under Chinese law), cannot adopt those contracts. In this situation, Chinese law generally treats the promoters collectively as a partnership with respect to third-party liabilities. This general approach is, however, not able to deal with the complexities that may arise without detailed legislative or judicial guidance. When pre-incorporation contracts are silent or ambiguous regarding who is bound – e.g. in a situation where the promoters make only conditional promises for the purpose of soliciting an offer that the company, if formed, could accept or reject – it is unfair to hold the promoters absolutely liable.

Probably for this reason, several provincial higher courts in China have issued some rather detailed judgments regarding pre-incorporation transactions and the promoter liabilities that follow. In this regard, the Shanghai municipal court made the following two clarifications. One, with respect to third-party debts incurred before the company incorporation, the courts should treat the promoters as partners who bear liabilities jointly and severally. Second, in case there is an unsuccessful incorporation, all promoters are jointly and severally liable to third parties for the external debts incurred in their attempts to incorporate; however, the promoters may share the liability among themselves according to the incorporation agreement.[130] In a judicial opinion issued after the promulgation of the 2005 new Company Law, the Shandong provincial court gave a more specific interpretation as to pre-incorporation transactions:[131]

---

129 See Liu Junhai (2008), p. 72; Chan (2009a).

130 Shanghaishi Gaoji Renmin Fayuan Guanyu Shenli Sheji Gongsi Susong Anjian Ruogan Wenti de Chuli Yijian (Opinions of the Shanghai Higher People's Court on Handling Several Questions Concerning Corporate Lawsuits), promulgated 12 June 2003.

131 Shandongsheng Gaoji Renmin Fayuan Guanyu Shenli Gongsi Jiufen Anjian Ruogan Wenti de Yijian (Provisional Opinions of the Shandong Provincial Higher People's Court on the Adjudication of Corporate Disputes), adopted on 26 December 2006, Part I.

1. Promoters shall be personally liable for contracts entered in their own names even though the contracts were for incorporation purposes. If the company, after its incorporation, elects to adopt the contracts or is already enjoying the rights under the contracts, the counterparties to the contracts may decide which responsible party it wishes to hold liable.
2. Companies should 'inherit' contracts signed by the promoters in the name of the company or 'preparation team' after incorporation. The court should not support claims of the counterparties unless they requested all the promoters to bear joint and several liabilities in the case of unsuccessful incorporation. However, if a promoter entered into contracts for his/her own interests – e.g. in order to transfer debts to the company, the company (after its establishment) and other shareholders may petition the court to waive the promoter's liability.
3. Between the promoters *inter se* the liability is shared in accordance with the promoters' agreement or the company's articles of association.

Broadly speaking 'third parties' should also include subscribers in case of failed incorporation. Article 95(2) of the Company Law mandates that promoters 'shall bear joint and several liability for refunding the subscription monies already paid by subscribers plus bank deposit interest'. Obviously, the law puts the subscribers in the position of creditors in case incorporation fails. However, subscribers may not claim damages beyond their original subscriptions plus interest.

4.11 SPECIAL INCORPORATION ISSUES CONCERNING ONE-PERSON LLCs

A one-person LLC is foremost a limited liability company under the Company Law, which means that its incorporation and registration process have, for the most part, to follow the rules and procedures for standardized LLCs, especially those concerning corporate names, articles of association and other registration documents, means of capital contribution, etc. However, the incorporation of a one-person LLC has some distinctive elements (or regulatory restrictions) that are worth special mention.

First, although either a natural person or legal person can establish a one-person LLC, a natural person may form only a one-person LLC, and this LLC is not allowed to establish a subsidiary one-person LLC.[132]

Second, with respect to capital contribution, the minimum registered capital is RMB100,000, a much higher amount than for a standard LLC. Further, the stakeholder must pay the entire registered capital in a single installment.[133]

Third, a one-person LLC shall declare in its company registration whether its single shareholder is a natural or legal person and so state in its business license.[134]

Fourth, and probably most important, there is a statutory 'presumption of guilt' under the Company Law with respect to the burden of proof in lawsuits brought by creditors against the single shareholder. For standardized LLCs, the law has a 'presumption of innocence' that grants LLC shareholders limited liability. If an LLC creditor wishes to pierce the corporate veil and ask the shareholders to be responsible for corporate debts, he or she must prove that the shareholders abused their shareholder status and the company's independent legal person status that in turn harmed the creditors' interests.[135] The same presumption applies for one-person LLCs. The single shareholder must prove that he/she maintained a separation between the company's financial affairs and his/her own personal finances; otherwise, the shareholder will lose the protection of limited liability and must assume liability personally.[136]

4.12 SPECIAL INCORPORATION ISSUES CONCERNING FOREIGN-INVESTED COMPANIES

4.12.1 Types of Foreign-invested Companies Permitted under Chinese Law

As noted in the preceding chapter, foreign investors can establish various forms of foreign-invested enterprises (FIEs), including companies. Originally, China only allowed foreigners to establish three types of companies: equity joint ventures, cooperative joint ventures, and wholly owned subsidiaries. And all in the form of limited liability companies

132 Company Law, Article 59, para. 2.
133 Company Law, Article 59, para. 1.
134 Company Law, Article 60.
135 Company Law, Article 20.
136 Company Law, Article 64.

(provided the foreigners were legal persons). Since the mid-1990s, the government has greatly relaxed the incorporation regime and now foreign investors can incorporate the following types of companies:

- Sino-foreign equity joint ventures (EJVs) under the PRC Law on Sino-Foreign Equity Joint Venture (EJV Law)[137] and its Implementing Regulations[138]
- Sino-foreign cooperative joint ventures (CJVs) under the PRC Law on Sino-Foreign Cooperative Joint Venture (CJV Law)[139] and its Implementing Rules[140]
- Wholly foreign-owned enterprises (WFOEs) under the PRC Law on Wholly Foreign-owned Enterprises (WFOE Law)[141] and its Implementing Rules[142]
- One-person limited liability companies (One-person LLCs) under the Company Law
- Standardized limited liability companies (LLCs) under the Company Law
- Foreign-invested joint-stock limited liability companies (FI-JSLC) under the Provisional Rules on Certain Questions Regarding the Establishment of Foreign-invested Joint Stock Limited Companies[143]

---

137 *Zhongwai Hezi Jingying Qiye Fa* (Law on Sino-Foreign Equity Joint Venture), first adopted by the National People's Congress on 1 July 1979, revised in April 1994 and March 2001, respectively, by the National People's Congress (hereinafter the EJV Law).

138 *Zhongwai Hezi Jingying Qiye Fa Shishi Tiaoli* (Regulations for Implementing the PRC Law on Sino-Foreign Equity Joint Venture), promulgated by the State Council on 20 September 1983, and most recently revised 22 July 2001 (hereinafter the EJV Implementing Regulations).

139 *Zhongwai Hezuo Jingying Qiye Fa* (Law on Sino-Foreign Cooperative Joint Venture), adopted 13 April 1988 by the National People's Congress and revised 31 October 2000.

140 *Zhongwai Hezuo Jingying Qiye Fa Shishi Xize* (Rules for Implementing the PRC Law on Sino-Foreign Cooperative Joint Venture), promulgated 4 September 1995 by the Ministry of Foreign Trade and Economic Cooperation.

141 *Waizi Qiye Fa* (Law on Wholly Foreign Owned Enterprises), adopted 14 April 1986 by the National People's Congress and revised 31 October 2000.

142 *Waizi Qiye Fa Shishi Tiaoli* (Implementing Rules for the Law on Wholly Foreign Owned Enterprises), promulgated 12 December 1990 by the Ministry of Foreign Trade and Economic Cooperation and revised 12 April 2001.

143 *Guanyu Sheli Waishang Touzi Gufen Youxian Gongsi Ruogan Wenti de Zanxing Guiding*, promulgated 10 January 1995 by the Ministry of Foreign Trade and Economic Cooperation (herein after the 'FI-JSLC Rules').

- Standardized joint-stock limited liability companies (JSLC) under the Company Law.

This is a bit confusing and needs some explanation. The confusion stems from two facts: first, China still maintains its traditional dualist regulatory system for domestic and foreign investors, and second, new regulatory and judicial practice has significantly eroded the dualist system after the promulgation of the Company Law in 1993. From the late 1970s to the mid-1990s, China only allowed foreign investors to establish EJVs, CJVs, and WFOEs. When the 1993 Company Law took effect, both regulators and courts gradually granted foreign investors national treatment; they allowed them to incorporate as Chinese citizens.

An illuminating court decision is *Hainan Pacific Oil Co. et al. v Asian-Pacific Oil Inc.* rendered by the Supreme People's Court of China (SPC).[144] The dispute was between Hainan Pacific Co. (hereinafter Hainan), a JSLC incorporated in Hainan Province, and Asia-Pacific Oil Inc. (hereinafter APO), a company registered in Thailand. The two companies concluded a stock transfer agreement so that APO could purchase 25.5 percent of the total shares of Hainan and nominate three members of the board of directors, the chief executive officer, and the chief financial officer. The contract stipulated it would fail if Hainan could not complete the registration procedures with the Hainan Administration of Industry and Commerce (HAIC).[145]

Hainan had secured the approval of the Province's Securities Commission in July 1994 and APO purchased its shares. In May 1995, HAIC approved the amendments to Hainan's registered capital and issued a new business license that recognized the equity interest of APO. Thereafter, Hainan submitted an application to the Ministry of Foreign Trade and Economic Co-operation (MOFTEC), but the ministry rejected the application based on eight points of regulatory non-compliance.[146]

On 4 October 1996, APO wrote to Hainan requesting the return of its investment because MOFTEC's rejection rendered its agreement with Hainan invalid. In 1998, MOFTEC rejected a second application because the ministry had received a letter from APO to end its share participation. APO sued and demanded the invalidation of its original agreement and return of the share price. One of APO's arguments was that, under

144 *Hainan Pacific Oil Co. et al. v Asia-Pacific Oil Inc.* PRC Supreme People's Court civil judgment (1999) Jing Zhong Zi Di 283 Hao.

145 Id.

146 Id.

MOFTEC's Rules on Foreign-Invested Joint-Stock Companies, the establishment of a foreign-invested joint-stock company must receive approval from MOFTEC.[147]

The Court held that neither the Company Law nor any laws and regulations in force prior to its promulgation prohibited foreign participation in domestic companies. It explained that foreign investment laws, such as the 1995 MOFTEC Rules, apply only when the domestic company wants to obtain the status of an FIE from MOFTEC. Therefore, the Court ruled that the agreement was valid and confirmed APO's shareholder status.[148]

Asian-Pacific Oil makes it clear that foreign investors may establish FIEs pursuant to one of the special FIE laws, or standardized (domestic) LLCs or JSLCs, according to the Company Law. Further, in accordance with a number of recently promulgated regulations, they may also acquire a portion (e.g. 10 percent) of the equity interest of a listed JSLC in the capacity of a Qualified Foreign Institutional Investor (QFII)[149] or a strategic foreign investor,[150] or become a shareholder in a Chinese company through a merger or acquisition.[151] In these cases, investees are not traditional FIEs but rather standardized LLCs or JSLCs that were originally but are no longer specially reserved for Chinese investors.

4.12.2 Incorporation Rules for Traditional Foreign-invested Companies

Despite the trend of convergence, China still maintains a separate regulatory regime, especially for the traditional foreign-invested companies (FICs) such as EJVs, CJVs, WFOEs, and FI-JSLCs. In fact, most

---

147 Id.

148 Id.

149 Under the *Hege Jingwai Jigou Touzizhe Jingnei Zhengquan Touzi Guanli Guanfa* (Administrative Measures for Domestic Securities Investment of Qualified Foreign Institutional Investors), promulgated by the China Securities Regulatory Commission, the People's Bank of China and the State Administration of Foreign Exchange on 24 August 2006. This replaces the old – and first – regulation on QFII issued in 5 November 2002.

150 Under the *Waiguo Touzizhe Dui Shangshi Gongsi Zhanlue Touzi Guanli Banfa* (Administrative Measures for Strategic Investment in Listed Companies by Foreign Investors) promulgated by the Ministry of Commerce, China Securities Regulatory Commission, State Taxation Bureau, State Administration of Foreign Exchange on 31 December 2005.

151 A later chapter of this book will examine domestic and foreign-related mergers and acquisitions.

foreign investors, because of path dependency or unfamiliarity with the new rules, still choose to incorporate their Chinese entities under the separate regime for foreign investment. In this sense, it is important to understand the rules in the relevant FIEs law insofar as it concerns incorporation.

Approval, registration, and capital requirements for traditional FICs in the form of LLCs

Although the 2005 Company Law switched from a pre-approval to a registration system, the pre-approval system is the basis establishing EJVs, CJVs, WFOEs, or FI-JSLCs.

To incorporate an EJV, the incorporators must submit an application to the PRC Ministry of Commerce (MOFCOM, formerly known as MOFTEC) for examination and approval. The application package must include a feasibility study, the EJV contract, articles of association, and the names of the chairman of the board, vice chairman, and directors.[152] MOFCOM shall decide whether to grant an approval within three months. If the application is approved, then the EJV has 30 days to apply to the relevant AIC for a business license. The approval processes for CJVs are almost the same except that the authorities shall decide within 45 days whether to approve. Furthermore, MOFCOM does not have a monopoly over the approval process for CJVs. The law clearly allows the State Council to delegate the power to other central ministries and local people's government.

WFOEs are now the most popular form of foreign-invested business vehicles in China.[153] Like CJVs, the incorporation of WFOEs is subject to the approval of MOFCOM or bodies delegated by the State Council. Before the formal incorporation starts, the foreign investors must first contact local government and explain the purposes of their intended investment. They can then file an application for establishment with the relevant approval authority, who has 90 days to decide whether the application merits approval. WFOEs are formally considered legal entities when they obtain business licenses from the relevant AIC after institutional approval.

---

[152] The newly issued Implementing Opinions on FICs cancelled the requirement to submit joint venture contracts. See *infra* note 154.

[153] According to a survey by the US–China Business Council, foreign investors established a total of 23,435 projects in China in 2009, of which 4,283 were EJVs, 390 were CJVs, 21 were FI-JSLCs, and 18,741 were WFOEs. See US–China Business Council, 'FDI in China', available at http://www.uschina.org/statistics/fdi_cumulative.html (accessed 1 October 2010).

Although the 2005 Company Law has significantly reduced the statutory minimum capital requirements, FICs, insofar as they are subject to separate regulatory regimes, have a high threshold of initial capital investment. This is proportionately linked to the FICs' total investment. For example, under a 1987 circular,[154] a joint venture with a proposed total investment (which includes registered capital and the borrowed assets of the firm after its establishment) of not more than US$3 million must have a registered capital of 70 percent of the total investment. If the total investment is between US$3 and 10 million, the registered capital should be at least 50 percent of the total investment but in no case lower than US$2.1 million. For projects in which the total investment is between US$10 and 30 million, 40 percent goes to registered capital. Finally, a total investment of more than US$30 million comes with a 'one-third rule' for the registered capital.

A rather unique capital requirement in China's FIE law is that a foreign party to an EJV or CJV should contribute at least 25 percent of the venture's registered capital. Interestingly, there is no ceiling for the foreign party's share of capital. The lawmakers have never disclosed their rationale for having such a requirement, although one could speculate that the purpose of the '25 percent rule' is to prevent the formation of joint ventures with *de minimis* foreign investment in order to enjoy the many preferential treatments granted by Chinese law to FIEs.

There are also special requirements regarding the methods and timings of FIE capital contribution. The investors can contribute in foreign currency, equipment, buildings, land-use rights, and intangible assets such as industrial property. However, the industrial property and technology contributed by the foreign party may not exceed 50 percent of its total capital contribution or 20 percent of the joint venture's total registered capital. As for the pace of payment, investors in EJVs and CJVs may pay their share in a single lump sum within six months from the issuance of the business license, or by installments with the initial payment varying according to the firm's registered capital. For EJVs and CJVs, investors must pay the first installment within three months from the license's issuance and must equal not less than 20 percent of the registered capital. For WFOEs, investors must pay the first installment within 90 days of the license's issuance and it must equal at least 15 percent of the registered capital. Now, the Registration Regulations have

---

[154] Provisional Rules on the Ratio between the Registered Capital and the Total Amount of Investment of Sino-Foreign Equity Joint Ventures, promulgated 1 March 1987 by the State Administration of Industry and Commerce.

brought the time for paying the sum total into conformity with the 2005 Company Law, under which foreign investors in LLCs must pay the remaining balance within two years of incorporation, unless it is an investment company where the period is five years.[155]

Approval and capital requirements for foreign-invested joint-stock limited companies

China has allowed foreign investors to establish joint-stock limited companies since it passed the FI-JSLC Rules in 1995. The law is still in force, even if the conditions for setting up an FI-JSLC are rather stringent – or even draconian – when compared with the rules relevant to establishing standardized JSLCs under the Company Law.

To establish an FI-JSLC, foreign shareholders must purchase and hold shares accounting for 25 percent of the company's total registered capital. In case of incorporation by share offer, one of the promoters, presumably the corporate promoter, shall have recorded profit for the last three years. The minimum registered capital is RMB30 million, tremendously higher than the RMB5 million requirement for JSLCs under the Company Law. Further, shares held by promoters are subject to a three-year lock-up period, which is significantly longer than the Company Law's one-year requirement. The approval and registration process is an arduous one: the promoters must first submit an application of incorporation to both the local government and MOFCOM, and then register with the SAIC to obtain a business license. Moreover, local governments and MOFCOM must also approve the conversion of existing EJVs, CJVs, or WFOEs into FI-JSLCs.

4.12.3 Regulatory Reform for FIC Incorporation after the New Company Law

As seen above, China created a separate regime for incorporating foreign-invested companies; it is, however, very complicated and even confusing. Indeed, the FDI regime and the revised national corporate law do send inconsistent messages to investors, as many of the rules regulating the same matters are remarkably different. Shortly after the adoption of the new Company Law, several central regulators jointly issued the Implementing Opinions on Several Issues Concerning the Application of Laws in Administering the Examination, Approval, and

---

155 Registration Regulations, Article 20, para. 3.

Registration of Foreign-invested Companies in China.[156] The Implementing Opinions not only clarify many procedural issues concerning FIC incorporation unanswered by the existing FIE and corporate laws, but also provide substantive rules on the operation and governance of FICs. These opinions represent the first substantial step toward creating a uniform regulatory framework for FICs in China as well as unifying the two separate regimes.

Governing laws for FIC incorporation

The Implementing Opinions make it crystal clear that the Company Law and the Registration Regulations govern FIC registration, unless the FIE *laws* provide otherwise.[157] For any issue not clearly addressed in the above laws and regulations, the applicable law shall be the relevant administrative regulations of FIE laws, decisions of the State Council, and other national rules concerning foreign direct investment.[158] Local rules that once filled the gaps where the national laws were silent are probably not applicable anymore.

Forms of FICs

It is unequivocally inferable from the Implementing Opinions that the authorities would permit the registration of not only traditional FIEs, but also standardized companies under the Company Law.[159] The articles of association of foreign-invested standardized LLCs and JSLCs must conform to the Company Laws not the FIE laws.[160] In displaying 'the instincts of a zoologist documenting biodiversity',[161] the Implementing Opinions prescribe 13 different designations for FICs formed as LLCs and 10 distinct designations for JSLCs, as shown in the following list:[162]

Legal suffixes of limited liability companies with foreign investment:

---

156 *Guanyu Waishang Touzi de Gongsi Shenpi Dengji Guanli Falu Shiyong Ruogan Wenti de Zhixing Yijian* (the Implementing Opinions on Several Issues Concerning the Application of Laws in Administering the Examination, Approval and Registration of Foreign-invested Companies), issued 24 April 2006 by the SAIC, MOFCOM, the General Administration of Customs (GAC), and the State Administration of Foreign Exchange (SAFE) (hereinafter the Implementing Opinions on FICs).

157 The FIE laws refer to the three basic laws adopted by the National People's Congress regarding EJVs, CJVs, and WFOEs.

158 Implementing Opinions on FICs, Article 1.

159 Implementing Opinions on FICs, Articles 3 and 6.

160 Implementing Opinions on FICs, Article 3.

161 Neumann (2006).

162 Implementing Opinions on FICs, Article 6, para. 1.

- LLC (Sino-foreign equity joint venture)
- LLC (Sino-foreign cooperative joint venture)
- LLC (foreign–foreign joint venture)
- LLC (solely invested by foreign legal person)
- LLC (solely invested by foreign non-legal person economic entity)
- LLC (solely invested by foreign natural person)
- LLC (equity joint venture between Taiwan, Hong Kong, or Macau investor and foreign investor)
- LLC (equity joint venture by Taiwan, Hong Kong, or Macau investor and Mainland investor)
- LLC (cooperative joint venture between Taiwan, Hong Kong, or Macau investor and Mainland investor)
- LLC (equity joint venture between Taiwan, Hong Kong, or Macau investors)
- LLC (solely invested by Taiwan, Hong Kong, or Macau legal person)
- LLC (solely invested by Taiwan, Hong Kong or Macau non-legal person economic entity)
- LLC (solely invested by Taiwan, Hong Kong, or Macau natural person)

Legal suffixes of joint-stock limited companies with foreign investment

- JSLC (Sino-foreign investment, unlisted)
- JSLC (Sino-foreign investment, listed)
- JSLC (foreign–foreign investment, unlisted)
- JSLC (foreign–foreign investment, listed)
- JSLC (investment by Taiwan, Hong Kong, or Macau investors and foreign investors, unlisted)
- JSLC (investment by Taiwan, Hong Kong, or Macau investors and foreign investors, listed)
- JSLC (investment by Taiwan, Hong Kong, or Macau investors and Mainland investors, unlisted)
- JSLC (investment by Taiwan, Hong Kong, or Macau investors and Mainland investors, listed)
- JSLC (investment by Taiwan, Hong Kong, or Macau investors, unlisted)
- JSLC (investment by Taiwan, Hong Kong, or Macau investors, listed)

In addition, the registrar has authority to add another suffix to the above legal suffix if needed to indicate some distinct feature of the company in question, such as 'foreign equity less than 25 percent', 'foreign acquisition of A-shares', 'foreign acquisition of 25 percent or above of the A-shares'.[163]

Capital requirements

The Implementing Opinions clarified – or revised – the capital contribution rules in the existing FIE laws and brought them more in line with the Company Law. In terms of the means of capital contribution, the Opinions emphasize that FICs shall observe the rules in the Company Law and Registration Regulations. FICs have considerable freedom to denominate their share capital in either RMB or foreign freely convertible currencies. Like standardized companies, shareholders can contribute in cash, tangible or intangible assets (with the latter two subjected to a 70 percent ceiling). The rules cancelled a previous requirement that the registered capital should come from the investors' 'self-owned' funds; now it is permissible to make capital contribution with borrowed funds. In terms of the timing of capital contributions, investors may make contributions by installments, provided that the first installment, which must be above the statutory minimum capital, is not less than 15 percent of total registered capital and paid within three months of the company's establishment. The investor must pay the remaining balance in accordance with the relevant rules in the Company Law. Capital contribution for FI-JSLCs must fully comply with the relevant rules in the Company Law, and thus ends the application of MOFTEC's 1995 promulgated rules for foreign-invested JSLCs.[164]

4.12.4 Company Law and Foreign-invested Companies in China: Some Observations

As noted by Bath (2007), for many years since China opened its door to international trade and investment, '[f]oreign investors were governed by a separate, relatively well-developed and well-documented legal regime relating specifically to foreign investment entities'.[165] Commentators once viewed this regime as advantageous for foreigners, as '[t]hey made their own assessment of the risks of investing and operating in China based on this regime and their assessment of the reliability of Chinese regulators and their Chinese partners'.[166]

---

[163] Implementing Opinions on FICs, Article 6, para. 2.
[164] Implementing Opinions, Articles 8–11.
[165] Bath (2007), p. 774.
[166] Bath (2007), p. 774.

The regulatory landscape has changed rapidly in recent years, which has led to a gradual erosion of the dualist system of regulation for Chinese and foreign investment enterprises. Firstly, the traditional benefits conferred upon the FIEs, such as preferential tax treatments, foreign trading rights, lower costs to access local infrastructural services, etc., are gradually diminishing. Secondly, as China gradually perfects its national corporate law, the position of investors will significantly improve, especially now that the 2005 Company Law is in effect. For example, the Company Law has now shifted to a registration-based system, in which companies will incorporate as long they meet the conditions listed in the Law. For the moment, the incorporation of traditional FIEs is still subject to regulators' discretionary approval power. With respect to the parties' rights and corporate governance issues, there are problems that 'include a regulatory regime which requires that certain decisions be taken by a unanimous decision of the board of directors, effectively giving the minority partner or partners a veto; the illiquidity of the equity interests, due to the statutory requirement that the consent of the other parties and the approval authorities be obtained for a transfer of an equity interest, and the difficulty of winding up or terminating the company'.[167] Thirdly, the Chinese government seems determined to merge the separate regimes and bring both under the umbrella of the Company and other related laws. The government enacted a number of legislative and regulatory measures in this direction recently, such as the 2006 Implementing Opinions on FICs, the 2007 Enterprise Income Tax Law, as well as a variety of ministerial rules issued by central regulators such as the CSRC, MOFCOM, and SAIC.

In short, a long-term perspective suggests that China will bring the separate regime for FIEs *into* a single legal framework under the Company Law. This will allow national treatment for foreign investors, but will also take away the current preferential treatment enjoyed by FIEs.

[167] Bath (2007), p. 777.

5. Shareholders and their rights

5.1 SHAREHOLDERS' RIGHTS IN GENERAL

Article 4 of the Company Law, an umbrella provision on shareholders' rights in China, states: 'The shareholders of a company shall enjoy such rights as earnings from assets, participation in major decision-making and selection of management personnel according to law'. This provision has given rise to some curious questions as to the nature of shareholders' interests, functions, rights, and powers in the company. Reading it together with the specific rights granted by other provisions of the Company Law to shareholders, one could have the impression that shareholders in China have more significant statutory rights than their counterparts in Anglo-American jurisdictions, especially with respect to 'participation in major decision-making'.[1] For example, it is the shareholders, not directors, who decide the policy concerning dividend distribution in China.[2] It is a separate question whether these rules are actually enforced to empower the Chinese shareholders. In addition, it has been argued that even those rules are not adequate to address the conflicts between minority and majority shareholders in a context where the state is often the majority shareholder in many companies.

Conceptually, corporate law theorists in China divide shareholder rights into 'self-benefit rights' (*zi yi quan*) and 'co-benefit rights' (*gong yi quan*) based on the purpose of exercising a particular right. A self-benefit right is exercised directly for a shareholder's personal and own interest. In contrast, a co-benefit right is one for all the shareholders' interests, involving mainly shareholder rights in corporate governance and management.[3] Specifically in the Company Law, shareholders' self-benefit rights include: right to transfer shares, right to dividends, right to distribution of residual assets, right to buy new shares (preemptive rights), and the right

---

[1] See also Wei (2006), p. 35 (noting that 'Compared with the situation in some other jurisdictions, the range of power of the shareholders' meeting in a Chinese company is much wider').

[2] Company Law, Article 38(6).

[3] Zhou Yousu (2006), p. 233; Liu Junhai (2011), p. 187.

of appraisal. Their co-benefit rights cover the right to vote, right to bring legal action, right to request or convene shareholders' meetings, proposal rights, enquiry rights, and the right to information.

5.2 WHAT DETERMINES A PERSON'S SHAREHOLDER STATUS?

5.2.1 Becoming a Shareholder in China

How and when does one become a shareholder in a Chinese company? This is a pressing question underlying many corporate law disputes in China. As there is no definition of shareholders in the Company Law, once such a dispute among the shareholders arises, a real question is often whether the person proclaiming to be an oppressed owner is really a shareholder at all. Indeed, published judicial decisions suggest that disputes over shareholder status constitute a large portion of the cases arising under the Company Law.[4]

Generally speaking, corporate law literature in China categorizes the requirements for legal recognition of shareholder status into two groups: conditions in substance (*shizhi yaojian*) and conditions in form (*xingshi yaojian*). Substantively, one can become a shareholder in a Chinese company through the two main ways. The first way to acquire the status of the shareholder is called *yuanshi qude*, or original obtainment of an equity interest, whereby a person turns into a shareholder by acquiring new shares offered by the company. A promoter, or a person who has subscribed to the shares of a company which is being incorporated, will become a shareholder after the company is successfully established. But a person could also buy shares offered by an established JSLC, or bring new investment in an established LLC, to become a shareholder therein.

The second way, *jishou qude,* or derivative acquisition of equity interest, means that the acquirer takes equity interest from a third party (other than the company) to become a shareholder. This could include purchasing such interest from a shareholder, accepting the equity interest as a gift from a shareholder, or inheriting the equity interest from a shareholder. In addition, the equity interest can be acquired by way of a law enforcement document such as a judgment or arbitral award.

---

[4] See Huai Xiaofeng (2007), Liu Lanfang (2009), Wang Zhenmin and Wu Ge (2011), and Wu Qingbao (2010).

Even if a person has done any of the above, his shareholder status might still be open to challenge if the formalities are not fulfilled. That is to say, there should be documentary proof to evidence the acquisition of the equity interest. This could include the following:

1. **Promoters' agreement**, which was concluded and signed by the promoters who undertake to contribute capital, time, and efforts to establish the company.
2. **Capital verification certificate**, which was issued by a lawfully established capital verification agency to certify the actual capital contribution by the shareholders.[5]
3. **Bank receipt**, which was issued to the subscribers of shares offered by a CLS under incorporation.[6]
4. **Capital contribution certificate**, which was issued by the company, upon its incorporation, to the shareholders.[7]
5. **Corporate charter,** which has the record of the basic information of the company and its shareholders. The articles of an LLC contain the names of the shareholders as well as the methods, amount, and timing of their capital contribution.[8] A CLS's articles should have the same information, not of all the shareholders, but of all the promoters.[9]
6. **Company's register of shareholders**, which is required by law to be set up in an LLC to record the shareholders' names, domicile, and capital contribution. Such a register would be unnecessary for public CLSs who could have hundreds of thousands of shareholders and whose shareholders can be traced though the computer system of the stock exchanges or other relevant institutions.
7. **Information registered with the official registrar**, which is sometimes the State Administration of Industry and Commerce (SAIC) but more often the local Administration of Industry and Commerce (AIC).
8. **Equity transfer agreement**, which was concluded between the acquirer and the existing shareholder for the sale of the equity interest.

---

[5] Company Law, Articles 29 and 90.
[6] Company Law, Article 89.
[7] Company Law, Article 32.
[8] Company Law, Article 25.
[9] Company Law, Article 82.

5.2.2 Judicial Practice on Equity Disputes

Does any of the above documentary evidence constitute conclusive proof of one's shareholder status? Which one of them should be weighted more than others if the disputants each possess some of them? Numerous judicial decisions have been rendered, but the courts at different levels and in different localities have not acted uniformly. A few cases decided after the adoption of the 2005 Company Law may illustrate the different approaches of local courts in treating disputes concerning shareholders' status.

In *Xue Lijuan v Xu Xiaolin* (2007) on shareholding disputes decided by the Beijing courts in 2006 and 2007,[10] the information in the relevant AIC suggested that the company in question was incorporated in November 2002 and had a total registered capital of RMB5 million, to which the plaintiff contributed 80 percent and the defendant contributed 20 percent. The company, however, only issued a capital contribution certificate to the plaintiff, which indicated that she contributed RMB5 million and was the only shareholder of the company. The defendant ceased to work for the company in November 2003 and his share in the company was transferred several times to others through resolutions of shareholders' meetings, presumably without the defendant's consent. The first instance court held that, although the AIC information showed that the defendant was a shareholder, because (1) the AIC information was not inconsistent with the information in both the company register of shareholders and the capital contribution certificate held by the plaintiff and (2) the defendant was not able to prove his capital contribution, and the 20 percent shareholding registered in the name of the defendant should actually belong to the plaintiff. Not surprisingly, this decision was overruled by the appellate court, which in this case was the Beijing No. 2 Intermediate Court. Although it was highly suspicious that the defendant had actually made the capital contribution, the appellate court ruled that, since it was clear from the AIC's registration information that the defendant was a shareholder holding 20 percent of the ownership of the company and that plaintiff did not raise any objection to this fact when the company was established, the 20 percent shareholding of the defendant must have been lawfully acquired and hence should be protected by the law.[11] In a casebook published by the Beijing judiciary, a judge who

[10] The facts and decisions of the case are summarized and discussed in Liu Lanfang (2009), pp. 18–25.

[11] Id, pp. 18–22.

commented on this case proposed the following guidelines on how the courts should allocate weight to the different pieces of evidence:[12]

1. The company's charter has the strongest evidentiary effect. The corporate charter was both signed by the shareholders and approved by the state, and serves as the basis for determining the rights and obligations of the shareholders, the company, and even the directors, supervisors, and managers. In addition, parties outside the company are expected to rely upon the published charter to understand the relationships and governance within the company.
2. Registration information with the AIC is of greater weight than the company's register of shareholders or capital contribution certificate, since this information (1) is based on the charter submitted by the company and (2) serves as a form of legal publicity so as to confer the power on the registered shareholder to defend against and challenge third parties.
3. Between the register of shareholders and the capital contribution certificate, the former should be given more weight. This is because the former is required by the law to be held in the company for public or shareholder inspection in case of need.

In *Li Ping v Su'an Construction Materials Ltd* (2006),[13] a local court took a slightly different approach in prescribing the ranking order of different forms of documentary evidence. In this case, the plaintiff purchased 52 percent of the company's equity ownership through an agreement with all the existing shareholders, shortly after the company was incorporated in February 2001. After the plaintiff made full payment according to the agreed terms, the shareholders amended the company's charter to reflect the accession of the plaintiff as a new shareholder. However, the defendant company never bothered to update this change with the AIC. The company also never convened a shareholders' meeting nor distributed any dividends after May 2001. The plaintiff, although a major shareholder, was denied any opportunity to participate in the company's management and even access to the company's business and financial information. The court held that the plaintiff must be treated as a lawful shareholder based on the equity transfer agreement and the corporate charter. In a published commentary on the case, two judges of the court mentioned the following considerations, which aided the court

---

12 Id, pp. 23–4.

13 The case was summarized and and commented upon in Huai Xiaofeng (2007), pp. 57–9.

in giving a balanced and fair assessment of the weight they believed should be ascribed to the evidence:

1. Recording of shareholders' information in the company's charter should have the strongest evidentiary effect and serve as prima facie evidence of a person's shareholder status.
2. That a person's name is included in the register of shareholders could serve as a basis for presuming his shareholder status. However, that a person's name is not listed there does not necessarily mean he is not a shareholder.
3. That a person is registered as a shareholder with the AIC will be helpful evidence and should be given more weight than other evidence such as the capital contribution certificate.
4. Whether a person has made an actual capital contribution is not a determining factor in deciding his shareholder status. Failure to make adequate capital contribution might give rise to legal liabilities under the law but does not necessarily annul his capacity as a shareholder.

In *Ni Xinghua v Changsheng Medical Materials Ltd et al.*, the plaintiff alleged that he was kicked out of the company by other shareholders during a reorganization process in which the company was converted from a shareholding cooperative enterprise, in which the plaintiff owned 7.81 percent of the equity interest, into an LLC. The defendants contended that the name of the plaintiff was borrowed to satisfy a policy requirement in the 1990s that a shareholding enterprise converted originally from a collective enterprise must have several shareholders. In fact, the enterprise was entirely funded by Mr. Zhu Shanben, currently the majority shareholder of the LLC, and the plaintiff didn't make any capital contribution to the company. Both the first instance court and the appellate court opined that the fact the plaintiff's name was registered with the AIC could not alone prove that he was a shareholder. Instead, a 'totality of evidence' approach should be adopted to decide a shareholder's status. From a substantive perspective, the plaintiff could not prove that he had made any capital contribution. On the formality aspect, he did not himself sign the enterprise charter. For these two reasons, the courts held that the plaintiff could not be treated as a shareholder.

5.2.3 SPC Judicial Interpretations on Equity Disputes

A reader could easily observe some inconsistencies in the courts' handling of such cases. Although the courts generally agreed that the corporate charter was the most important evidence, the weight given to each piece of evidence varies from court to court. In addition, while the evidence was normally presented to the court in the form of paper documents, some courts seemed to be more interested in looking at the 'true intention' of the parties behind the papers than ranking the evidence according to a certain criterion. As disputes in this regard had grown rapidly, the SPC promulgated two judicial interpretations in recent years to provide several nationally applicable rules for the lower courts to follow, one being the 2011 Company Law Interpretation III and the other the 2010 FIE Interpretation I. The following principles are provided in the above two interpretations:

Cause of action

The courts will accept and adjudicate disputes involving shareholder status, on the condition that the company concerned should be named as the defendant and the other persons with material interested in the disputed equity named as third parties in the action.[14]

Burden of proof

A party seeking judicial confirmation of his status as a shareholder has the burden to prove the following facts: (1) he has made a capital contribution or subscribed to make capital a contribution in accordance with the law and is not in violation of any mandatory provisions of the laws or administrative regulations, or (2) he has acquired or otherwise succeeded to the equity interest in the company without violating any mandatory provisions of the laws or administrative regulations.[15] On the other hand, if a person's shareholder status is challenged by another person in a lawsuit, after the plaintiff produces evidence that gives rise to reasonable doubt as to whether the defendant has performed his capital contribution obligation, the burden of proof is on the defendant to prove the obligation has been honored.[16]

In a published commentary on the Company Law Interpretation III, the Civil Division II of the SPC, which handles corporate and commercial cases at the SPC, restates the need to look at both the conditions in substance and conditions in form.[17] In terms of ranking of the documentary evidence, it opines that (1) the corporate charter should be given the

---

[14] Company Law Interpretation III, Article 22.
[15] Company Law Interpretation III, Article 23.
[16] Company Law Interpretation III, Article 21.
[17] SPC Civil Division II (2011), p. 345.

heaviest weight and constitute a sufficient basis for determining shareholder status; (2) the register of shareholders of the company should serve as prima facie evidence, which might be successfully challenged by counter-evidence that proves the self-claimed shareholder does not meet other more important substantive or formal conditions; and (3) registration with the AIC is important evidence, especially for a bona fide third party, but does not have the determining effect.[18]

It is submitted that the SPC Company Law Interpretation III suggests an approach that is more oriented towards substantive conditions. Under this, as long as a person can prove that he has actually made a capital contribution or acquired the equity interest in a way not inconsistent with the mandatory rules of the law, the court will very likely treat him as a shareholder. Since the Interpretation does not specify the scope of evidence, presumably any lawful form of evidence will be admissible, which can include but is not limited to the corporate charter, register of shareholders, and registration information with the AIC. That said, the SPC Civil Division II has also pointed out that a distinction has to be made between capital contribution and shareholder status. If the documents were properly presented, 'then even though the shareholder has not fulfilled his obligation for making a capital contribution, he shall be treated as a shareholder'.[19]

On the other hand, it could happen that a person has lawfully made a capital contribution or otherwise succeeded to and obtained the equity interest, but the company fails to issue a capital contribution certificate, enter his name in the register of shareholders, and/or carry out the registration with the competent AIC. In such cases, a legal remedy is available under the Interpretation III that enables the shareholder to institute a legal action in the court to compel the company to perform those obligations.[20]

The anonymous shareholder

The existence of *Yinming Gudong*, or anonymous or undisclosed shareholders, is understood to be widespread in China.[21] In a society that is undergoing rapid transformation, it is understandable that some investors would maintain anonymity so that they can hide their wealth and

---

[18] SPC Civil Division II (2011), pp. 353–4.

[19] SPC Civil Division II (2011), p. 355.

[20] Company Law Interpretation III, Article 24.

[21] SPC Civil Division II (2011), p. 371 (noting the relationship between the actual investor and nominal investor has always been among the hottest and most difficult issues in corporate law disputes).

investment to avoid resentment. More often, anonymity is used – lawfully or unlawfully – to overcome some legal barriers, such as the requirements that prohibit government officials from owning equity interests in certain business entities.

The Company Law does not explicitly address the problem of shareholder anonymity. On the surface, its rules seem to suggest that the identity of all shareholders shall be disclosed within at least a limited scope of persons, examples being the mandatory rules of registration of shareholder information with the AIC and the establishment of a register of shareholders in an LLC. As common sense, knowing who your fellow shareholders are is a fundamental right of a shareholder. The anonymity of some shareholders gives rise to legal uncertainty that disadvantages both the other shareholders and third parties such as the company's creditors. However, given the existence of shareholders whose identity was unknown, the courts had no other choice but to devise a legal theory to distinguish different types of anonymous shareholders and recognize some of them. This task falls on Article 25 of the SPC's Company Law Interpretation III, which provides the following three rules:

1. In the case that an actual investor and a nominal investor of an LLC enter into a contract to provide that the actual investor makes a capital contribution and actually enjoy the rights and benefits of the investment and that another person (the nominal investor) is to hold the nominal title of shareholder, if a dispute concerning the validity of the contract arises between the actual shareholder and the nominal shareholder, the court should uphold the validity of the contract unless it was an illegal contract or one concluded under fraud or coercion according to Article 52 of the PRC Contract Law.[22]
2. If a dispute over vesting of the investment rights and interests arises between the actual investor and the nominal shareholder, if the actual investor asserts rights – on the grounds that he has actually performed the capital contribution obligation – against the nominal shareholder, he will have the support of the court. On the other hand, the court will not support the nominal shareholder who is only able to prove that his name is included in the company's register of shareholders or registered with the AIC as a shareholder.[23]

[22] Company Law Interpretation III, Article 25, para. 1.
[23] Company Law Interpretation III, Article 25, para. 2.

3. However, the actual investor must obtain the consent of at least one-half of the other shareholders of the company if he requests that the company change the shareholder's identity, issue him a capital contribution certificate, list his name in the register of shareholders, record his information in the corporate charter, and carry out registration with the AIC.[24]

This provision has legitimized the substantive conditions-oriented approach already practiced by Chinese courts. It obviously suggests that, since the Company Law does not prohibit anonymous shareholders, freedom of contract should override other concerns. The meeting of minds of the actual investor and the nominal shareholder should hence be treated as a binding internal arrangement within – and only within – the company. The doctrine of privity of contract dictates that this contract could not be used against third parties, especially those outside the company. That is to say, the shareholder's rights should still be legitimately exercised by the nominal shareholder before the title is legally transferred to the actual investor.[25] However, any legal transfer of title is subject to the restriction imposed by rule no. 3 above, which was drafted, according to the SPC, by reference to Article 72 of the Company Law that limits the transferability of equity interest by LLC shareholders.[26]

Interpretation III grants a legal remedy to the actual investor whose economic interest is harmed by the nominal shareholder if the latter transfers, pledges, or otherwise disposes of the equity concerned. In such a case, the court might invalidate the nominal shareholder's said transaction upon a request of the actual investor.[27] This, however, has to be done pursuant to Article 106 of the PRC Property Law, which subjects the actual investor's right to that of the bona fide third party. That is, the bona fide purchaser's reliance interest based on the registration information with the AIC shall take precedence over the actual investor's claim of economic ownership. In any case, the nominal shareholder is liable for any losses as a result of such a transaction.[28] The court may also apply Article 106 to handle disputes involving multiple transfer of the same equity interest by one shareholder.[29] If the second transfer occurs after a delay in updating the registration information to reflect the

---

[24] Company Law Interpretation III, Article 25, para. 3.
[25] SPC Civil Division II (2011), p. 371.
[26] Id.
[27] Company Law Interpretation III, Article 26, para. 1.
[28] Company Law Interpretation III, Article 26, para. 2.
[29] Company Law Interpretation III, Article 28, para. 2.

accession of the acquiring shareholder (who acquired the equity through the first, lawful, transfer), the directors, senior management personnel, or de facto controller, who are at fault for failing to carry out the registration of change in a timely manner, might be held liable to the acquiring shareholder before a court of law.[30]

The anonymous shareholder in an FIE

The SPC's FIE Interpretation I of 2010 provides several rules to deal with disputes involving anonymous shareholders in a foreign-invested enterprise (FIE):

1. The court normally will not support the actual investor's request for judicial confirmation of his shareholder status or court-ordered change of the shareholder, unless the following conditions are met: (1) the actual shareholder has made the investment; (2) the shareholders other than the nominal shareholder recognize the actual investor's status as a shareholder; and (3) the court has secured the consent of the FIE examination and approval authority (which is the PRC Ministry of Commerce) for the change of shareholder.[31]
2. A contract that specifies that one party shall make the actual investment and the other party shall serve as the nominal shareholder in an FIE shall be held valid by the court unless such contract is otherwise void according to PRC laws or administrative regulations. The court shall not invalidate the contract merely because it was not approved by the competent FIE approval authority. This means that the court will help the actual investor request the nominal shareholder to honor its obligations in the contract, including returning the investment income and benefits to the actual investor.[32]
3. The court may apply the frustration of contract doctrine to terminate the contract between the actual investor and the nominal shareholder and hold the latter liable for any damage caused if the actual investor claims that he could not realize the objectives of the contract.[33]
4. The court, however, will not support the actual investor in making a direct request to the FIE for a distribution of the profits or the exercise of other shareholder rights.

---

[30] Company Law Interpretation III, Article 28, para. 2.
[31] FIE Interpretation I, Article 14.
[32] FIE Interpretation I, Article 15.
[33] FIE Interpretation I, Article 16.

Given that the FIE laws are special laws to the Company Law, the disputes concerning the anonymous shareholders will apply the FIE Interpretation I first. The Company Law Interpretations will be applied only when specific rules cannot be found in the FIE Interpretation.

5.3 SHAREHOLDERS' INFORMATIONAL RIGHTS

5.3.1 Basis for Shareholders' Rights to Information

Knowledge of certain corporate information is necessary for shareholders to exercise their rights. This is especially true for minority shareholders who do not run and control the company. A shareholder in China has a statutory right to inspect corporate books and records. A shareholder in an LLC generally has the right to inspect and reproduce the corporate charter, the minutes of shareholders' meetings, the resolution of the meetings of the board of directors, and resolutions of the meetings of the supervisory board and the financial and accounting reports.[34] If the shareholder wishes to go further to inspect the more important account books, he shall make a written request to the company to state a proper purpose for inspection (note, however, that he does not have the right to reproduce the account books in whatever form). The request might be, as it often was, rejected by the company if the company believes the purpose is improper and may harm the lawful interests of the company. In such a case, the company shall reply to the shareholder in writing to state the reasons for the refusal within 15 days from the date of the written request of the shareholder.

The rule for shareholders in a JSLC is simpler – and hence more vague. It states 'shareholders shall have the right to inspect the corporate charter, register of shareholders, counterfoil of corporate bonds, minutes of shareholders' meetings, minutes of the meetings of the board of directors, minutes of the meetings of the supervisory board, and financial and accounting reports'.[35] Obviously a shareholder of a JSLC does not have the statutory right to inspect the account books, no matter whether he has proper purposes or not. One explanation for the reduction of protection levels for JSLC shareholders is that JSLCs are already subject to the mandatory disclosure requirements in securities law and hence much of the useful information is already available. However, publicly available information apparently does not include account books.

---

[34] Company Law, Article 34, para. 1.
[35] Company Law, Article 98.

5.3.2 Proper Purposes for Inspection

The Company Law does not define a 'proper purpose'. Liu Junhai (2011) observes that a proper purpose would be one related to the shareholder's interest as an investor, such as those to ascertain the financial condition of the company, the propriety of dividends, the value of shares, whether there has been mismanagement or illegal activities conducted by the directors, the reasons for the fall of the share price, the necessity and feasibility of a fundamental corporate change, information in aid of a shareholder lawsuit, or information to help clarify the financial and accounting reports of the company.[36] On the contrary, an improper purpose would be one unrelated to the interest of the shareholder as an investor. In *Yao Jianguo v Jinghua Textile and Clothing Ltd* (2006),[37] the plaintiff was a shareholder and director of the defendant company before he stopped working for the company in September 2005, to establish another company (Lihua Ltd). In June 2006, a law firm sent, on behalf of the plaintiff, a letter to the company requesting inspection of account books, which was rejected by the company. The court, after finding that the defendant company and Lihua Ltd were bidding for the same project in July 2006, ruled that the purpose of inspection was improper because Lihua, for which the plaintiff served as the legal representative, was in competition with the defendant company.[38]

5.3.3 Remedies if Inspection is Denied

Under Article 34 of the Company Law, if the company wrongfully denies a shareholder the right to inspect its books and papers, the shareholder may petition the court to enforce such right of inspection.[39] The court will order the company to make the requested documents accessible to the shareholder. Consequently, the shareholder may sue the company to claim compensation for any losses incurred as a result of this refusal. In addition, under urgent circumstances, the shareholder may apply for judicial preservation of the documents pursuant to Chapter 9 of the PRC Civil Procedure Law.

---

36 Liu Junhai (2011), p. 257.

37 The case was summarized and commented upon in Liu Lanfang (2009), pp. 125–33.

38 Liu Lanfang (2009), id, pp. 126–7.

39 Company Law, Article 34, para. 2.

5.3.4 Liberal Judicial Activism in Inspection Disputes

Articles 34 and 98, the two provisions on shareholders' informational rights in the Company Law, give rise to questions that cannot be answered by a textual interpretation of the rules. For example, is the list of documents exhaustive? Can a shareholder request to inspect and reproduce documents not listed in the two provisions? Can the company reject a request on the ground that the shareholder has not performed his capital contribution obligation?

Although the law is rather vague in this regard, numerous cases suggest that the courts tended to adopt a more liberal approach to accommodate the inspection demand of the shareholders. In a scholarly case note, the authors – who were judges of a court in Beijing – radically argued that:

> The essential nature of shareholders' informational rights suggests that all carriers of corporate information should be covered by the said rights ... We suggest that judges go beyond the stated scope of information in the Company Law by (1) adopting an expanded interpretation of the rules [of the Company Law] based on the legislative intent, or (2) relying on the corporate charter to expand the scope of information accessible to shareholders.[40]

In *Jin Yaping et al. v Fulin Printing Ltd* (2006),[41] the three plaintiffs were shareholders of the defendant company incorporated in Zhuji City, holding in aggregate 7.4 percent of the company's total equity interest. In March 2006, a law firm representing the three plaintiffs made a written demand to the company requesting to inspect the company's financial reports, account books, and other documents. In May 2006, the company held a shareholders' meeting that passed a resolution to provide the plaintiffs with several – but not all – financial reports, but not any account books requested by the plaintiffs. The defendant company argued, *inter alia*, that it was improper for the plaintiffs to request to inspect the original receipts and invoices in relation to the company's sales, which was obviously beyond the scope of documents permitted in Article 34 of the Company Law. The Zhuji court was not convinced by this argument. On the scope of corporate information accessible to shareholders, it held that the fact that the Company permitted shareholders to inspect the financial reports and account books should not be

---

[40] Liu Lanfang (2009), p. 115.

[41] The facts and decision of the case are summarized and commented upon in Huai Xiaofeng (2007), pp. 126–30.

interpreted as barring the shareholders from inspecting other documents. The court maintained that, as a matter of fact, to understand the account books, it was necessary for the shareholders to examine also the source accounting documents such as the original receipts and invoices.[42]

From the company's perspective, there is a need to strike a balance between shareholders' informational rights and the company's interest in keeping certain information confidential. The above pro-shareholder approach of the courts then gives rise to a concern that the company's business secrets might be prejudiced. The broader context was the rampant eruption of accounting scandals in Chinese firms in recent years, which led to the widespread conviction that even the account books were not necessarily trustworthy,[43] and shareholders seeking information should verify the accounting books with the source accounting documents such as the original receipts and invoices. In this light, the 'expanded interpretation' adopted by courts in the above-mentioned cases was meant to provide a type of equitable remedy for oppressed shareholders to maximize their access to the corporate information which was not under their control. However, without an SPC judicial interpretation or other national laws to help define the scope of documents permissible for inspection, the legal uncertainty seems to be obvious. From a practical perspective, lawyers should advise their corporate clients to define improper purposes to exclude business secrets from the reach of inspection, set preconditions for making an inspection demand, and limit the number of inspections per year.

5.4 SHAREHOLDERS' VOTING RIGHTS

Voting is one of the shareholders' fundamental rights. Shareholders' power in a company is most importantly and ultimately embodied in their rights to choose or remove their representatives in the power center of the structure of centralized management (which comprises the board of directors and the supervisory board in Chinese companies) and to examine and approve proposals that might have a fundamental impact on their investment. Specifically, they should have the rights to (1) attend the shareholders' meeting in person or by proxy; (2) elect and remove members of the board of directors and the supervisory board; (3) vote on the soundness of fundamental corporate decisions, including corporate

42 Id, p. 127.
43 Armstrong (2011). See also Cheng Weibing (2006).

budgeting, charter amendments, change in the registered capital, major transactions, and profit distribution; (4) vote to approve or disapprove fundamental corporate changes, such as mergers, divisions, dissolution and changes to the form of the company; (5) propose resolutions and ask questions; (6) be informed of the procedural and operational rules concerning the shareholders' meeting, including voting procedures and methods. These rights will be examined in detail in the next chapter.

5.5 SHAREHOLDERS' RIGHTS TO TRANSFER EQUITY INTERESTS

5.5.1 Right of Transfer in General

The freedom to convey or transfer his equity interest in a company is a fundamental right of the shareholder. In the absence of valid restrictions on transferability, corporate equity interest is freely transferable. The restrictions may be imposed by the law, corporate charters, agreements among shareholders, or stock exchange rules. This section discusses the transferability of equity interest in LLCs. The transfer of shares of JSLCs, which is much less bound by restrictions, but still subject to a complicated body of corporate and securities laws, will be dealt with later in a separate chapter in this book.

5.5.2 Restrictions on the Transferability of Equity Interests in LLCs

The shareholders of an LLC may freely transfer all or part of their equity interests among themselves.[44] However, because of the close personal and working relations among the shareholders in an LLC, even the transfer of equity of a single shareholder to an outsider might have profound implications for the control of the company. For this reason, the Company Law not only imposes certain legal restrictions on equity transfer in LLCs but also permits the companies to set restrictions on the transfer through the corporate charters or agreements among shareholders.

The first legal restriction is related to other shareholders' approval of the transaction. Article 72 of the Company Law requires the deal to be approved by more than half of the other shareholders (note it is

44 Company Law, Article 72, para. 1.

'one-shareholder-one-vote' in such a case), when a shareholder transfers his equity in the firm to an outsider. The selling shareholder should notify in writing other shareholders of the proposed transfer, who then have 30 days to decide whether to approve it. The law treats the other shareholders' failure to reply within 30 days as consent to the proposed transfer. Further, if the proposed deal was killed because the majority of the other shareholders did not agree to it, the dissenting shareholders then have the legal obligation to purchase the equity interest in question. A refusal to make such purchase will also be deemed as consenting to the deal.[45]

The transfer of equity to outsiders is constrained by the other shareholders' preemption rights, which provide existing shareholders with a right of first refusal to purchase such equity interest 'under the same conditions'.[46] This often means buying the equity at a set price or at the price it is offered to a third party. If two or more shareholders are interested in the said equity but fail to reach an agreement through consultation, they shall exercise their preemption right in proportion to their respective ratio of capital contribution at the time of the transfer.[47]

The right also applies to court-ordered equity transfers in judicial enforcement procedures. The court should notify the company and all the shareholders of the enforcement. If the other shareholders do not offer to buy the equity within 20 days, they shall be deemed to have forfeited their preemption right.[48]

5.5.3 Effect of the Transfer

The transfer of equity interests of an LLC involves a two-step process. In the first step the seller and the buyer reach an agreement in which the terms of the sale are specified. In the second step the parties have to cooperate to carry out the delivery to make sure the buyer becomes a shareholder of the company. The company's cooperation is essentially important. In fact, the company is under the legal obligations to (1) cancel the capital contribution certificate of the seller; (2) issue a new capital contribution certificate to the buyer; and (3) revise details of shareholders and their capital contribution in the the corporate charter and registry of shareholders.[49] It is important to note that the charter

---

45 Company Law, Article 72, para. 2.
46 Company Law, Article 72, para. 3.
47 Company Law, Article 72, para. 3.
48 Company Law, Article 73.
49 Company Law, Article 74.

amendments can be done by the company directly based on the equity transfer agreement, without the usual need to have a shareholders' meeting convened and a resolution passed by a two-thirds majority of the voting rights.[50]

A dishonest seller might sell the same equity to different buyers by taking advantage of the time lag between the conclusion of the equity transfer agreement and the registration of the first buyer's information with the AIC. If the seller does this or disposes of the equity that is already transferred to the first buyer in any other way and the first buyer requests the court to invalidate the seller's transactions with others, the court is mandated by the SPC's Company Law Interpretation III to apply Article 106 of the PRC Property Law.[51] Article 106 gives the legal owner the general right to claim back the property, but this is subject to the lawful right of the bona fide third-party buyer. That is to say, a bona fide third-party buyer shall acquire the legal ownership of the disputed property if (1) he was in good faith at the time of receiving the assigned property; (2) the property was assigned at a fair value; or (3) the registration of the assigned property has been completed as required by the law or has been delivered to the assignee if no registration is legally required.[52] Obviously, this SPC Interpretation aims to protect the reliance interest of third parties who have acquired the disputed equity ownership in good faith. If the ownership of such a third party has been duly registered, he will be treated as a shareholder, overriding even the claim of the first buyer. A party – such as the first buyer – who has suffered losses because the company did not complete the registration in time is entitled to sue not only the seller but also the company's directors, senior management personnel or the actual controllers if they are at fault for this.[53]

---

50 Id. According to Article 104 of the Company Law, an amendment to the corporate charter has to be adopted by two-thirds of the voting rights held by the shareholders. If this requirement is applied equally to equity transfer in an LLC, it would be contradicting Article 72 which permits the transfer to be approved by more than half of the other shareholders.

51 Company Law Interpretation III, Article 28.

52 Company Law Interpretation III, Article 28, para. 1.

53 Company Law Interpretation III, Article 28, para. 2.

5.6 SHAREHOLDERS' APPRAISAL RIGHTS

The appraisal remedy provided in the Company Law offers an exit strategy for shareholders who are not satisfied with certain corporate decisions, allowing them to sell back their equity interests to the company at a fair value. A shareholder of an LLC who has voted against a resolution passed by the shareholders' meeting may request the company to buy back his equity interest 'at a reasonable price' under any of the following circumstances:[54]

1. the company has not distributed profits to shareholders for 5 consecutive years, although it has been profitable during the same period and satisfies the conditions for making profit distribution provided in the Company Law;
2. a merger, division, or sale of major assets occurs; or
3. the company's term of operation stipulated in the company's charter has expired or other trigging events for the company's dissolution have emerged, but the shareholders' meeting has passed a charter amendment to renew the company's existence.

The appraisal rights eventually have to be considered and evaluated by the court. The company has 60 days from the date of the adoption of the charter amendment to reach an equity repurchase agreement with the dissenting shareholder. Absent such an agreement, the shareholder can bring a legal action in the court to enforce his appraisal rights.[55]

The statutory appraisal remedy is less comprehensive for JLSC shareholders and covers only their objections to issues relating to corporate mergers and divisions.[56] The rationale is easy to understand: these shareholders have the more liquid capital markets to trade their shares. In contrast, LLC shareholders can only transfer their equity interest through individually negotiated transactions.

In practice, minority shareholders have often been discouraged from making use of it by the cumbersome procedures and heavy burden of proof. Courts have asked the dissenting shareholders to identify the scope of assets and prove the fair value of their equity interests. In *Hua Yefang and Chen Guoqiang v Zhongxing Jialian Ltd*,[57] two Beijing courts

---

[54] Company Law, Article 75, para. 1.

[55] Company Law, Article 75, para. 2.

[56] Company Law, Article 143, para. 1(4).

[57] The case was summarized and discussed in Liu Lanfang (2009), pp. 166–74.

dismissed the dissenting shareholders' claim for appraisal on the ground that the dissenters were not able to define the scope of the company's total assets, despite the fact that there was no way for the plaintiffs, being the oppressed minority shareholders, to have access to the company's account books and other financial documents to figure out the actual total assets of the company.

5.7 SHAREHOLDERS' OTHER RIGHTS

In addition to the above rights, shareholders' other important rights include the right to dividends and the right to bring legal actions against the company and its directors, supervisors or senior officers, and other shareholders. These rights will be examined in separate chapters in later parts of this book.

6. The general corporate governance and management structure

6.1 CHINESE CHARACTERISTICS OF CORPORATE GOVERNANCE

Corporate governance has become a highly fashionable topic in China since the outset of the twenty-first century, when a listed company, popularly known as YinGuangXia, was disclosed by the media to have committed a RMB745 million fraud through massive fabrication of sales receipts and false disclosures perpetrated by a few 'core' insiders. This case caused losses to thousands of minority shareholders and is considered one of the biggest corporate scandals in recent decades of PRC history.[1] It revealed some fundamental weaknesses in the management, regulation, and supervision of the country's enterprises. As a Standard & Poor's report noted, '[c]orporate governance since then has been placed at the very top of the government's agenda', and 'the mandate to improve corporate governance is a top priority amongst all sectors, including government bodies, regulators, intermediaries, corporations, and investors'.[2] In the following years, various government agencies issued numerous laws and normative documents to standardize the corporate governance practice of Chinese enterprises.

As a general note, several 'Chinese characteristics' of corporate governance will be pointed out. First, China has set up a hybrid system of corporate governance institutions, borrowed from both the Anglo-American model and Germanic-Japanese model. In terms of internal governance, the typical organizational structure of a company comprises three tiers of control, namely the shareholder's meeting, the board of directors, and the supervisory board. In addition, a JSLC is legally required to have a management team. Partially as a solution to the agency problem stemming from the separation of ownership and control in modern corporations, Anglo-American jurisdictions install independent

1 Standard & Poor's (2003), p. 1.
2 Standard & Poor's (2003), p. 1.

directors on the board, Germanic-Japanese jurisdictions set a supervisory board to monitor the management board, but listed companies in China must have both. As observed in Tan and Wang (2007)[3],

> The coexistence of the supervisory board and the independent directors demonstrates a strong feature in the mentality of China's corporate reform, namely, an approach of 'crossing the river by feeling the stones', because, although the reformers were eager to learn from foreign experience, they were unsure as to which model was suitable to China. As such, legal institutions from both the 'insider' model and the 'outsider' model were transplanted into Chinese soil without a proper evaluation of their suitability.

A second feature is the political impact of dominant state ownership on the governance of companies. Most of those companies were converted from traditional SOEs and are said to have been suffering from political control by the government or even the Chinese Communist Party. One commentator thus concludes that 'the corporate governance system adopted by the Chinese listed firms can be best described as a control-based model, in which the controlling shareholders – in most cases, the State – tightly control the listed companies through concentrated ownership and management friendly boards'.[4] Indeed, the 'grabbing hand theory' suggests that the government uses SOEs 'to serve political and social objectives, which has a negative impact on the firm's economic performance'.[5] One could argue, of course, that this theory is overly simplistic, as the state might have a larger stake in converting the SOEs into normal, commercial entities. Another strand of literature, the 'helping hand theory', maintains, however, that the government may 'generate a positive effect on firm performance because [it helps] secure scarce resources in the quasi-market economy and mitigate agency problems in firms with poor corporate governance'.[6]

Thirdly, culture also plays important roles in the corporate governance of Chinese companies. Hamilton (2006) points out that it is fundamentally wrong to characterize Chinese private firms by holding them up against similar firms of Western capitalism without considering the cultural aspects. Embedded in its own hierarchical and harmonious cultural tradition, 'the Chinese family firms is [*sic*] in fact … a "political

---

[3] p. 147.
[4] Liu Qiao (2006), p. 429.
[5] Chang and Wong (2004), p. 618.
[6] Chang and Wong (2004), p. 618.

infrastructure" in which "power differentials" … lie behind the disparities in economic roles and rewards in the family business'.[7]

In short, the governance practice of Chinese enterprises is an evolving process, the direction of which has been shaped by many factors. This chapter, as the beginning of the part of this book on corporate governance in China, outlines the general allocation of corporate powers among various governance and management institutions in a company – including the shareholders' meeting, the board of directors, the supervisory board, and the management.

6.2 SHAREHOLDERS' GENERAL MEETING

Shareholders, as the electorate of the 'corporate republic',[8] play an important role in corporate governance. Although shareholders do not participate in the day-to-day management of the company and cannot act on behalf of the company, they are entitled to elect directors and supervisors, vote on major corporate transactions and decisions, and amend the corporate charter and other bylaws. The exercise of all these powers depends almost entirely on the proper functioning of the shareholders' meetings.

6.2.1 Convening the General Meetings

Voting at shareholders' meetings is the only direct way for shareholders to exercise the right of 'participation in major decision-making and selection of management personnel' provided in Article 4 of the Company Law. A shareholder has a right to attend and vote at a shareholders' general meeting, which can be either a regular (annual) general meeting or an extraordinary general meeting.[9] It is up to the corporate charter of an LLC to stipulate the frequency of general meetings, but a JSLC must have an annual general meeting.[10]

In an LLC, the general meetings should be convened regularly in accordance with its charter. An extraordinary general meeting of the LLC may be called by shareholders holding one-tenth or more of the voting rights, by one-third of the directors, or by the supervisory board or the

[7] Hamilton (2006), p. 224.

[8] English Jurist William Blackstone once described the company as the 'little republic'.

[9] Company Law, Article 40.

[10] Company Law, Article 101.

supervisor in the case where the company does not have a supervisory board.[11] A JSLC must hold an annual general meeting. The extraordinary general meeting of a JSLC can be convened within two months of any of the following events: (1) the number of directors falls below two-thirds of the quorum prescribed in the Company Law or the corporate charter; (2) uncovered losses reach one-third of the paid-up capital of the company; (3) the meeting is requested by shareholders who aggregately hold 10 percent or more of the company's shares; (4) a meeting is deemed necessary by the board of directors; (5) a meeting is proposed by the supervisory board; and (6) other events provided in the corporate charter.[12]

In both LLCs and JSLCs, the general meetings should first of all be convened by the board of directors and chaired by the chairperson of the board.[13] If the chairperson is unable or fails to perform his duties, the vice chairperson should chair the meeting. In the case where the vice chairperson also is unable or fails to perform duties, a director appointed by more than half of the board of directors shall chair the meeting.[14] In LLCs without a board, the executive director performs the relevant duties.[15] Further, if the board or executive director is not able to or fails to convene a meeting, the supervisory board (or the supervisor in LLCs that have not established a supervisory board) should take over the responsibility. If the supervisory board or supervisor does not act, the Company Law then empowers shareholders holding 10 percent or more of the voting rights to 'do-it-yourself' – convening and chairing the meeting directly.[16] However, there is a contemporaneous ownership requirement imposed on those JSLC shareholders, who must have held their shares for 90 or more consecutive days.[17]

The above mechanisms are established in the Company Law with a view to ensuring that the general meetings are not delayed or spoiled by the insiders of the company. In contrast, the 1993 Company Law had a 25 percent shareholding threshold for LLC shareholders to call a special meeting, and such a right was not even enjoyed at all by JSLC

---

[11] Company Law, Article 40.

[12] Company Law, Article 101.

[13] One exception is that the first meeting after the establishment of an LLC should be convened by the shareholder who has made the largest amount of capital contribution. See Company Law, Article 39.

[14] Company Law, Art 41, para. 1; Article 102, para. 1.

[15] Company Law, Article 41, para. 2.

[16] Company Law, Article 41, para. 3.

[17] Company Law, Article 102, para. 2.

shareholders. Further, neither did shareholders have any power to convene a meeting themselves under the 1993 Law.[18]

6.2.2 Powers of the General Meeting

In the law on the books at least, the Company Law practices 'shareholders centralism' in allocating corporate decisional powers.[19] Articles 37 and 99 define the shareholders' meeting as the company's *quanli jigou*, or organ of power. Serving as the 'parliament' or general assembly of the corporate republic, the shareholders' meeting has the following powers:[20]

1. to decide on the company's business strategy and investment plans;
2. to elect and remove directors and supervisors who are not representatives of the employees;
3. to decide on the remuneration of directors and supervisors;
4. to review and approve the reports of the board of directors;
5. to review and approve the reports of the supervisory board or the supervisor;
6. to review and approve the annual financial budget and financial accounting plans of the company;
7. to review and approve the profit distribution plans or loss recovery plans of the company;
8. to pass resolutions on increase or reduction of the registered capital of the company;
9. to pass resolutions on the issuance of corporate bonds;
10. to pass resolutions on company merger, division, dissolution, liquidation, or change of the corporate form;
11. to amend the corporate charter; and
12. to exercise any other powers given to the shareholders' meeting by the corporate charter.

In addition, several special powers are given to the shareholders' meeting of a listed company. When the company, within one year, purchases or sells major assets, or provides guarantees to outsiders, if the transactional value exceeds 30 percent or more of the company's total assets, the Company Law requires the transaction to be approved by a two-thirds absolute majority of the voting rights of the shareholders presented in the

[18] 1993 Company Law, Article 43, 104, and 105.
[19] Liu Junhai (2011), pp. 468–9.
[20] Company Law, Articles 38 and 100.

meeting.[21] Further, in line with Article 38(12) of the Company Law, the CSRC Model Corporate Charter confers upon the general meeting the powers to (1) pass resolutions on hiring or dismissal of the accounting firms for the company; (2) to review and approve the plans to change the usage of the funds raised; (3) to review (but not approve) the company's stock incentive plans.[22] The annotation following this Model Charter provision indicates that all these are exclusive powers of the general meeting and may not be delegated to the board of directors or any organs or individuals.[23]

The wide range of powers given to the general meeting of shareholders is remarkable in a comparative light. Calling the general meeting the 'highest body' of the company is not uncommon in civil law jurisdictions,[24] but very few modern legal systems would actually treat it as the 'supreme' decision-making organ of the company. In Germany, it was permissible for the general meeting to give instructions on matters relating to the conduct of business until 1937, but it 'has … since 1937 lacked the general power to decide on competences within the company, so that the prevailing opinion no longer regards the general meeting as the "highest body"'.[25] In the U.S., the separation of power is significantly more tilted toward the management. In contrast, the powers possessed by the general meeting of Chinese companies are more real and meaningful. As observed by Mathias M. Siems, '[b]y contrast with this internationally predominant legal position [of downgrading the status of the general meeting in the corporate structure], in China the general meeting shares responsibility for the conduct of business'.[26] The separation of power between the general meeting and the management will be further examined in the part on the powers and duties of the board of directors.

6.2.3 Voting in the General Meeting

Decision-making in the general meeting is generally dominated by capital, not by heads. In an LLC, the default rule is that the amount of voting rights exercisable by a shareholder at a meeting is based on his

---

21 Company Law, Article 122.

22 CSRC Model Corporate Charter, Article 40(11), (14), and (15).

23 CSRC Model Corporate Charter, annotation to Article 40.

24 Siems (2008), p. 151 (noting that 'in France, Japan and China the "highest body" terminology is quite common').

25 Siems (2008), p. 151.

26 Siems (2008), p. 154.

percentage of the capital contribution.[27] The Company Law, however, permits LLC shareholders to make a different voting rule in the corporate charter.[28] Shareholders' meetings in a JSLC follow the principle of 'one share, one vote'.[29] Treasury shares – namely those held by the company – are not entitled to vote.[30] In addition, as JSLCs only issue common shares at this stage, realistically only common shares carry voting rights.[31]

As a general rule, resolutions of a general meeting in a JSLC shall be passed by a simple majority of votes cast by shareholders present at the meeting. A mandatory two-thirds majority of votes is required for amending the corporate charter, increase or reduction in the registered capital, corporate mergers, division, dissolution, or change of corporate form.[32] Further, under Article 122 of the Company Law, major transactions, in which a listed company purchases or sells major assets or provides security to others in excess of 30 percent of the total assets within one year, must also be approved by two-thirds or more of the voting rights. There is, however, no such requirement for LLCs, who are permitted to freely specify the methods of deliberation and voting procedures of the meeting in their corporate charters, as long as an absolute majority – that is, two-thirds – voting requirement is imposed for approval of charter amendments, increase or reduction of the registered capital, and merger, division, dissolution, or change of corporate form.[33]

Shareholders are allowed to vote in person or in absentia to a limited extent. A shareholder may attend the meeting in person, and may also send an authorized representative to vote on his behalf, as long as a proper power of attorney stating the scope of authorization is submitted to the company.[34] However, no shareholder is allowed to mail their proxy votes to the company. While this may make it logistically difficult for some shareholders to cast their votes, the difficulty can be alleviated by the increasingly popular online voting system, which was formally introduced by the CSRC in 2004 to enable shareholders to participate in

---

27 Company Law, Article 43.
28 Company Law, Article 43.
29 Company Law, Article 104.
30 Company Law, Article 104.
31 Note that the Company Law does not prohibit the establishment of other classes of shares in a JSLC.
32 Company Law, Article 104.
33 Company Law, Article 44.
34 Company Law, Article 107.

meetings by means of remote communication. Both the Shenzhen Stock Exchange (SZSE) and Shanghai Stock Exchange (SSE) have established networks with thousands of securities companies for shareholders to vote.[35]

6.2.4 Procedural Rules: Time, Place, Notice, and Quorum of the Meeting

The Company Law does not mandate the time of the shareholders' general meetings nor impose geographical restrictions on the location at which a meeting may be held. There are, however, stringent rules on the procedures of convening the meetings. For JSLCs, a notice concerning the time, place, and agenda of the meeting shall be given to each shareholder 20 days before the annual general meeting. In case of a special meeting, the notice should be given 15 days in advance.[36] In any case, the general meeting shall not pass resolutions on any matter not notified in advance to the shareholders. A default 15-day requirement is also imposed for shareholders' meetings in LLCs, but the law permits the corporate charter or a shareholders' agreement to make a different rule in this regard.[37]

Interestingly, there is no specific quorum requirement in the Company Law for any type of shareholders' meeting. Thus, in theory, absent a provision to the contrary, any number of shareholders could constitute a quorum. While a high quorum requirement might have certain characteristics that allegedly protect the minority shareholders, the Chinese approach of non-provision of an explicit rule offers flexibility to firms that may instead make quorum rules in their corporate charters.[38]

The technical rules concerning the meeting procedures might be of crucial importance if a dispute arises over whether a particular decision should be taken or the legality of the decision. For example, a defective notice could lead to the invalidation of the meeting by the court. Under

---

35 Details on online voting can be found at http://www.sse.com.cn and http://www.szse.cn.

36 Company Law, Article 103.

37 Company Law, Article 42.

38 Note that Article 22 of the Special Regulations Governing Joint Stock Limited Company Offering and Listing Shares Overseas promulgated by the State Council in 1994 mandates a quorum of 50 percent of the total voting rights for a valid shareholders' general meeting to be held. This set of administrative regulations apply, however, only to Chinese companies which are to offer and list shares in a foreign stock market.

Article 22 of the Company Law, a resolution passed by the shareholders' meeting is void if it violates national laws or administrative regulations. If the convening procedures and voting methods of a meeting violate national laws, administrative regulations or the corporate charter, a legal remedy is available for the shareholders who may request a court to revoke the resolution.[39]

Particularly, non-compliance with or abuse of the procedural rules could create a ground for the courts to void a shareholders' resolution. In *Junhao Ltd v Zhongshe Ltd*,[40] the plaintiff was a shareholder of the defendant, an LLC incorporated in 2003. The plaintiff requested the court to revoke a resolution adopted by a special shareholders' meeting held on 17 April 2006. Although the company's charter provided that a notice for a general meeting should be given to shareholders 10 days in advance, the notice sent out by the defendant's legal representative gave shareholders only five days to prepare for the meeting. The plaintiff and another shareholder (a third party in the case) showed up at the meeting venue, but were refused entry to the meeting because they did not sign the attendance list arranged by the company management. Even without the plaintiff's presence, the meeting was effectively attended by half of the shareholders. On the impact of the late notice, the appellate court held that, although the corporate charter provided for 10 days for general meetings, it had no mention of a time period required for special meetings. Given that special meetings were normally for urgent matters, it was acceptable to have a shorter period of time for sending the notice. Further, given that the plaintiff and the other shareholders appeared at the meeting venue in time, whether the notice was late became irrelevant. The court, however, invalidated the resolution on another ground: signing up for attendance was not a mandatory procedure provided in either the Company Law or the company's charter. Since the two shareholders showed up, they should be permitted to attend the meeting. Had they been able to join the discussion, they would have had the chance to shape the resolution in their own favor.[41]

6.2.5 Voting Methods: Straight Voting vs. Cumulative Voting

Two voting methods are provided in the Company Law for JSLC shareholders. Straight voting, which is the default voting method, is

---

[39] Company Law, Article 22, paras. 1 and 2.

[40] The case was summarized and discussed in Liu Lanfang (2009), pp. 285–95.

[41] Id, pp. 290–91.

based on a traditional and rigid understanding of the one-share-one-vote principle, which unreservedly favors the majority shareholders. For minority shareholders, this is not the end of the world, as the law offers an alternative voting mechanism, the cumulative voting method, which redresses the imbalance to a certain extent. Article 106 of the Company Law defines cumulative voting as a system in which the number of voting rights attached to each share is the same as the number of directors or supervisors to be elected and the voting rights of a shareholder can be pooled and used together. Plainly speaking, it is 'the privilege of multiplying the number of shares held by the number of directors [and supervisors in the Chinese context] to be elected and casting for a single candidate or distributing the product among two or more candidates'.[42] In doing so, the minority shareholders have a better chance to secure representation on the board of directors and the supervisory board. 'Without cumulative voting, holders of a bare majority of the shares may elect the full board and thus control the corporation without any representative of other interests being present at board meetings.'[43]

A controversial question is whether cumulative voting is mandatory or should be made mandatory for companies in China. Stating that 'the cumulative voting system may be adopted in accordance with the corporate charter or shareholders' resolution when the shareholders' meeting elect directors and supervisors', Article 106 does not seem to be imposing a mandatory method but rather suggesting an opt-in approach, namely a company may choose to adopt cumulative voting through the corporate charter or a shareholders' resolution. The Code of Corporate Governance for Listed Companies in China requires, in light of this spirit, that 'the election of directors should fully reflect the opinions of minority shareholders', and that 'cumulative voting should be adopted in listed companies that are more than 30 percent owned by controlling shareholders'.[44] Fortunately, for listed companies in China, the code has not been regarded as an enforceable law, and as such only '[c]ertain Chinese listed companies have already included the cumulative voting system in their articles of association'.[45]

---

42 Cox and Hazen (2003), p. 348.

43 Id, p. 349.

44 Code of Corporate Governance for Listed Companies, issued by the CSRC and then State Economic and Trade Commission, 7 January 2001, Article 31.

45 CSRC (2011), p. 43.

6.3 BOARD OF DIRECTORS

As noted at the outset of this chapter, China's hybrid regime of corporate governance features a two-tier board system, comprising a board of directors with decision-making functions and a supervisory board that monitors the directors and managers. The functions and powers of the two boards are examined in this and the following sections.

6.3.1 Board Composition and the Term of the Directors

All companies, even including wholly state-owned companies, are required by Company Law to have a board of directors,[46] unless it is an LLC of few shareholders or small size, which could appoint an executive director (*zhixing dongshi*) instead of a full board.[47]

The Company Law stipulates the range of the number of directors as from three to 13 for LLCs and five to 19 for JSLCs.[48] Under normal circumstances, these directors shall be elected by the general meeting of the shareholders. However, if the LLC is established by two or more state-owned enterprises (SOEs) or state investment entities, there should be employee representatives on the board. Employee representatives on the board are encouraged but not required for other types of LLCs and JSLCs.[49] Any board must have a chairperson director and may have one or more vice chairpersons.[50]

The term of appointment of the directors is a matter for the corporate charter to decide, provided that each term does not exceed three years. However, as there is no limit on the re-election of directors, in theory one could serve as a director indefinitely.[51] Further, a director whose term of office has expired could continue his directorship until a new director is appointed under the following circumstances: (1) no election was held in time upon expiration of the term of office of the director, or (2) a director resigned during his term of office, resulting in the number of directors falling below the statutory quorum.[52]

---

46 Company Law, Article 45, para. 1; Article 109, para. 1.
47 Company Law, Article 51.
48 Company Law, Articles 45 and 109, respectively.
49 Company Law, Article 45, para. 2; Article 109, para. 2.
50 Company Law, Article 45, para. 3; Article 110, para. 1.
51 Company Law, Article 46, para. 1; Article 109, para. 2.
52 Company Law, Article 46, para. 2; Article 109, para. 2.

6.3.2 Qualifications of Directors

The Company Law does not define 'director'. Implicitly, a person becomes a director according to the formal procedures of appointment, and there is no explicit legal basis for de facto directors. Thus under Company Law, a person is either a director or not a director. This clear position apparently denies the existence of 'shadow directors' who control the company's business to a significant extent by virtue of their position vis-à-vis the company, without letting their names appear in any corporate records or legal documents.

The law also does not specify the positive qualifications of directors, i.e. those persons who are suitable for a directorship. A director must be a natural person who has attained age 18 (16 under certain circumstances as provided in the GPCL). As inferred from Article 147 of the Company Law and provided in Article 95 of the Model Charter, corporate directorship is not allowed. Apart from that, one's nationality, gender, or age would not constitute a general barrier to one's directorship.

Apparently, the law does not require the director to be also a shareholder, leaving it a matter for the corporate charter to decide.[53] Requiring directors to own equity interest in the company is, however, a popular practice and many JSLCs now compensate their directors in stock rather than cash.

There is, however, a long list of negative qualifications denying eligibility of directors enumerated in the Company Law, the Model Charter, and the Listed Company Directors Selection and Conduction Guidance adopted by the Shanghai Stock Exchange (hereinafter the SSE Directors Guidance).[54] A person shall not act as a director of a company in any of the following circumstances:[55]

1. He is a person with no or limited capacity for civil acts according to China's civil law;
2. He was convicted for corruption, bribery, encroachment of property, misappropriation of property, or disruption of the order of the socialist market economy, and not more than five years has elapsed since expiry of the execution period;

---

[53] Articles 25 and 82 authorize the shareholders' general meeting to insert any items it may consider necessary into the corporate charter.

[54] The SSE Directors Guidance, known as Shanghai Zhengquan Jiaoyisuo Shangshi Gongsi Dongshi Xuanren yu Xingwei Zhiyin, was promulgated by the Shanghai Stock Exchange on 25 August 2009.

[55] Company Law, Article 147.

3. He was deprived of his political rights for being convicted of a crime and not more than five years has elapsed since expiry of the execution period;
4. He, as a director, factory manager, or manager of a company or enterprise which was liquated upon bankruptcy, was personally responsible for the bankruptcy, and not more than three years has elapsed since the date of completion of the bankruptcy liquidation;
5. He, as the legal representative of an enterprise, was personally responsible for the revocation of the enterprise's business license by the authority or for the close-down of the enterprise by order of the authority, and not more than three years has elapsed since the enterprise was closed down or its business license revoked;
6. He has a relatively large amount of personal debts due and unsettled.

Additionally for listed companies, a person cannot act as a director if he has been banned by the CSRC from entering the securities market, or he has been subject to administrative penalties of the CSRC or disciplinary measures of a stock exchange in the past three years, or is in a period that is regarded by the stock exchange to be unsuitable for him to be a company director.[56] If any of the above situations occurs, the election or appointment of the person as director shall be voided, and the director should be removed from office.[57]

6.3.3 Appointment and Removal of Directors

Normally directors are elected in the shareholders' general meeting. There is not much guidance in the Company Law as to how the directors should be elected, indicating that the legislators wisely wished to leave this as a matter for the corporate charter to decide. The Code of Corporate Governance for Listed Companies ('Code of Corporate Governance') requires the charter to ensure a formal and transparent board nomination and election process.[58] In particular,[59]

1. The listed company should disclose detailed information of the candidates for directorship prior to the general meeting to ensure shareholders have adequate knowledge of the candidates.

---

[56] Model Charter, Article 95; SSE Director Guidance, Article 8.
[57] Company Law, Article 147, paras. 2 and 3.
[58] Code of Corporate Governance, Article 28.
[59] Code of Corporate Governance, Articles 29, 30, 31, and 32.

2. The candidates should provide a written undertaking to accept the nomination and warrant the truthfulness and completeness of the disclosed information about the candidate, as well as to promise to perform their duties in earnest once elected.
3. The election process should thoroughly reflect the opinions of minority shareholders. Listed companies are encouraged to adopt the cumulative voting system, and they are obligated to adopt cumulative voting if over 30 percent of the shares are owned by controlling shareholders.
4. Once directors are elected the company should sign appointment agreements with them to prescribe the respective rights and duties of both the company and the directors.

Regarding the removal of directors, one of the concerns has been about whether a director can be removed without cause. On this point the Company Law is not clear. The 1993 Company Law contained a provision stating that 'the shareholders' meeting may not remove a director before the expiration of his period of office without cause'.[60] This provision was deleted by the current 2005 Company Law. The deletion could arguably be understood as the lawmakers no longer wanted to prohibit the general meeting from removing a director without cause, or that the lawmakers would rather leave this matter for the corporate charter to decide. It seems the latter understanding has prevailed at least insofar as listed companies are concerned, as nothing has changed for them so far. Indeed, Article 95 of the Model Charter still provides that the general meeting may not remove a director before his term of office expires. Of course, pursuant to Article 147 of the Company Law and the relevant CSRC and stock exchange rules, if a director falls under a circumstance enumerated in the above-mentioned negative qualifications of directors, his directorship must be terminated by the company, which is considered as a removal 'with cause'.

The election of employee directors takes place in a separate process. Candidates for such directorships shall be 'democratically elected by company employees via the employees' representative congress, employees' congress or other means'.[61] There is, however, no serious implementation of these provisions in practice. As a survey of the China Academy of Social Sciences has pointed out, very few listed companies in China

[60] 1993 Company Law, Article 47, para. 2.
[61] Company Law, Article 45, para. 2; Article 109, para. 2.

have employee representatives on their board, and there were no such directors in any of the top 100 listed companies in China as of 2008.[62]

6.3.4 Convening a Board Meeting

It is primarily the duty of the chairperson of the board to convene and preside over a board meeting. If the chairperson is unable or fails to perform his duties, the vice chairperson shall take over the duty to convene and chair the meeting. If the vice chairperson is also unable or fails to perform his duties, a director designated jointly by more than half of the directors shall then convene and chair the meeting.[63] These emergency plans are provided in the 2005 Company Law in response to the deadlocks created by the 1993 Company Law, which rested the power to convene a board meeting exclusively in the hands of the chairperson. Only when the chairperson could not perform his duties because of some unexplained 'special reasons' was he to authorize the vice chairperson or another director to call and chair the meeting. One-third or more of the directors could propose a meeting of the board but did not have the power to actually convene one.[64] One can reasonably deduce from these provisions what the chairperson would do if he is faced with the resentment of the majority of the directors and a meeting is expected to result in board resolutions not in his favor. But under the 2005 Company Law, the chairperson is not able to unduly delay a meeting.

Certain players in a JSLC have additional powers to call a board meeting. The Company Law mandates two regular board meetings for a JSLC, but shareholders holding one-tenth or more of the voting shares, one-third or more of the directors or the supervisory board may propose a special board meeting. The chairperson of the board is then obligated to respond within 10 days of receipt of the proposal to convene and chair such a meeting.[65]

---

[62] 'Shekeyuan Zuixin Baogao Cheng: Zhongguo Baiqiang Shangshi Gongsi Jihu Meiyou Zhigong Dongshi' ('A survey of the China Academy of Social Sciences claims that there are almost no employee directors on the board in China's top 100 listed companies'), available at http://www.civillaw.com.cn (accessed 30 March 2012).

[63] Company Law, Articles 48 and 110.

[64] 1993 Company Law, Articles 48 and 114.

[65] Company Law, Article 111, para. 2.

6.3.5 Attending and Voting at Board Meetings

It is an implicit requirement that the board of directors exercises its powers collectively by meeting. A director must join this collective decision-making process to perform his duties. In the Chinese context, he has no power of his own to act on the company's behalf. A JSLC director could attend the meeting in person or authorize someone to represent him at the meeting, but his representative must be another director.[66] In this digital age, a board meeting could be held in the form of a teleconference or videoconference, so that the directors do not have to travel to the same location for the meeting. A resolution could also be adopted by way of a circular instead of convening a meeting, which requires the directors to sign and return the circular within a given period of time.[67]

Procedurally, the director is entitled to receive a notice of the two statutorily required regular meetings 10 days prior to the meeting.[68] The law is silent about the notice period for special board meetings, which is normally a matter for the corporate charter to decide.[69]

If the director properly participates in the meeting, his vote is equally as important as that of any other director since board meetings follow the 'one-person-one-vote' rule.[70] Notably, a mandatory quorum requirement, which is a majority of the directors, exists for board meetings in JSLCs, whereby a valid meeting must have more than half of directors present. Further, a board resolution has to be passed by more than half of all directors, no matter whether they have attended the meeting or not. That is, if a board has 19 directors, 10 directors must be present for a valid meeting to be held, and all 10 of them must unanimously vote for a resolution for its adoption by the board.

The right to vote comes with an important restriction for directors in listed companies. In brief, a director is prohibited from voting on a resolution if he is affiliated with – or a related party to – an enterprise involved in the resolution matter. He may also not be represented by another director on this matter. 'Affiliation' or 'related-party relationship'

---

66 Company Law, Article 113, para. 1.

67 Liu Junhai (2011), p. 488.

68 Company Law, Article 111.

69 Model Charter, Article 116. In an interesting contrast, in the U.S., unless otherwise required by the Articles of Incorporation, no notice is needed for regularly scheduled board meetings, but a two-day advance notice should be given for special meetings. See Model Business Corporation Act (MBCA), §8.22(a) and §8.22(b).

70 Company Law, Article 112, para. 2.

is defined as 'the relationship between the controlling shareholder, de facto controlling person, director, supervisor or senior management executive of a company and an enterprise under their director or indirect control, or any other relationship that may lead to the transfer of any interest of the company'.[71] In such a case, a valid board meeting may be held if attended by more than half of the directors without such affiliation, and a resolution can only be passed by more than half of the unaffiliated directors. The company will have to submit the resolution matter to the shareholders' general meeting when the number of unaffiliated directors is less than three.[72]

The Company Law says little about the procedures for calling and conducting board meetings in LLCs. Apart from requiring the board to keep minutes of the meeting and follow the rule of one-director-one-vote, it permits the corporate charter to make rules for the board's 'method of deliberation and voting procedures'.[73]

6.3.6 Director's Liability for Illegal Board Decisions

The decisions on the matters deliberated at the board meetings shall be put into board minutes, which shall be signed by all the directors present at the meeting.[74] Consequently, a liability is imposed on the directors with respect to the resolutions adopted. That is, when a resolution of the board violated the provisions of laws, administrative regulations, the corporate charter, or the resolution of the shareholders' meeting and caused the company to suffer serious losses, the directors who participated in adopting the resolution should bear compensation liability to the company. There is only one way for a director to get out of this: if he proves before the dispute settlement tribunal that he expressed his objection to the resolution and such objection is recorded in the minutes of the meeting, then he will be exempt from liability.[75]

6.3.7 Judicial Interference to Revoke Illegal Board Actions

Pursuant to Article 22 of the Company Law, board resolutions, like the resolutions passed by the shareholders' meeting, are void if they violate

---

[71] Company Law, Article 217 (4).
[72] Company Law, Article 125.
[73] Company Law, Article 48.
[74] Company Law, Article 49, para. 2; Article 113, para. 2.
[75] Company Law, Article 113.

the laws and administrative regulations.[76] Implicitly, any shareholder shall have the right to bring a legal action for rescission of such resolutions. The Company Law does not hint whether other stakeholders, such as the company's creditors or employees, or third parties negatively affected by these resolutions, also have the right to sue the company for this. Obviously it does not prohibit such lawsuits.

The shareholders clearly have the right to ask the court to revoke a resolution if the procedures for convening the board meeting or the method of voting at the meeting violate laws, administrative regulations, or the corporate charter, or if the contents of the resolution contradict the corporate charter. For instance, if a director of a listed company, in violation of Article 125 of the Company Law, did not abstain from voting on matters concerning related transactions in which he was an interested party, the shareholders could petition the court to revoke the resolution. In all such cases, the suing shareholder should take the legal action within 60 days of the adoption of the resolution; otherwise, his petition will be rejected by the court.[77]

Technical rules, especially those concerning the notice of board meetings, can be crucially important. A party not happy with the resolution passed by the board meeting may challenge the adequacy of notice with the view to persuading the courts to invalidate the relevant board actions. Courts are sometimes reluctant to allow this to easily happen, especially when the procedural violations are considered insignificant. Further, courts normally treat attendance at a meeting as waiver of notice. In *Xinke Yuntong v Zhongbiao Ltd*,[78] a case tried in Beijing in 2005 and 2006, the plaintiff was a shareholder of Zhongbiao and it sued on behalf of Mr. Li, who was a director (of course, one nominated by the plaintiff) and the general manager of Zhongbiao. It requested the court to invalidate a board meeting on the ground of inadequate notice. The company's charter required a 10-day advance notice for board meetings, but Mr. Li was only given telephone notice on the day before the meeting. A resolution was adopted at the meeting to remove Mr. Li from the position of the general manager. Mr. Li showed up at the meeting but did not sign on the resolution. Both the first-instance court and the appellate court ruled that, although there were some defects in the procedures for convening the meeting, such as that the notice was not served in accordance with the corporate charter, the board meeting was

[76] Company Law, Article 22, para. 1.

[77] Company Law, Article 22.

[78] The facts and court rulings of this case were summarized and discussed in Liu Lanfang (2009), pp. 322–30.

still a valid one because (1) Mr. Li attended the meeting anyway in the capacity of a director; and (2) the delay of the notice would not negatively affect the director's exercise of his right to vote as the resolution was simply about the dismissal of the general manager, a matter for which a decision could be formed quickly.[79]

6.3.8 Authority and Powers of the Board of Directors

We now come to probably the most important aspect of the system of the board of directors in China, which concerns the key functions and powers of the board of directors. Under Articles 47 and 109 of the Company Law, the board 'is accountable to the shareholders' meeting'. As a collegiate body, it is granted the statutory powers to:

1. convene the shareholders' general meeting and report on its work to the general meeting;
2. implement the resolutions of the general meeting;
3. decide on the company's business operation plans and investment proposals;
4. formulate the company's annual financial budget and financial accounting plan;
5. formulate the company's profit distribution plan and loss recovery plan;
6. formulate the plans for increase or reduction of the company's registered capital and issuance of corporate bonds;
7. formulate the plans for merger, division, dissolution, or change of the corporate structure;
8. decide on the establishment of the company's international management organs;
9. appoint and remove the general manager (also known as the chief executive officer or CEO in some situations) of the company and decide on his remuneration; decide, based on the recommendations of the general manager, on the appointment and dismissal of the company's deputy general managers, and chief financial officer, as well as on their remunerations;
10. formulate the basic management system of the company;
11. perform any other duties and exercise powers granted by the corporate charter.

---

[79] Liu Lanfang (2009), p. 325.

Indeed, in line with point (11) above, the Model Charter gives additional powers for the board of listed companies to:

1. formulate plans for major acquisitions and share repurchase;
2. decide, within the authorization of the shareholders' general meeting, on the company's external investment, buying and selling assets, mortgage of assets, external guarantee, related-party transactions, etc.;
3. appoint and dismiss the board secretary and decide on his remuneration;
4. manage the company's information management;
5. recommend that the general meeting hire or dismiss the company's outside auditor;
6. listen to the general manager's work report and inspect his work performance;
7. perform any other duties and exercise powers given by the corporate charter.

Conceptually, the above powers can be categorized into three groups: decisional powers, appointment powers, and oversight powers. The decisional powers make the board of directors a 'management board' to some extent, by virtue of which the board has the power to set the course of the company by determining its business operation plans and investment plans, to make the company's financial budget and accounting plans, and to formulate plans concerning profit distribution and loss recovery, change in the registered capital, issuance of corporate bonds, and fundamental changes of corporate form and structure. The appointment powers entitle the board to select corporate officers and to determine their compensation, among which the most important function of the board is to choose the company's general manager (chief executive officer). In addition, the board has authority to determine the company's management structure and overall management system. The oversight authority subjects the general manager – and implicitly the whole management team – to the supervisory power of the board.

6.3.9 Separation of Powers between the Board and the General Meeting

Looking at the allocation of decisional power in Chinese companies with a critical eye, one may not find a clear separation of powers between the board of directors and the general meeting. In contrast, the shareholder-centered nature of corporate governance in China has produced a 'mixture of competences' in the allocation of functions and powers between the board and the general meeting.[80] For example, the general meeting is in charge of 'determining the company's business strategy (*jingying fangzhen*) and investment plans (*touzi jihua*)',[81] while the board has the power to 'decide on the company's business operation plans (*jingying jihua*) and investment proposals (*touzi fangan*)'. It is not clear where to draw a line between 'business strategy and investment plans' and 'business operation plans and investment proposals'. The authority to decide profit distribution rests exclusively in the hands of the general meeting, although the board has the power to initiate dividend distribution plans.

Giving shareholders' general meetings so much power to intervene in the running of the company's business is a distinctive feature of corporate governance in China, especially in light of the international trend of resting the management of the business and control of the company on the directors.[82] What explains the far-reaching statutory powers granted to the general meeting? It is submitted that the purpose behind these powers is to favor the majority shareholder, which, in the Chinese context, is often the state. The powers of the general meeting could only be exercised collectively through voting by the shareholders, and the passage of a resolution must be supported by at least a simple majority of the voting rights based on the percentage of the equity interest held by the shareholders. Since the state is the single or largest shareholder in the SOEs, giving some key decisional powers to the shareholders' meeting, which is usually controlled by the majority shareholders, could desirably undermine the independence of the board to prevent the latter from making decisions that are not in the interest of the state. On the other hand, since the state as a shareholder retains only the most important powers on fundamental corporate decisions, it does not need to involve itself in making decisions for the day-to-day management of the company.[83] However, the general meeting's possession of such comprehensive powers does not necessarily entail better protection of the minority shareholders. In fact, the interests of minority shareholders are often overlooked in such a system.

---

[80] See Siems (2008), p. 154.

[81] Company Law, Article 38(1).

[82] Siems (2008), pp. 152–4 (noting 'In most countries, it is accordingly taken as a basic tenet that the conduct of business is incumbent on the board of directors and other members of the management'. See p. 153).

[83] Siems (2008), p. 154; Gu Mingkang (2010), p. 143.

6.3.10 Board Committees

The Company Law does not have any mention of the sub-units of the board, but the Code of Corporate Governance encourages listed companies to establish, under the board of directors, a corporate strategy committee, an audit committee, a nomination committee, a remuneration and appraisal committee, and other special committees in accordance with resolutions of shareholders' general meetings.[84] Most listed companies have also adopted bylaws for the special committees. The committees are responsible to the board. Without independent decision-making powers, all their recommendations and proposals must be reviewed and approved by the full board.[85] They may solicit professional opinions from outside intermediary institutions at the company's expense.[86]

Briefly, the corporate strategy committee looks at the long-term strategic development of the company and makes recommendations to the board accordingly.[87] The audit committee is responsible for proposing to appoint or dismiss the company's outside auditor (note that it is in the authority of the general meeting to actually appoint or dismiss the auditor), supervising the company's internal auditing, liaising between the internal auditor and outside auditor, reviewing and approving the company's financial information and disclosure, and reviewing the company's internal control system.[88] The nomination committee is the company's search body, in charge of setting the hiring criteria for directors and managers, searching suitable candidates to fulfill vacancies of the board or the management team, and reviewing the qualifications and eligibility of those candidates.[89] Finally, the Code of Corporate Governance tasks the remuneration and appraisal committee with reviewing and recommending to the full board the compensation of directors

---

[84] Code of Corporate Governance, Article 52.

[85] Code of Corporate Governance, Article 58.

[86] Code of Corporate Governance, Article 57.

[87] Code of Corporate Governance, Article 53. The bylaws of some listed companies have conferred upon the corporate strategy committee the functions and powers to review the major investment and fundraising proposals, as well as major asset investment and management projects, which are required to be approved by the board of directors. See Article 8 of the Working Rules of Board Special Committees of SANY Heavy Industry Co. Ltd, available at http://www.sse.com.cn (accessed 30 March 2012).

[88] Code of Corporate Governance, Article 54.

[89] Code of Corporate Governance, Article 55.

and senior management executives. It also generally oversees the company's compensation policies.[90]

The Code of Corporate Governance requires listed companies to have all their committees comprised solely of directors. The majority of the audit committee, nomination committee, and remuneration and appraisal committee must be formed by independent directors. Those committees must also be chaired by independent directors.[91]

6.3.11 Chairperson of the Board

The board of directors must have a chairperson, which is normally the most influential position in the company. It is up to the corporate charter of an LLC to decide the methods and procedures for appointing the chairperson and deputy chairpersons, but the chairperson and vice chairpersons of the JSLC board must be elected by over half of all the directors.[92] Under Company Law, the chairperson has the following functions and powers on top of the normal rights and powers given to the directors:

1. *Chairing the shareholders' general meeting*: The general meeting is to be convened by the board of directors, but it could only be presided over by an individual, which is naturally a task of the chairperson of the board.[93] As noted previously, the chairperson can no longer monopolize this power after the 2005 Company Law took effect, as the vice chairperson or a director appointed by a majority of the directors will take over to make sure the general meeting goes smoothly if he fails or is unable to chair the meeting.
2. *Convening and chairing board meeting*: It is also the chairperson's authority to call and chair the board meetings. Like at the general meeting, the vice chairperson or a director designated by a majority of the directors will take this authority if the chairperson does not exercise it.
3. *Examining the management team's implementation of board resolutions*: The chairman reviews the management team's work to verify whether they have faithfully implemented the board's resolutions. Although the chairperson cannot interfere with the daily

---

90 Code of Corporate Governance, Article 56.
91 Code of Corporate Governance, Article 52.
92 Company Law, Article 110, para. 1.
93 Company Law, Articles 41 and 102.

management of the company, this authority still confers upon him a tremendous power to influence managerial decisions.

The authority of the chairperson was significantly downgraded by the 2005 Company Law. Under the 1993 Company Law, only the chairperson could be the company's legal representative.[94] This provision, until it was abolished by the new law, was the source of a major governance dilemma in Chinese companies, making it legally almost impossible for companies to oust an unwelcome chairperson. The 1993 Law also permitted the companies to 'authorize the chairperson to execute part of the duties and powers of the board of directors when the board is not in session'.[95] Needless to say, the delegation of the authority of the full board to an individual could entirely eliminate the checks and balances within the corporate governance structure of a company. All these provisions are gone in the 2005 Company Law. Now the position of the chairperson can be assumed by either the chairperson of the board, the executive director of an LLC (which does not have a board), or the general manager.[96] The board is also not permitted to delegate its powers to the chairperson.

6.3.12 Board of Wholly State-owned Companies (WSOCs)

Although WSOCs have only one shareholder and do not need to have a shareholders' general meeting,[97] they are mandated by the Company Law to establish a board of directors, which, according to the language of the Law, has the same functions and powers possessed by the board of directors in ordinary LLCs and JSLCs. The directors are appointed by the State-owned Assets Supervision and Administration Commission (SASAC).[98]

What is notable about the WSOC board is that the Company Law attempts to establish a co-determination system in the board by mandating the installation of employee representatives on the board. The employee members of the board are elected by the employees democratically.[99] An annotation of the Company Law edited by the Legislative

94 See Ch. 3, section 3.2.2 above.
95 1993 Company Law, Article 120.
96 Company Law, Article 13.
97 Company Law, Article 67.
98 Company Law, Article 68.
99 Company Law, Article 68.

Commission China's National People's Congress explains the rationale behind this provision as:[100]

> The requirement of having employee representatives on the WSOC board … reflects the fundamental goal of our socialist country to rely wholeheartedly on the working masses and to safeguard the lawful rights and interests of the workers.

Despite this somehow hilarious explanation, the SASAC, which legally serves the role of the state shareholder in SOEs, has made rules to shrewdly downplay the importance of this requirement and even disincentivize would-be candidates for the directorship. According to the Administrative Rules on Employee Directors in Wholly State-owned Companies under Experiment promulgated by the SASAC in 2006,[101] an employee director could be nominated by the company's trade union or by self-nomination, and elected by the employees through democratic processes. The WSOC must have at least one employee director. The employee director is not entitled to remunerations or any form of bonus in the capacity of a director, and he is not given any special power. Still, he must bear personal liability for illegal or mistaken board actions as required by the Law or corporate charter. Consequently, those privileged and high-paid 'employees' such as trade union leaders or Chinese Communist Party officials, who represent more of the state and the management, are more likely to run and be appointed as the employee directors.

6.4 INDEPENDENT DIRECTORS

The original design of the two-tier board structure in the 1993 Company Law was meant to establish checks and balances within the company by having the supervisory board monitoring the management board (the board of directors). As will be examined below, the supervisory board system appeared to be a failure at least from the perspective of the 1993 Company Law. Disappointed at the poor corporate governance of China's listed companies and the ineffectiveness of the supervisory boards, the CSRC issued, in August 2001, the *Guidelines on the Introduction of the*

---

[100] An Jian (2005), p. 105.

[101] Chinese pinxin title of the rules is: Guoyou Duzi Gongsi Dongshihui Shidian Qiye Zhigong Dongshi Guanli Banfa (Shixing), Guo Zi Fa Qun Gong [2006] 21 Hao, promulgated on 3 March 2006, available at http://www.sasac.gov.cn/gzjg/qzgz/200603130062.htm (accessed 12 March 2012).

Independent Directors System in Listed Companies.[102] Although it is not the CSRC's first mention of independent directors in its regulations,[103] the major change this time is that the *Guidelines*, for the first time, mandate that '[a]ll domestically listed companies shall amend their articles of association and … appoint qualified persons to be independent directors'.[104] Specifically, 'By June 30th, 2002, at least two members of the board of directors shall be independent directors; and by June 30th, 2003, at least one third of [the] board shall be independent directors'.[105] The installation of independent directors into the board of directors of listed companies was further required by the Code of Corporate Governance issued on 7 January 2002 and the 2005-amended Company Law.[106]

6.4.1 Independence Requirements

The *Guidelines* define an independent director as one 'who holds no posts in the company other than the position of director, and who maintains no relations with the listed company and its major shareholder that might prevent him from making objective judgment independently'.[107] This general (positive) definition is followed by certain negative qualifications, the presence of which would disqualify a director from being independent:[108]

1. An employee of the listed company or its affiliated enterprises, or his/her direct relatives and major social relationships (direct relatives refer to their spouse, father, mother and children, etc.; major

---

[102] *Zhongguo Zhengquan Jiandu Guanli Weiyuanhui Guanyu Fabu <Guanyu Zai Shangshi Gongsi Jianli Duli Dongshi Zhidu De Zhidao Yijian> De Tongzhi* (The China Securities Regulatory Commission Notice on Issuing the Guidelines for Introducing Independent Directors Listed Companies), Zhengjianfa (2001) No. 102, 16 August 2001, English text available at http://www.csrc.gov.cn/en/jsp/detail.jsp?infoid=1061947864100&type=CMS.STD (accessed 12 February 2006) (hereinafter the Guidelines on Independent Directors).

[103] The CSRC indicated in its *Guidelines on Articles of Association of Companies* issued in 1997 that 'companies may set independent directors according to their needs'.

[104] Guidelines on Independent Directors, Article I:3.

[105] Id.

[106] Article 123 of the Company Law stipulates, 'Listed companies shall appoint independent directors; the specific measures shall be provided by the State Council'.

[107] Guidelines on Independent Directors, Article I:1.

[108] Guidelines on Independent Directors, Article III.

social relations refer to their brothers, sisters, father-in-law, mother-in-law, daughter-in-law, son-in-law, spouse of their brothers, sisters, and their spouse's brothers and sisters, etc.);

2. A shareholder who holds more than 1 percent of the outstanding shares of the listed company directly or indirectly;
3. A natural person shareholder who is one of the 10 largest shareholders of the listed company, or such person's direct relative;
4. An employee of a unit which holds more than 5 percent of the outstanding shares of the listed company directly or indirectly, or of the unit which ranks as one of the five largest shareholders of the listed company, or such employee's direct relative;
5. A person meeting any of the three above-mentioned conditions in the immediate proceeding year;
6. A person providing financial, legal or consulting services to the listed company or its subsidiaries;
7. A person stipulated as not qualified as an independent director in the articles of association;
8. A person determined by the CSRC as not qualified.

In brief, the independent directors are required to be independent of the company and its major shareholders and employees, as well as its major professional services providers. Obviously absent here is an independence requirement in connection to major business relationships, namely companies with which the listed company has significant transactions. In contrast, the *Final NYSE Corporate Governance Rules* (2003) mandate that a director is not 'independent' if he is 'an executive officer or an employee, or whose immediate family member is an executive officer, of a company that makes payments to, or receive payments from, the listed company for property or services in an amount which, in any single fiscal year, exceeds the greater of $1 million, or 2% of such other company's consolidated gross revenues'.[109] Singapore's Code of Corporate Governance 2005, issued by the Ministry of Finance of Singapore, has a similar guideline.[110] The UK Combined Code of Corporate Governance also

---

[109] New York Stock Exchange, *Final NYSE Corporate Governance Rules* (2003), available at http://www.nyse.com/pdfs/finalcorpgovrules.pdf (accessed 15 February 2005).

[110] See Code of Corporate Governance 2005, Article 2.1(d), available at http://www.ccdg.gov.sg:/news:/pdf/AnnexE_Code_of_Corporate_Governance_2005.pdf (accessed 14 February 2006).

presumes that a director is not independent if he has a 'material business relationship with the company'.[111]

6.4.2 Nomination, Election, and Retirement of Independent Directors

An independent director is to be nominated by the board of directors, the supervisory board, or a shareholder or shareholders who independently or jointly have more than 1 percent stake in the company. The nominee, before the election in the shareholders' meeting, shall issue a public statement that she or he has no relationship with the listed company that may affect her/his independent objective judgment. The CSRC intervenes before the election, as it requires listed companies to submit the nomination for examination and approval by the CSRC. A nominee objected to by the CSRC can only serve as candidate for an ordinary directorship and not independent directorship. If elected, an independent director is not to occupy the position for more than six years. He or she may be removed by the shareholders' meeting, upon request of the board of directors, on failing to attend the board meeting in person three consecutive times. The independent director may also resign before the term expires, but the notice of resignation is to take effect only 'after the subsequently appointed independent director fills the vacancy', indicating that 'forced labor' is possibly intended in the *Guidelines*.[112]

6.4.3 Powers of Independent Directors

The *Guidelines* grant a variety of powers to independent directors. A proposed related-party transaction (defined as a transaction concluded between the listed company and related parties, which is in excess of RMB3 million or 5 percent of the company's net assets) should be approved by independent directors before it is submitted to the board of directors for discussion. The independent directors may appoint outside auditors and consultants and solicit proxies before the shareholders' meeting. They can also propose to the board of directors to call an extraordinary shareholders' meeting or a meeting of the board of directors, as well as to hire or dismiss the company's accounting firm.[113] In addition, the independent directors may issue 'independent opinions' with

---

[111] See UK Combined Code on Corporate Governance (2003), A.3.1, available at http://www.fsa.gov.uk/pubs/ukla/lr_comcode2003.pdf (accessed 14 February 2006).

[112] *CSRC Guidelines on Independent Directors*, *supra* note 27, Article IV.

[113] Id, Article V.

regard to matters relating to appointment and replacement of directors and senior management executives, remuneration for directors and senior managers, and any significant existing or new loans or fund transfers between the listed company and its shareholders, actual controllers, and affiliated enterprises, as well as any other events the independent directors consider detrimental to the interest of the minority shareholders.[114]

6.4.4 Evaluating the Chinese System of Independent Directors

Now almost all of China's over 2,300 listed companies have installed independent directors on their boards. On average, each company has three such directors.[115] Has the system proven to be effective, or at least more effective than the supervisory board?

It is important to observe, from a global perspective, that there is a lack of empirical evidence on the efficacy of the independent directors in relation to improved corporate governance and firms' performance.[116] Bhagat and Black (1998) surveyed the literature on independent directors and concluded that '[t]here remains no convincing evidence that the composition of the board of directors affects overall firm performance'.[117] As Tan (2003: 378) observes,

> There is a tendency to think that simply having independent directors improves corporate governance. The reality is sometimes the opposite. Unless there are independent directors who are truly independent, and have the strength and ability to perform an effective monitoring function, the presence of independent directors acts as a smokescreen and a snare for the unwary investor who may pay a higher price for the equity on the basis of a supposedly better corporate governance structure.

However, in spite of the debate on the link between board composition and corporate performance, countries undergoing institutional transitions still compete to appoint independent directors to the corporate board.[118] Since the independent director system was implemented in 2002, China has accumulated only four years of experience in this area. It is hence too early to evaluate the effectiveness of the system in that country. However, China, a leading emerging economy, provides an interesting 'research

---

114 Id, Article VI.
115 Yang (2005), p. 2.
116 Tan (2003); Baysinger and Butler (1984).
117 Bhagat and Black (1998), pp. 299–300.
118 Peng (2004), p. 453.

laboratory' for corporate governance theorists.[119] There are a few signs showing that the independent directors have played a more effective role than the supervisory board in serving as checks and balances to the management. Using the optimistic words of a CSRC official stated in the 2005 OECD Policy Dialogue on Corporate Governance in China,

> As Chinese independent director system has not [been] established too long and experienced independent directors are [needed badly], we have to wait a longer time to witness the obvious effect of independent directors' significance on corporate governance; however, we are deeply convinced that the establishment of [an] independent director system has already made Chinese people and companies take a big step in better understanding the idea of corporate governance.[120]

The purpose of the independent director system, however, cannot be confined to merely educating the 'Chinese people and companies' on corporate governance; the system itself should be part of a purported good corporate governance structure.

A joint survey by the Association of Board Secretaries of Listed Companies of Shanghai and Shanghai Jinxin Institute of Securities Research conducted in 2003, two years after China's formal launch of the independent director system, demonstrated that independent directors helped improve corporate governance, especially in terms of bringing professional expertise and protecting minority shareholders.[121] The empirical research of the Research Center of Corporate Governance Center of Nankai University shows that the degree of perfection of independent directors has an obviously positive relationship with the profitability, market valuation, and financial security of listed companies. It has a negative relationship with the scale of illegal activities of companies.[122] Although the data is still limited and rudimentary, it is increasingly recognized that independent directors can make a difference in firms' governance and performance in China.

---

[119] Peng (2004), p. 453.

[120] Yang (2005), p. 2.

[121] *Securities Daily* (2003). The survey shows that over 90 percent of the secretaries of boards of directors took the view that the independent directors can play a 'certain' role in preventing listed companies from making misrepresentation and fabricating documents, improving corporate governance structure, enhancing disclosure and transparency, and protecting the interest of minority shareholders.

[122] Li Weian *et al.* (2004).

6.4.5 Explaining the (Limited) Efficacy of Independent Directors in Chinese Companies

Compared with the total failure of the supervisory board, the independent director system has been regarded – albeit with limited empirical evidence – as conducive to good corporate governance. At least in theory, this limited success can be explained from the following perspectives.

First of all, any meaningful – no matter how limited – check and balance imposed on the management of China's listed companies is supposed to have a positive effect on corporate governance, as poor governance practices in those companies are rampant. According to an 'incomplete' survey by the *Beijing Modern Business Daily*, a newspaper based in Beijing, 10 senior management executives of several of China's listed companies disappeared with corporate funds through collusion with related parties and other corporate officers under their direct control, causing the loss of over RMB10 billion (about 1.2 billion U.S. dollars) to those corporations. In the first month of 2005, 14 senior management executives of listed companies either disappeared or were arrested by the police, causing enormous damage to the companies.[123]

In state-owned companies, the state, after all, is only an abstract owner. It is common in China for agents appointed by the state to manage the companies, who were civil servants and government officials before appointment, to not always align their own interest with that of the state. Thus the agency problems in China's listed SOEs feature the 'absence of [an] effective ultimate principal'.[124] This has led to one model of insider control, namely the so-called *guanxiren kongzhi* [key-person control].[125] The key person is usually the chief executive officer (CEO), chairman of the board, or a senior executive manager of the company. Appointing them, the government often loses control of their activities. As a result, the key person usually becomes the super-sovereign and the sole commander of the company. Having virtually the ultimate decision-making power over all corporate affairs, he is, in fact, endowed with the power of control, execution, and supervision.[126] In other cases – no matter whether the company is an SOE or a private enterprise – if the key person is appointed and controlled by the parent company, he acts solely as the representative of the controlling shareholder, having no or little regard to

---

[123] Chen Hua (2005).
[124] Clarke (2003), p. 499.
[125] Tan and Wang (2006).
[126] Tan and Wang (2006).

the proprietary rights of minority shareholders.[127] The board of directors comprising of insiders, selected by the key person on behalf of the state or the controlling shareholder, cannot effectively monitor the activities of the key person.

It is reasoned that, at least from a theoretical point of view, the independent directors, not working in the company on a full-time basis and hence less subject to the control of the key person, would impose constraints on the exercise of power by the key person. As noted above, the empirical surveys also disclose that, so far, the installment of independent directors on the board has a positive correlation with the performance of the listed companies.

6.4.6 Limits on the Effectiveness of Independent Directors

Although the independent director system is, overall, more effective than the supervisory board, the surveys mentioned above all point out that there is a tremendous gap between the current performance of independent directors and the expectation of the public.[128] This is hardly surprising. Indeed, given the significant limits on the functions of independent directors, as discussed below, it is not easy for one to sustain his optimism on the effectiveness of this system.

Independence

The biggest problem is still how independence is to be maintained. Although independent directors are outsiders, their independence is somehow constrained by their nomination. The *CSRC Guidelines for Independent Directors* prescribe that they should be nominated by the board of directors, the supervisory board, or a shareholder or shareholders who separately or jointly own more than 1 percent stake in the outstanding shares of the company, and elected by the shareholders' meeting. It is, however, difficult to believe that the CSRC is not aware of the high concentration of ownership as well as the dysfunction of supervisory boards in China's listed companies. A survey of the *China Securities Daily* shows that 67.5 percent of the independent directors were nominated by the board of directors, while 27.5 percent were directly nominated by the controlling shareholders.[129] Further, 52.5 percent of the independent directors under survey said their remuneration was determined by the company's 'senior management executives', while

---

127 Tan and Wang (2006).

128 *China Securities Daily* (2005); *Shanghai Securities News* (2004).

129 *China Securities Daily* (2005).

37.5 percent of those under survey revealed that it was the 'controlling shareholders' who decided their remuneration.[130] Clearly, for a significant portion of the independent directors, their constituency is the controlling shareholders.

Will this constituency base affect the independence of the outside directors? Although those directors appear to be more independent than the inside directors, they are far from being as 'independent' as one would expect from an outsider who is really free from influence from inside the company. As one independent director pointed out, in many listed companies, the controlling shareholders wish that independent directors would be satisfied to serve as 'ornaments' of the corporate Christmas tree, 'raising just their hands'.[131] Not surprisingly, 65 percent of the independent directors in the survey of the *China Securities Daily* indicated that they never said 'no' in the meetings of the board of directors. A full 100 percent of them indicated that they did, at least 'occasionally', vote 'yes' when they should have voted 'no' based on the merits of the proposal.[132]

The legal framework, designed by the CSRC, has created the problems that undermine the effectiveness of independent directors. The CSRC is certainly aware of the extensively reported problems of high-ownership concentration and key-person control in China's listed companies. Nevertheless, it still imposes no restrictions on the power of the controlling shareholders to nominate independent directors, and grants no special privilege to minority shareholders who are the major victims of the agency problems associated with the key-person control model.

The independence of independent directors is further undermined by the *guanxi* based cultural environment, which is still pervasive in contemporary Chinese society. *Guanxi* requires one to show respect for the feelings of – or 'give face' to – others, especially to one's friends. As one commentator observes:

> In the Chinese culture with a history of several thousand years, the concept of 'saving face for friends' or 'giving no cold face to friends' is so persistent that it has huge impact on every interaction between people. Affected by this special cultural environment, it is inevitable that an independent director would be very reluctant to offend his friend, namely the chairman or CEO of

---

[130] *China Securities Daily* (2005).

[131] *Shanghai Securities News* (2004a) (comment by Prof. Dong Ansheng relating his career as an independent director in several listed companies).

[132] *China Securities Daily* (2005).

the company, although the chairman or CEO has committed something which is detrimental to the interest of the company and its shareholders.[133]

Access to corporate information and other facilities

Apart from independence, the access to corporate information for independent directors is limited, or controlled, by the management of the company. A survey conducted in 2004 demonstrated that about 90 percent of independent directors relied primarily on corporate management to obtain information, through either the brochure produced by the company or briefing by senior management executives of the company.[134] That is to say, very few independent directors had actually employed the tools granted by the Law, such as proxy contest, the right to hire external independent auditors, or direct communication with the company's employees or other stakeholders, to supervise the corporate management.

Regarding independent directors' access to information, the legal regime does not offer much help. The *CSRC Guidelines for Independent Directors* mandate that listed companies must provide independent directors with adequate access to corporate information. It is further required that, 'when the independent director performs his/her duties, the relevant persons concerned in the listed company shall cooperate actively and shall not turn down the independent director's proper request, nor shall they hinder the independent director's work or conceal the information'.[135] In addition, 'the company shall make the necessary working facilities available to the independent directors for them to perform their duties'.[136]

The key question here is whether these requirements can be enforced. As noted above, an overwhelming majority of the independent directors mainly depends on the senior corporate officers for information, and is hence influenced, or even controlled by the corporate management in terms of access to information. When the corporate management is determined to withhold negative information from conscientious independent directors who have doubts about the disclosure of corporate information, those directors normally have no other choice but to offer their resignation. They cannot resort to China's corporate law regime, including the *CSRC Guidelines for Independent Directors*, as the system provides no legal solution if the listed company refuses to provide

---

133 Xie Chaobin (2004), p. 320.
134 *China Securities Daily* (2005).
135 *CSRC Guidelines for Independent Directors*, Article VII:3.
136 *CSRC Guidelines for Independent Directors*, Article VII:2.

information. Clearly, when thc requirements are not associated with enforcement measures, their legal effects are essentially minimized.

Similarly, although the *Guidelines* require the company to provide the necessary facilities for the independent directors to perform their duties, they do not specify the consequences of violation by the company. For instance, though the *Guidelines* provide that the independent directors can appoint outside auditing or consulting institutions to review the financial affairs of the company, this provision is unlikely to be implemented if the management of the company does not cooperate by bearing the necessary auditing or consulting cost. In a high-profile case in 2004, which is also believed to be the first case in which the independent directors challenged the management of the company, the four independent directors of Lianhua Gourmet Power Co., a company listed in the Shanghai Stock Exchange, requested the management to retain independent outside auditors to review the illegal use of RMB949 million of the listed company's funds by its largest shareholder. The request was simply ignored by both the management and the controlling shareholder, resulting in a situation that is characterized as '*buliao liaozhi*' in Chinese, meaning 'settling a matter by leaving it unsettled'.[137]

Liability of independent directors

The independent directors are assigned a number of rights and duties by the *Guidelines*. From the legal perspective, rights and duties must be associated with liabilities. In other words, the directors face certain legal consequences should they fail to perform their duties. With regard to duties, the *Guidelines* require that:

> The independent directors shall bear the duties of good faith and due diligence and care towards the listed company and all the shareholders. They shall earnestly perform their duties in accordance with laws, regulations and the company's articles of association, shall protect the overall interests of the company, and shall be especially concerned with protecting the interests of minority shareholders from being infringed. Independent directors shall carry out their duties independently and shall not subject themselves to the influence of the company's major shareholders, actual controllers, or other entities or persons who are interested parties of the listed company.[138]

But what are the legal consequences if the independent directors fail to fulfill their duties? The *Guidelines*, again, do not specify the consequences of violation, except that an independent director shall be

---

[137] *China Securities Daily* (2005).

[138] *CSRC Guidelines for Independent Directors,* Article I:2, *supra* note 27.

removed if he or she fails to attend the board's meeting in person three times consecutively.[139] Of course, an independent director is also subject to the legal liabilities imposed by the Company Law on any director who violates his duty of good faith and loyalty.[140]

A judicial case decided in 2002 revealed that if an independent director fails to perform legal duties, he might be subject to the disciplinary actions of the CSRC. Lu Jiahao, a former independent director of a listed company called Zhengbaiwen, was fined by the CSRC RMB100,000 because he did not take corrective actions when the company made a false disclosure to the public. Lu brought the CSRC to the Beijing Number One Intermediate Court. Although the court rejected the claim of Lu on the ground of procedural error, the case still serves as an alarm to independent directors, reminding them of the high risks involved in this job.[141]

The current question for China's independent directors is, however, not how harsh the punishment should be. If the harsh liability is not associated with proper institutions to support the independent directors to perform their duties, e.g. ensuring that administrative and judicial remedies are available to the independent directors or shareholders if the corporate management refuses to provide the independent directors access to corporate information and facilities, it can only prevent more able persons from getting into the pool of independent directors, which badly needs more talent. In fact, there was a race to resignation by independent directors in 2002 after the *Lu Jiahao* case was decided.[142]

In conclusion, the creation of independent directors for China's listed companies was the CSRC's direct response to the virtually complete failure of the supervisory board system, as discussed in the following section. Empirical studies, rudimentary as they are, still suggest that independent directors have contributed to the improvement of corporate governance. One has to attribute this to the extremely poor quality of corporate governance in China's listed companies prior to the establishment of the independent director system in 2001. The independent directors are able to exercise some checks and balances on the power of the manager or the representative of the controlling shareholder.

As the independent director system has been in place in China for only a decade, it is still too early to assess the effectiveness of this institution, especially because it was imported into China from the origin countries

139 *CSRC Guidelines for Independent Directors*, Article IV:5.
140 Company Law, Articles 147–53.
141 Gu (2003), pp. 70–71.
142 Gu (2003), p. 71.

(mainly the U.S. and UK), which have a very different legal and cultural environment than the transplant country. Although the institution has achieved limited success, it is not easy for observers to be optimistic about the role of independent directors in corporate governance in China, unless certain fundamental defects, which are deeply rooted in the economic, political, and legal environment surrounding China's enterprise sectors, are cured. Those problems include, most notably, the lack of true independence of the independent directors and the weak enforcement measures in relation to violation of the legal rules giving powers and privileges to independent directors.

6.5 SUPERVISORY BOARD

6.5.1 Composition and Meeting of Supervisory Board

It is a statutory requirement that a company have a supervisory board (SB) or at least a supervisor. An LLC with relatively few shareholders or one of smaller scale may appoint one or two supervisors instead of a supervisory board.[143] The SB should be composed of no less than three supervisors.[144] The chairperson of the SB, who has the authority to convene and preside over the SB meeting, is elected by more than half of all supervisors. The SB of a JSLC may also have a vice chairperson. To prevent the chairperson from abusing his position, the Law mandates that, in a JSLC, when the chairperson fails or is unable to perform his duties, the vice chairperson shall take over the duty to convene and chair the meeting. If the vice chairperson suffers from the same problem, a supervisor jointly designated by more than half of all directors shall take over to ensure the SB meeting is smoothly convened and chaired.[145] For the SB meeting in an LLC, if the chairperson is unable to or fails to perform his duties, a supervisor jointly appointed by more than half of the supervisors will immediately take over to convene and chair the meeting.[146] The supervisors, like directors, serve three years for each term but may be re-elected upon the expiration of their term of office. Even after his term is expired without re-election, a supervisor may continue to hold his position until his replacement assumes duty.[147] The

---

143 Company Law, Article 118.
144 Company Law, Articles 52 and 118.
145 Company Law, Article 118, para. 3.
146 Company Law, Article 52, para. 3.
147 Company Law, Article 53.

supervisors, like the directors, exercise their supervisory powers collectively. That is, a supervisory board of an LLC must meet at least once a year, and a JSLC supervisory board must meet every six months. In addition, any supervisor may call for a special SB meeting.[148] Resolutions will be adopted by a simply majority, unless the corporate charter of an LLC provides otherwise.[149]

The co-determination feature is more obvious in the SB. The composition of the supervisory board shall include representatives of shareholders, who are elected by the shareholders' general meeting, and 'an appropriate percentage of employee representatives', which means at least one-third of the supervisors should be democratically elected by the employees of the company.[150] Supervisors, like directors and managers, must meet the eligibility requirements stipulated in Article 147 of the Company Law. Directors and senior management executives are expressly prohibited from serving as supervisors.[151]

The SBs in wholly state-owned companies (WSOCs) are subject to a separate regulatory regime. The number of supervisors on the SB in a WSOC must not be less than five, with one-third of the supervisors being employee representatives. The normal supervisors and the SB chairperson are appointed by the SASAC, but the employee supervisors shall be elected democratically by the employees.

6.5.2 Authority and Powers of Supervisory Board

The SB was intended to be the only internal watchdog over the management. The SB oversees the board of directors and managers to ensure they comply with state laws and company policies. Specifically, PRC Company Law 1993, before it was amended in 2005, granted the SB the following powers:

1. examining the financial affairs of the company;
2. supervising the conduct of directors and managers in their performance of duties that is in violation of laws, administrative regulations, or the corporate charter;
3. demanding the directors and senior manager to correct their wrongdoings that injure the corporate interest; and

---

[148] Company Law, Articles 56 and 120.
[149] Company Law, Article 120, para. 3; Article 56, para. 2.
[150] Company Law, Article 52, para. 2.
[151] Company Law, Article 52, para. 4; Article 118, para. 4.

4. proposing the convening of an extraordinary shareholders' meeting.[152]

The 2005 revisions to the Company Law added to or clarified the arsenal of the SB, making it substantial:[153]

1. proposing, to the general meeting, to remove directors or senior management executives who have violated any laws, administrative regulations, the corporate charter, or resolutions of the shareholders' meetings;
2. convening and presiding over the general meeting as required by the law if the board of directors fails to fulfill this duty;
3. making proposals to the general meeting;
4. conducting investigations or, when necessary, hiring an outside intermediary (such as an accounting firm or law firm) at the expense of the company to conduct an investigation, if it discovers any irregularities in the company's business;
5. bringing legal actions against directors and senior management executives pursuant to Article 152 of the Company Law; and
6. attending the board meeting, asking questions and providing advice to the board in relation to the resolution matters.

6.5.3 Assessing the Chinese Supervisory Board in a Comparative Light

It is common knowledge that the Chinese supervisory board was inspired by the two-tier board structure in Germany. However, it is essentially important to note that the SBs in Chinese companies are significantly different from their counterparts in Germany in terms of both the statutory powers and the supervisory practice. According to the German Stock Corporation Act:[154]

> The supervisory board is responsible for appointing and dismissing members of the management board (§ 84(1)) and representing the corporation in its dealings with such board (§90), including entering into employment agreements with its members (§112). The management board reports to the supervisory board, though the latter is independently entitled to inspect the

---

[152] Company Law (1993), Article 54.

[153] Company Law, Articles 54 and 55.

[154] *The Germany Stock Corporation Act*, translated (with an introduction) by Hannes Schneider and Martin Heidenhain, The Hague: Kluwer Law International (1996).

> books, records and properties of the corporation (§111(2)). The supervisory board must consent to certain business decisions of the management board if required by the articles or the supervisory board's rules. The supervisory board may not, however, encumber the management board's ability to manage the corporation with excessive consent requirements. If the supervisory board withholds consent, the management board may nevertheless act if it can obtain a three quarters majority of votes cast at the shareholders' meeting (§111(4)).[155]

Clearly, compared with its counterpart in China, the SB in public corporations in Germany has a much broader power base, although it is also expected to refrain from excessively interfering with the board of directors (the 'management board'), which is vested with the authority to manage the day-to-day operation of the business. In essence, the management board in a German stock corporation is legally accountable to the SB to a very large extent as the directors of the management board have to (a) be appointed and removed by the SB and (b) seek consent from the SB regarding important business decisions. China's SB apparently does not possess such a wide range of powers. For instance, a Chinese SB's statutory powers do not include any authority to control the appointment or business decision-making of the management board. Hence, as a matter of law, it is impossible for the SB to act 'as supervisory organ in the sense of checks and balances, which appoints, control, advises – and where necessary also dismisses – the Management Board',[156] as prescribed in the German corporate governance structure.

In practice, the effectiveness of a typical SB is, first of all, undermined by its composition. The membership of the SB consists of 'political officers', leaders of the non-functional trade union, or close friends and allies of the senior management executives.[157] According to a survey of the Shanghai Stock Exchange Research Center on the educational background of supervisors serving in corporations listed in the Shanghai Stock Exchange, the overall professional quality of supervisors was inferior to the members of the board of directors.[158] Further, the study found that supervisors, appointed by the executives who also determine the supervisors' compensation, had virtually no independence from the

---

155 Schneider and Heidenhain (1996), p. 10.

156 Berlin Initiative Group, 'German Code of Corporate Governance', Berlin: 2 June 2006, part I:6, available at http://www.gccg.de/eng_German-Code-of-Corporate-Governance.pdf (hereinafter GCCG).

157 Tenev and Zhang (2002), p. 100; Dahya *et al.* (2003), pp. 313–16; SSE (2004), p. 44.

158 SSE (2003), p. 160.

management.[159] In addition, the SB had limited access to corporation information, rendering it impossible to make informed decisions. Last but not least, because of the highly concentrated leadership (in the hands of the either the state or other controlling shareholders), many SBs were at best a 'censored watchdog', not allowed to speak against the management or controlled by the controlling shareholder or the government.[160]

The old SB system provided in the 1993 Company Law was widely regarded as a failure. This was publicly admitted by one senior official of the China Securities Regulatory Commission ('CSRC'), China's chief watchdog on the capital markets:[161]

> It is sometimes argued that more authority should then be given to the supervisory boards, which sit on top of the boards of our listed companies. However, experience has shown that this system of supervision is not effective as it is often unclear whose interest is being represented by the supervisory board. In many cases, the supervisory board duplicates the authority of the board itself but without corresponding responsibilities. In fact, the presence of a supervisory board may give the illusion of certain checks and balances in the listed company when none existed.

Given that the new Company Law has tremendously strengthened the power base of the SB, the new SB has, of course, been expected to help improve corporate governance of Chinese companies. Professor Zhao Xudong has, however, pointed out that even the new SB is '*xingtong xushe*' (performing practically no function), and he radically – maybe wisely – suggested abolishing the SB system and making the board of directors a direct and more effective supervisory body to oversee the management.[162]

6.5.4 Relationship between Independent Directors and Supervisory Board

Lastly, it is useful to note the different roles played by the independent directors and the SB in China's corporate governance system. They are, of course, expected to complement each other – otherwise, why would

---

159 SSE (2004), p. 44.

160 Dahya *et al.* (2003), p. 315. See also SSE (2004), p. 44.

161 Cha (2001).

162 Zhao Xudong Jiaoshou Dadan Jianyi quxiao Jianshihui ('Professor Zhao Xudong boldly suggested abolishing the supervisory board'), Legal Daily, 11 March 2011, available at http://www.legaldaily.com.cn/bm/content/2010-03/11/content_2079635.htm (accessed 30 March 2012).

the lawmakers codify both of them? In the Chinese discourse of corporate law, the independent directors oversee the board of directors and the management by voting in the board meeting, and thus provide '*ex ante* supervision' in the company. In contrast, the SB, because it has no right to participate in the decision-making process, is believed to be able to render '*ex post* supervision'.[163] One could easily differentiate the two roles by comparing the respective powers of the two governance organs.

6.6 THE MANAGER AND SENIOR MANAGEMENT EXECUTIVES

6.6.1 The Concepts of 'Manager' and 'Senior Management Executives'

The term 'manager' (*jingli*) as used in Company Law is often referred to as the 'general manager' or even 'chief executive officer' (CEO) in practice. He is the person who has the authority to implement board resolutions and carry out the day-to-day operations of the company. The manager is appointed by and accountable to the board of directors.[164] He is subject to the same eligibility criteria as set out in Article 147 of the Company Law.

The Company Law has also introduced the frequently mentioned concept of '*gaoji guanli renyuan*', or senior management executives, which is akin to the concept of 'officers' in English and American corporate law. Senior management executives include the manager, deputy manager(s), chief financial officer, board secretary, as well as any other person as provided in the corporate charter.[165]

Notably there is no clear separation of the chairperson of the board and the general manager. Arguably, the Company Law might even encourage a convergence of the two roles. Article 115 provides that the board of a JSLC can decide to appoint a director (including the chairperson) as the manager. Article 69 permits the SASAC to appoint a director as the

[163] See CSRC (2011), p. 79. The supervisors may attend board meetings and ask questions or provide advice to the board, but may not vote on the resolution matters. See Company Law, Article 55.

[164] Company Law, Articles 50 and 114.

[165] Company Law, Article 217(1); Model Charter, Article 124, para. 3, and the annotation.

manager. Finally, Article 51 allows the executive director of an LLC with relatively fewer shareholders and smaller scale to serve as the company manager.

6.6.2 Powers of the Manager

The (general) manager has the following functions and, arguably, powers under the Company Law:[166]

1. taking charge of the company's business production and operation and implementing the resolutions of the board of directors;
2. implementing the annual business operation plans and investment proposals;
3. drafting the plans for the establishment of the company's internal management structure;
4. drafting the basic management system of the company;
5. formulating the specific rules and bylaws of the company;
6. proposing to the board of directors to hire or dismiss the deputy manager(s) and chief financial officer;
7. deciding to hire or dismiss management personnel other than those to be hired and dismissed by the board of directors;
8. attending the board meeting as an observer;
9. exercising other functions and powers delegated by the board of directors.

Despite the long list of the managerial powers provided in the Company Law, the Law makes clear that these are not compulsory. In fact, it is entirely up to the corporate charter to make rules for the functions of the manager, even though those rules may be inconsistent with the listed powers above.[167]

6.6.3 Board Secretary

The 'board secretary' provided for listed companies by Article 125 of the Company Law is essentially a functional equivalent of the 'company secretary' foreseen in the laws of other jurisdictions. They are one of the 'senior management executives' often mentioned in corporate laws and regulations. Many non-listed companies also have such a position. In practice, many board secretaries also hold the position of 'deputy general

---

[166] Company Law, Article 50; Article 114, para. 2.

[167] Company Law, Article 50.

manager' in order not to be misunderstood as an insignificant administrative assistant. The board secretary has the following functions and powers:[168]

1. Preparing and organizing the shareholders' general meeting and board meeting;
2. Maintaining and storing the company's records and information of shareholders;
3. Managing the company's information disclosure;
4. Assisting the directors, especially the independent directors, to perform their duties;
5. Helping establishing rules and procedures to improve the corporate governance of the company;
6. Managing the company's investor relations and public relations;
7. Managing the restricted sale of shares and monitoring share transfer matters of the company to ensure directors, supervisors, and senior management executives of the company comply with the legal restrictions on share transfer;
8. Conducting the training of directors, supervisors, and senior management executives;
9. Advising the directors, supervisors, and senior management executives on their fiduciary duties;
10. Reporting to the stock exchange in case fiduciary duties have been violated;
11. Attending, as an observer, meetings convened by the general manager and other meetings that concern major corporate matters.

The board secretary is guaranteed a more independent position than other senior management executives by the CSRC and stock exchanges. The Code of Corporate Governance requires that 'no institutions or individuals shall interfere with the board secretary's work'.[169] The Administrative Measures of the Shanghai Stock Exchange (SSE) on the Board Secretary of Listed Companies (Rev. 2011)[170] provides that the board secretary is the designated contact person of the listed company for the

---

[168] See generally, Company Law, Article 125, and the SSE Administrative Measures, *infra*, note 169.

[169] Code of Corporate Governance, Article 90.

[170] Shanghai Zhengquan Jiaoyisuo Shangshi Gongsi Dongshihui Mishu Guanli Banfa (Xiuding), promulgated by the Shanghai Stock Exchange on 15 April 2011, available at http://www.sse.com.cn (accessed 12 March 2012).

SSE, who cannot be removed by the listed company without cause.[171] The secretary should report immediately to the SSE when/if he is obstructed by others in his performance of duties.[172]

171 Id, Articles 3 and 9.
172 Id, Article 24.

7. Fiduciary duties of directors, supervisors, and management executives

7.1 INTRODUCTION TO FIDUCIARY STANDARDS AND RULES IN CHINA'S CORPORATE LAW

In the sense that business companies in China share all the fundamental attributes of modern corporations,[1] they also suffer from the same generic agency problems,[2] subject, of course, to the strong characteristics produced by China's social, economic, and political milieu. The first agency problem involves the conflict between the shareholders and the directors and the hired managers. In many cases, SOEs in China face an ownership vacuum, or at least have the problem of 'strong managers, weak owner'.[3] Private Chinese companies with separation of ownership and management are also plagued by the typical conflict between the firm's owners and its hired managers as the latter tend to pursue their personal interests. The second agency problem arises from 'the conflict between, on one hand, owners who possess the majority or controlling interest in the firm and, on the other hand, the minority or noncontrolling owners'.[4] In SOEs under strong control of the government, which is also the largest shareholder, or in private companies dominated by majority shareholders, the state agency concerned or majority shareholder look toward the subsidiaries as cash cows for ready milking, necessarily at the expense of the minority shareholders who do not have access to corporate resources.[5]

---

[1] See generally Chapter 1, section 1.5.

[2] Kraakman *et al.* (2009), p. 36.

[3] Tan and Wang (2007), p. 149. See also Mark Roe, *Strong Managers, Weak Owners: The Political Roots of American Corporate Finance* (Princeton University Press, 1994).

[4] Kraakman *et al.* (2009), p. 36.

[5] Tan and Wang (2007), p. 151.

As a partial solution to these agency problems, the 2005 Company Law, for the first time, officially unveils a framework of fiduciary duties 'resembling common law fiduciary duties'.[6] Like the major other jurisdictions, China has now adopted in its corporate law a mixture of rules and standards, under the umbrella of 'fiduciary duties', to minimize the 'agency costs' arising out of the separation of ownership and control. Not surprisingly, this has been regarded as a successful move to transplant an Anglo-American doctrine into Chinese law, as remarked by Professor Nicholas Howson:[7]

> [I]n October 2005 China introduced Anglo-American-style corporate fiduciary duties into the nation's corporate law. In addition, and as in the 1994 Company Law (but in a different article), the 2005 Company Law sets forth in accompanying Article 149 a number of bright-line prohibitions, violation of which would constitute breach of loyalty-type obligations.

For analytical purposes, it is useful here to distinguish between 'rules' and 'standards'. As Kraakman *et al.* (2009) point out:[8]

> The most familiar pair of regulatory strategies [in addressing agency problems] constrains agents by commanding them not to make decisions, or undertake transactions, that would harm the interests of their principles. Lawmakers can frame such constraints as *rules*, which require or prohibit specific behaviors, or as general *standards*, which leave the precise determination of compliance to adjudicators after the fact.

In the particular context of fiduciary duties, Cahn and Donald (2010) note that:[9]

> A 'standard of conduct' prescribes how a person should act to fulfill a function or task, and it operates as an open-ended measure against which the quality of performance can be assessed *ex post*. A 'rule', by contrast, names something specific that the management must do or not do. Standards flexibly adapt to acts and procedures that are not foreseen in their entirety when the standard is written, but standards can also create legal risks for directors because the scope of their requirements is often difficult to foresee. Rules, on the other hand, offer bright lines that are easy to apply, but for the same reason they can also be easy to evade – given that their parameters are clear

---

[6] Anderson and Guo (2006a) (noting that 'the Chinese framework [of management duties] appears to be patterned on common law concepts').

[7] Howson (2008), p. 198.

[8] Kraakman *et al.* (2009), p. 39 (emphases original).

[9] Cahn and Donald (2010), pp. 332–3.

and inflexible – unless they are arranged with sufficiently contiguous density, and often fail to account for changing circumstances.

7.2 FIDUCIARY DUTIES AS CODIFIED AND UNDERSTOOD IN CHINA

With Articles 148, 149, 150, 152, and 153, China appeared probably to be the first major jurisdiction that systematically – not yet entirely – confided the contents and enforcement of fiduciary duties.[10] Article 148 of the Company Law requires the senior personnel in a company to act in accordance with due care and loyalty: [11]

> Directors, supervisors and senior management executives shall abide by laws, administrative regulations and the corporate charter, and have a duty of loyalty (zhongshi yiwu) and duty of care (qinmian yifu) to the company.

This provision sets forth a general, statutory, standard of corporate fiduciary duties in China. Other than this, there are no general principles or guidelines to elaborate upon the contents of the standards of fiduciary duties. As Professor Nicolas Howson has observed with respect to the duty of care, 'the 2005 statutory formulation passes upon the opportunity to … articulate a specific *standard* for the duty of care prong, or any instruction to regulators or judges who might be employed as a "business judgment rule" for newly authorized duty of care inquiries'.[12]

An interesting comparison is the articulation of the general standard for directors' 'duty to promote the success of the company' in the UK Companies Act 2006, which reads:[13]

> Article 172 Duty to promote the success of the company
>
> (1) A director of a company must act in the way he considers, in good faith, would be most likely to promote the success of the company for the

---

[10] After the 2005 PRC Company Law, the United Kingdom codified its body of directors' duties in Part 10 of the Companies Act 2006.

[11] Company Law, Article 148, para. 1 (Chinese pinxin added). There is a similar general standard of fiduciary duty in Article 33 of the Code of Corporate Governance, which states, 'Directors should act in the best interest of the company and all the shareholders, performing their duties loyally, in good faith and diligently'.

[12] Howson (2008), p. 198.

[13] UK Companies Act 2006, Article 172(1).

benefit of its members as a whole, and in doing so have regard (amongst other matters) to

(a) the likely consequences of any decision in the long term,
(b) the interests of the company's employees,
(c) the need to foster the company's business relationships with suppliers, customers and others,
(d) the impact of the company's operations on the community and the environment,
(e) the desirability of the company maintaining a reputation for high standards of business conduct, and
(f) the need to act fairly as between members of the company.

One may easily notice the words such 'good faith', 'benefit', 'success', 'fairly', which feature a high degree of flexibility and uncertainty; all require clarification and interpretation in a specific context. Likewise, the duty of loyalty in the U.S. requires a director to act 'in the good faith belief that her actions are in the corporation's best interest'.[14] Flexible terminology like 'good faith', 'best interest', 'fair', 'reasonable', and 'adequate' also compels judicial interpretation. That is to say, in applying a standard of fiduciary duties, courts everywhere will always have to interpret the doctrine and terminology to determine, on the facts and context of each case, whether the standard was met.[15] China in theory is not an exception, but whether the Chinese judiciary is able to undertake such a task is an open question.[16]

Although it is overwhelmingly agreed that the doctrine of fiduciary duties in Chinese corporate law has its Anglo-American origins, it can also find part of its roots in Chinese civil law, which was styled after the Continental legal family. The majority view is that the relationship between the company and its directors, supervisors, and executives is based on an agency-based 'contract of mandate' (*weiren hetong*, officially called *weituo hetong* in the PRC Contract Law), in which the principal

---

14 *Stone, ex rel. AmSouth Bancorporation v. Ritter*, 911 A 2d 362, 370 (2006), cited in Cahn and Donald (2010), p. 344.

15 Cahn and Donald (2010), p. 343.

16 See below, Chapter 8 on judicial enforcement of shareholders' rights and management duties. See also Howson (2008), p. 202 (noting 'the application of fiduciary duties requires extraordinary flexibility and complex fact analysis, and thus a demanding level of technical competence among the judicial corps (or state regulator) wielding the doctrine').

and the agent agree that the agent will handle the principal's affairs.[17] Leading civil law textbooks in China have suggested that 'the mandatory [agent] shall perform the duty of care of a good manager [*shangliang guanli ren*] in contracts of mandate with remunerations'.[18]

Since the modern civil law system on the Chinese Mainland was, to a large extent, built upon the civil law of the Republic of China (ROC), which was systematically imported into China before 1949 and still applies and is evolving in Taiwan today, Chinese academic writing is accustomed to use laws, judicial decisions, and scholarly opinions in Taiwan to interpret concepts in contemporary PRC civil law. The above treatment of the mandatory/agent as a 'good manager' with a duty of care in Chinese textbooks on civil law is just such an example. Article 535 of the ROC Civil Code states, 'The mandatory who deals with the affair commissioned, shall be [acting] in accordance with the instructions of the principal and with the same care as he would deal with his own affairs. If he has received the remuneration, he shall do so with the care of a good administrator'.[19] Article 192 of the ROC Company Law, governing the legal relationship between the company and its directors, was largely derived from Article 535 of the Civil Code. It provides, 'The relationship between a company and its directors, unless otherwise stipulated in this law, shall be [understood] in accordance with the civil code stipulations for mandate (*weiren*)'.[20]

Since the doctrine of fiduciary duties has been formally introduced but the doctrine of 'mandate' is here to stay, it will be interesting to see how Chinese courts will reconcile the two in disputes on director/management duties. Some pragmatic academics and judges in China have optimistically – but probably mistakenly – understood the two as having the same result. After the PRC Trust Law, a much hailed but rarely used national basic law, was adopted in April 2001, they now have further reason to believe that the two doctrines can co-exist in China's corporate law. Article 25 of the Trust Law requires the trustee to 'be attentive to duties and perform his obligations honestly, trustworthily, prudently and effectively'. Professor Liu Junhai thus writes:[21]

---

17 PRC Contract Law, Article 396. Leading textbooks on civil law in China suggest that *weiren* and *weituo* mean the same and can be used interchangeably. See Wang Liming (2010), p. 483; Guo Mingrui (2007), p. 507.

18 Wang Liming (2010), p. 485; Guo Mingrui (2007), p. 508.

19 The bilingual versions of the ROC Civil Code were provided at the website of the ROC Ministry of Justice (http://mojlaw.moj.gov.tw).

20 Translation provided in Howson (2008), p. 203.

21 Liu Junhai (2011), pp. 506–7.

> The generally agreed view in our country is that the relationship between the company and its directors, supervisors and senior management executives is one of contractual relations based on *weituo* (*weiren*). The directors, supervisors and senior management executives should perform both the obligations conferred upon [them] by the Contract Law and the contract of mandate, and the obligations arising from the provisions in the Company Law and its special laws. Although the respective duties of the directors, supervisors and senior management executives are a bit different, they share the common duty of being honest, trustworthy, and diligent.
>
> The Anglo-American legal family usually relies on the concept of fiduciary duties to interpret the legal relationship between the company and its directors and senior executives. As our country adopted the Trust Law in April 2001 and the trust obligations stipulated in the Trust Law are higher than the obligations in the contract of mandate under the Contract Law, we could also use trust obligations to describe the relationship between the company and its directors, supervisors and senior executives in our country. Of course, no matter one uses the contract of mandate or the trust obligations to explain the relationship between the company and its directors, supervisors and senior executives, it will lead to the same result though from different paths. [In this sense], the two paths do not [have] fundamental differences.

The zeal to embrace fiduciary duties in Chinese corporate law, however, ignores a basic fact in the development of the duties in their origin countries: they are not just some plain and simple rules that could be easily copied from the statute book of one jurisdiction and pasted into that of another. Indeed, these rules and standards of great longevity were developed by courts over several centuries in Anglo-American jurisdictions, and, instead of being plain rules, they are embedded in a vast body of common law (case law), which is probably impossible to transplant into a civil law tradition. As Professor Paul L. Davies remarks, 'These rules for directors were developed by the courts at an early stage, often on the basis of analogy with the rules applying to trustees. The substantial corpus of learning on the nature and scope of these general fiduciary duties and duties of skill and care has remained until now largely within the common law'.[22]

Despite the incorporation of some of the rules of fiduciary duties into Chinese legislation, it is still an open question whether Chinese courts could apply these duties in a way that is roughly in line with both the fundamental principles and legal reasoning for applying such duties in their origin countries. As will be seen in later sections, Chinese courts, because of their lack of understanding of the common law in which the fiduciary duties are embodied, often resort to the traditional doctrines and legal reasoning in their own civil law system to interpret and apply the

---

22 Davies (2008), p. 477.

newly established 'fiduciary duties' in the PRC Company Law. Of course, there is probably nothing wrong with this per se, but eventually we will have a doctrine of fiduciary duties that are full of Chinese characteristics.

7.3 DUTY OF LOYALTY

An advantage of Chinese corporate law as the product of a civil law jurisdiction is that the legislators can freely – and almost exclusively – impose legal obligations on the 'subjects', i.e. actors of the society. A wide range of rules on management duties are now included in the Company Law and rules enacted by the CSRC and the stock exchanges.

7.3.1 Rules in the Company Law

First, paragraph 2 of Article 148 sets forth a general prohibition for all directors, supervisors, and senior management executives, which reads: 'Directors, supervisors and senior executives shall not take advantage of their positions and powers to collect or accept bribes or other illegal income, and shall not encroach upon the property of the company'. This is explicitly a statutory provision of a duty of loyalty that applies to the 'key players' inside a company, namely all the directors, supervisors, and senior management executives. It covers the typical conflicts of interest situations in a company. The key players, holding company offices, possess certain decision-making powers and also have unique access to company resources, information, and secrets. These key players will be subject to civil and/or criminal liability if they use their position to gain personally or to gain advantage for someone else with a view to seeking or accepting bribes or other illegal income. They are also prohibited from expropriating the company's property in any form.

In addition, under Article 142, all the key players in a JSLC are required to declare their shareholdings and report any changes. A one-year lock-up period applies to the key players who are not allowed to trade in their company shares within one year from the date the company was listed on a stock exchange. Shares transferred by a key player each year during his term of office may not exceed 25 percent of the total shares he owns in the company. His shares are also subject to a six-month 'freezing period', running from the date of his departure from the company during which no transfer is allowed. Further, the PRC Securities Law discourages the key players of a listed company from engaging in short-swing transactions.[23] If a key player engages in trading of their company shares within a span of six months, the earnings generated by the transaction will be disgorged to the company.

Article 149 of the Company Law provides a number of additional bright-line prohibitive rules, the violation of which would constitute breach of the duty of loyalty by only the directors or senior management executives (and not the supervisors). In essence, a director or senior management executive must not do the following under Article 149 of the Company Law and Article 97 of the Model Charter:

1. He shall not misappropriate the company funds, or deposit company funds in a bank account opened in his personal name or in the name of another individual.[24] Obviously this is flagrant stealing of corporate money and a plain breach of the director's or executive's duty of loyalty, which very likely will also lead to punishment of the wrongdoers under the PRC Criminal Law.
2. He shall not lend company funds to others or use company property as collateral to provide security for others, without the consent of the shareholders' general meeting or of the board of directors.[25] This especially refers to a director or executive who has the authority to dispose of corporate assets and uses this position to gain advantage for someone else, regardless of whether he has received anything in return. In the Chinese context, because a director does not have managerial rights unless he also serves as a senior management executive, such wrongdoing is most often committed by executives. Such a transaction could, however, be approved or ratified by either the general meeting or the board of directors.
3. He shall not enter into a contract or transaction with the company in violation of the corporate charter or without the consent of the shareholders' general meeting.[26] This provision covers the typical self-dealing transactions where the director/executive and the company are on opposite sides of the deal. Often such transactions are concluded on terms unfair to the company. In essence, the effect of an unfair transaction is the same as if the director or executive has appropriated the financial difference between the transaction's fair

23 PRC Securities Law, Article 47.
24 Company Law, Article 149(1) and (2).
25 Company Law, Article 149(3).
26 Company Law, Article 149(4).

value and the transaction's concluded price. But even if he can prove the 'fairness' of the transaction, it will still be voided by the court if the deal violated the corporate charter or was not approved by the general meeting. Such deals are often related-party transactions, whereby the controlling shareholder (or actual controller) of the company orders the company's board or management to sign and perform contracts preferential to the controlling shareholder but at the expense of the minority shareholders. In such a case, the controlling shareholder or actual controller, together with the directors or executives concerned, also violate Article 21 of the Company Law.

4. He shall not use his position to seek or seize, for himself or for other persons, commercial opportunities that belong to the company without consent from the general meeting.[27] This is apparently the Chinese version of the 'usurping corporate opportunity' doctrine, which prohibits the director or executive from seizing for himself or someone else desirable business opportunities that the company likely would have taken and profited from. The court will invoke the corporate opportunity doctrine only when the director's or executive's taking of the opportunity was not approved by the general meeting. It is not clear in the law what would be the consequence if the director/executive takes the opportunity for himself after presenting it to the company and the company declines to take it. It is, of course, likely that a wise court would interpret this as an 'approval' by the company.
5. He shall not operate for himself or any other person the same type of business as that of the company without the consent of the general meeting.[28] This is a statutory recognition of the non-compete clause in many private contracts. The directors and senior management executives are thus prohibited from pursuing a similar profession or business in competition against the company. Of course, as with other types of conflict of interests, disloyal competition may be approved or ratified by the general meeting of shareholders. It also refers to the situation where the director/executive is competing with the company while still on the payroll. Competition after the director or executive has ended his employment with the company is not governed by the Company Law. In fact, it might largely depend on whether the company has a

[27] Company Law, Article 149(5).
[28] Company Law, Article 149(5).

non-competition agreement with said director or executive. It is also important to note that this non-compete provision could be related to the corporate opportunity doctrine above, as the competitive business the director/executive runs might also be a desired opportunity for the company.

6. He shall not accept commissions for transactions between the company and other parties and turn them into personal gains.[29] This is to be distinguished from taking bribes referred to paragraph 2 of Article 148 of the Company Law. Here the other party in the transaction is understood to have no intention to bribe the director or senior management executive. He is assumed simply mistakenly to believe that the director/executive was a broker for the transaction who deserved the commission. It is not relevant whether the director/executive who pocketed the commission also held the same belief.
7. He shall not disclose company secrets without authorization. The unique decision-making and leadership position of the directors and supervisors provide them with access to all the key information and business secrets of the company.
8. He shall not harm the interest of the company in related-party transactions.

7.3.2 Disclosure Plus Consent

The above prohibitions could be generally classified into two groups, i.e. whether they are absolutely prohibited or could be approved/ratified. The director/executive is 'absolutely prohibited' from engaging in taking bribes, commissions, and other illegal income, expropriating company property, misappropriating company funds, or depositing the funds in the personal name of his or other individuals, harming company interest in related-party transactions, or arbitrarily disclosing confidential information. Other acts can be put into the 'approvable group' as they are conditional upon the in-advance-approval or after-the-fact-ratification of the board or the general meeting. That is to say, an act of the director or supervisor that otherwise violates the duty of loyalty may be validated if it is approved in advance or ratified afterward ('consent'). In line with the shareholder-centered nature of China's corporate law, all transactions with such conflict of interest must be approved by the general meeting with one exception: lending company funds to or providing security for

---

[29] Company Law, Article 149(6).

others may be consented to by the board of directors. Implicitly, to obtain the consent, a full disclosure of the nature of the conflict and material facts of the transaction to the general meeting or board would be necessary.

Conflicted interest transactions shall only be approved by disinterested holders of the voting rights. In the case the board's consent could suffice, it is important to note that, especially in listed companies, the board approval or ratification could only be passed by the majority of disinterested directors under Article 125 of the Company Law.[30] It has been suggested, however, that the court should adopt an 'expanded interpretation' of Article 125 and apply it to non-listed companies.[31] As noted above, most of such transactions must be approved by the general meeting. Similarly, interested shareholders shall recuse themselves under certain circumstances. Based on Article 16 of the Company Law, a company's investment in another enterprise or provision of security for others may be approved by either the board of directors or the general meeting. But if the company provides security for a shareholder or the de facto controlling person of the company, it must be approved by the general meeting in the form of a resolution.[32]

7.3.3 Legal Consequences for Violating the Rules

A violation of any of the prohibitive rules above might lead to the following legal consequences. First, all the gains (profit) as a result of the

---

30 See also Ch. 6, section 6.3.5 above.

31 Liu Junhai (2011), pp. 490–91.

32 Any other forms of company approval other than a formal resolution would be regarded as invalid by the courts. In *Weiyan Ltd v Xu Naihong and Others* (2006), the defendant, Mr. Xu, was a deputy general manager of the plaintiff, a Japanese-invested LLC. During his term of office at Weiyan Ltd, the defendant formed another company and served as the legal representative of the company, which had a similar scope of business to that of the plaintiff. The defendant argued that he was approved by the defendant's legal representative, in an approval letter that even carried the official stamp of the plaintiff, to serve as another company's executive director and general manager. The court, which was a basic court in Wuxi City, Jiangsu Province, ruled that Mr. Xu violated the duty of loyalty rule that a senior management executive of a company 'shall not operate for himself or any other person the same type of business as that of the company without the consent of the general meeting'. The approval letter signed by the company's legal representative together with corporate seal was not the same as a resolution of the general meeting. The facts and decision of the case were summarized and discussed in Huai Xiaofeng (2007), pp. 322–9.

violation shall belong to the company – that means the wrongdoer will have to disgorge such gains.[33] Second, the wrongdoer might be sued by the company or shareholders for damage under Article 150 of the Company Law. If the court invalidates the transactions, restitution will follow and the wrongdoer might also be ordered to return the corporate property he illegally possessed. In addition, the wrongdoer might be subject to administrative and criminal liability. In particular, a criminal offence for breaching the duty of loyalty was introduced by the National People's Congress by way of Amendment (VI) to the PRC Criminal Law in June 2006.

7.3.4 Lack of the 'Fairness' Factor

The disclosure and approval requirements above appear to be procedural in nature. A legalistic interpretation of the requirements will lead to the following understandings:

1. The courts will void any transactions in the 'absolutely prohibited group'.
2. The courts will dismiss a claim that challenges a transaction of the 'approvable group' if the statutorily required consent is obtained from the general meeting or the board, regardless of whether the transaction is fair to the company.
3. On the other hand, the courts will invalidate a transaction that is not approved or ratified by the board or the general meeting, regardless of whether the transaction is actually fair or not to the company.

This legalistic and rigid interpretation, which might very likely be adopted by courts in China, demonstrates a major loophole in the legal test under the duty of loyalty rules examined above. By contrast, under U.S. law, the director or executive concerned will avoid self-dealing problems if the conflict-of-interest transaction (1) was ratified by an impartial director approval or impartial shareholder approval and he disclosed the material facts to the board or general meeting; or (2) was proven to be basically 'fair' to the company.[34] That is, if the self-dealing transaction is found to be fair to the company, it will be allowed to stand by the courts. This is true whether or not the transaction was approved or ratified by the board or general meeting. However, it will not be a surprise if some Chinese courts opt for ignoring a rigid textual reading of

---

[33] Company Law, Article 149, para. 2.
[34] Cox and Hazen (2003), p. 210.

those disclosure and approval requirements as seen above with the view of determining the case based on the 'fairness' of the transaction. As we have demonstrated in some judicial cases in previous chapters, more than one Chinese court has avoided rigid application of vague text in the law by adopting a so-called 'expanded approach of interpretation'.[35]

7.4 DUTY OF CARE

7.4.1 General Standard

Apart from mentioning the duty of care in Article 148, the Company Law has neither a clear definition nor guiding principles as to how to understand this duty. One textbook in China defines it as follows:[36]

> The duty of care, also known as the duty of good management or duty of attention, means that the directors, supervisors and senior management executives shall exercise the rights granted by the company prudently, seriously and diligently, and act with the kind of prudence, care and diligence and skills that a reasonably prudent person would behave like under similar circumstances.

Other leading corporate law textbooks or treaties have adopted rather similar definitions.[37] There is little doubt this kind of definition was borrowed from American corporate law.[38] Indeed, § 4.01(a) of the ALI Principles of Corporate Governance has an almost identical provision about the duty of care: 'A director or officer has a duty to the corporation to perform the director's or officer's functions in good faith, in a manner that he or she reasonably believes to be in the best interests of the corporation, and with the care that an ordinarily prudent person would reasonably be expected to exercise in a like position and under similar circumstances'.

The Company Law does not define the basic standard of care and diligence. As noted above, China treats the legal relationship between the

---

[35] See e.g. Ch. 5 above.

[36] Zhou Yousu (2006), p. 391.

[37] See Liu Junhai (2011), p. 513; Shi Tiantao (2006), p. 401; Gan Peizhong (2007), p. 405.

[38] The leading textbooks noted above rely heavily on the relevant rules, concepts, principles and explanations in American corporate law to interpret the duty of care in Chinese Company Law. See Gan Peizhong (2007), pp. 405–7; Shi Tiantao (2006), pp. 400–403; Liu Junhai (2011), pp. 513–14.

company and its directors as one based on the contract of mandate, in which the mandatory must act with the duty of care of a 'good manager', although the specific requirements for a good manager have not been spelled out. Two judges of the PRC Supreme People's Court (SPC), in their academic writing, have boldly – but not surprisingly – suggested Chinese courts adopt the 'three criteria of the duty of care decided in the case law of Anglo-American countries', which are interpreted by them as the following:[39]

1. *Good faith.* The directors and executives must act in good faith, which is understood as a subjective standard. That is to say, whether the good faith standard is met depends on the mental state of the director or executive when he was committing the alleged wrongdoing. Here, an essential factor would be whether he understood the consequences of his action and had bothered take due care to ensure negative consequences would not ensue.[40]
2. *Care.* The director or executive should act as an ordinarily prudent person would reasonably do in a like position under similar circumstances. He would however need to exercise the necessary care of an expert if he does have such professional capabilities.[41]
3. *Reasonable belief that his action is in the best interest of the company.*[42]

One has no difficulty in discerning the similarities between the above standard and the one provided in ξ 8.30(a) of the Revised Model Business Corporation Act (RMBCA), which provides that, '[a] director shall discharge his duties as a director … : (1) in good faith; (2) with the care an ordinarily prudent person in a like position would exercise under similar circumstances; and (3) in a manner he reasonably believes to be in the best interests of the corporation'.[43]

---

39 Xi and Jin (2008), pp. 468–9.
40 Xi and Jin (2008), p. 469.
41 Id.
42 Id.
43 Note this provision has been replaced by ξ 8.30(a) of the new Model Business Corporation Act (MBCA), which simply requires a member of the board of directors to act '(1) in good faith, and (2) in a manner the director reasonably believes to be in the best interests of the corporation'.

7.4.2 Return to the Civil Law Doctrine of Tort Liability

It is, however, not difficult to discover a doctrinal misunderstanding in the two SPC judges' interpretation of the American duty of care. That is, the standard of care enumerated in the RMBCA is basically an 'objective one', rather than the 'subjective standard' understood above:[44]

> [T]he director will be held to the standard of care that would be exercised by a 'reasonable person' in the director's position. Consequently, a director who is simply less smart, less able or less innately diligent than an 'ordinary' reasonable director will nonetheless have to meet this higher ordinary standard.

The difference here may be only linguistic in nature. After all, the two judges' interpretation above also requires the director/executive to behave with the care an ordinarily prudent person in a like position would exercise, which was a literal reproduction of the relevant American corporate law rules in Chinese. 'Subjective standard', a rather peculiar expression, is used here to emphasize a key element in the Chinese doctrine of the duty of care as understood by the courts, which is the mental fault of the wrongdoers. In doing so, the application of fiduciary duties was casually translated into the application of the traditional doctrine of general tort liability that has long existed in Chinese civil law. In essence, a cause of action for general tort liability requires the following four key elements:[45]

- An infringing action (*jiahai xingwei*), which is essentially illegal and harmed the civil rights and interests of the injured. The action is characterized as 'illegal' to presume the presence of a duty. Harming others by breaching any laws, which is defined here in its broadest sense, would constitute an illegal action.[46]
- Injury (*sunhai shishi*) in the form of economic losses, or physical, mental, or emotional damage.[47]
- Causation (*yinguo guanxi*), which means it can be proven that there is a causal link between the injury and the infringing action.[48]
- Fault (*guocuo*), which means the infringer is at fault. Fault was the subjective mental state of the infringer when committing the

---

44 Emanuel (1997), p. 175.
45 Wang Liming (2004), pp. 834–53.
46 Id, p. 836.
47 Id, pp. 838–43.
48 Id, pp. 843–7.

infringing action, which could either be based on the infringer's intention or negligence.[49]

Not coincidentally, Judge Xi and Judge Jin explicitly stated in their academic writing that the duty of care liability would require the showing of the following four factors:[50]

- *Jiahai xingwei*: The director or senior executive violated laws, administrative regulations, or the corporate charter in their conduct of corporate affairs.
- *Guocuo*: The director or senior executive must be mentally at fault when he failed to meet the duty of care, which was a result of either intention or negligence.
- *Sunshi*: The company must have suffered financial losses, which include both direct and indirect losses.
- *Yinguo guanxi*: The losses suffered by the company must be caused by the breach of the duty of care.

It is fairly reasonable to say that the above view is the judicial practice in China. In *Xiangjia Ltd v Tai Jianying* (2007),[51] the defendant, Mr. Tai Jianying ('Tai'), was hired by the plaintiff in August 2004 as its manager. On 31 August 2005, Tai signed, on behalf of the plaintiff, a sale contract with Baiqiang Ltd in which the plaintiff was committed to provide goods worth RMB16,310 to Baiqiang. The contract was signed by the representatives of Baiqiang without affixing Baiqiang's corporate stamp. Tai left the plaintiff on 30 September 2005. The goods were delivered to Baiqiang but Baiqiang never made any payment to the plaintiff. The plaintiff, however, also never attempted to go after Baiqiang through litigation, arbitration, or any other effective means. In a beautifully written judgment, which linguistically constructed an accommodation of the common law duty of care and the doctrine of tort liability in Chinese civil law, the court ruled that:[52]

> Tai Jianying ('Tai'), as the company's hired manager in charge of business operations, should meet his obligations and conduct the company's affairs with diligence and care, otherwise he should be liable for the losses suffered

49 Id, pp. 847–53.

50 Xi and Jin (2008), p. 470.

51 The facts and decision of the case were summarized and discussed in Liu Lanfang (2009), pp. 432–5.

52 Id, pp. 433–4.

by the company. This liability would be established if the following four constituent elements were shown: (1) he violated laws, administrative regulations or the corporate charter in managing the company's business; (2) he was subjectively at fault; (3) the company suffered losses; and (4) there is a causal link between the violations and the losses suffered by the company. In the case in question, Tai's signing the contract and performing the contractual obligations on behalf of the company were actions that he had taken to execute his managerial duties in good faith, which did not violate any national laws, administrative regulations or provisions in the corporate charter. Baiqiang Ltd. was a legal person enterprise lawfully registered with the company registration authority, which had secured in its own name a contract for building a construction project. Xiangjia Ltd. could certainly benefit from the sale contract for supplying concrete to the project, and the payment of the price was also guaranteed to a certain degree. For these reasons, Tai had already exercised the due care required for an ordinarily prudent person in signing and performing the sale contract. As such, Tai should not be expected to be liable for any loss as a result of his actions above. Further, the economic loss which Xiangjia Ltd. had asked Tai to compensate was actually because Baiqiang Ltd. did not perform its obligation of making payment under the sale contract. [Under normal circumstances], Xiangjia should raise claims to Baiqiang in time after the payment was delayed. An economic loss would be incurred only when Xiangjia still could not get paid after it tried to pursue its claims through litigation, arbitration or other effective means. Since Xiangjia Ltd. had never raised any claim [against] Baiqiang, the economic loss claimed by Xiangjia had actually never been incurred. Furthermore, there is no direct causal link between Tai's above actions and Xiangjia Ltd.'s alleged loss. It is thus ruled that this court will not support the plaintiff Xiangjia Ltd.'s claims for compensation by Tai.

7.4.3 Rules on Duty of Care

Unlike the duty of loyalty, the duty of care does not have a list of specific rules in the Company Law. This task falls on the Model Charter, which imposes the following obligations on the directors:[53]

1. exercising the rights granted by the company prudently, seriously, and diligently to ensure that the company's business conduct complies with the requirements of national laws, administrative regulations as well as state economic policies and does not go beyond the scope of business as defined in the company's business license;
2. treating all the shareholders equally;

[53] Model Charter, Article 98.

3. familiarizing themselves on a timely basis with the business operation situations of the company;
4. signing a written confirmation of the regular reports of the company and guaranteeing the truthfulness, authenticity, and completeness of the information disclosed;
5. faithfully providing information and materials (as requested) to the supervisory board and not obstructing the supervisory board's exercise of powers and duties.

Although there is no systematic provision of rules on the duty of care in the law, certain legal provisions are worth mentioning as they may, arguably, require the directors or senior executives to perform functions in accordance with the duty of care. One such example is Article 151 of the Company Law, which obligates the directors, supervisors, or senior executives to attend the shareholders' general meeting upon request and take and answer inquiries from the shareholders. They also have the statutory obligation to assist the work of the supervisors by faithfully providing materials and information to the supervisory board or supervisor and may not obstruct the supervisory board from exercising their powers. As noted above, this obligation has been incorporated into the Model Charter as part of the key players' duty of care. A further mandate is in the SPC's Company Law Interpretation III, Article 13 of which indicates that the directors and senior executives are under a duty of care to collect the unpaid capital contributions from the shareholders concerned. If the directors and executives failed to urge the shareholders to perform their capital contribution obligations, the courts, upon the request of other shareholders, could order them to pay on behalf of those shareholders concerned.[54]

7.5 BUSINESS JUDGMENT RULE, OR THE LACK THEREOF?

There is no mention of the business judgment rule ('BJR') whatsoever in any of the corporate law legislations in China, but Chinese judges and scholars seem to truly like the rule and prefer to see it being applied in corporate litigation in China, although they have publicly admitted that the BJR was a creation of American corporate law.[55] For the purpose of

---

[54] Company Law Interpretation III, Article 13, para. 4.

[55] See e.g. Xi and Jin (2008), p. 476 (stating 'the business judgment rule is a legal institution created by American courts to exempt directors from bearing

comparison, a leading definition on the BJR in the ALI Principles of Corporate Governance is provided below:

> ALI Principles. ξ4.01(c): A director or officer who makes a business judgment in good faith fulfills the duty [of care] if the director or officer:
>
> (1) is not interested in the subject of the business judgment;
> (2) is informed with respect to the subject of the business judgment to the extent the director or officer reasonably believes to be appropriate under the circumstances; and
> (3) rationally believes that the business judgment is in the best interests of the corporation.

In essence, the BJR is a presumption that the directors or executives acted on an informed basis, in good faith and in the honest belief that the action taken was in the best interest of the company. The courts will thus not easily second-guess business decisions of the company and 'will abstain from reviewing board decisions unless those decisions are tainted by fraud, illegality, or self-dealing'.[56]

Chinese jurists' understanding of the BJR is largely in line with the above spirit. Immediately after the new Company Law was promulgated in 2005, two SPC judges, one of them being a Vice President of the SPC, published an article in the *People's Court Daily* to encourage Chinese courts to 'respect the principle of party autonomy in private law' and apply the business judgment in judicial resolution of disputes.[57] This article states, among things, that:[58]

> The key to the trial of corporate disputes by the people's courts is to stick to the principle of safeguarding the autonomy in private law, respect the self-governance and self-control of decision-making of the corporate bodies, and properly handle the relationship between lawful judicial interference and the company's self-governance … . A major problem of the [1993] Company Law is that it has left very little room for corporate self-governance, having the law to decide on both the big and trivial matters of the company. The practice has shown that making the law decide on everything is not only impractical but also impossible. The numerous differences in corporate activities necessarily mean that corporate governance could not follow the

liability for reasonable mistakes in business operation'. See also Liu Junhai (2011), pp. 517–18; Gan Peizhong (2007), pp. 411–13; Shi Tiantao (2006), pp. 403–8.

56 Bainbridge (2009), p. 109.

57 Li and Wang (2005).

58 Id.

> same pattern at all. For these reasons, the people's court, when stepping in to look at the internal legal relations inside a company, must be cautious enough to leave enough room for corporate self-governance. The people's courts should not substitute judicial power for the company's ordinary business judgment, but should instead respect the ordinary business judgment. Judges are not always able to make wise and fair decisions under all circumstances, even though they have the good will to do so. Generally speaking, a company's internal affairs should be carried out by the company in accordance with its charter. As long as self-governance does not pose barriers to transactional security and social stability, we should respect the companies to make decisions based on commercial considerations, respect their freedom in declaring intention and carrying out civil acts, and recognize the legal effect and corporate self-governance. The people' courts should intervene to replace the business judgment with judicial judgment only when issues relating to the health of the corporate structure or transactional security are concerned, such as that the controlling shareholders, directors or senior executives abuse the autonomy of private law and the freedom of carrying out civil acts and therefore harm the rights and lawful interests of the parties in corporate legal relations.

In Xi and Jin (2008), the judges advocated that the Supreme People's Court should enact a judicial interpretation to incorporate the BJR into Chinese law for three reasons:

> (1) The BJR is suitable for dealing with the complexities of business operation of the companies. As the company's scale expands its operation becomes increasingly complicated, and therefore it is impossible to expect the directors to make all decisions correctly.
> (2) The BJR is consistent with the nature of commercial decision-making. Market risks and uncertainties predetermine that business decisions cannot always only bring benefits to the company, and one simply could not predict in advance the negative consequences of a decision before it was made. If the requirement is that a business judgment should always be correct, the results would be that commercial opportunities will be missed, corporate operational efficiency will be reduced and the protection for the company and the shareholders will be undermined.
> (3) The BJR is consistent with nature of the operation of the corporate organs. It positively encourages the directors to be more risk-taking in business operation to bring value for the company and its shareholders.[59]

Despite influential SPC judges' enthusiastic embracing of the BJR, neither judicial interpretations nor typical cases related to the BJR have emerged in China. It is hence still an open question, from a doctrinal

---

[59] Xi and Jin (2008), p. 476.

perspective, how Chinese courts will consider the constituent elements of the BJR in judicial practice.

7.6 FIDUCIARY DUTIES OF SUPERVISORS

As noted previously, supervisors are also governed by the general standards of fiduciary duties provided in Article 148 of the Company Law. They are, however, explicitly excluded from Article 149, which provides a list of prohibitive rules on the duty of loyalty. This certainly does not mean that there are no prohibitive rules for the supervisors in this regard. More likely, the legislators meant to leave the corporate charter to provide the list. The specific rules could also be inferred from the supervisory powers provided in Articles 54 and 55 of the Company Law. The supervisors will be liable to the company if they failed to exercise their powers when they should do so.

7.7 LEGAL REMEDIES AND LIABILITIES FOR BREACHING FIDUCIARY DUTIES

Breach of fiduciary duties by the directors, supervisors, and senior management executives will lead to civil, administrative, and criminal liability under the corporate law, CSRC rules, or PRC Criminal Law.

7.7.1 Civil Liability in Corporate Law

The old 1993 Company Law was often attacked for giving shareholders' rights without providing remedies to enforce the rights (*you quanli wu jiuji*). In particular, it stipulated a limited range of duties for the directors, supervisors, and senior executives, but failed to name the consequences, the liability those key players should bear once the duties were violated. A significant improvement of the new 2005 Company Law is that it now provides not only the consequential liability for violating fiduciary duties but also the judicial avenues for enforcing those rights. The range of civil liability in the Company Law includes the following:

- The disgorgement by *directors or senior executives* of ill-gotten gains resulting from loyalty breaches (Article 149, paragraph 2);
- The liability to compensate the company for *losses* caused by *directors, supervisors, or senior executives* who, when discharging

corporate duties, violate PRC laws, administrative regulations or the corporate charter (Article 150).

- The liability of directors to compensate the company for *serious losses* caused by a board resolution they adopt which violated PRC laws, administrative regulations, or the corporate charter. In such a case, a director who is present at the board meeting when the resolution is passed is deemed to have 'participated' in adopting it unless he can prove that his objection to the resolution is entered in the minutes of the meeting (Article 113, paragraph 3).

The company and shareholders may seek judicial enforcement of the above civil liability through either direct or derivative actions. The procedures for direct and derivative actions will be examined in the next chapter.

7.7.2 Administrative Liability

Competent state authorities, such as the CSRC or SAIC (and its local counterparts), may implement administrative penalties against directors, supervisors, or senior executives if authorized by the law. The CSRC has a wide range of powers to impose fines and warnings against the key players in listed companies. A more significant power of the CSRC is career related. That is, it can ban the wrongdoers from 'entering the securities market'.[60] It will be illegal for a person under such a ban to engage in securities business or hold the position of a director, supervisor, or senior manager in any listed company.[61]

The CSRC sometimes can be rather stern in enforcing the administrative liability as can be seen in the unfortunate story of the retired Associate Professor Lu Jiahao. Lu was an independent director of Zhengzhou Baiwen Co. Ltd, a company that almost collapsed because of a corporate scandal created by its management. The CSRC, after an investigation that revealed that the company had inflated its profits by RMB19 million through falsifying financial documents, imposed administrative penalties on almost the whole board and management team, including Lu. Lu was condemned and fined RMB100,000 by the CSRC for being 'directly responsible' for the accounting fraud, implying that he

---

[60] See, generally, the CSRC Provisions on Banning the Entry into the Securities Market, promulgated on 3 March 2006.

[61] Id, Article 4.

violated his duty of care.[62] Lu later challenged the CSRC before courts in Beijing but his claim was dismissed for procedural reasons. Greatly feeling wronged, Lu, however, confessed to the media that he always treated the 'independent director' as an honorary title and never received any remunerations from the company. Of course, he also did not participate in the company's business operation, including meetings of the board.[63] Perhaps this was why the CSRC believed Lu had violated his duty of care to the company.

7.7.3 Criminal Liability

In June 2006, a new offense was added by the National People's Congress to the PRC Criminal Law, which reads:[64]

> Article 169-1. Where any director, supervisor or senior management executive of any listed company breaches his duty of loyalty and takes advantage of his corporate position to make the company undertake any of the following actions so that the listed company suffers material losses, he shall be sentenced to fixed-term imprisonment of not more than three years or criminal detention, and/or shall be fined; he shall be sentenced to a fixed-term imprisonment of not less than three years but not more than seven years and shall be fined in the case the company suffers extraordinary material losses:
>
> (1) providing funds, goods, services or any other assets gratuitously to any entity or individual;
> (2) providing or accepting funds, goods, services or other assets under obviously unfair terms;
> (3) providing funds, goods, services or any other assets to any entity or individual who obviously does not have the ability of repayment;
> (4) providing guarantee to any entity or individual who obviously does not have the ability of repayment, or providing guarantee to any entity or individual without justifiable reasons;
> (5) waiving any credit or undertaking any debt without justifiable reasons;
> (6) harming the interests of the listed company by any other means.
>
> The controlling shareholder or actual controlling person who instructs the director, supervisor or senior management executive to conduct any of the

---

[62] CSRC documents Zheng Jian Fa Zi [2001] 19 Hao, 27 September 2001.

[63] 'Huaping Dongshi Lu Jiahao Zhuanggao Zhengjianhui An' ('The Law Suit of Vase Director Lu Jiahao against the CSRC'), *Sina Finance,* available at http://www.sina.com.cn (accessed 12 March 2012).

[64] Amendment (VI) to the Criminal Law of the People's Republic of China, adopted by the Standing Committee of the National People's Congress on 29 June 2006, Article 9 (adding Article 169-1 to the Criminal Law).

> acts as described in the preceding paragraph shall be punished according to the preceding paragraph.

This offence, now designated as '*beixin sunhai shangshi gongsi liyi zui*' (the 'crime of breaching the loyalty duty to harm the interests of the listed company'), has been expected to serve as a deterrent to serious loyalty breaches. Conversely, even in corporate disputes involving civil liability only, the courts may rely on the above descriptions of loyalty breaches by treating them as statutory prohibitions in addition to those listed in Article 149 of the Company Law.

8. Shareholders' litigation

8.1 SHAREHOLDERS' RIGHTS TO SUE: DIRECT VS. DERIVATIVE SUIT

8.1.1 Advantages of Private Enforcement

As noted in the previous chapter, shareholders have now gained avenues under the Company Law to protect their rights and enforce duties of the management (including the directors, supervisors, and senior executives) through administrative actions, criminal prosecution, or civil litigation. The first two punish the wrongdoer, but generally do not provide compensation to the harmed shareholders. Civil litigation, known as private enforcement, enables shareholders to sue the wrongdoer before a court of law to seek damages. From a macro perspective, private enforcement appears to be more efficient and provide a more effective deterrent to violations of shareholders' rights. La Porta, Lopez-de-Silanes, and Shleifer (2006) also found that, by examining the securities laws of 49 countries, private enforcement is more positively correlated to financial development than public enforcement. For example, in relation to equity offerings, '[p]ublic enforcement plays a modest role at best in the development of stock markets. In contrast, the development of stock markets is strongly associated with extensive disclosure requirements and a relatively low burden of proof on investors seeking to recover damages resulting from omissions of materials information from the prospectus'.[1] One may certainly hold a different view about the macro impact of this, but one thing is clear from the shareholders' perspective: private enforcement – and probably only private enforcement – may help them and the company recover the losses suffered. By contrast, fines associated with administrative and criminal liabilities, no matter how large the amount, go to the state rather than the shareholders or the company. Needless to say, this gives the shareholders the strong motivation to bring legal actions against the wrongdoers if the legal procedures are not too complicated and costly.

---

[1] La Porta, Lopez-de-Silanes, and Shleifer (2006), p. 20.

Private enforcement is especially meaningful in the Chinese context as the effects of public enforcement have been discounted by a variety of factors. As Anderson and Guo (2006b) succinctly observe,

> Public enforcement resources are insufficient to identify and prosecute most violators. Furthermore, enforcement efforts by government agencies, such as the China Securities Regulatory Commission (CSRC) and the State Administration for Industry and Commerce, may be susceptible to political influence, local protectionism and other forms of corruption, and similar problems. To make matters worse, administrative and criminal penalties in China have not been severe enough to deter bad corporate governance practices in Chinese companies. The government is often reluctant to impose heavy administrative penalties on offenders for fear of negatively impacting the company's performance and criminal prosecution is only invoked in particularly serious circumstances. Potential violators may rationally choose to run afoul of the laws because the illicit gains they foresee are larger than the likely penalties.

It is thus hoped that 'the threat of shareholder lawsuits under the [2005] Company Law should render management and controlling shareholders less likely to seek illicit gains by violating corporate governance provisions'.[2]

8.1.2 Direct Suit vs. Derivative Suit

Under the Company Law two litigation techniques are now available to shareholders to vindicate their interests in the company, especially when fiduciary duties are breached by the key players in a company, such as the directors, supervisors, senior management executives, and sometimes even the controlling shareholders. The techniques are the direct suit and derivative suit rules designed for shareholders to bring legal actions against those key players in accordance with the Company Law.

Article 153 of the Company Law prescribes the rule for direct suits, which reads:

> In the event that a director or senior management executive violates the provisions of laws, administrative regulations or the corporate charter and harms the interests of the shareholders, the shareholders may bring a legal action in a people's court.

Article 153 thus permits a shareholder to sue in his personal capacity to ensure his rights as a shareholder. This happens when an act of the key players directly affects the shareholder. The cause of action belongs to

---

2 Anderson and Guo (2006b).

the shareholder in his individual capacity, which means the suit is not directly on behalf of the company and for the company's interest. For example, the shareholder may directly sue the directors or officers for the following reasons:

- to enforce his informational rights
- to compel payment of dividends declared but not distributed to him
- to compel the repurchase of his equity interest in the company under the circumstances prescribed in the Company Law
- to challenge the denial or dilution of voting rights
- to compel the holding of a shareholders' meeting
- to stop the management from engaging the company in an acquisition deal
- to compel dissolution of the company
- to redress the oppression of, or fraud on, minority shareholders
- to recover investment losses from wrongdoers in insider trading.

Thus the direct suit is a mechanism for shareholders to vindicate their own financial and limited participation rights in the company. Its general legal basis is the 'proper plaintiff rule' in Article 108(1) of the PRC Civil Procedure Law, which states, 'the plaintiff shall be a citizen, legal person or organization that has direct interest in the case'. 'Direct interest' is the Chinese expression of standing or *locus standi*. It does not deal with the situations in which the interests of the company, not those of the shareholders, are directly harmed. When the company sues, it must only be represented by its legal representative or a person appointed by the legal representative.[3] Shareholders are thus not entitled to bring a lawsuit in these cases, as they could not demonstrate to the court their own sufficient connection to and harm from the infringement actions. Individual directors, supervisors, and senior executives have fiduciary duties to the company.[4] When they encroach upon the property of the company, steal corporate funds, take kickbacks or bribes, transact with the company, or trap the company in unfair related-party transactions, the separate and independent legal personality of the company suggests it is the company whose interests are directly harmed and who should initiate a legal action against the wrongdoers before the court. Unfortunately, sometimes the company has no intention to pursue such an action, simply

---

3 PRC Civil Procedure Law, Article 49.

4 As clearly stated in Article 148 of the Company Law, the key players 'own the duty of loyalty and duty of care to the company' (*dui gongsi fuyou zhongcheng yiwu he qinmian yiwu*).

because the company is controlled by the directors or senior executives who have committed the wrongdoing, or by the majority shareholders who instruct the directors or executives to do so. Shareholders are indirectly affected, but they don't have the standing to sue under both Article 153 of the Company Law and Article 108 of the Civil Procedure Law.

In this sense, the introduction of derivative suits by the 2005 Company Law is a major breakthrough in the development of shareholders' protection in China. This peculiar form of action, embodied in Article 152 of the Company Law, permits an individual shareholder to bring suit, in the interest of the company, against the individual wrongdoer who has injured the interests of the company. Detailed rules of the Chinese mechanism for derivative suits will be examined in the following sections. Suffice it to say that, as Reisberg (2007) notes, since derivative suits 'operate to deter mismanagement by imposing the threat of liability [on the key players in the company]', they provide a strong incentive for key players to act in the interest of the company and the shareholders, so as to reduce agency costs and enhance corporate governance.[5] Further, from the perspective of private enforcement, derivative actions are practically the only legal tool possessed by shareholders to deal with insider wrongdoing. When insiders (the key players including the directors and senior executives) breach their duties to the company, the company itself will rarely take action against them as the company is actually controlled by the insiders. Giving shareholders the standing to sue the insiders is then the best choice to redress the injury to the company.

8.2 DEVELOPMENT OF SHAREHOLDERS' LITIGATION IN CHINA

8.2.1 Shareholders' Right to Sue: From the 1993 to 2005 Company Law

Before the recent development brought by the new Company Law, legal provisions concerning private enforcement contained in the 1993 Company Law were vague and rudimentary, and for all intents and purposes unenforceable. One terse provision, Article 111, provided the only legal basis for private enforcement. It allowed shareholders to bring a lawsuit

---

[5] Reisberg (2007), p. 23.

to 'enjoin such violation or infringement' if a resolution adopted by the shareholders' meeting or board of directors 'violates national laws or administrative regulations to infringe upon the rights and interests of the shareholders'.[6]

Due to its inherent defects, Article 111 was rarely relied upon by the courts to solve civil corporate disputes. The court, for a long time, took a much easier approach; it simply rejected almost all private enforcement initiatives.[7] For example, in the *Hongguang* case, a listed company committed serious misrepresentation in its initial public offering disclosure and subsequent disclosures, resulting in severe losses to thousands of investors. The China Securities Regulatory Commission (CSRC) sanctioned the company for its false disclosure. But when one investor launched a lawsuit in Shanghai in 1998 to recover her personal losses, her claim was dismissed by the courts five times from 1998 onward, chiefly on the grounds that the court did not have subject matter jurisdiction over such a case.[8] In the following years, hundreds of shareholders' suits were rejected by courts around China on the same or similar grounds. The real reason underlying the rejection was that the courts were not willing to adjudicate such cases in the absence of clear guidance from the statute and judicial interpretations.[9]

The 1993 Company Law also granted a wide range of powers to shareholders, many of them unknown to investors in Anglo-American jurisdictions. Those important powers, however, could only be exercised by the shareholders' general meeting, which reaches decisions on a majority or supermajority vote. Based on this, a dominant shareholder could have unfettered control over the assets and management of the company, exploiting the minority shareholders, who were introduced into the company as a result of the corporatization of traditional SOEs. In such a system, the controlling shareholder, the state, or its surrogate

---

[6] Article 111, 1993 Company Law.

[7] Here we do not refer to those disputes between shareholders such as share transfer cases.

[8] '"Zhongguo Zhengquan Minshi Jiufen Diyi An" Hongguang An Dacheng Tiaojie Xieyi' ('Hongguang case, "China's first securities civil dispute case", ended with an settlement agreement'), *Legal Daily* (China), 21 March 2003, available at http://old.chinacourt.org/html/article/200302/21/38309.shtml (accessed 22 January 2014). See also Anderson and Guo (2006b).

[9] Judge Li Guoguang, then a Vice President of the Supreme People's Court, once commented that 'it is difficult for the court to accept and try cases for which there is no applicable law'. See 'Li Guoguang Gaojie Touzizhe: Dui Susong Fengxian Yingyou Xinli Zhunbei' ('Li Guoguang warns investors to be mentally ready for litigation risks'), *Shanghai Securities Daily*, 10 January 2003.

companies established to hold shares in state-owned enterprises, did not need private enforcement. The minority shareholders, having little power in the corporate governance structure, were also denied access to private litigation, in order not to disrupt the state's control of the companies.

In stark contrast with the 1993 Company Law, the 2005 Company Law offers minority shareholders a host of legal remedies. Unlike the 1993 Law that allowed minority shareholders to seek an injunction but did not grant them civil remedies, the 2005 Law expressly requires the wrongdoer to pay 'compensation'. In particular, the 2005 Law significantly strengthens the shareholders' power to launch direct lawsuits against corporate directors and senior officers. It also introduces derivative actions into China's company law regime. Under Article 152, any shareholder of a limited liability company or shareholders of a joint-stock company holding more than 1 percent of the outstanding shares of the company for more than 180 consecutive days may bring lawsuits in their own name on behalf of the company against corporate directors, senior executives, or any parties infringing the rights and interests of the company.

The shift of the focus of shareholder protection – though partial only – from public enforcement to private enforcement represents arguably the single most important rule of law development in China's corporate law system. Judicial protection would enable minority shareholders to monitor the management in a more efficient way and ensure more careful and faithful corporate decisions. Compared with the 1993 Law, the new rules are clearer, more practical, and more enforceable, and thus more likely to bring about effective and just settlement of corporate legal disputes.

8.2.2 Judiciary in Shareholders' Litigation: From Passivity to Assertiveness

In the sense that access to the judiciary is an important mechanism to ensure that laws are effectively enforced and congruence is achieved, judicial resolution of disputes concerning shareholders' rights is an indispensable part of the rule of law in this area. As noted above, courts in China were initially cold to minority shareholders, refusing to adjudicate most of the cases filed. In 2001, a number of corporate scandals were discovered and investors rushed to courts for help. They were frustrated by the judiciary's reluctance to process securities litigation. In the wake of the formation of a wave of shareholders' lawsuits, the Supreme People's Court (SPC) issued on 21 September 2001 the famous (or infamous) notice requiring all lower courts not to accept securities lawsuits concerning insider trading, fraud, market manipulation, and the like, based on the 'constraints created by the current legislative and judicial conditions'.[10] A shock to investors, professionals, and scholars, the notice fueled much debate over China's commitment to the rule of law and the role of the Chinese judiciary in protecting investors' rights.[11]

The ban, although characterized as being 'temporary', was a strong move of the nation's top court and naked violation of the rule of law even by Chinese standards. It is an established rule of law principle in the civil law tradition that the court should not refuse to adjudicate simply because there is no current legislation applying to it.[12] Although this principle has not been expressed in such a way, it may be inferred from Article 108 of the PRC Civil Procedure Law, which provides, 'A lawsuit must meet the following conditions: (1) the plaintiff must be a citizen, legal person or any other organization, who has a direct interest in the case; (2) there must be a specific defendant; (3) there must be a concrete claim, a factual basis, and a cause for the lawsuit; and (4) the lawsuit must be within the scope of civil lawsuits to be accepted by the people's courts and within the jurisdiction of the people's court with whom the lawsuit is filed'. As long as the plaintiff satisfies the above conditions, there is no legitimate reason for the court to refuse to take the case.[13]

The reasons given by the SPC through several media interviews, however, suggest that the judicial ban was a rational and pragmatic decision. First, there was an issue of lack of judicial coordination. Investors would have to initiate different lawsuits against the same defendants across multiple jurisdictions, and different lower courts would almost certainly render conflicting rulings due to the absence of coherent criteria. Second, there was a concern about overloading the entire court system with securities litigation. Third, court leaders acknowledged the lack of experienced judges and the absence of a national uniform standard regarding evidentiary rules. Lastly, there was concern over

---

10 See Zuigao Renmin Fayuan Guanyu She Zhengquan Minshi Peichang Anjian Zanbu Shouli de Tongzhi (Notice of the Supreme People's Court on the Temporary Ban on Private Securities Lawsuits), Fa Ming Chuan, Court Doc. No. 406, 21 September 2001.

11 Chen Zhiwu (2003), p. 462.

12 An example is Article 4 of the French Civil Code, which provides, 'A judge who refuses to give judgment on the pretext of legislation being silent, obscure or insufficient, may be prosecuted for being guilty of a denial of justice'. Translation of Professor Georges Rouhette, available at http://www.legifrance.gouv.fr (accessed 12 April 2012). The same principle was also embodied in a decision of a court of Taiwan. See Liu Junhai (2011), p. 974.

13 Yao Hong (2007), pp. 164–6.

protecting state assets, fearing that the assets of the listed SOEs would be substantially stripped away by small investors.[14]

Four months later, a second notice by the SPC lifted the ban partially, allowing Chinese courts to accept private securities cases concerning misrepresentation. It sets up relevant judicial standards and a definition for 'misrepresentation', but confines a court's subject matter jurisdiction only to misrepresentation claims. Moreover, it preconditions judicial acceptance of these cases on the prior penalty report of the CSRC establishing the facts and evidence. Arguably, this breaches the principle of adjudication independence guaranteed by the PRC Constitution and was alleged to be a re-writing of the Securities Law enacted by the National People's Congress.[15] Nevertheless, a wave of lawsuits flooded the courts following the promulgation of this notice.

On 9 January 2003, the SPC released the most comprehensive judicial interpretation on misrepresentation cases to date, the Provisions Concerning the Adjudication of Civil Compensation Securities Cases Based upon Misrepresentation ('PSL Rules'). The Provisions are a response to requests from the legal community for more detailed procedures and substantive rules. Despite its many limitations (e.g. limiting claims to those based on misrepresentation and preconditioning private lawsuits on the prior investigation and administrative decision of a PRC government agency), this judicial interpretation has opened the door for private securities litigation in China. The issuing of three judicial interpretations within a short period of time demonstrates that, subject to resource – and sometimes ideological – constraints, the judiciary is becoming more assertive in protecting private shareholders.

The first adjudicated private securities lawsuit is the *Daqing Lianyi* case, the first instance judgment of which was issued by the Harbin Intermediate Court on 19 August 2004. An appeal by the defendants to the Heilongjiang Provincial High Court was dismissed on 21 December 2004. Daqing Lianyi (DL) was a listed company converted from an SOE. It was penalized by the CSRC in March 2000 for fraudulently overstating profits in its IPO prospectus and 1997 annual report. The ruling asked the defendant to pay a considerable amount of damages to the investors, and the underwriter was held jointly liable. As one commentator remarked, despite the strong stereotype of the Chinese judiciary as weak and lacking independence, 'the Heilongjiang High Court has demonstrated a great degree of independence by ruling boldly against a listed company.

---

14 Wang Jiangyu (2004), p. 43.
15 Chen Zhiwu (2003), p. 466.

In addition, the judges have shown a considerable level of judicial competence and innovation in handling this unprecedented private securities litigation case. It may, therefore, be envisaged that in future, local courts will play a more significant role in shaping the evolution of law in China'.[16]

Recent developments suggest that the SPC was ready to completely lift the ban on securities litigation. In practice, since June 2007, courts in China had already begun accepting investors' lawsuits for other types of corporate and securities fraud, following a speech of SPC Vice President Xi Xiaoming, which called for judicial trial of those relevant cases by reference to the principles and procedures of the PSL rules.[17] The SPC, with the help of the CSRC, is in the process of drafting new judicial interpretations on securities litigation concerning other types of market fraud. These judicial interpretations, together with the private enforcement rules in the Company Law, will form a rather comprehensive and complete framework for shareholders' litigation in China.

8.3 PROCEDURAL RESTRICTIONS IN DERIVATIVE LITIGATION

8.3.1 Umbrella Provision

The mechanism for derivative suits is chiefly provided in Article 152 of the Company Law, which, over the years, has been supplemented by and elaborated upon by SPC interpretations, court decisions, and the writing of judges and influential scholars. It is useful to reproduce the long and awkward-sounding Article 152 here:

> If a director or senior management executive is in the circumstances specified in Article 150 [of the Company Law] hereof, the shareholders in the case of a limited liability company, or the shareholders, in the case of a joint stock limited company, who hold one percent or more of company shares individually or aggregately for more than 180 consecutive days, may request in writing the supervisory board or the supervisor (in the case of a limited liability company without a supervisory board) to file a lawsuit with a

---

[16] Xi Chao (2006b), p. 496.

[17] Zhengquan Minshi Peichang Qiaoran Quanmian Jiejin, Neimu Jiaoyi Deng Jiangbei Li'an ('The Ban on Securities Civil Litigation was Silently Lifted, and Insider Trading and Other Civil Lawsuits will be Accepted'), *Caijing Online*, 2 September 2007, available at http://www.caijing.com.cn (accessed 22 January 2014).

> people's court. If a supervisor is in the circumstances specified in Article 150 hereof, the aforementioned shareholders may request in writing the board of directors or the executive director (in the case of a limited liability company without a board of directors) to file a lawsuit with a people's court.
>
> If the aforementioned supervisory board, supervisor, board of directors or executive director refuses to bring a lawsuit after receipt of the written request of the shareholders as specified in the preceding paragraph, or fails to bring a lawsuit within 30 days of the date of receipt of the request, or if the matter is urgent and the company will suffer irrecoverable losses if a lawsuit is not instituted at once, the shareholders specified in the preceding paragraph shall have the right to bring a lawsuit in a people's court directly in their own name in the interests of the company.
>
> If any other person infringes upon the lawful rights and interests of the company and thereby causing losses to the company, the shareholders specified in Paragraph One of this Article may bring a lawsuit in a people's court in accordance with the provisions of the preceding two paragraphs.

Obviously, a shareholder who wishes to initiate a derivative suit must satisfy a number of procedural requirements. Those related to the cause of action, the plaintiff's standing to sue, status of the company in the lawsuit, demand on board, and litigation expenses will be examined in the following sections.

8.3.2 Cause of Action

The cause of action for statutory derivative suits against directors and senior executives is provided in Article 150 of the Company Law, which states: 'If a director, supervisor or senior management executive violates the provisions of laws, administrative regulations or the corporate charter in his performance of duties relating to his position in the company, thereby causing losses to the company, he shall be liable for compensation'.

Article 150 covers a wide range of duties of the key players, including, but not limited to, their fiduciary duties of loyalty and due care provided in Articles 148, 149, and other relevant rules.[18] Generally speaking, Article 150 establishes a fault liability in tort law, under which the key players shall make compensation when '(1) there must exist the fact that the company is injured; (2) the injury must be the result of the wrongdoer's acts of breaching of the provisions of the laws, administrative regulations and the corporate charter in his execution of company

---

[18] For detailed discussion of fiduciary duties see Ch. 7 above. See also An Jian (2005), p. 216.

duties [which includes certainly the breach of fiduciary duties]; (3) there must be a causal link between the illegal acts and the injury; and (4) the wrongdoer must be at fault, which means he was either intentional or negligent in performing the harming acts'.[19] A textual reading of Article 150, however, suggests 'a derivative action should not be allowed against directors, supervisors and/or senior officers if they caused losses to the company while not in the course of performing company duties'.[20]

Paragraph 3 of Article 152, which offers shareholders the right to launch derivative suits against third parties, might cause confusion in practice. Since any third party other than the directors or senior executives could harm the interests of the company in various ways, 'any other person' might be broadly construed to be the company's controlling shareholder, a creditor who refuses to perform on a contract signed with the company, or an outsider who has inflicted harm upon the company. If the company refuses to sue, the shareholders, subject to fulfilling the preconditions examined below, can sue in the interest of the company. Insofar as the controlling shareholder is concerned, paragraph 3 should be read together with Articles 20 and 21 of the Company Law, which provide, respectively, that the shareholders, including the controlling shareholder, should be liable to compensate the company for any losses caused by their abuse of their limited liability and the company's independent legal personality or by their misconduct in related-party transactions.

An interesting question is whether the plaintiff should manifest the legal action as a 'derivative suit' in the complaint. Given the existence of the preconditions for initiating the derivative suit (which will be examined below), the court is supposed to conduct a screening of the pleadings to make sure the preconditions are satisfied. But the courts could be flexible sometimes. In *Dongfeng Automobile Trading Ltd and Inner Mongolia Automobile Building Factory v Inner Mongolia Wuzi Group Ltd et al.* (2007),[21] a case finally decided by the SPC, the plaintiffs, minority shareholders of a company, seemingly filed a direct suit against the company's controlling shareholder, chairman of the board of directors, and general manager, alleging that they sold the major assets of the company to a related party at a price tremendously below the

---

19 An Jian (2005), p. 216.

20 Li Xiaoning (2007), p. 286.

21 SPC Doc. No. Zuigao Renmin Fayuan (2007) Min Yi Zhong Zi Di 49 Hao. The facts and court decisions at the first-instance and appellate levels are summarized and discussed at Wu Qingbao (2010), pp. 253–74 (hereinafter the *Dongfeng Automobile* case).

market value of the assets. The defendants pointed out the plaintiffs, being merely shareholders, had no standing to sue. This view was supported by the Provincial Higher Court of the Inner Mongolia Autonomous Region, but was reversed by the SPC. The SPC, without even mentioning the fact that the plaintiffs filed procedurally a direct suit, ruled that because the complaint met all the procedural requirements for derivative actions, it should be treated as a derivative suit.[22]

8.3.3 Eligible Plaintiff-shareholders and their Standing to Sue

The plaintiff-shareholder in a derivative suit is a self-appointed representative for the company. Although the shareholder sues in the interest of the company (*wei gongsi liyi*), he must file the suit in his own name (*yi ziji de mingyi*) and serve as the named plaintiff in the suit. He cannot even claim that he does this on behalf of the company as there is no way he could be given a power of attorney by the company.

If many shareholders wish to launch derivative suits against the company, the board and management will be overloaded with lawsuits and may not have much time to spend on managing the company's business affairs. This might be a manageable situation in LLCs as their shareholders are capped at 50.[23] Such generosity, however, cannot be taken for granted by the shareholders of JSLCs, as there are simply far too many of them. Thus a contemporaneous ownership requirement is imposed upon JSLC shareholders should they wish to initiate derivative suits.

The contemporaneous ownership requirement in Article 152 is basically a rule of standing, under which the shareholders may not commence a derivative action unless they are shareholders owning at least 1 percent of the company's total shares at the time the suit is filed. Moreover, the holding period of the shares must be at least 180 consecutive days. According the SPC's Company Law Interpretation I, this means the plaintiff-shareholders must have already owned those shares, either individually or aggregately, for 180 or more days uninterruptedly when the derivative proceedings were instituted.[24] However, neither the Company Law nor the SPC interpretation mentions whether the plaintiff should also be a shareholder at the time the cause of action arose. Judges

---

22 Wu Qingbao (2010), p. 266.

23 See Huang Hui (2007), p. 237 (discussing the reasons why the law was less restrictive about derivative suits launched by LLC shareholders).

24 Company Law Interpretation I, Article 4.

Xi and Jin, in their academic writing, argue for the continuous ownership requirement:[25]

> We are of the view that our country should adopt the principle of shareholding at the time [of the transactions] to qualify the plaintiff's shareholder status. If the plaintiff is a shareholder when the lawsuit was filed, he may not bring a derivate suit for the illegal actions or resolutions of the company before he became a shareholder. He could only sue for tortious acts or illegal resolutions [which] occurred after he became a shareholder.

It is, however, submitted that this interpretation has no legal basis in the corporate law legislations. Apart from the contemporaneous ownership requirement for the plaintiff's shareholder status at the time the suit is filed and the 180 days' holding period requirement, there is no rule requiring the plaintiff also be a shareholder at the time the illegal actions took place. A textual reading of the relevant rules would lead to the conclusion that the plaintiff does not need to be a shareholder at that time but he must still prove he suffered losses caused by the wrongdoers' action even though he was not a shareholder then.

Notably H-share holders have been carved out of the derivative action regime under a series of special arrangements, which, ironically, were meant to afford better legal protection to those shareholders. H-shares are shares issued by companies incorporated in Mainland China that are listed and traded on thc Stock Exchange of Hong Kong (SEHK).[26] H-share companies have to comply with certain portions of the company ordinance and securities regulations and listing rules of Hong Kong, but they are also bound by PRC law. The Chinese authorities issued in August 1994 a special model corporate charter for H-share companies, which is entitled the Mandatory Provisions for Articles of Association of Companies to be Listed Overseas ('Mandatory Provisions').[27] As the name of the model charter suggests, these provisions are mandatory for H-share companies. In particular, Article 163(1) of the Mandatory Provisions requires that a dispute or claim concerning company affairs between the company and its foreign capital shareholders (e.g. H-share

---

25 Xi Xiaoming and Jin Jianfeng (2008), p. 302.

26 Wang Jiangyu (2009), p. 387.

27 Dao Jingwai Shangshi Gongsi Zhangcheng Bibei Tiaokuan, promulgated by the State Council Securities Commission (SCSC) and the State Commission for Restructuring of the Economic System (SCREC). The SCSC was the predecessor of the CSRC. The SEREC was abolished but part of its powers and functions are exercised by the National Development and Reform Commission (NDRC) today.

holders), between the foreign capital shareholders and the company's directors, supervisors, and executives, or between the foreign capital shareholders and domestic capital shareholders (e.g. PRC national shareholders based in Mainland China) must be submitted to arbitration by the parties concerned. The arbitral award shall be binding upon the company, shareholders, directors, supervisors, managers, and other senior executives. This provision, if still viewed as good law, will exclude H-share holders from bringing derivative actions in a PRC court and thus put them in a less favorable position vis-à-vis shareholders of the same company in Mainland China.[28]

8.3.4 Status of Company in Derivative Litigation

The status of the company in the derivative suit is a matter of formality only, since the suit is essentially one conducted between the plaintiff-shareholder and the wrongdoing directors, executives, or third parties. It only matters when the court decides how to express the title of the judgment. Thus a judgment in the form of 'Shareholder vs. Director and Company' entails that the company is made a defendant by the court, and 'Shareholder and Company vs. Director' means the company is treated as a plaintiff. The company might also be joined as the third party by the courts in some cases.

The Supreme Court of China took a rather open attitude to the position of the company in derivative actions. In *CAS Institute of Software and Xiangtou Group Ltd v Zhongke Software Group Ltd* (2006),[29] the SPC reasoned that, in indirect suits such as derivative actions, the plaintiff-shareholders were actually exercising the company's own right to sue. The company does not need to participate in the litigation, but it might choose to participate. In the case where the company was willing to take part in the litigation, as its status was indeed a complicated and controversial question, the court was of the view that 'people's courts

[28] One could, however, argue that Article 163(1) of the Mandatory Provisions is no longer good and hence should not be invoked as a bar to H-share holders' initiation of derivative suits for two reasons: (1) the new derivative suit rules in the 2005 Company Law, since they were made much later in time, should override Article 163(1); and (2) the constitutionality of Article 163(1) as a rule of law becomes questionable after the 2005 Company Law came into being since the ministries of the State Council do not have the authority to make any rules to contravene national laws.

[29] SPC Doc. No. (2006) Min Er Zhong Zi Di 227 Hao. The case is reported in SPC Civil Division II (2011a), pp. 311–17.

may define the status of the company in the litigation based on the actual situations of the cases', although the SPC indicated clearly that it did not prefer to see the company treated as a defendant.[30]

8.3.5 Preconditions: Demand and Board Control of Derivative Litigation

Given that a derivative suit is about the interests of the company and the recovered money – if any – will also go to the company, it is only logical that the company should be given an opportunity to review the claim and decide whether to bring suit before a shareholder is allowed to launch a derivative action. Article 152 thus provides that shareholders may not file a derivative suit unless they first make a demand on the board of directors or the supervisory board. The demand requirement entails the following specific rules:

1. A demand should be made on the supervisory board (or the supervisor in an LLC without a supervisory board) if the shareholder sues the directors or senior executives.
2. A demand should be made on the board of directors (or the executive director in an LLC without a board of directors) if a supervisor is the named defendant in the suit.
3. The supervisory board (or supervisor) or the board of directors (or the executive director) on whom the demand is served has 30 days to respond after receiving the demand. If they decide not to proceed with a lawsuit, the shareholder is then entitled to bring a derivative suit.
4. The demand is excused if the matter is urgent and a delay in lodging a lawsuit would cause irreparable injury to the company.

Although the demand requirement is procedural in nature, Chinese courts have been treating it as a substantive rule in derivative litigation. That is, the courts are rather stringent about requiring the plaintiff to fulfill the preconditions. In *Xu Hongwei v Beijing Printing Group Ltd* (2007),[31] the plaintiff, a minority shareholder, filed a derivative action against the controlling shareholder. The plaintiff-shareholder alleged that, because the company, under the defendant's instructions, had moved the major

[30] Id, p. 316.

[31] Beijing Number One Intermediate Court Doc. No. (2007) Yi Zhong Min Chu Zi Di 1273 Hao. The facts and court decision of the case are summarized and discussed in Liu Lanfang (2009), pp. 375–82.

assets of the company from its registered place of business, an urgent situation had thus emerged, and so there was no longer the need for him to fulfill the preconditions by making a demand on either board. The court unhesitatingly dismissed the claim on the grounds that the plaintiff was not able to prove that the situation was 'urgent enough' to waive his having an obligation to meet the preconditions of Article 152 of the Company Law.[32] In *Hantang Co. v Chen Shihua, et al.* (2006),[33] the first derivative suit involving a foreign party tried by the Beijing Number Two Intermediate Court after the 2005 Company Law took effect, the plaintiff, a major shareholder of a company, sued three directors of the company, alleging that they defrauded the company in a related-party transaction. Although the factual elements of fraud were quite clear, the court nevertheless quickly dismissed the plaintiff-shareholder's claim on the grounds of its failure to meet the preconditions of making a demand.[34]

8.3.6 Litigation Expenses

As previously noted, the nature of derivative litigation decides that any recovered money, if the plaintiff-shareholder wins, runs to the company. The sole benefit the plaintiff-shareholder could expect to receive is the increase in share price resulting from the recovery. Of course, it is unlikely that the plaintiff will sue for money – he may simply only wish to undo the harmful behavior of the directors and improve the management and governance of the company. The question is, if the plaintiff-shareholder has won the derivative suit, will he even be reimbursed the expenses that many believe he deserves since he has just undertaken the effort and expense of a lawsuit to defend the interests of the company? Unfortunately, there is no mention of this issue in the Company Law and related regulations. The usual Chinese rule is that the losing party will be ordered by the court to pay for the winning party's 'case acceptance fee', which is the fee charged by the court that tries the case,[35] but each party pays its own attorney fees and other expenses. In any event, there are no national rules in China's corporate law providing for payment of the

---

32 Id, p. 380.

33 Beijing Number Two Intermediate Court Doc. No. (2006) Er Zhong Min Chu Zi Di 03768 Hao. The facts and court decision of the case are summarized and discussed in Liu Lanfang (2009), pp. 382–7.

34 Id, p. 384.

35 See Susong Feiyong Jiaona Banfa [Administrative Measures on Payment of Litigation Fees], adopted by the State Council on 8 December 2006, effective as of 1 April 2007, Article 29.

plaintiff's legal fees by the company in derivative litigation. Understandably, this could become a strong disincentive for potential plaintiff-shareholders to launch derivative suits.

Local courts have appeared to be more proactive in awarding reimbursement for successful plaintiff's legal fees. Even before the 2005 Company Law took effect, the provincial higher courts of Jiangsu and Shanghai had made rules for indemnifying the plaintiffs in derivative litigation. The Jiangsu court rules provided 'that in derivative actions if the court supports the plaintiff's derivative claims, reasonable litigation fees such as the attorney's fees and travel costs should be borne by the company; if the court does not support the derivative claims, the litigation costs should be paid by the plaintiff shareholder; if the court partly supports the claims, the plaintiff shareholder and the company should bear the costs pro rata'.[36] One may hope that someday the SPC might incorporate these obviously American-born rules into a nationally applicable judicial interpretation.

8.4 DERIVATIVE SUITS AGAINST THIRD PARTIES (INCLUDING CONTROLLING SHAREHOLDERS)

Pursuant to paragraph 3 of Article 152, a shareholder may bring suit against 'any other person' who has harmed the company's interests and caused its losses. As noted previously, any other person could be construed to refer to a controlling shareholder, a creditor, or any third party that has done injury to the company. For example, the SPC judicial interpretation on administrative litigation provides that an investor in a foreign-invested enterprise (FIE) may sue the government in its own name if it believes that the FIE's rights or interests were harmed by the administrative actions of the government.[37]

In many cases the third party is the controlling shareholder or actual controlling person of the company. When a derivative claim involves a controlling shareholder, the courts will have to apply the Company Law's two substantive rules on shareholders' obligations. Article 20 mandates that 'If a shareholder of the company abuses his shareholder's rights, thereby causing losses to the company or other shareholders, he shall be

[36] Quoted in Li Xiaoning (2007), p. 297.

[37] Zuigao Renmin Fayuan Guanyu Zhixing Zhonghua Renmin Gongheguo Xingzheng Susongfa Ruogan Wenti De Jieshi [SPC Interpretations on Several Issues Concerning the Application of the PRC Administrative Litigation Law], promulgated and took effect on 10 March 2000, Article 15.

liable for compensation'.[38] Article 21, targeted particularly at the key players in a company such as the controlling shareholder, actual controlling person, directors, supervisors, and senior executives, provides that these key players shall not harm the interests of the company in related-party transactions; otherwise, they are liable for the damage caused.

An interesting question is to whom the demand is to be submitted if a minority shareholder wishes to bring a derivative suit against the controlling shareholders. According to Article 152, the plaintiff-shareholder should make a demand on the supervisory board (or the supervisor) in the case where a director is the named defendant, and on the board or directors (or the executive director) if a supervisor is the defendant. The law does not say who should be given the demand when the controlling shareholder is sued. In *Zhejiang Hexin et al. v Guangxia Holding Ltd* (2007),[39] a written notice was sent by the would-be plaintiff-shareholder 'to the company' generally, addressed to neither the supervisory board nor the board of directors. The Zhejiang Provincial Higher Court ruled that, since the written notice had been circulated among all the senior executives and discussed by the directors and supervisors, the preconditions were regarded as having been met.[40] Later, an SPC judge, in an academic commentary on this case, indicated that, if the controlling shareholder was sued, the proper corporate organ on whom the demand should be made was the board of directors. As long as a notice was served on the board of directors and the board refused to bring a legal action, the shareholder-plaintiff should be able to launch the derivative suit.[41]

8.5 DEFICIENCIES OF CHINA'S DERIVATIVE LITIGATION MECHANISMS

The introduction of derivative suits in the 2005 Company Law was a major breakthrough in the development of shareholder protection laws in China. Shareholders, especially the minority ones, have thus acquired a useful weapon to hold wrongdoing corporate insiders liable. At this stage,

---

[38] Company Law, Article 20, para. 2.

[39] Zhejiang Higher Court Doc. No. (2007) Zhe Min Er Chu Zi Di 5 Hao. The facts and court decision of the case are summarized and discussed in Wu Qingbao (2010), pp. 242–52.

[40] Id, p. 246.

[41] Id, p. 250 (comments of Judge Du Jun).

it is premature or even naïve to talk about 'disadvantages', such as the possibility of abuse or excessive use of derivative suits by shareholders. In a country that does not have a long and strong tradition of protecting minority shareholders, the top priority should be nurturing as many good investor protection mechanisms as possible.

That said, it is important to point out several intriguing deficiencies of the derivative suit rules in Chinese law. The first is an obvious contradiction that looks technical on the surface but may be caused by problems deep underneath. On the one hand, the lack of indemnification rules for the plaintiff's legal expenses could have strong deterrent effects and prevent potential plaintiff-shareholders from engaging in derivative litigation. On the other hand, board control of derivative litigation is rather weak under the Company Law. A demand on the board constitutes a mere procedural obstacle that is easy to overcome. The language of Article 152 with respect to the demand requirement 'suggests that as long as the company itself refuses to bring an action, the shareholder will be able to bring the derivative action, regardless of the reasoning behind the company's decision'.[42] Under Article 152 the court also does not seem to have the power to dismiss a derivative claim on grounds other than non-compliance with the procedural preconditions. By contrast, in other jurisdictions such as Australia and the U.S., the court is given the power to apply the business judgment rule to review the merit of the case and decide whether the derivative suit can proceed or be terminated.[43]

A further concern is about the capabilities and impartiality of the courts in China. One commentator has described the popular and conventional perception of the Chinese judiciary as follows: 'China's weak legal infrastructure, lack of precedent, and lack of knowledge by the courts on these corporate topics make lawsuits a very slow and likely unsuccessful choice. If the threat of a lawsuit is minimal, then the deterrent effect on fraudulent behavior by senior management and the [board of directors] is also very unlikely'.[44] Anecdotal evidence, as seen from some of the corporate disputes tried by Chinese courts, might suggest that this is rather overgeneralized and unfair criticism, even though one admits the problems of the Chinese judicial system, typical characteristics of an emerging economy. On the other hand, optimists may take comfort from the 'new analytic framework for understanding and promoting judicial independence in China' developed by Professors

---

42 Huang Hui (2007), p. 244.

43 Id, pp. 245–6.

44 Trifiro (2007), p. 292.

Fu Yulin and Randall Peerenboom, which argues that although Chinese courts were biased towards the government in political cases or politically sensitive cases, they appeared to be more neutral and impartial in economic and civil cases.[45]

[45] Fu and Peerenboom (2010), p. 120 (stating 'there is a greater role in economic matters for commercial and administrative litigation'). See also generally Howson (2010a).

9. Offering and trading of shares in joint-stock limited companies

9.1 THE CONCEPT AND CLASSIFICATIONS OF SHARES IN CHINA

9.1.1 Forms of Shares

The term 'share' or 'share of stock' could refer to either *gufen*, one of the equal units of capital in a company, or *gupiao*, which simply means the share certificate. A joint-stock limited company (JSLC) is required by the Company Law to divide its capital into such equal units, or shares.[1] A limited liability company (LLC) does not need – and is not required by the law – to issue shares. It can instead state the percentage of each shareholder's equity interest in the shareholders' agreement and the corporate charter.

Although the issuance of shares in China became an electronic process featuring paperless and digitalized transactions a long time ago,[2] the Company Law still defines *gupiao* or share certificate as if we were still in the age of paper-based transactions. Thus, 'the shares of a company shall take the form of share certificates, which are vouchers issued by the company to certify the shares held by their holders'.[3] Further, 'share certificates shall be in paper form or other forms prescribed by [securities regulatory authorities]'.[4] A share certificate 'shall clearly state the following particulars: (1) the name of the company; (2) the date of establishment of the company; (3) the class and face value of the share certificate and the number of shares it represents; and (4) the serial

1 Company Law, Article 126.

2 The Shanghai Stock Exchange (SSE) started completely digitalizing transactions for stock trading in May 1991, making China one of the first stock markets to abandon paper-based transactions. See Lu Yi (2011). See also CSRC (2008), p. 15.

3 Company Law, Article 126, para. 2.

4 Company Law, Article 129, para. 1.

number of the share certificate'.[5] In the age when securities issuance and trading are fully computerized, one would wonder to what extent these rules still make sense.

A company may issue either registered shares (*jiming gupiao*) or bearer shares (*wujiming gupiao*). However, the Company Law mandates that shares issued to promoters and legal person shareholders of the company must be registered shares and those shares must be held by the real owners who are prohibited from using a 'street name' to hold the shares.[6] Companies that issue registered shares are required to establish a register of shareholders to record (1) the name and domiciles of the shareholders, (2) the number of shares held by each shareholder, (3) the series numbers of the share certificates, and (4) the date on which each shareholder acquired the shares.[7] Obviously, the trading of registered shares is procedurally very troublesome according to the law on paper, but computerization has made it much easier now to fulfill the formalities. As a result, all the publicly issued shares these days are registered shares,[8] for which the shareholders' information can be easily located in the networks linking stock exchanges, securities registration and clearing companies, and securities companies (which are investment banks, brokers, and dealers in China). In any case, the distinction between registered shares and bearer shares has become increasingly insignificant and irrelevant in practice with the advance of communication technology.

9.1.2 Types of Shares in China – All Shares Are Not Created Equal

Though both the Company Law and Securities Law are curiously silent on the classification of corporate shares, it remains the most distinctive feature of Chinese securities markets. The shares, in addition to their universal classification as ordinary shares, preference shares, etc., are also defined by the status and nationality of their shareholders. There are two classes of shares in China's stockmarket, which include A-shares and B-shares. A-shares could be further divided into state shares, legal person shares, and individual shares. B-shares were originally the only shares available for foreign investors. As many China-incorporated companies are listed on stock exchanges overseas nowadays, H-shares, N-shares,

---

[5] Company Law, Article 129, para. 2.

[6] Company Law, Article 130.

[7] Company Law, Article 131.

[8] That today shares issued by JSLCs in China are all registered shares can be further strengthened by the practice that all JSLCs only issue shares in electronic share distributing networks maintained by stock or equity exchanges, which require the provision of real names of shareholders.

L-Shares, and S-shares have joined the family of foreign capital shares. The basic rationale for this class distinction is for purposes of controlling the transferability of the different types of shares and maintaining the government's leading role in the economy. The characteristics of the different types of shares are discussed in the following.

A-shares

A-shares, originally a nickname given by the marketplace and practitioners to distinguish them from foreign capital B-shares, has now become almost the official name for domestic capital shares – the main body of corporate shares – in China's JSLCs. Including state shares, legal person shares, and individual person shares, A-shares are now also available to Qualified Financial Institutional Investors (QFIIs) in the public market and foreign investors through approved mergers and acquisitions.

> State shares (*Guojia Gu*): These shares refer to shares held by central governmental agencies, local governments, or authorized institutions on behalf of the state. According to relevant regulations, they shall include: the shares converted from the net assets of SOEs that have been transformed into stock companies; shares initially issued by various companies and purchased by central or local governmental departments investing on behalf of the state; and shares initially issued by companies and purchased by investment companies, asset management companies, and economic entities authorized to make investments on behalf of the state.[9] State shares legally were not eligible for trading on open markets such as a stock exchange or an over-the-counter (OTC) market until after the 2005-launched 'non-tradable shares reform', which will be examined in the next section. Even before that, they could be transferred upon approval of the central authorities such as the Ministry of Finance, the CSRC, and the State-owned Assets Supervision and Administration Commission (SASAC). Sales of state shares to foreign investors have been allowed since 2002 as a result of several post-WTO reform programmes.[10]

> Legal person shares (*Faren Gu*): These are shares of a JSLC owned by another company or organization with a 'legal person' status. The legal person shares can be indirectly held by the state if the

[9] Fang Liufang (1995), p. 203.
[10] Wang Jiangyu (2004), pp. 25–9.

shareholders are state-owned enterprises (SOEs). They originated from the shares 'allocated to SOEs that contribute capital to the restructuring company before the [initial public offering]',[11] but, '[o]ver time, a multiplicity of legal persons evolved, so that [legal person] shares come in a wide variety of different types'.[12] Basically, this class includes shares held by domestic entities in which the state is the majority owner but has not the entire ownership. There are five types of ownership for legal person shares: state-owned legal person shares, collective enterprise legal person shares, private enterprise legal person shares, foreign-invested enterprise legal person shares, and institutional legal person shares.[13] Trading of legal person shares through stock exchanges was prohibited before the aforementioned 2005 reform, albeit this could be done upon case-by-case approval from relevant authorities. Like state shares, legal person shares were allowed to be sold to foreigners according to several laws issued after China's accession to the WTO.[14]

Individual person shares (*Geren Gu*): These refer to shares that may only be owned by Chinese residents and legal entities established in China. A-shares resemble classic stock and may be freely traded and transferred within domestic markets. For a long time, until a few years ago, these shares were the only type of equity that were traded among domestic investors at the two stock exchanges and were not accessible to foreign investors. After China's accession to the WTO, regulations were passed to allow QFIIs to have a limited holding of these individual A-shares and trade them in China's stockmarket.[15]

Foreign capital shares (*Waizi Gu*)

B-shares (*B Gu*): Officially known as 'domestically listed foreign capital shares' (*Jingnei shangshi waizi gu*), these are shares of Chinese companies issued to international investors. They are denominated in Chinese currency (the Renminbi) but could be purchased only with foreign currencies (U.S. dollar in Shanghai

---

11 Green (2003), p. 15.
12 Walter and Howie (2003), p. 77.
13 Fang Liufang (1995), p. 204.
14 Wang Jiangyu (2004), pp. 25–9.
15 Id, pp. 21–5.

Stock Exchange and Hong Kong dollar in Shenzhen Stock Exchange). As a very cautious early step of the Chinese government's effort to internationalize its companies and capital markets, B-shares were originally reserved for overseas investors and off-limits to individual and institutional Chinese investors. In February 2001, a new policy was implemented to allow domestic individual investors to buy and trade B-shares using their foreign currencies. The B-shares market, however, is still highly illiquid. Despite many years of development, the market remains small in terms of both the number of listed companies and market capitalization. Probably for these reasons, it has been significantly marginalized in the years following 2001.[16]

Overseas listed shares (*Jingwai Shangshi Gu*): These are shares issued by China-incorporated companies listed on stockmarkets outside Mainland China. Though subject to Chinese laws and the CSRC insofar as registration and initial approval are needed for the companies to go abroad, they are not part of the Chinese securities market but rather components of the stockmarket in which their shares are listed and traded. They currently include H-shares, N-shares, L-shares, and S-shares, all alphabet designations coined by the marketplace using the first letter of the place where the shares are listed. Thus H-shares are offered by Chinese companies listed on the Stock Exchange of Hong Kong (SEHK). They can only be purchased and traded by Hong Kong local investors and international investors. Likewise, N-shares are listed on the New York Stock Exchange (NYSE). Some of them are issued through IPOs but many others are denominated in Renminbi and subscribed for in U.S. dollars. Dividends are declared in Renminbi but paid in U.S. dollars. As such, many N-shares are not traded directly on stock exchanges but were issued by way of American Depository Receipts (ADRs).[17] In addition, L-shares are Chinese company shares listed on the London Stock Exchange (LSE) according to a Memorandum of Understanding between the UK and China in 1996. S-shares are offered on the Singapore Exchange (SGX). In some unofficial documents such as speeches of CSRC officers, H-shares are used to refer to all overseas listed shares of Chinese companies, simply because Hong Kong listed shares constitute the vast majority of Chinese corporate shares circulated overseas.

---

16 Id, p. 21.
17 Id, p. 17.

In addition, there is also a group of shares termed 'red-chip' shares in Hong Kong and other financial centers (known as 'dragon-chip' shares in Singapore). A red-chip company is defined as a China-controlled company that is, however, incorporated outside the PRC. The HKEx identifies a company as red-chip if '(i) the company has at least 30 per cent shareholding held in aggregate directly by Mainland China entities [defined as state-owned organizations and entities controlled by Chinese provincial or municipal authorities], and/or through companies which are controlled by Mainland China entities or (ii) the company has below 30 per cent but 20 per cent or above shareholding held in aggregate directly by Mainland China entities, and/or through companies which are controlled by Mainland China entities, and there is a strong influential presence, on a judgmental basis, on the company's board of directors'.[18] It is important to note that the red-chip shares legally are not regarded as shares issued by Chinese companies since the issuers were incorporated in foreign jurisdictions.

9.1.3 Not Different Classes of Shares

It is important to note that A-shares (with the sub-classifications of state shares, legal person shares, and individual person shares), B-shares, H-shares, etc., do not represent different classes of shares. The distinction between them is also not one between, for instance, ordinary shares (common stock) and preference shares (preferred stock), which arises as a result of the investors' dividend expectations, voting rights, and priority in liquidation. By contrast, all the aforementioned different types of shares legally belong to the same class, namely the common stock class. However, in practice, the corporate charters of H-share companies do authorize separate 'class meetings' for H-share holders and A-share holders as if they are shares of different classes.[19]

An interesting question is whether Chinese companies can issue preference shares. The Company Law is notoriously ambiguous in this regard. On the one hand, there is no explicit prohibition on issuing preference shares by JSLCs. Following the rule of law principle of *Omnia praesumuntur legitime facta, donec probetur contrarium* (All things are presumed to be lawfully done, until it is shown [to be] in the

[18] Hong Kong Exchange (HKEx), 'China Stock Markets Web: Glossary', available at http://www.hkex.com.hk. See also Wang Jiangyu (2009).

[19] Notices of the annual and extraordinary general meetings of H-share companies can be found on the website of Hong Kong Exchange and Clearing Limited at http://www.hkex.com.hk.

reverse), which is widely recognized in China, JSLCs are supposed to be able to lawfully offer preference shares. On the other hand, Article 132 of the Company Law provides that 'the State Council may formulate separate regulations for the offering of other types of company shares than those provided in this Law', indicating that the issue of any other class or type of shares shall be based on administrative regulations. In China's regulatory environment, authorities such as the CSRC or SAIC would be very reluctant – or might even refuse – to approve and register such share offerings without a clear 'legal basis'. On the other hand, Chinese companies themselves are not keen on issuing preference shares at this stage simply because they are not willing to undertake the legal obligation to distribute dividends to any shareholders on a regular basis.

9.1.4 Mixed Ownership and Limited Share Tradability

A typical domestically listed Chinese company normally has a mixed ownership structure, with its share capital divided into the above three categories of shares. Each of the three major groups (state, legal persons, and individuals) holds about one-third of the total outstanding shares. The structure becomes slightly more complex as many companies also issue B-shares to foreigners and other foreign capital shares. But for most listed JSLCs, all or the overwhelming majority of shares are still domestic A-shares. As noted in CSRC (2008), at the end of 2004, 'the total shares of listed Chinese companies were 714.9 billion, of which 454.3 billion shares, or 64% of the total, were non-tradable. Of the non-tradable shares, 74% were state-owned.'[20] In summary, this shareholding structure has the following characteristics.

First, it ensures that the state remains the dominant shareholder in most of the listed companies. Second, it made the Chinese stock market a segmented market with low float ratio. It was insulated in the sense that the public market was only for the individual person shares. That is to say, only one-third of the total shares issued by the listed companies were tradable, which means two-thirds remained legally frozen in terms of transferability in the public market before they were 'rescued' by the 2005 reform. This mixed ownership formed by the three different types of shares, popularly called the 'split shareholding structure' (*guquan fenzhi*) in China, was long regarded as 'a material cause of the Chinese stock market's deficiencies and corporate governance problems'.[21]

20 CSRC (2008), p. 204.
21 Wang and Chen (2006), p. 305.

Wang and Chen (2006) point out three deficiencies caused by the split structure. First, it generated a conflict of interest between the non-tradable shareholders and the tradable shareholders, which led to inevitable distortions in the market. The second deficiency was related to the erosion of the capital market pricing mechanism. As a result of the split 'actual … share prices were only based on a minority of the total numbers of shares'. The third deficiency, in relation to corporate governance, is that the split structure 'impeded the development of both a scientific evaluation standard and an effective incentive mechanism'.[22]

9.1.5 Non-tradable Share Reform in 2005–2007

On 29 April 2005, the CSRC, presumably after having accumulated sufficient political capital, launched the historical Split Shareholding Structure Reform by kicking off a pilot reform programme 'under the leadership of the [Chinese Communist Party] and the State Council'.[23] The Administrative Measures on the Split Shareholding Structure Reform were issued in September 2005 to formally and completely implement the reform for all the listed companies in China.[24]

The CSRC wisely designed the reform as a process of negotiations between the holders of tradable shares and those of the non-tradable shares, thus avoiding government intervention in the shareholding reform of specific companies. The central part of the negotiations was about how much compensation the owners of the non-tradable shares were willing to give the holders of tradable shares in exchange for the trading rights of the non-tradable shares through the following bargaining process:[25]

> The process typically started with a proposal for floating the non-tradable shares put forward by the holders of non-tradable shares, which would then be revised by all shareholders. This would be followed by a vote on the proposal by all shareholders and by holders of tradable shares respectively … The proposal could only be passed if at least two-thirds of the shareholders voted and at least two-thirds of holders of tradable shares endorsed the proposal, a measure to protect the interest of small shareholders in the negotiation process

---

22 Id, pp. 306–7.

23 CSRC (2008), p. 205.

24 Shangshi Gongsi Guquan Fenzhi Gaige Guanli Banfa, promulgated by the CSRC on 4 September 2005, CSRC Doc. No. Zheng Jian Fa [2005] 86 Hao, available at http://222.73.229.9/cs/zhs/xxfw/flgz/regulations/listedco/listed20050905.htm (accessed 1 March 2011).

25 CSRC (2008), p. 206.

> … The design and implementation of the reform were based on market-oriented principles.

The non-tradable share reform was a remarkable success. By the end of 2007, 98 percent of listed companies had completed the process and converted their non-tradable shares, legally, into tradable ones.[26] As an OECD report observes, '[i]n contrast to earlier reform efforts, the market reaction was positive' this time.[27] In the sense that the reform programme had legally eliminated the distinction between tradable and non-tradable shares, it will have profound implications for capital markets development in China, especially with respect to share transferability, the market for corporate control, and new financial products.

9.2 EVOLUTION OF THE REGULATION OF INITIAL PUBLIC OFFERING OF SHARES

This and the next few sections provide a comprehensive examination of the legal and regulatory framework of IPOs in China, focusing on the required substantive and procedural conditions, the sponsorship system, the underwriting system, the price consultation system, as well as the role of the China Securities Regulatory Commission (CSRC), which is the principal regulator of China's securities markets, in the IPO process.

Initial public offering, popularly known as IPO, refers to the process through which a company issues its shares to the public for the first time. IPO is one of the principal channels for a business to raise capital, and it is a necessary step for a privately held enterprise to 'go public', i.e. become a publicly held and traded company, with which a variety of economic advantages are associated.

In 2007, China became the largest IPO market in the world, with 240 companies raising US$62 billion over the year. This was a remarkable achievement amid the global credit crisis, which had already started in 2007, and in light of the fact China had not recognized the concept of publicly traded shares until 1991. Notably, the offering of Industrial and Commercial Bank of China (ICBC), which harvested US$19.1 billion in October 2006 through a simultaneous A- plus H-share listing, remains the largest IPO in the world. It remained as the world's biggest IPO

---

[26] Id, p. 208.
[27] OECD (2010), p. 82.

market in 2011, outshining significantly other financial centers such as the U.S. and Hong Kong in that year.[28]

Public offering of shares is subject to a set of very stringent legal and regulatory rules in China. Many of the rules are unnecessarily burdensome, often making equity financing in China more costly than it should be. Other rules, restrictive as they are, might simply reflect the characteristics of China as an emerging market economy. In either case, international investors have an interest in knowing the rules. This is not only because foreign-invested companies in China (which are legally PRC-incorporated enterprises) may wish to get financed through IPO, but also because the Chinese government may soon permit foreign-incorporated multinationals to offer shares publicly in China and list in the Shanghai Stock Exchange.

Between 1990 and 2000, China implemented an administrative approval regime for public offering of shares, which was largely centered on the infamous 'quota system'. Each year the regulator – which was initially the People's Bank of China (PBC) and later the CSRC – stipulated the amount of total shares that might be issued to the public by companies in China. Provincial governments and central ministries with joint-stock companies under them negotiated the size of quotas they could receive, and recommended companies that might issue shares to the CSRC. Only then could the recommended companies deal with the CSRC directly and go through a process individually for approval.[29] Obviously, this is a planned economy style of share issuance.

A new system, termed *hezhun zhi*, has been in place since March 2001.[30] It is essentially an *ex ante* review and approval system, under which the CSRC requires potential issuers to fulfill certain substantive conditions and procedural rules, as well as mandatory information disclosure requirements. The major difference from the quota system is that there are no longer quota restrictions. At least in theory, an unlimited number of companies and amount of shares could be issued to the public every year, as long as the CSRC determines that they meet the 'going public' requirements.

From a comparative perspective, the new approval system, as China's securities regulatory approach, is in stark contrast with the registration system adopted in most advanced market economies. The philosophical

---

[28] 'China's IPO market the world's biggest despite slump', Reuters newswire, 4 January 2012, available at http://www.reuters.com (accessed 12 June 2012).

[29] Fang Liufang (1995), pp. 178–93; Peng Bing (2005), pp. 90–91.

[30] Peng Bing (2005), p. 90.

approach to securities regulation determines the mission or goals of the regulators. It also indicates the orientation of administrative and judicial policies on the relationships between the regulator and the regulated, as well as the line between legal and illegal behaviors in the market. For example, the mission of the U.S. Securities and Exchange Commission (SEC) is to 'protect investors, maintain fair, orderly, and efficient markets, and facilitate capital formation'.[31] Put very simply, it is the so-called 'disclosure philosophy'. The adoption of the disclosure approach in the U.S. followed a battle of conflicting regulatory philosophies in the late 1920s and early 1930s.[32] The liberal view preferred a non-interventionist, anti-fraud approach, namely 'stern enforcement of the penal laws without even the power somewhere to enjoin frauds'.[33] 'Any preventive law, even of the purely injunction type, would not work ... and would only hinder honest business.'[34] At the other extreme, the merit doctrine based on state blue-sky laws of the 'merit standards' endorsed government revocation of securities issuance upon administrative finding that 'the enterprise or business of the issuer ... or the security is not based upon sound principles, and that the revocation is in the interest of the public welfare', or that the issuer 'is in any other way dishonest' or 'in unsound condition or insolvent'.[35] Eventually, the Securities Act of 1933 adopted the disclosure approach based on Louis D. Brandeis' publicity philosophy.[36] As the SEC points out, 'The laws and rules that govern the securities industry in the United States derive from a simple and straightforward concept: all investors, whether large institutions or private individuals, should have access to certain basic facts about an investment prior to buying it, and so long as they hold it. To achieve this, the SEC requires public companies to disclose meaningful financial and other information to the public'.[37]

As will be seen in the following, China's securities regulation adamantly practices 'merit standards', especially with regard to securities issuance. Under the PRC Securities Law and a huge body of CSRC rules, public offering of securities is subject to a complicate, paternal, *ex ante* review and approval system administered by the CSRC. It is a typical

---

31 SEC (2012).

32 Loss and Seligman (1995), pp. 22–33.

33 Id, p. 25.

34 Id, p. 25.

35 Id, p. 25 (quoting the original legislative bills of the 1933 Securities Act, S. 875 and H.R. 4314, 73d Cong., 1st Sess. §§6(c), (e), (f) (1933)).

36 Id, p. 25.

37 SEC (2012).

merit-based system, with strong disclosure requirements. It differs from the registration system mainly in that, as will be illustrated in detail below, the CSRC looks at certain substantive conditions in addition to the disclosure requirements, such as whether the issuer is a profitable company, its business prospects, its scope of business, its corporate governance, etc.

Institutionally, the CSRC approval system is supported by several sub-systems, including the sponsorship system, the underwriting system, the information disclosure system, the price consultation system, as well as the CSRC internal review system. In terms of the legislative framework, public offering of shares is governed by the Company Law and the Securities Law, together with a variety of administrative rules issued by the CSRC, including the following:

- CSRC Administrative Measures on Initial Public Offering and Listing of Shares (hereinafter IPO Measures),[38] which form the major body of rules governing IPO practice in China.
- CSRC Administrative Measures on Securities Offering and Underwriting (hereinafter Underwriting Measures),[39] and
- CSRC Administrative Measures on Securities Offerings by Listed Companies (hereinafter New Offering Measures).[40]

These rules mainly apply to companies offering and listing their shares in the two main boards in the Shanghai Stock Exchange (SSE) and Shenzen Stock Exchange (SZSE), but most of them also apply to going public and listing on ChiNext board, China's newly established Nasdaq-style board of growth enterprises.

9.3 SUBSTANTIVE REQUIREMENTS FOR IPO

9.3.1 General Principles of Public Offering in China

Public offering of securities shall be carried out in accordance with the so-called '*sangong yuanze*', namely the three principles of openness,

---

[38] Shouci Gongkai Faxing Gupiao Bing Shangshi Guanli Banfa, promulgated by the CSRC in May 2006.

[39] Zhengquan Faxing Yu Chengxiao Guanli Banfa, promulgated by the CSRC in September 2006 and recently revised 18 May 2012.

[40] Shangshi Gongsi Zhengquan Faxing Guanli Banfa, promulgated by the CSRC in May 2006.

fairness, and impartiality.[41] Shares of the same type/class in the same issue shall be offered on the same conditions and at the same price.[42] Shares may be issued at or above par value, but not below par value.[43] Further, as China implements an IPO system that combines the characteristics of both the merit-based system and the disclosure-based system, the issuer must also disclose true, accurate, and complete information in connection with the offering.

9.3.2 Qualifications of the Issuer

A qualified issuer must be a joint-stock limited company (JSLC) that has already been established for over three years.[44] As we have already learned in previous chapters, in China, a JSLC – and only a JSLC – may offer shares to the public and get its shares listed and traded on a stock exchange. Although share offering and listing are practically combined in one process in China, they are legally two separate things. To offer shares for public subscription, an approval from the CSRC must be obtained. With the 2005 revision of the PRC Securities Law, the CSRC has returned the power of approving listing of companies to the stock exchanges. Both the Shanghai Stock Exchange (SSE) and the Shenzhen Stock Exchange (SZSE) examine applications for listing from JSLCs according to their own Listing Rules. A company whose shares are listed on a stock exchange is called a 'listed company'. A listed company could obtain large amounts of low-cost capital through initial and subsequent offerings of shares to the public, which means the supply of capital from an almost unlimited number of investors. Being a JSLC, however, does not necessarily mean that it is also a listed company. There are currently over 2500 companies listed on China's two stock exchanges, which constitute a tiny portion of JSLCs incorporated in China.

Under the IPO Measures, the JSLC must have continuously operated for three or more years before it can be approved to be an issuer of shares.[45] A JSLC younger than three years could publicly offer shares only upon approval by the State Council, China's cabinet, which only gives important state-owned enterprises (SOEs) such a privilege.[46]

---

41 Securities Law, Article 3; Company Law, Article 127.
42 Company Law, Article 127.
43 Company Law, 128.
44 IPO Measures, Articles 8 and 9.
45 Id, Article 9.
46 Id.

The three-year establishment requirement raises a curious question concerning the legality of the IPO Measures in China's legislative structure in the sense that it might be inconsistent with the national Company Law. Under Article 78 of the Company Law, a JSLC might be established either by way of promotion, which means that the promoters subscribe to the entire share capital, or by way of share offering (also called 'incorporation by IPO'), which means a sale of possibly more than 65 percent of the shares to the public, followed by company registration. That is, the Company Law permits the IPO even before the JSLC is officially established. The compulsory three-year establishment requirement under the IPO Measures thus contradicts Article 78 of the Company Law. At this stage, the IPO Measures allow the use of the incorporation by the IPO method only when it is an LLC being converted into a JSLC. In China's legislative structure, the Company Law, a basic law promulgated by the National People's Congress, has a much higher binding force than rules issued by the CSRC, and the CSRC is not allowed to make rules that are inconsistent with the national laws. As such, it's legally not clear on what grounds the CSRC makes such a requirement, although it's unlikely that the issuers would ignore this requirement and rely directly on Article 78 of the Company Law to offer shares to the public.

The CSRC permits only one exemption from the three-year requirement, which is the situation of the so-called *zhengti biangeng*, literally meaning complete conversion or restructuring as a whole. When it is a complete conversion of an LLC into a JSLC, the three-year period is counted from the date when the LLC was established.[47] This advantage of *zhengti biangeng* is embodied in paragraph 2, Article 9 of the IPO Measures, which states, 'In the event of a company limited by shares converted from a limited liability company based on conversion of shares from net assets at original book value, the period of continuous operation shall be counted from the date of establishment of the limited liability company'. That is to say, in the case where the original enterprise is an LLC, it could have the benefit of counting the period of continuous operation from the date of the LLC's own establishment. This opens the door for an accelerated IPO, especially for some state-owned enterprises (SOEs) that had taken the form of an LLC for years before they became JSLCs.

It is hence necessary to explain what is such a complete conversion. Basically, it is the change of the business form – and only a change of form – for an LLC to become a JSLC. When an LLC's own resources satisfy the requirements for establishing a JSLC, it can simply change its

[47] Id, Article 9, para. 2.

registered business form into a JSLC upon fulfilling, among others, the following conditions: (1) the number and qualifications of the LLC's own shareholders are eligible for being shareholders of a JSLC, so that the reincarnation does not need to involve new shareholders; (2) the LLC's own capital meets the registered capital requirement for JSLC incorporation; (3) the LLC's entire original net asset value is converted into the share capital of the new JSLC, so that the paid-up capital of the JSLC does not exceed the net asset value of the LLC; and (4) the JSLC takes all the rights and obligations of the LLC, including all its claims and debts.

In addition, the issuer must meet the following conditions:

- Capital adequacy and integrity: The issuer's registered capital has been fully paid up, the transfer of titles of assets contributed has been completed, and there is no major dispute on the title of its main assets;[48]
- Legality: The issuer's business operation complies with the laws, administrative regulations, and its own articles of association, as well as the state's industrial policy;[49]
- Business operation ability: There is no significant change in the issuer's core business, directors, and senior management personnel, and there is no change in the company's actual controller, during the past three years;[50]
- Clarity in shareholding structure: There is no significant ownership dispute over the shares of the issuer, especially no major disputes in relation to shareholdings held by the controlling shareholders and actual controllers.[51]

9.3.3 Independence of the Issuer

The IPO Measures place heavy emphasis on the independence of the issuer. This is largely a response to the ambivalent relationship between listed companies and their parent companies in China, in which the listed company became a sham for its parent company to raise funds from the capital market, which was to be used in an irresponsible way by the

---

48 Id, Article 10.
49 Id, Article 11.
50 Id, Article 12.
51 Id, Article 13.

parent through, among others, related-party transactions or straightforward assets stripping. In many cases, the parent and the listed subsidiary shared the same assets, business operation, and management personnel.

The IPO Measures require that the issuer have an integral business operation system and the ability to engage in independent market-oriented operations.[52] Specifically, the assets owned independently and intact by the issuer are sufficient to maintain its independent business production and operation.[53] The personnel of the issuer must be independent of its controlling shareholders or actual controlling persons. In particular, the senior management executives of the issuer may not hold any position other than the position of a director or supervisor in the controlling shareholders, actual controllers, or companies controlled by the above two, and they may not be on the payroll list of the controlling shareholders, actual controllers, or companies under their control.[54] The issuer should be financially independent, meaning it has its own financial accounting and decision-making systems.[55] Further, the issuer should have its independent governance organizations, which exercise business management powers and duties independently.[56] Finally, the business of the issuer should be independent. It should not have any competing business or obviously unfair related-party transaction with its controlling shareholders, actual controllers, or enterprises under the control of the above two.[57]

9.3.4 Standardized Operation of the Issuer

The section 'Standardized Operation in the IPO Measures' is a hybrid of rules concerning corporate governance, corporate internal control, fiduciary duties, and related-party transactions. Generally, the issuer must have established a sound corporate governance structure including proper systems for shareholders' general meeting, board of directors, board of supervisors, independent directors, and board secretary.[58] The qualifications of the directors, supervisors, and senior executives should be in conformity with laws, administrative regulations, and the corporate

---

52 Id, Article 14.
53 Id, Article 15.
54 Id, Article 16.
55 Id, Article 17.
56 Id, Article 18.
57 Id, Article 19.
58 Id, Article 21.

charter. A person shall be disqualified from his capacity as a director, supervisor, or other senior management positions if he is currently subject to a market-entry ban by the CSRC, or administrative penalties by the CSRC within the past 36 months, or open reprimand by the stock exchange within the past 12 months, or if he has been subject to a criminal or administrative investigation although the specific conclusion is still pending.[59] These key players are required to understand corporate and securities laws relating to IPO, and familiarize themselves with their legal obligations and duties (including fiduciary duties).[60]

Further, the issuer should also have in place a sound internal control system that is able to ensure the reliability of financial reports, legality of business operation, and operational efficiency and results.[61] The issuer must not, within the most recent 36 months, have been involved in illegal offering of securities, or received an administrative penalty for violation of administrative rules, or made materially defective or fraudulent submissions to the CSRC in order to obtain official approvals. The issuer should also not be under an ongoing criminal investigation.[62]

Lastly, the issuer must have in place a rigorous treasury system that is able to prevent misappropriation of corporate funds by controlling shareholders or actual controllers through loans or other means. The issuer's articles of association shall specify the limit of authority and procedures for approving external guarantees, and the company must not have extended illegal guarantees to the controlling shareholders, actual controllers, or enterprises controlled by them.[63]

9.3.5 Finance and Accounting Requirements

In general, the issuer should maintain good financial status, having quality assets, a reasonable assets–liability balance, good profitability, and normal cash flow.[64] An unqualified report must be issued by a certified public accountant with respect to the effectiveness of the issuer's internal control system.[65] All the related-party transactions must be

---

59 Id, Article 23.
60 Id, Article 22.
61 Id, Article 24.
62 Id, Article 25.
63 Id, Articles 26 and 27.
64 Id, Article 28.
65 Id, Article 29.

properly disclosed.[66] In addition, the issuer must meet the following financial conditions:[67]

1. Within the past three accounting years, it has reported profits in each year, with an aggregate amount of profit exceeding RMB30 million;
2. Its cumulative cash flow generated within the past three accounting years exceeds RMB50 million, or its cumulative business revenue in the past three accounting years exceeds RMB300 million;
3. Its minimum share capital is not less than RMB30 million before the IPO;
4. The value of its intangible assets (excluding land-use rights, marine cultivation rights, and mining rights) must not exceed 20 percent of the net assets at the end of the most recent accounting year; and
5. There are no unrecovered losses at the end of the most recent accounting year.

Lastly, the CSRC requires that the issuer does not have significant risks in repayment and is not involved in significant contingent events such as guarantees, litigation, or arbitration that might aversely affect its operation as a going concern.[68] Furthermore, the issuer's continuous profitability must not be adversely affected by any of the following circumstances: (i) there have been or will be significant changes in the issuer's business model or type and structure of products or services; (ii) there have been or will be significant changes in the issuer's industry position or the business environment of its industry, which will have significant adverse impacts on the issuer's profitability going forward; (iii) the issuer's business revenue or net profit of the issuer in the last accounting year relied heavily on related parties or clients with material uncertainty; (iv) the issuer's net profit in the last accounting year comprised mainly returns derived from off-balance sheet investment income; (v) there exist the risks of significantly adverse changes in the issuer's acquisition or use of intellectual property rights or technologies such as trademarks, patents, know-how, and franchises; and (vi) there are other circumstances that may have a significantly adverse impact on the continuous profitability of the issuer.[69]

---

66 Id, Article 30.
67 Id, Article 33.
68 Id, Article 35.
69 Id, Article 37.

9.3.6 Use of Funds Raised through IPO

The IPO Measures stipulate a principle that the funds raised through the IPO must be used for specified purposes, mainly for developing the company's core business. Unless the issuer is a financial institution, the funds cannot be used to purchase, hold, and trade in financial assets. The issuer is prohibited from using the proceeds to invest in companies that engage in securities trading.[70]

The rules in the IPO Measures on the issuer's use of IPO funds demonstrate strong paternalism by setting not only specific restrictions and directions on the specific uses of the money. For example, it is required that 'the amount of funds raised and the project they are to be invested in shall be commensurate with the issuer's existing production and operation scale, financial position, level of technology, and management capabilities'.[71] The use of funds should also comply with 'state industrial policy, investment regulation, environmental protection, [and] land management', along with other laws.[72] The board of the issuer is required to present an analysis of the investment project to ensure its market prospects and profitability.[73] Further, the use of the funds should not give rise to intra-industry competition or have an adverse impact on the independence of the issuer.[74]

9.4 IPO PROCESS

9.4.1 Starting the Process

The IPO process must be kicked off by the JSLC, which will later be called the issuer. Under China's corporate laws, the plan to issue new shares must be endorsed by a resolution of the shareholders' general meeting, which determines the type and quantity of shares to be offered, the offerees, the price or pricing method, use of proceeds, etc.[75] However, the initiation of the offering plan must come from the company's board

---

70 Id, Article 38.
71 Id, Article 39.
72 Id, Article 40.
73 Id, Article 41.
74 Id, Article 42.
75 Company Law, Article 134; IPO Measures, Article 45.

of directors, which shall pass a resolution on the specifics of the plan and present it to the general meeting for approval.[76]

As noted above, the issuer normally should be an already established JSLC. In many cases, the enterprise that wishes to raise money from the capital market has yet to be converted into a JSLC. The enterprise could initially be a traditional state-owned enterprise, a collectively-owned enterprise, a privately-owned enterprise that is not registered under the Company Law, a foreign-invested enterprise, or a standardized LLC registered under the Company Law. Naturally, the first step is to restructure such an enterprise into a JSLC. In practice, it could be a partial restructuring (*bufen gaizhi*), whereby the original enterprise uses only its quality assets as capital contributions to establish a subsidiary JSLC in which the original enterprise remains as the controlling shareholder. It could also be a complete restructuring (*zhengti gaizhi*), whereby the original enterprise dissolves and deregisters itself immediately after investing all its assets to incorporate a JSLC. In this case, the JSLC takes all of the original enterprise's assets and liabilities. Lots of house-cleaning work needs to be done before an IPO-eligible JSLC is established, which provides tremendously lucrative business for investment bankers and lawyers.

9.4.2 Sponsorship and Guidance

Article 11 of the PRC Securities Law sets forth the requirement for sponsorship (*baojian*) in a public offering and listing of shares. Sponsorship involves documented due diligence examination of the issuer's offering documents and information disclosure by qualified sponsoring institutions (*baojianren,* or sponsors). Since 2004, sponsorship has been relied on as a market-oriented tool by the CSRC to shift some supervisory responsibility originally reserved for the regulators to external verification of the information provided by the issuer by professional intermediaries (e.g., the securities companies, accounting firms, law firms). The sponsorship system was finalized with the promulgation of the *Measures for the Administration of the Sponsorship System of Issuance and Listing of Securities* in 2008 (hereinafter the Sponsorship Measures).[77]

Under the sponsorship system, a CSRC-licensed sponsoring institution (which is normally a securities company licensed to underwrite securities

---

[76] IPO Measures, Article 44.

[77] Zhengquan Faxing Shangshi Baojian Yewu Guanli Banfa, adopted by the CSRC on 14 August 2008 and revised on 13 May 2009.

offerings) must be hired by the issuer for initial or follow-on public offering of securities.[78] For a particular offering project, the sponsoring institution shall appoint an employee, who is a CSRC-licensed 'sponsoring representative' (*baojian daibiaoren*), to be responsible for the sponsorship work. If the securities offered reach a certain amount, a maximum of two sponsoring institutions may undertake joint sponsorship.[79]

The sponsor is required to conduct a comprehensive due diligence review of the issuer's business, in particular the risks and problems faced by the issuer.[80] The due diligence work shall be conducted according to the CSRC's *Guidance on Due Diligence Investigation Performed by Sponsoring Representatives* (issued May 2006), which emphasizes the independent opinion of the sponsor and the need to examine related-party transactions.

The sponsor is also charged with the responsibility of *fudao*, or guidance work.[81] This is basically a training job that requires the sponsor to coach the issuer about current knowledge concerning the laws, economics, and business in relationship to securities offering, corporate governance, and information disclosure. The 'students' will comprise the issuer's directors, supervisors, and senior executives, shareholders that own 5 percent or more of the company's shares (or their legal representatives), and actual controllers (or their legal representatives). The new Sponsorship Measures have removed a previous requirement that the guidance work must last for at least one year, but still retained the power of the local representative office of the CSRC to decide whether the guidance work is acceptable.[82]

The sponsor's coaching and investigation work will result in an offer sponsorship letter, which is an indispensable part of the application package submitted to the CSRC. The letter is required to have the following information:[83]

- An item-by-item account of whether the contemplated offering complies with the relevant provisions of the Company Law and Securities Law;

---

78 Sponsorship Measures, Article 2.
79 Id, Article 6.
80 Id, Articles 23 and 24.
81 Id, Article 25.
82 Id, Article 26.
83 Id, Article 31.

- An item-by-item account of whether the contemplated offering complies with the relevant CSRC rules, as well as the factual basis and verification procedures for each conclusion reached;
- The main risks faced by the issuer;
- An assessment of the issuer's growth prospects;
- A brief description of the sponsor's internal review procedures and the internal review opinion concerning the contemplated offering;
- The affiliation relationship between the sponsor and the issuer;
- The undertakings.

The sponsoring institution is required to make certain undertakings.[84] First, it must demonstrate that it has good reason to firmly believe that (1) the issuer complies with all the relevant laws; (2) the issuer's application and information disclosure documents have no false record, misleading statement, or material omission; (3) the basis for the opinions expressed by the issuer and its directors in the application and disclosure documents is complete and reasonable; and (4) there is no substantial difference between the application and information disclosure documents and the opinions expressed by the intermediaries concerned. Further, undertakings must be made to ensure that the sponsoring representatives and persons concerned have diligently fulfilled their duties, that the sponsoring documents have no false records, misleading statements, or material omission, and that the professional services provided and the professional opinions issued by the sponsor comply with laws, administrative regulations, CSRC rules, and industrial practices. Finally, the sponsor must make an undertaking to 'voluntarily' accept the supervision of the CSRC.

The sponsorship system was first tested in the Qionghua scandal after it was put into place. Jiangsu Qionghua High-Tech Co Ltd ('Qionghua'), a paper and packaging company, was one of the first eight companies to successfully launch their IPO and get listed on China's newly established SME (Small and Medium Enterprise) Board established in May 2004 by the Shenzhen Stock Exchange (SZSE). Qionghua was listed on 25 June 2004. On 1 July 2004, the media began to question the external guarantees provided by Qionghua, and the SZSE immediately asked Qionghua to explain the transactions. It was discovered that, before Qionghua's IPO and listing, it intentionally misrepresented its treasury bond investments at the total value of RMB35.55 million. Because the counterparties to the transactions were subject to liquidation receivership,

[84] Id, Article 33.

the investments were bound to suffer a significant loss. These facts were not disclosed in Qionghua's IPO prospectus. Apart from the issuer's legal liability, one of the key issues in the scandal was the liability of the sponsor, Minfa Securities Company, and the sponsoring representatives. On 9 July 2004, the SZSE issued a public warning against Qionghua. On 15 July 2004, the CSRC launched an investigation into Qionghua's misrepresentation case and, at the same time, decided to punish the two sponsoring representatives by refusing to accept any offering application sponsored by them for three months.[85]

The Qionghua scandal raised serious doubt in the market about the sponsorship system. Despite the criticism, the CSRC has still decided to shift some supervision responsibilities to the sponsors in preparation for the eventual adoption of the registration system for public offerings.

It is also important to note the obligation of post-offering continuing guidance (*chixu dudao*) by the sponsors. Even after the IPO is complete, the sponsor should continue to monitor the issuer possibly for up to four years.[86] During the monitoring period the sponsor shall urge and push the issuer to comply with their undertakings and legal obligations, particularly focusing on related-party transactions, internal control, use of funds raised through IPO, and external guarantees provided by the issuer.[87]

9.4.3 CSRC Review and Approval

Government approval has always been an essential part of the public offering of shares in China. An offering without state approval might trigger administrative and criminal as well as civil liabilities. For example, according to Article 188 of the Securities Law, a company unlawfully issuing securities without state approval shall be ordered to cease the issuance and return the funds raised plus deposit interest to the investors, as well as pay a fine of 1 to 5 percent of the funds it has illegally raised. Article 179 of the PRC Criminal Law provides that any person issuing securities without state approval may be sentenced to a fixed-term imprisonment of not more than five years and be fined from 1 to 5 percent of the funds illegally raised. Responsible individuals such as management executives or directors may also be given fixed-term imprisonment for up to five years.

---

[85] See 'IPOs: Who Vouches for the Sponsors?' *China Daily* Online, 14 December 2011, available at http://www.chinadaily.com.cn/business/2011-12/14/content_14264691.htm (accessed 12 March 2012) and various news reports.

[86] Sponsorship Measures, Article 36.

[87] Id, Article 35.

Generally speaking, the state is becoming increasingly less interventionist in share issuance, although the final say on whether an offering can go ahead is still firmly rested in the hands of the CSRC. From 1990 to 2000, IPOs were regulated under the quota system, under which Chinese securities supervisory authorities established each year a total amount of shares companies were allowed to issue to the public. The CSRC decided the allocation of quotas to the provinces and various ministries, which would then select enterprises in their jurisdictions to fulfill the quota and submit their application for public offering to the CSRC for preliminary review and final approval.[88] A salient characteristic of the quota system is that the total amount of shares, as well as largely the total number of issuers and amount of capital to be raised, was pre-decided. That is to say, once the quota was fully filled, no other companies could issue shares to the public, even though they might have better assets, management, and business prospects.

The quota system was abandoned in 2001. Since March 2001, China has been implementing the new *ex ante* review and approval system ('RAS'), under which an application will go through three steps once filed with the CSRC: (1) preliminary review by the CSRC's Department of Public Offering Supervision; (2) formal review by the Share Offering Review Committee (SORC), which is formed under the auspices of the CSRC to examine the documents submitted by the issuer and recommended by the sponsor; and (3) final decision by the CSRC.

At the preliminary review stage, the IPO Measures require the CSRC to 'consult the People's government at the provincial level of the place of registration of the issuer on whether it consents to the share offering in question, and consult the National Development and Reform Commission on whether the investment project of the issuer to be funded by the proceeds is in line with the State's industrial policy and investment management rules'.[89] Not surprisingly, this requirement casts doubt on the independence of the CSRC in reviewing applications, although it can be argued that consultation does not give the provincial governments and the NDRC the veto power. There is, however, no doubt that the opinions given by the other ministries will be seriously taken into consideration by the CSRC in its review of an application.

The SORC was established in 1999, when it consisted of 80 members. A panel of nine members was established to review a particular application. Initially, the identity of the members of the panel was kept strictly

---

88 Fang Liufang (1995), pp. 178–93; Peng Bing (2005), pp. 90–91.
89 IPO Measures, Article 49.

confidential, as well as the time of the meeting. In December 2003, the CSRC reshuffled the SORC, reducing the size of the full committee from 80 members to 25 and the size of the panel from nine members to seven. After the launch of the ChiNext board, an SORC especially for the ChiNext was also established, comprising 35 members. Five 'yes' votes are needed for an application to be approved. To improve transparency, the CSRC now makes known to the public, before each meeting, the time of the meeting, and the names of the panel members, as well as information about the applicants. Voting results are also published on the CSRC's website shortly after the meeting.[90]

It is important to note that it is the CSRC, not the SORC, that has the final decision-making power with respect to an application. That is to say, the authority of the SORC is to make recommendations to the CSRC, which 'shall render a decision to approve or disapprove an application for offering in accordance with the statutory criteria and issue the relevant approval documents accordingly'.[91] This provision further evidences that the Quota System is no longer applicable as the CSRC is supposed to approve – and has no legitimate reasons to disapprove – applications that meet the statutory conditions.[92] Once an application is approved by the CSRC, the issuer must issue shares within six months, otherwise the approval document will expire and become void.[93]

Offering shares to the public without CSRC approval, called 'illegal issuance of securities' by the government, will result in severe legal consequences of administrative and criminal liabilities. Under Article 188 of the Securities Law, such an issuer 'shall be ordered by the [CSRC] to cease the offering, shall return the funds it has raised plus the deposit interests to the investors, and shall be fined for up to five percent of the funds it has illegally raised'. 'The persons in charge or directly responsible' for the illegal issuance – referring to the key players in the company – will be given a warning as well as fined up to RMB300,000.

On criminal punishment, those who are in charge or directly responsible might be sentenced to fixed-term imprisonment of not more than five

---

[90] For rules concerning the PORC see generally Zhongguo Zhengquan Jiandu Guanli Weiyuanhui Faxing Shenhe Weiyuanhui Banfa (CSRC Measures for the Share Offering Review Committee), adopted by the CSRC on 8 May 2006 and revised on 13 May 2012.

[91] IPO Measures, Article 50.

[92] This is, however, certainly not the case in reality as the CSRC still considers the applications on a case-by-case basis and suspends the processing of IPO applications for various reasons.

[93] Id.

years or criminal detention, and might also be fined up to 5 percent of the funds 'illegally raised'.[94] This is, however, not the end of the story, as the Chinese authorities have often published the names of individuals who were responsible for the illegal issuance with much heavier offences – a group of crimes under the umbrella of 'illegally raising funds' (*feifa jizi zui*) in the PRC Criminal Law. For example, illegal issuance of shares can be prosecuted by the state under Article 192 of the Criminal Law, which stipulates the offence of 'raising funds by means of fraud' (*jizi zhapian zui*), so that a person who 'unlawfully raises funds by means of fraud' normally shall be imprisoned for not more than five years and fined up to RMB200,000. However, if the amount of money involved is extraordinarily huge, or if there are other extraordinarily serious circumstances, he may be subject to fixed-term imprisonment for above 10 years or even life imprisonment, as well as a fine up to RMB500,000. More unfortunately for him, if his illegal issuance is characterized as involving not only an extraordinarily huge amount of money but also 'causing extraordinarily serious damage to the interests of the state and the people', the person may be subject to the death penalty under Article 192 of the Criminal Law.

9.4.4 Underwriting

Under China's corporate and securities law, all forms of public offering must be underwritten by a securities company.[95] Article 28 of the Securities Law provides that underwriting may be conducted on an 'agency or fully-underwritten basis'. Underwriting on an agency basis refers to the underwriting method in which a securities company sells securities on behalf of the issuer and, at the end of the underwriting period, returns all unsold securities to the issuer. Underwriting of securities on a fully underwritten basis means that a securities company purchases all securities of the issuer pursuant to an agreement between them, or purchases all unsold securities at the end of the underwriting period.[96]

In essence, the two underwriting methods provided in Article 28 of the Securities Law point to the three classic types of underwriting: standby underwriting, whereby the issuer offers its securities to the public, and the underwriter undertakes to purchase any securities not purchased by the public; best-effort underwriting, whereby the underwriter agrees to

[94] PRC Criminal Law, Article 179.
[95] Company Law, Articles 88 and 135.
[96] Securities Law, Article 28.

use its best efforts to find buyers for the securities offered by the issuer; and firm-commitment underwriting, whereby the issuer sells its securities to the underwriter at an agreed price and the underwriter then resells the securities to brokerage firms or to the public at a profit.

Standby underwriting, known as *yu'e baoxiao*, is the most commonly used underwriting method for public offerings in China.[97]

In the case of underwriting on an agency basis, the securities firm is prohibited from reserving for its own account securities underwritten by it. On the other hand, if the total amount of shares actually sold to investors fails to reach 70 percent of the proposed quantity of shares offered to the public at the end of the underwriting period, this will be deemed as a failed offering, and the issuer must refund the issue price plus bank deposit interest.[98] This is certainly a significant legal risk associated with underwriting on an agency basis. The risk is shared by both the issuer and the underwriter, as the IPO Measures require the lead underwriter to 'assist the issuer' in refunding the share price and bank interest.[99] Further, a failed offer also damages the reputation of the underwriter. For this reason, even in underwriting on an agency basis, the underwriter is under full pressure to market the shares.

In either form of underwriting, the underwriting period shall not exceed 90 days.[100] The securities firm is also required by the Securities Law to verify the truthfulness, accuracy, and completeness of the public offering documents, and to suspend or stop the sale if false records, misleading statements, or material omissions are discovered.[101]

If the total par value of securities offered to the public exceeds RMB50 million, an underwriting syndicate must be formed.[102] The underwriting syndicate agreement and the underwriting agreement may be signed after the offer price is determined. The lead underwriter is required to establish a special department within it to assist the issuer to deal with matters concerning information disclosure, marketing, book-keeping, pricing, placement, and settlement.

Lastly, the underwriting process is monitored by the CSRC. Before the underwriting commences, the underwriter shall report the offering plan

---

97 Article 40 of the Underwriting Measures requires the use of underwriting on an agency basis (best-effort underwriting) in the case where a listed company sells shares in a non-public offering or right offering.

98 Securities Law, Articles 34 and 35.

99 IPO Measures, Article 40.

100 Securities Law, Article 33.

101 Securities Law, Article 31.

102 Securities Law, Article 32.

and the underwriting plan to the CSRC. Ten days after the securities are listed, the lead underwriter shall submit a report to the CSRC on the basic issues of the underwriting as well as the performance of the new securities in the market.[103]

9.4.5 Pricing Consultation

A variety of methods have been adopted to price shares in the history of the Chinese stockmarket. A common feature was that all the methods put the CSRC in the driver's seat for determining the IPO price. In the early 1990s, the issuers had no power with respect to either the quantity of shares to be offered or the pricing of the shares. The price for every offering was determined by the CSRC based on various considerations. The CSRC alternatively used the fixed-price method and price/earnings ratio (P/E ratio) pricing method in the 1990s. From 2000–2001, the CSRC allowed the issuers and underwriters to negotiate the offer prices. Between 2001 and 2004, the P/E ratio method was adopted again.

In December 2004, the CSRC officially introduced the price consultation system for IPO (*xunjia zhidu*), replacing government approval of the price with a book-building process. The new method has been finalized in the 2006-promulgated Underwriting Measures. The measures mandate that the offer price of an IPO 'shall be determined by making an inquiry to the specified institutional investors', which include mutual funds companies, securities companies, trust and investment companies, finance companies, insurance companies, qualified foreign institutional investors, and institutions or individual investors recommended by the underwriter.[104] With the revision of the Underwriting Measures in May 2012, issuers are now allowed again to determine the offer price through negotiations with the lead underwriter.[105] In short, now the IPO price can be determined by the following methods:[106]

- Price consultations
- Negotiations between the issuer and the lead underwriter
- Any other lawful and plausible method.

---

[103] Underwriting Measures, Article 50.

[104] Underwriting Measures, Article 5, para. 2. Individuals recommended by the underwriting have been allowed to participate in price consultations after the Underwriting Measures were revised in May 2012.

[105] Underwriting Measures, Article 5, para. 1.

[106] Id.

The Underwriting Measures provide a two-stage price consultation process: a preliminary price consultation and a book-building price consultation.[107] The issuer and the lead underwriter determine a price range (*qujian*) through a preliminary consultation with the consultation participants, and then determine the final offer price within the range through an off-line book-building process with the prospective placement participants. The issuer and its lead underwriter are responsible for respectively reporting to the CSRC and making public announcements after determining the offer price range and final offer price.[108] After the revision of the Underwriting Measures in May 2012, the two-stage process is no longer compulsory as now the issuer and the lead underwriter may directly determine the offer price after the preliminary consultation stage, without entering the book-building stage.[109]

The Underwriting Measures have mandated the amount of feedback that must be successfully collected from the consultation participants. At the end of the preliminary price consultation, the issuer and the lead underwriter should suspend the offering if, in case the quantity of the shares offered to the public is less than 400 million, there are less than 20 price consultation participants providing valid price quotations, or, in case there are more than 400 million publicly offered shares, there are less than 50 consultation participants providing valid price quotations.[110]

9.4.6 Sale of Shares

Under the Underwriting Measures, the shares may be sold through two channels: off-line offering and online offering. An off-line offering involves the sale of securities to specified investors, and it may include a strategic placement and/or an institutional placement. If the quantity of the shares offered exceeds 400 million, the issuer and underwriter may sell directly a certain amount of shares to strategic investors ('strategic placement').[111] The purpose of strategic investment is to attract long-term investors who also have the interest and capabilities to help the issuer improve its business operation and corporate governance. However, the strategic investors must promise to hold the shares for at least 12 months.[112] The issuer and underwriter may also place shares with

---

107 Underwriting Measures, Article 13.
108 Id, Article 20.
109 Id, Article 14.
110 Id, Article 33.
111 Id, Article 23.
112 Id, Article 24.

institutional investors who participated in the price consultation process ('institutional placement').[113]

Ordinary investors can subscribe to the shares through online offering, which involves the sale of securities via the electronic networks of stock exchanges. Under the Underwriting Measures, off-line offering and online offering should be conducted simultaneously, although when the offering is made the online offer price has not yet been determined. In this situation, investors participating in online offering should subscribe to the shares based on the upper limit of the price span.[114]

If the size of the offering reaches a certain scale, the issuer and its underwriter are required to a establish a claw-back mechanism (*huibo jizhi*), which may be activated, upon completion of the offering, to adjust the relative sizes of the off-line offering and online offering based on their respective ratios in the total subscriptions. The activation of the claw-back mechanism is determined on the basis of the preliminary success rate in the online offering and the preliminary placement ration in the off-line offering.[115]

9.4.7 Greenshoe Option

The Underwriting Measures have introduced, for the first time, the Greenshoe option.[116] This price stabilization arrangement was already adopted in the simultaneous share offerings of the Industrial and Commercial Bank of China (ICBC) on the domestic and Hong Kong markets in September 2006. The Greenshoe, formally known as the stabilization and over-allotment clause, gives the lead underwriter the right to sell additional shares of up to 15 percent of the original total number of offered shares if demand for the shares exceeds the original amount offered. It is the only market tool allowed by the CSRC to stabilize the price of a new issue post pricing. Under the Underwriting Measures, the issuer and its underwriter may adopt the Greenshoe option where more than 400 million shares are offered in an IPO.

---

113 Id, Article 26.
114 Id, Article 31.
115 Id, Article 32.
116 Id, Article 49.

9.5 INFORMATION DISCLOSURE IN SHARE OFFERING

9.5.1 Basic Principles of Information Disclosure

Arguably since the Securities Law was promulgated in 1998, the focus of securities market regulation in China has, in part, been gradually shifting from pure administrative control to compulsory information disclosure. As a result, securities regulation in China now combines the characteristics of both the merit-based system and the disclosure system.

In accordance with the Securities Law, the IPO Measures, and the CSRC Administrative Measures for the Information Disclosure of Listed Companies (hereinafter the Disclosure Measures),[117] once an application for offering is approved, the issuer shall publicize the offering documents prior to the offering. The issuer may not offer any securities before the documents are properly disclosed. Further, prior to the disclosure of information according to the law, no informed persons may publicize or leak such information.

The issuer is required to disclose 'any information which has a material impact on the investment decision of investors'.[118] Students of American securities regulation could easily find the similarities between this standard of disclosure and the substantial likelihood of materiality by the U.S. Supreme Court in *TSC Industries, Inc. v Northway, Inc.*[119] and *Basic Inc. v Levinson*,[120] which is expressed as 'a fact is material if there is a substantial likelihood that the disclosure of [an] omitted fact would have been viewed by the reasonable investor as having significantly altered the total "mix" of information made available'.[121] The CSRC's materiality standard is embedded in the following general principles for information disclosure provided in the Securities Law, Company Law, CSRC rules, and stock exchange rules:[122]

---

[117] Shangshi Gongsi Xinxi Pilu Guanli Banfa, promulgated by the CSRC and took effect on 30 January 2007.

[118] IPO Measures, Article 54.

[119] 426 U.S. 438 (1976).

[120] 485 U.S. 224 (1988).

[121] Soderquist and Gabaldon (2004), p. 158.

[122] CSRC (2011), p. 52. On the legal provisions see particularly, Securities Law, Articles 20, 63, 68; IPO Measures, Chapter 4; Underwriting Measures, Chapter 5; and Disclosure Measures.

- Principle of authenticity. The information disclosed should be truthful, objective, consistent, and contain no false statements.[123]
- Principle of accuracy. The information should be 'accurate and may not use vague expressions or misleading statements' that cause confusion or misunderstanding.[124]
- Principle of completeness. The issuer has the duty to speak in the disclosed documents the whole truth and not to omit material information from the documents.[125]
- Principle of timeliness. The issuer has the duty to disclose the most recent information and to update the information when necessary without delay.
- Principle of equality. The information should be disclosed to all the investors on an equal basis and must not give only some investors more privileged access to the information.[126]

9.5.2 Disclosure Documentation

The issuer and its underwriter shall submit to the CSRC, the stock exchange (if listing is the goal) as well as make known to the public, among others, the following documents: a prospectus, a summary prospectus, and an offer announcement.

The prospectus is the single most important legal document. Before the prospectus is published according to law, the issuer must file a submission draft of the prospectus with the CSRC. The draft must closely follow the CSRC Guidelines on Contents and Formats for Information

---

123 CSRC (2011), p. 52. For reference, Article 2.5 of the Shanghai Stock Exchange Listing Rules provides: 'A listed company and the relevant person with disclosure obligations shall disclose information based on facts or judgments and opinions derived from facts. Such information should reflect realities and contain no misrepresentations' (hereinafter SSE Listing Rules).

124 CSRC (2011). Article 2.6 of SSE Listing Rules requires the listed companies and person with disclosure obligations to 'disclose information objectively with no exaggeration and no misleading statement'.

125 Article 2.7 of the SSE Listing Rules provides 'The information disclosed by the listed company and the relevant persons with disclosure obligations shall be complete in contents and properly formatted, and contain all the relevant documents without material omissions'.

126 Article 2.4 of the SSE Listing Rules provides 'The listed company and the relevant persons with disclosure obligations shall publicly disclose material information simultaneously to all the investors to ensure that all the investors have equal access to the same information, and shall not reveal or leak such information only to any individual investors or any group of investors'.

Disclosure by Companies Offering Securities to the Public (No. 1): Prospectus (hereinafter the Prospectus Guidelines). According to Article 54 of the IPO Measures, the aforementioned CSRC Guidelines form the minimum requirements on information disclosure in this regard, and the issuer is mandated to disclose any information that has a material impact on the investment decisions of investors. However, the CSRC may authorize the omission from the prospectus of the information otherwise required if the information concerns state secrecy, commercial secrecy, or if the disclosure may cause serious harm to the interest of the company.

In an IPO, the issuer and all of its directors, supervisors, and senior executives shall sign the prospectus to certify the truthfulness, accuracy, and completeness of the information disclosed in the prospectus. The sponsor and sponsoring representatives shall verify the truthfulness, accuracy, and completeness of the information and sign the verification opinion.[127] This clearly stated responsibility not only subjects the key players of the company to administrative liability but will also help the courts to clarify their duties related to disclosure in both civil and criminal cases.

In relation to the IPO disclosure, the 2012-revised Underwriting Measures now provide a 'quiet period' of time extending from the time the CSRC accepts the offering application until the application is approved by the CSRC and the prospectus is published in CSRC-designated places, during which the issuer and any person involved in the proposed offering must not market – or entrust any other person to market – the shares in any open manner or disguised open manner.[128]

9.5.3 Pre-disclosure

The 2005 revision of the Securities Law has introduced, for the first time, the pre-disclosure system,[129] which is elaborated upon in the IPO Measures. Pre-disclosure requires the issuer to disclose the submission draft of the prospectus on the CSRC's website after CSRC's acceptance of the application documents but before the SORC holds a formal meeting to examine the documents.[130] The pre-disclosed draft prospectus is, however, legally not deemed an official document. That is, it shall

---

127 IPO Measures, Article 55. Article 24 of the Disclosure Measures also requires the key players to be responsible for the periodical reports.

128 Underwriting Measures, Article 53.

129 Securities Law, Article 21.

130 Underwriting Measures, Article 58.

not contain price information and the issuer may not issue shares based on it.[131] Although the issuer and its directors, supervisors, and senior executives are similarly required to certify the truthfulness, accuracy, and completeness of the information on the pre-disclosed document, they should place the following statement in a conspicuous place in the documents:[132]

> The company's application for offering has yet to be approved by the CSRC. This prospectus (submission draft) does not have the legal validity for share offer and is for advance disclosure purpose only. Investors shall base their investment decision on the full text of the prospectus to be announced officially.

9.6 REFORMING CHINA'S IPO REGIME

The IPO regime in China is at its crossroad. For many years, public offerings of securities have been subject to tight administrative control. As the numbers of issuers and investors have grown rapidly in recent years, it has become increasingly difficult for this planned economy-style regulatory approach to deal with the complexity of the new landscape.

Although China still adopts a merit system, two new trends have emerged in the course of reforming China's IPO regime since 2001. First, administrative examination of applications for new offerings is increasingly becoming institutionalized and rule-oriented. Although the CSRC still has the final say as to whether an offering can go ahead, the use of the SORC indicates a limited degree of checks and balances within the CSRC with respect to the approval power. Arguably, SORC demonstrates an increased willingness to rely on the wisdom and integrity of independent experts, who are supposed to follow pre-established rules to make decisions. Further, in December 2003, the CSRC released new rules to abolish the confidentiality requirement that kept the identity of committee members unknown to the public, and replaced the SORC members' anonymous voting with real-name voting. These reform measures have improved the transparency of the share offering approval system.

Second, the market-driven reform is increasingly shifting the supervision responsibility from the regulators to financial intermediaries. This is, in particular, evidenced in the sponsorship system. The sponsor, who will also be the issuer's (lead) underwriter, is now under the obligation to

---

[131] Id, Article 60, para. 1.
[132] Id, Article.

'educate' the issuer with respect to securities and legal compliance knowledge, as well as to verify the information disclosure of the issuer. The sponsor must also undertake continuous coaching and supervisory responsibility to ensure that the issuer establishes sound corporate governance and complies with the listing and disclosure rules. The share price could also be decided through the more market-driven book-building process. All these supervisory powers used to belong to the province of the regulatory authority of the CSRC.

Despite the market-oriented trends, the current IPO system is constrained by several defects. First, the combination of the characteristics of both the merit system and the disclosure system places an onerous burden on the issuer, making the application process for share issuance costly, time-consuming, and unpredictable. Second, vesting the final decision-making power for IPO with the regulators creates huge rent-seeking activities for regulatory officials. The *Wang Xiaoshi* case and the *Wang Yi* case, both involving CSRC officials who provided illegal benefits to business companies in exchange for bribery, evidenced that the system, which gives the regulator the power to conduct substantive examination of the issuer's nature of business, financial standing, corporate governance as well as business prospects, is very easily abused by unscrupulous officials. Third, the CSRC is overloaded with the review job for hundreds of applications every year, which its limited resources are not able to handle. And fourthly, even the highly regarded sponsorship system has its problems, as the scarcity of CSRC-licensed sponsors make them monopolizers in the market. As a result, the quality of sponsoring in many of the submitted applications has turned out to be disappointingly low.

The chief problem lies in the CSRC's examination and approval power. Given the stated purpose of the system is 'to protect the lawful rights and interests of investors and the public interest' by giving the CSRC such mighty approval power to ensure the quality of the issuers,[133] it is supposed to be matched with a CSRC responsibility to guarantee the aforesaid quality. However, the CSRC undertakes no such responsibility, although many notorious offering scandals were discovered after the issuers successfully obtained CSRC approval to go public.

What reform measures could be taken to overcome the above-mentioned defects in the system? A suggestion that has been forcefully advocated by scholars and practitioners in China is actually a fundamental change of the system, which, if adopted, will lead to the abolition of

133 IPO Measures, Article 1.

the CSRC's review and approval power and the establishment of an American style disclosure-based registration system. In fact, the CSRC has indicated, on numerous occasions, that stock issuance in China will eventually adopt the registration system.

It is, however, unrealistic to expect such a switch to occur any time soon. As long as the institutional, legal, and regulatory frameworks that are necessary for supporting the registration system do not appear in China, adoption of such a system would be rather detrimental than beneficial to the securities markets in China. It is submitted that, before formally adopting the registration system, China must firstly work to set up a legal and regulatory framework for the securities markets that could achieve the following objectives: first, to ensure that complete, accurate, and true information could be disclosed by the issuers; second, to ensure that the regulators are able enforce the laws and punish the wrongdoers in an effective way; and third, to ensure that corporate governance rules and fiduciary duties owned by corporate insiders can be enforced by investors through private enforcement.

9.7 LISTING OF SHARES

9.7.1 Markets for Listing and Trading Shares in China

Subject to the restrictions that will be examined later in this chapter, the relatively free transferability of shares of JSLCs determines that there must be markets for those shares, no matter if the shares were publicly offered and listed on a stock exchange, or privately placed. The shares, once offered, will be traded in China's developing *duocengci ziben shichang* [multi-layered capital markets], which are in the process of establishing market infrastructures and networks comprising of both stock exchanges and over-the-counter markets.[134] At the current stage, the places and networks for stock listing and trading consist of the following markets:

- The Main Board (*Zhuban*) of the Shanghai Stock Exchange (SSE). The SSE was founded on 27 November 2007 with its Main Board, which is still the only listing and trading board in the SSE today. The Shanghai Main Board is, however, the market for the large,

[134] CSRC (2008), p. 295.

blue-chip companies in China. It is the only main board now to accept applications for listing on the main board.

- The Main Board of the Shenzhen Stock Exchange (SZSE). The SZSE was founded 1 December 1990. It stopped accepting new listing requests in 2000 but still remains a trading place for companies already listed.
- The Small and Medium-sized Enterprise Board (SME Board; *Zhongxiao Qiye Ban*) under the SZSE. It was established on 27 May 2004 and initially was intended to be modeled after Hong Kong's Growth Enterprise Market (GEM). The CSRC, however, only allows the SME Board to use the rules and requirements of the main board (the so-called 'two non-changes': no change in the laws and no change in the listing requirements), which has made the SME Board far from being any kind of innovation. For this reason, the SME Board was usually regarded as a section of the SZSE Main Board. Nevertheless, it has developed its own trading system (including a price determination mechanism, trading position disclosure, price fluctuation definitions, surveillance, stock codes, and index) and is becoming a separate listing and trading place for small-scale companies in China.
- ChiNext, China's official Growth and Enterprise Board (*Chuangye Ban*) under the SZSE. The ChiNext was established on 23 October 2009 and its first trading day was 30 August 2009. As the second board modeled after the NASDAQ in the U.S. and Hong Kong's GEM, it is aimed at start-ups and high-tech firms and has attracted about 300 listed companies in less than three years. The listing requirements are more relaxed than those of the main board.
- Stock Transfer Agent System (STAS; *Daiban Gufen Zhuanrang Xitong*). Nicknamed as the 'third board', the STAS was established in June 2001, initially for the purpose of accommodating the companies that listed and traded their shares in the STAQ and NET systems, two OTC markets closed down by the government in 1998. In addition, it now provides a share-trading platform for companies that are delisted by the SSE and SZSE, as well as for non-listed JSLCs based in the Zhongguancun Science and Technology Park.
- 'Black Markets' (*Gupiao Dixia Heishi*). Most of these supposedly illegal markets were formed by investors in the early 1990s for trading JSLC shares that were not yet listed on stock exchanges.[135]

---

135 Peng Bing (2005), pp. 174–6; CSRC (2008), p. 7.

For a long time, the black markets also provided a trading place for employee shares that were issued in the early days of some JSLCs but refused by the authorities to be listed on stock exchanges because the shares were not publicly offered.

- Equity Exchanges (*Chanquan Jiaoyisuo*). A number of equity exchanges have been established in China, especially in the past decade, for trading of all kinds of equity interests other than shares listed on the approved stock exchanges. They are membership based and only members can trade – often on behalf of other enterprises – in the exchanges. Now every province in China has established one or more equity exchanges, but the more influential ones are the China Beijing Equity Exchange and Shanghai United Assets and Equity Exchange.

9.7.2 Listing Shares on a Stock Exchange

After the IPO, the shares offered may be listed on a stock exchange, either the Shanghai Stock Exchange (SSE) or the Shenzhen Stock Exchange (SZSE). Although listing of shares with a stock exchange is legally not part of the IPO process, offering and listing of shares are now combined in the one 'going public' process in China. Listing provides benefits to companies and their shareholders of accessibility, transferability, reputation in the public market, and uniformity in corporate governance. Once a company is listed, it will be much easier for it to issue new shares to raise further funds from the market. Due to these incentives, it is fair to say that the ultimate goal of 'going public' is to get the shares listed.

Listing of shares used to be subject to CSRC approval before the new Securities Law took effect in 2006. Article 48 of the Securities Law has returned this power to the stock exchanges by providing that 'An application for listing of shares for trading shall be submitted to a stock exchange, and examined, verified and approved by the stock exchange according to law'. However, Article 50 of the Securities Law still specifies the following minimum conditions for exchange listing of shares: (i) CSRC approved public offering has been completed; (ii) total share capital of the issuer is not less than RMB30 million; (iii) total shares offered to the public account for 25 percent or more of the total outstanding shares of the company; where the company's share capital exceeds RMB400 million, shares held by the public shall constitute 10 percent or more of the total outstanding shares; and (iv) the company has not committed any significant illegal act within the most recent three years, and there is no false record in the company's financial and accounting reports.

Stock exchanges are permitted by the Securities Law to make listing requirements that are higher than the minimum conditions provided for in Article 50 of the Securities Law. For instance, both SSE and SZSE stipulate that the total share capital of the issuer shall not be less than RMB50 million.[136] The ChiNext, however, has a much lower threshold. Under the SZSE's ChiNext Listing Rules, which were enacted based on the 2009-issued CSRC Interim Measures for the Administration of Initial Public Offering of Shares and Listing thereof on the Growth Enterprise Board,[137] the issuer's total share capital shall reach RMB30 million – which is lower than the requirement of RMB50,000 for the main board – in order to get its shares listed on the ChiNext.[138]

The listing of a company's shares is based on a service contract between the listed issuer and the stock exchange. However, the contractual nature of the relationship between these two must not be taken for granted in the Chinese context. Because of the tight control of the stock exchanges by the Chinese government, there was once a prevailing view that the exchanges were agencies of the government rather than market-based self-regulatory entities. As noted in a report of the Law Committee of the National People's Congress (NPC) to the NPC Standing Committee in the course of the Standing Committee's discussion of the draft amendments to the 1998 Securities Law in 2005,[139]

> There are now two views [on the role of the stock exchanges]. One view holds that, the stock exchanges are administratively under the CSRC. Therefore, its review and approval of listing requests and decisions to suspend or delist companies are all administrative acts, which shall be subject to laws of administrative reconsideration and litigation. Another view however asserts that, in international best practice, stock exchanges are all membership-based self-regulatory organizations which accept listing requests and decide to

---

136 See e.g., SSE Listing Rules, Article 5.1.1.

137 Shouci Gongkai Faxing Gupiao Bingzai Chuangye Ban Shangshi Guanli Zanxing Banfa, adopted by the CSRC on 21 January 2009 and effective as of 1 May 2009.

138 Shenzhen Zhengquan Jiaoyisuo Chuangye Ban Gupiao Shangshi Guize (Listing Rules for the Growth Enterprise Board in the Shenzhen Stock Exchange), 2012 version, Article 5.11 ('ChiNext Listing Rules').

139 'Quanguo Renda falu Weiyuanhui Guanyu "Zhonghua Renmin Gongheguo Zhengquanfa (Xiuding Cao'an)" Xiugai Qingkuang De HuiBao' ('Report of the Law Committee of the National People's Congress on the Draft Amendments to the PRC Securities Law'), 23 August 2005, reprinted in An Jian (2005), p. 428.

> suspend listing or delist companies in accordance with their own listing rules. Disputes arising out of the parties' discontent with the stock exchanges shall be resolved according the principles of civil relations. After careful research and deliberation, the Law Committee is of the opinion that, the stock exchanges [in China], as the organizers of the securities markets, review and approve listing applications based on statutory listing conditions and the exchanges' own listing rules. These are self-regulatory activities. If a listing application is approved, the stock exchange should sign a listing agreement with the applicant, which is a civil law relationship and forms the basis for the parties' rights and obligations.

The package of the listing contract includes not only the listing agreement signed before the listing takes place but also all the relevant rules of the stock exchange. By subscribing to such a contract, the issuer incorporates these rules into its corporate charter and bylaws, and accepts the regulatory powers of the stock exchange.

9.8 RESTRICTIONS ON SHARE TRANSFERABILITY

9.8.1 Methods of Share Transfer

As emphasized at the beginning of this book, giving shareholders the right to transfer their ownership interests is a fundamental attribute in modern corporations. This is also an accepted principle in China. Subject to the restrictions discussed as follows, shares of JSLCs are in principle freely transferable. Shares of companies listed on the main boards, SME Board, or ChiNext of the two stock exchanges will be traded in the public markets under the public, centralized trading mechanism of the stock exchanges, which is based on aggregate auctions (*jizhong jingjia*) and continuous auctions (*lianxu jingjia*).

JSLC shares can also be transferred through block trading (*dazong jiaoyi*) or negotiated transfer (*xieyi zhuanrang*). Block trading applies to transfer transactions of a high volume or value. A transaction involving a sale of half a million shares or a value of RMB3 million will be able to apply the rules of block trading, which can be conducted on a more confidential basis in a separate market for big investors.[140] The method of negotiated transfer allows the buyer and seller to conduct arm's length negotiations between themselves without entering the centralized public market. It is used for mergers and acquisitions, transfer of shares between

---

[140] See SSE Trading Rules, Article 3.7.1 onwards.

parties with controlling relationships, foreign investors' strategic investment in a listed company, or any other transactions approved by the CSRC.

It is important to stress that, insofar as listed companies are concerned, the venues for share trading are severely regulated. Article 40 of the Securities Law provides that 'securities that are listed and traded on a stock exchange shall be traded by the method of public, centralized trading or other methods approved by the [CSRC]'. Over the years, relevant rules of the CSRC have generated an understanding that all the shares of listed companies could only be transferred in a stock exchange, no matter if the shares themselves are listed or not.[141] The shares of non-listed companies are in theory not in the province of the CSRC's regulatory power, and they can be transferred in other trading platforms such as the equity exchanges.

9.8.2 Legal Restrictions on Share Transferability

The general principle of free transferability of JSLC shares is constrained by the following restrictions provided in the Company Law, Securities Law, and CSRC rules.

Lock-up restrictions for key players in a company

The following restrictions are imposed on the transferability of shares held by the following key players in a JSLC:[142]

1. Shares owned by the promoters of a company may not be transferred within one year of the date of establishment of the company.
2. Shares issued by the company before its IPO may not be transferred within one year of the date of the listing of its shares on a stock exchange.
3. A director, supervisor, or senior executive of a company may not transfer more than 25 percent of the company shares he owns each year during his term of office.
4. A director, supervisor, or senior executive of a company may not transfer his company shares within one year of the date of the listing of the shares on a stock exchange.

---

[141] Xing Haibao (2010), p. 98.

[142] Company Law, Article 142.

5. A director, supervisor, or senior executive of a company may not transfer his company shares within six months after he leaves his company post.

In addition, a foreign investor who purchases A-shares of a listed company pursuant to the Administrative Measures for Strategic Investment of Foreign Investors in Listed Companies is not allowed to transfer the purchased shares within three years after the purchase.[143]

Share holding and trading restrictions for securities service providers

Securities service providers are subject to the following restrictions on their buying or selling of shares:[144]

1. Securities service firms and personnel who issue audit reports, asset valuation reports, legal opinions, or other documents for a share offering may not buy or sell the shares in question while the offering is being underwritten and for six months after the expiration of the underwriting period. This restriction applies to service providers such as accounting firms, asset valuation firms, and law firms, as well as the responsible individuals in those firms.
2. In addition, securities service firms and personnel who issue audit reports, asset valuation reports, legal opinions, or other documents may not buy or sell the listed shares in question from the date on which they accept the mandate from the listed company until five days after the aforementioned documents are made public.

Permanent share holding and trading restrictions for regulators and semi-regulators

Article 43 of the Securities Law imposes restrictions on holding and trading of shares by business personnel of stock exchanges, securities companies and securities registration and settlement bodies, and staff of securities regulatory authorities, as well as other persons prohibited by law and administrative regulations from participating in share trading. These persons may not hold or trade shares directly or under false names or other persons' names, and may not accept shares from other persons as

---

[143] Waiguo Touzizhe Dui Shangshi Gongsi Zhanlue Touzi guanli Banfa, jointly promulgated by the PRC Ministry of Commerce, CSRC, State Administration of Taxation, SAIC, and State Administration of Foreign Exchange on 31 December 2005, Article 5(3).

[144] Securities Law, Article 45.

a gift. Shares originally possessed by these persons must be transferred to others after they become such personnel.

These restrictions aim to address the conflict of interest problems in China's capital markets, indicating that the lawmakers considered the above persons as regulators, semi-regulators, or administrators in the securities markets. The rationale was stated by NPC's Working Group on Securities Law revision for the restrictions:[145]

> These persons are involved in the supervision and administration of securities activities, including making of the relevant policies and laws on securities transactions, review and approval of share offering, and inspections and investigations of securities activities. If they also hold and trade securities, there will be a major conflict of interest with their official duties and powers.

Disgorging short-swing profits

Under Article 47 of the Securities Law, if a director, supervisor, senior management executive, or shareholder owning 5 percent or more of the total shares of a listed company sells company shares within six months after purchase of the shares, or purchases the shares within six months after selling the shares, any gains so obtained are regarded by the Law to belong to the company. The board of directors of the company is obliged to recover such gains. A cause of action for derivative suit is conferred upon the shareholders to sue the key player who is involved in such short-swing transactions. One should note, however, that this is not a prohibition as such – the key player may freely engage in short-swing transactions as long as the gains are confiscated by the company.

Share repurchase restrictions

JSLCs are generally not allowed to buy back their own shares unless for the following reasons: (1) reducing the company's registered capital; (2) merging with another company that owns this company's shares; (3) awarding the shares to employees; and (4) being requested by a shareholder to buy back company shares owned by the shareholder since he objects to a resolution of the shareholders' general meeting on the merger or division of the company.[146] Shares repurchased for awarding to employees will have to be distributed to the employees within one year. In addition, the number of shares repurchased may not exceed 5 percent of the company's total outstanding shares, and the repurchase should be

---

[145] NPC Working Group (2006), p. 50.

[146] Company Law, Article 143, para. 1.

paid out of the company's after-tax profits.[147] Shares repurchased for other purposes shall be cancelled within 10 days of the repurchase.[148]

Restrictions by the CSRC for investigating illegal securities activities
Article 180(7) of the Securities Law authorizes the CSRC, when investigating major violations of securities law such as securities market manipulation or insider trading, 'to restrict trading in securities by the parties involved in the incident under investigation'. The period of the restriction is limited to not more than 15 trading days, and may be extended by another 15 trading days if the case is complex. Based on this, the CSRC enacted the Implementing Measures for Restricting Securities Trading in 2007 to prescribe the specific procedures for the authorized restrictions.[149]

9.9 INSIDER TRADING LAW

9.9.1 Development of Insider Trading Law in China

Rules prohibiting persons who possess inside information were put in China's corporate and securities law almost at the same time that capital markets were re-established in the PRC, even before the 1993 Company Law was promulgated.[150] The national Securities Law, in its first version adopted in 1998, contained five articles dealing with insider trading, all of which are incorporated and further refined in the 2005 revision to the Securities Law. Meanwhile, the NPC amended the PRC Criminal Law several times to criminalize insider trading. Arguably, these rules have not been effectively and rigorously enforced by the regulators and courts in China as insider trading remains pervasive in the secondary market, despite the waves of government-launched 'wars' against such trading.[151]

---

[147] Company Law, Article 143, para. 3.

[148] Company Law, Article 143, para. 2.

[149] Xianzhi Zhengquan Maimai Xingwei Shishi Banfa, promulgated by the CSRC on and effective as of 18 May 2007.

[150] The CSRC promulgated its first set of rules against fraudulent securities activities, Jinzhi Zhengquan Zhaqi Xingwei Zanxing Banfa (Interim Measures on the Prevention of Securities Fraud), issued by the CSRC and approved by the State Council Securities Committee on 15 August 1993, effective as of 2 September 1993. The measures were abolished on 15 January 2008 by State Council Order 516.

[151] See e.g. 'China Steps Up Insider Trading Crackdown', *Financial Times* online, 14 May 2007; 'The Battle Against Insider Trading', *Wall Street Journal*

On 1 December 2011, Guo Shuqing, the new CSRC chief, announced that one of the top priorities of the CSRC would be cracking down on insider trading in his first public speech as the country's chief securities regulator.[152] A few months later, China's Supreme People's Court (SPC) and Supreme People's Procuratorate (SPP) jointly issued the Interpretation on Several Issues Concerning Application of Law in Handling Criminal Cases Regarding Insider Trading and Disclosure of Inside Information (hereinafter the 'Insider Trading Interpretation').[153] Meanwhile, the CSRC has accelerated investigation of insider trading cases. All these have given the market a hope that the authorities were serious about prosecuting insider trading this time.

From a legislative perspective, China's insider trading law is rather good: it is both comprehensive and straightforward, especially when compared with its counterpart, the short and obscure Rule 10b-5 in the Federal securities law in the U.S. The general principle on regulating insider trading is provided in Article 73 of the Securities Law, which reads:

> Informed persons with inside information on securities trading and persons that unlawfully obtained inside information are prohibited from using such inside information to engage in securities trading activities.

Under the umbrella of Article 73, China's insider trading law is centered around three key concepts: informed persons, insider information, and illegal use of the information to trade. Basically, the law prohibits persons with knowledge of inside information, broadly known as 'insiders', to trade securities based on such information while it is still 'inside'.

9.9.2 Definitions of Persons Involved in Insider Trading

Informed persons

Two groups of persons are governed by the insider trading law in China: the 'informed persons' and 'persons that unlawfully obtained inside information'. It is notable that the Securities Law does not use the term

---

online, 27 June 2007; and 'China Launches War Against Securities Insider Trading', *China Daily* online, 22 May 2009.

152 Speech of Chairman Guo Shuqing at the Ninth Forum on SME Financing, 1 December 2011, available at http://www.csrc.gov.cn/pub/newsite/bgt/xwdd/201112/t20111201_202480.htm (accessed 3 June 2012).

153 Guanyu Banli Neimu Jiaoyi, Xielu Neimu Xinxi Xingshi Anjian Juti Yingyong Falu Ruogan Wenti De Jieshi, promulgated by the SPC and SPP on 29 March 2012 and effective as of 1 June 2012.

'insiders' or 'corporate insiders'. 'Informed persons' appears to be a broader and more inclusive concept, covering both corporate insiders and persons outside the company, such as the 'constructive insiders' defined by the U.S. Supreme Court in *Dirks v SEC.*[154] Informed persons who have knowledge of inside information include the following:[155]

- Directors, supervisors, and senior management executives of the issuer of securities.
- Shareholders owning 5 percent or more of a company's shares, and the directors, supervisors, and senior management executives of such company, as well as the actual controlling person of such company and its directors, supervisors, and senior management executives.
- A company of which the issuer is the controlling shareholder as well as such company's directors, supervisors, and senior management executives.
- Persons who can obtain a company's relevant inside information because of their position in the company.
- Staff members of the securities regulatory authorities (such as the CSRC) and other persons who in the performance of their statutory duties administer securities issuance and trading.
- Relevant staff members of the sponsors, underwriters, stock exchanges, securities registration and settlement companies, and securities services providers.
- Other persons stipulated by the securities regulatory authorities of the State Council.

As can be seen, the definition of informed persons in the Securities Law is broad enough to encompass a wide range of persons who may get involved in securities trading based on non-public information, including both the key players and the employees of a company, the substantial shareholders of a company, constructive insiders such as the accountants, lawyers and investment bankers, and regulatory officials.

Persons who have unlawfully obtained inside information

The Securities Law does not identify the persons who 'unlawfully obtained inside information' mentioned in Article 73. This task was recently done by the SPC and SPC in the Insider Trading Interpretation.

[154] 463 U.S. 646 (1983).

[155] Securities Law, Article 74.

Now it is clear that Chinese courts will define such persons as the following:[156]

- Persons who have obtained inside information by means of stealing, cheating, fraudulently extracting, eavesdropping, luring by promise of gain, spying, or under-the-table deals.
- Near relatives of or other persons who have close personal relationships with the informed persons of inside information if they, during the inside-information-sensitive period, engage in, or expressly or impliedly procure others to engage in, or tip the inside information to other persons who trade securities on the basis of the information tipped. The courts, however, must also check two more conditions to determine whether those persons have unlawfully obtained inside information. First, the suspected trading activities are obviously irregular. Second, the traders could not justify the irregular trading with any legitimate reasons or sources of information.
- Persons who have contact or intercourse with the informed persons of inside information, if they, during the inside-information-sensitive period, engage in, or expressly or impliedly procure others to engage in, or tip the inside information to other persons who trade securities on the basis of the information tipped. Here the courts also need to check the two conditions mentioned above.

Tippers and tippees?

The Insider Trading Interpretation does not expressly use the concepts of 'tippers' and 'tippees' found in American securities regulation. Tippers are corporate insiders and outsiders with a confidentiality duty who knowingly make improper tips of the inside information, and tippees are those who do not have a confidentiality duty but knowingly trade on improper tips.[157] As can be seen, these concepts are embodied in the definitions of the near relatives or people who have close relationships or contact with the informed persons.

---

[156] Insider Trading Interpretation, Article 2.

[157] *Dirks v SEC*, *supra* note 154. See also Loss and Seligman (1995), pp. 821–30.

9.9.3 Definition of Inside Information

The Securities Law contains both a general definition of inside information and a long list of types of information that are mandatorily classified as inside information by the law. In general, inside information refers to 'non-public information, which, in the course of securities trading activities, pertains to a company's business operations and finances or has material impact on the market price of the company's securities'.[158] Pursuant to Articles 75 and 67 of the Securities Law, the following types of information constitute inside information as required by the law:

- A major change in the company's operational policies or scope of business;
- A decision of the company on a major investment or acquisition of major assets;
- Entry into an important contract by the company that may have a material effect on the assets, liabilities, rights and interests, and business results of the company;
- The incurrence of major debts by the company or default on a major liability;
- The suffering by the company of major losses or major damage;
- Major changes with respect to the external conditions of the company's production and operation;
- A change in the directors, one-third or more of the supervisors, or the general manager of the company;
- A relatively big change in the shareholding of shareholders who originally own 5 percent or more of the company's shares or in the circumstances of control by the company's actual controlling persons;
- A decision by the company to reduce capital, merge, divide, dissolve, or file for bankruptcy;
- The incurrence of any major company litigation, or the annulment or invalidation of resolutions of the shareholders' general meeting or the board of directors by dispute resolution bodies according to law;
- The undertaking by judicial authorities of an investigation of the company as a suspect in a criminal case, or the subjection by judicial authorities to coercive measures of a director, supervisor, or

---

158 Securities Law, Article 75.

senior management executive of the company as a suspect in a criminal case;

- The plan of a company to distribute dividends or increase capital;
- Major changes in a company's capital structure;
- Major changes in security for the company's liabilities;
- A single mortgage, sale, or write-off of the major assets used in the company's operation exceeding 30 percent of the value of such assets;
- Potential liability for compensation of major damages to be assumed according to law arising from the acts of directors, supervisors, or senior management executives of a company;
- A plan concerning the takeover of a listed company;
- Other important information determined by the CSRC to have a clear impact on the trading prices of securities.

9.9.4 Duties of Insiders and Prohibited Insider Trading Activities

As noted above, Article 73 of the Securities Law generally prohibits informed persons with inside information on securities trading or persons who have unlawfully obtained inside information, who may be loosely called 'insiders', to trade on the basis of such information. The specific rules of conduct for such persons are contained in Article 76, which stipulates:

> An informed person with knowledge of inside information about securities trading or a person who has unlawfully obtained inside information may not, before the inside information has become public, buy or sell securities of the company in question, or reveal the information or advise other people to buy or sell the securities.

Three specific duties are thus imposed on the insiders. Basically, before the information is disclosed to the public, the insiders shall not (1) trade on the securities themselves; (2) leak the information to others; and (3) advise others to trade the securities. For convenience one could summarize them as the three duties of 'no trading, no leaking and no procuring'. This is, to some degree, similar to the 'disclose or abstain rule' in American securities law.[159] Under Article 76, disclosure is actually not an option, as the insider has a duty not to leak the non-public information at all.

---

159 *SEC v Texas Gulf Sulphur Co.*, 401 F.2d 833 (2d Cir. 1968).

According to the Securities Law and the Insider Trading Interpretation, certain transactions are carved out as exceptions to activities that may otherwise be regarded as insider trading. In general, securities trading that can be explained by legitimate reasons or based upon information from legitimate sources will not be treated as insider trading by the court. Particularly, the following transactions are exempt. First, takeover transactions are generally excluded. This means the purchase of the shares of a listed company by a person (natural person, legal person, other any other organization) who holds (or jointly holds with other persons) 5 percent or more of the company's shares for the purpose of acquiring the control of the company. Further, if the trading is carried out according to pre-concluded written contracts, instructions, or plans, or is based on information that was already disclosed by others, the traders will be exempt from the insider trading duties.[160]

9.9.5 Legal Liabilities of Insiders

Persons involved in insider trading are subject to a host of administrative, civil, and criminal sanctions and liabilities. As in most other parts in China's corporate and securities law, insiders' administrative and criminal liabilities are more clearly defined than their civil liability. As a matter of fact, prior to the revision of the Securities Law in 2005, only administrative liability and criminal liability were available for punishing wrongdoers in securities frauds such as insider trading, market manipulations, and misrepresentations.

On administrative liability, the CSRC is authorized by the Securities Law to impose a fine for the amount of not more than five times the illegal gains.[161] If convicted criminally an insider may also be sentenced to fixed-term imprisonment of not more than 10 years.[162]

Investors injured by insider trading are more concerned with the civil liability, which in theory may enable them to recover any losses caused by the wrongdoers' trading activities. Article 76 of the Securities Law now generally confers a private cause of action upon individual investors by providing that 'the doer shall bear liability for compensation according to law where an act of insider trading causes loss to investors'. In the absence of detailed rules on how to determine who is hurt by insider trading, how to calculate the losses, and determine the causal link, courts

---

[160] Securities Law, Article 76, para. 2; Insider Trading Interpretation, Article 4.

[161] Securities Law, Article 202.

[162] Criminal Law, Article 180.

are very unwilling to take private enforcement cases. The 2012 Insider Trading Interpretation is one for criminal cases. Reportedly, the SPC started to draft a judicial interpretation for dealing with civil disputes in insider trading cases almost a decade ago, but both the draft interpretation and the estimated time of its release remains inside information within the SPC.

10. Financial affairs, accounting, and profit distribution

10.1 CORPORATE FINANCIAL AND ACCOUNTING SYSTEMS

The Company Law largely leaves other laws to regulate a company's internal financial and accounting affairs. Article 164 provides that 'a company shall establish its own financial and accounting systems in accordance with laws, administrative regulations and rules of the treasury department [Ministry of Finance] of the State Council'. China's accounting system underwent revolutionary changes during 1992–2002, moving basically in the trend to converge with international accounting standards. The China Auditing Standards for CPA issued by the PRC Ministry of Finance in 2006 marked China's full embracing of the international best practices on accounting and auditing. As the CSRC notes,[1]

> These new auditing standards cover almost all items of international auditing criteria … [They] are based on the structure of international auditing standards and cover nearly all of its items. They adopt all the basic principles and core procedures of the international standards. Major aspects such as the auditing objective and principle, evaluation and risk management, access to auditing evidence and evidence analysis, drafting and report of auditing conclusions, as well as formulation of professional responsibilities are in conformity with international auditing standards.

In addition, a few provisions in Chapter 8 of the Company Law (entitled 'Financial Affairs and Accounting of Companies') emphasize the company's obligations to report and disclose information, some of which are also provided in other parts of the Company Law as well as in the Securities Law. In particular, each company is under the obligation to prepare its financial and accounting reports in accordance with state accounting rules at the end of each financial year, which shall be audited

[1] CSRC (2011), p. 67.

by an accounting firm.[2] An LLC is obligated to deliver its financial and accounting reports to each of its shareholders within the time limit specified in its corporate charter. JSLCs do not need to make such individual delivery to each of their shareholders, but must make the reports readily available at the company for the perusal of shareholders 20 days before the annual general meeting of the shareholders. A JSLC with publicly offered shares should make a public announcement about its financial and accounting reports.[3]

10.2 VARIOUS RESERVE FUNDS IN A COMPANY

Companies in China are required or encouraged to maintain several contingency reserve funds. These are important matters for shareholders and other stakeholders such as the creditors and employees, as the use of the funds may directly affect their financial interests.

First, it is mandatory that each company establish a 'statutory common reserve fund' (*fading gongjijin*) and allocate 10 percent of its after-tax profits to this fund if the company decides to distribute for a given year. The company does not need to make such allocations when the cumulative amount of such reserve exceeds 50 percent of its registered capital.[4] A company, upon the approval of its shareholders' meeting, may also establish a discretionary common reserve fund (*renyi gongjijin*).[5] In addition, the premiums earned from the issuance of shares above par shall enter into the capital common reserve (*ziben gongjijin*) account.[6] These reserves normally will be used for making up the company's losses, expanding the company's business, or increasing the company's registered capital, except that the capital common reserve may not be used for making up the company's losses.[7]

---

[2] Company Law, Article 165.
[3] Company Law, Article 166.
[4] Company Law, Article 167, para. 1.
[5] Company Law, Article 167, para. 3.
[6] Company Law, Article 168.
[7] Company Law 169. The 1993 Company Law used to require companies to set aside part of their profits for a statutory common welfare fund for the protection of company employees. The requirement was canceled by the 2005 Company Law.

10.3 DISTRIBUTION OF DIVIDENDS UNDER THE COMPANY LAW

10.3.1 Order of Dividend Distribution and Forms of Payment

The distribution of after-tax profits ('dividends distribution') takes the following order under the Company Law:[8]

1. Making up the losses suffered by the company in the previous year;
2. Allocating 10 percent of the profits to the statutory common reserve fund;
3. Allocating some profits to the discretionary reserve fund according to a resolution – if any – of the shareholders' meeting;
4. Distributing the profits to the shareholders.

In theory, dividend distribution in China may take one or several of the following forms: cash dividends, stock dividends, property dividends (dividends in kind), and liability dividends.[9] Cash dividends (*xianjin guli*) are paid out in cash. For shareholders of listed companies the payment is sent directly to his stock trading accounts via the electronic funds transfer system maintained between the stock exchanges and the securities companies. A stock dividend (*gupiao guli*), essentially not a dividend at all, is the issuance of additional shares of a JSLC to its shareholders at no charge to the shareholders. As the payment of stock dividends is made to all the shareholders in proportion to their shareholding, it does not alter the equity structure of the company. Therefore, a shareholder does not really get an increase of his wealth for both the market capitalization of the company, and his share of the ownership of the company remains the same. However, stock dividends could increase the liquidity of the shareholder's wealth as he could sell the additional shares for cash. A company may also pay property dividends (*caichan guli*) to shareholders in the form of tangible or intangible assets, such as products, services, or securities of other entities held by the company. Lastly, liability (*fuzhai guli*) dividends are paid in the form of notes payable in cash to the shareholders on a due date in the future. Liability dividends basically convert the shareholders' rights to dividends into claims as creditors of the company.

---

8 An Jian (2005), p. 238.
9 Zhou Yousu (2006), p. 457; Zhao Xudong (2006), p. 464.

Listed companies in China usually pay cash or stock dividends to their shareholders as forms of dividend payment. Indeed, the CSRC Model Charter stipulates that listed companies may only use cash or stock for profit distributions.[10]

10.3.2 Power to Propose and Approve Dividend Distributions

It is clear in Articles 38 and 100 of the Company Law that only the shareholders' meeting of a company has the power to review and adopt a resolution to approve the plans for distributing profits. Articles 47 and 109 further make it clear that the board of directors has the power to formulate the company's profit distribution plans. It is less clear whether the board's formulation power is an exclusive one. In particular, the question is whether shareholders can also make a proposal to the shareholders' meeting for distributing profits, which, if adopted by the shareholders in the form of a resolution, will compel the company to distribute profits. It is submitted that, at least in JSLCs, the shareholders should be able to do this given that (1) Article 103 of the Company Law permits shareholders who individually or aggregately hold 3 percent or more of company shares to submit written proposals for the shareholders' meeting to consider and (2) the law does not limit the scope of shareholders' self-proposed items. It certainly will not be violating any law if the shareholders' meeting decides to make profits distributions based on a proposal of certain shareholders.

However, the Supreme People's Court (SPC), in *Hu Ke v Siwen Ltd* (2006),[11] opined that, on dividend distribution, the court should allow the board of directors and the shareholders' meeting to take proper actions first, rather than directly render a judicial decision to compel the company to distribute profits. The plaintiff was one of the four founders of Siwen Ltd, the defendant, owning 25 percent of its equity interest. The company was incorporated in 1998. By 2004, it had undistributed profits of more than RMB100 million. The Higher People's Court of Henan Province, the first-instance court in this case, ruled that the defendant had violated the Company Law and harmed the interest of the minority shareholder by refusing to distribute the huge amount of profits it had accumulated. The defendant was ordered to pay dividends to the plaintiff in proportion to his 25 percent shareholding in the company. The decision was overruled by the SPC, which held that the power to decide

---

10 Model Charter, Article 151.

11 SPC Doc. No. (2006) Min Er Zhong Zi Di 110 Hao, reprinted in SPC Civil Division II (2011a), pp. 293–8.

whether and how to distribute dividends was within the province of powers and duties of the board and the shareholders' meeting. Specifically, the SPC emphasized that the profit distribution plan should be formulated by the board and approved by the shareholders' meeting. There was hence no legal basis allowing a shareholder to directly ask the court to compel any form of dividend distribution.[12]

10.3.3 Abolition of the Principle of Proportionality

In principle, the dividends of a company should be distributed to shareholders in proportion to their shareholdings. Using the phrase in the Company Law, 'shareholders should receive dividends in proportion to "their paid-up capital contributions in an LLC"[13] and "their shareholdings in a JSLC"'.[14] Indeed, in the 1993 Company Law it was compulsory for companies to pay dividends in accordance with the principle of proportionality.[15] The 2005 Company Law canceled this compulsory requirement by allowing company shareholders to make rules for themselves in this regard. Thus, an LLC should in principle distribute dividends based on the principle of proportionality and grant its shareholders the preemptive rights to subscribe for new capital contributions, 'except where all shareholders agree not to receive dividends in proportion to their paid-up capital contributions or not to exercise the preemptive rights to subscribe for new capital contributions in proportion to their paid-up capital contributions'.[16] The same principle applies to JSLCs, which should distribute dividends in proportion to the shareholdings of their shareholders 'unless the corporate charter of the companies stipulates that the profits shall not be distributed in proportion to the shareholdings'.[17] These changes were viewed as another milestone in developing business companies' 'self-governance' in China.

10.3.4 Remedies When the Company Refuses to Distribute Dividends

It can be inferred from various provisions of the Company Law that companies in China are not under any compulsory legal obligation to make dividends distributions. In other words, it is up to the companies –

12 Id, p. 298.
13 Company Law, Article 35.
14 Company Law, Article 167, para. 4.
15 1993 Company Law, Article 33.
16 Company Law, Article 35.
17 Company Law, Article 167, para. 4.

via the board of directors and the shareholders' meeting – to decide when and how to distribute dividends to its shareholders.

For LLC shareholders, if the company refuses to distribute dividends, there is only one remedy available, that is, requesting the company to repurchase its equity interest in the company 'at a reasonable price'. Under Article 75 of the Company Law, the repurchase request may be posted to the company if all the following conditions are met: (1) the company has not distributed profits to shareholders for five consecutive years; (2) the company has been profitable in each of those five years; (3) the company satisfies the requirements for distribution of profits stipulated in the law; (4) the shareholders' meeting adopts a resolution not to distribute dividends; and (5) the requesting shareholder has voted against the resolution. The company and the requesting shareholder have 60 days after the adoption of the shareholders' resolution to conduct consultations. In the case where an agreement cannot be reached through consultations, the shareholder may bring a legal action before the court to compel the company to buy back his equity interest within 90 days after the adoption of the resolution.

It is notable that there is no such repurchase obligation imposed on JSLCs. There is even no chance for a court to apply Article 75 to JSLCs by analogy, as the lawmakers indicated clearly during the congressional debates in 2005 that Article 75 should be applied only to LLCs as JSLC shareholders could choose to leave the company simply by selling their shares.[18]

10.4 CSRC POLICY ON DIVIDEND DISTRIBUTIONS IN LISTED COMPANIES

Listed companies in China are notoriously known for their unwillingness to distribute dividends. Reportedly, the average dividends/profits ratio (the percentage of dividends distributed in the profits earned each year by the listed companies) declined from 88.96 percent in 2001 to 16.30 percent in 2010. One hundred and seventy-three listed companies never distributed cash dividends in the past decade.[19]

---

18 An Jian (2005), p. 417.

19 '173 Jia Shangshi Gongsi Shinian Wei Xianjin Feihong, Zai Rongzi 400 Yi Yuan' ['173 Listed Companies Never Distributed Cash Dividends in the Past 10 Years, but Raised Another RMB40 billion during the Same Period']. *East Daily*, 15 November 2011, available at http://sc.stock.cnfol.com/111115/123,1325,11138801,00.shtml (accessed 18 June 2012).

The CSRC, proclaiming itself the protector of investors in China, has a long-held view that the generally low levels of dividends paid by listed companies are detrimental to the development of China's capital markets. For this reason, it has constantly put into the markets, often unsuccessfully enforced, controversial regulatory measures to press listed companies to adopt more generous dividend policies. The Administrative Measures for the Issuance of New Shares by Listed Companies promulgated in 2001 required listed companies to explain why they had not paid dividends to shareholders for the past three years. Following a policy paper issued in 2004, *Several Provisions on Strengthening the Protection of the Rights and Interests of Public Shareholders*,[20] the new Administrative Measures on Securities Offerings by Listed Companies (the 'New Offering Measures') were issued by the CSRC in 2006, which initially required a listed company to pay out at least 20 percent of their annual average profit for the past three consecutive years in the form of cash dividends to shareholders. The minimum amount was raised to 30 percent by the amendments to the New Offering Measures in 2008. Listed companies that refuse to make such dividends distributions will not be allowed to float new bonds or sell additional shares.[21]

The CSRC's most recent movement on dividend policies was the promulgation of the *Circular on Further Implementing Cash Dividend Distribution by Listed Companies* in May 2012.[22] The new circular requires that the IPO prospectus contain information about the issuer's dividend policy and plans for payments of dividends in the next three years, together with strategic plans for generating long-term returns for the company. Now listed companies must formulate dividend policies that shall be provided in their corporate charters. The company's dividend policy and its implementation must also be fully disclosed in its periodical reports.

---

[20] Guanyu Jiaqiang Shehui Gongzhonggu Gudong Quanyi Baohu De Ruogan Guiding, promulgated by the CSRC on and effective as of 7 December 2004 (hereinafter the CSRC Investor Protection Provisions).

[21] New Offering Measures, Article 8(5).

[22] Guanyu Jinyibu Luoshi Shangshi Gongsi Xianjin Fenhong Youguan Shixiang De Tongzhi, adopted by the CSRC on 4 May 2012.

11. Mergers, acquisitions, and takeovers

11.1 KEY DEFINITIONS

Any discussion of fundamental corporate changes in China cannot start without clarifying the key concepts involved and distinguishing them from each other. Jargon such as *shougou*, *jianbing*, *goubing*, and *hebing* frequently appear in newspapers, books, journals, and legislation concerning corporate activities, but the distinctions are not precise, and often the terms are used interchangeably. They are loosely grouped under the term 'mergers and acquisitions' (M&A) in China to refer to the combination of two or more business companies or one company's purchase of a large amount of stock or assets from another company.

The Company Law has a few provisions loosely defining corporate combinations. Article 173 defines two types of mergers (*gongsi hebing*). A merger by absorption (*xishou hebing*) is effected by the absorbing of one or more existing companies by another. The absorbing company survives and continues the combined business, while the absorbed – or the merged – company will be dissolved. This form of merger is popularly known as *Jianbing*, namely one company swallows another. A merger by new establishment (*xinshe hebing*), which is essentially a consolidation in American corporate law,[1] refers to the creation of a new company by combining two or more existing companies. Only the 'consolidated' company survives and continues with the assets and liabilities of the original – also called the 'constituent' – companies, while all the original companies are legally dissolved. Therefore, conceptually the key distinction is whether a new company is formed to replace the constituent companies that cease to exist. In practice, however, this distinction is often blurred, as a number of variations could be generated on the basis of these two legally prescribed forms of merger.

Shougou, or acquisition, is a broad concept covering the purchase of equity interests or assets by one company from another. It could refer to the acquisition of either a small or large amount of other companies'

[1] 'A consolidation is the uniting or amalgamation of two or more existing corporations to form a new corporation'. Cox and Hazen (2003), p. 606.

stock or assets. If a merger (including consolidation) is typically understood as the joining together of two or more companies to become one, an acquisition is merely a sale of assets or equity interests. However, if the size of the purchase is large enough, the transaction will essentially be a merger or consolidation. One such example is the acquisition by Lenovo, a Chinese computer manufacturer, of the personal computer division of IBM in 2005. Although the transaction was literally characterized as an acquisition of assets, it was actually a merger of the personal computer business of IBM, which operated like a subsidiary with certain operational autonomy, into Lenovo. One may even argue that this is actually a consolidation, as the new Lenovo was moved to the U.S. and re-incorporated in New York after the acquisition.

Takeover refers to the acquisition of the controlling interest of a company by another. In essence, it is the acquisition of the entire company. In China, *shangshi gongsi shougou* especially refers to the acquisition – or takeover – of a listed company by purchasing its shares through tender offer or negotiated share transfer agreements.

11.2 PROCEDURAL ISSUES ON CORPORATE COMBINATIONS

Under the Company Law, a corporate combination, be it a merger by absorption or merger by new establishment (consolidation), must go through the following statutory procedures:

1. Board formulation of merger plan. According to Articles 47 and 109 of the Company Law, it is in the power of the board to draft the plan for corporate merger or consolidation.
2. Shareholders' approval. The merger plan must be submitted to and approved by the shareholders' general meeting of each constituent company. Under Articles 44 and 104 of the Company Law, a resolution for adopting the merger plan must be endorsed by shareholders holding two-thirds or more of the total voting rights.
3. Conclusion of the merger agreement. After the general meetings approve the merger plan, 'the parties to the merger shall enter into a merger agreement' in accordance with Article 174 of the Company Law. It is, however, unspecified in the law about who are 'the parties'. Naturally, the parties are understood as the combining

companies.[2] That is, the agreement shall be signed by the legal representative of the company or his authorized representative. However, the Company Law does not provide any guidance as to the main terms of the merger agreement.

4. Public announcement and notice to creditors. Each constituent company shall make a public announcement of the proposed merger on a newspaper within 30 days of the shareholders' approval. Each company must also notify its own creditors within 10 days of the shareholders' approval.[3]
5. Regulators' approval. Not all corporate combination transactions need government approval, but some of them do. Normally the merger of LLCs would not involve regulatory interference. Approval is required if it is a merger involving state-owned assets, FIEs, or listed companies. Depending on the types and ownership of the companies involved in the mergers, the regulators could be the SASAC, NDRC, SAIC, and/or CSRC.
6. Settlement of debts. Creditors of the company are vested with the statutory right of objection in merger transactions. Specifically, the creditors, within 30 days of receipt of the written notice, or within 45 days from the date of the public announcement of the merger, are entitled to request the company to repay the debts owed to them, if the debts are due; or to provide corresponding guarantees, if the debts are not due.[4] Impliedly, the proposed merger may not proceed if the company fails to reach agreements with its creditors for settlement of debts. In any case, the surviving company (or the new company in the case of a consolidation) is legally required to assume all the claims and debts of the combining companies.[5]
7. Registration. A merger almost certainly involves changes in the particulars of corporate information that are legally required to be registered with the company registrar (AICs). The surviving company in a merger by absorption will have to update the registration information at least about the changes in registered capital. The new company after a consolidation must go through all the requisite registration process. Further, all the dissolved companies must undergo de-registration.[6]

---

[2] Zhou Yousu (2006), p. 472.

[3] Company Law, Article 174.

[4] Company Law, Article 174. See also Liu Junhai (2011), p. 593.

[5] Company Law, Article 175.

[6] Company Law, Article 180; Company Registration Regulations, Article 39.

11.3 LIBERALIZATION OF CROSS-BORDER M&A IN CHINA

China is now one of the biggest markets for M&A activity in the world. Chinese M&A, however, has a rather short history. This is understandable in the sense that mergers or acquisitions could only happen between business enterprises with independent legal personality, which was lacking in China before the mid-1980s.[7] Before the national Company Law was adopted in 1993, a few laws were issued by the Chinese government for restructuring and reforming SOEs. These regulations were more administrative than commercial in nature as they were mainly concerned with the government's reallocation of resources among state enterprises in different places and at different administrative levels. The provisions on corporate merger and consolidation in the 1993 Company Law, applying to all types of companies irrespective of their nature of ownership, opened the door for domestic M&A activity. In addition, the Securities Law of 1998 set out a more comprehensive framework for takeover of listed companies in China.

M&A, or *goubing*, became popularly known in China when foreign investors were legally permitted to have access to China's nascent M&A market about a decade ago. The Chinese government has always been proactive in attracting foreign direct investment (FDI, or greenfield investment), but was initially rather hostile toward foreign takeover of Chinese companies via M&A, largely out of concern for sovereign control over the national economy. The two earliest foreign purchases of equity ownership of Chinese companies both occurred in May 1995. One involved the acquisition of 25 percent of the shares of Beilu Motors Co., Ltd by two Japanese companies, and the other was the purchase of 20 percent of the shares of Jiangling Motors Co., Ltd by Ford Motor Company. The two acquisitions triggered tremendous volatility in China's stockmarket and quickly caught the attention of Chinese regulators. A month later, the central government issued a circular mandating that 'no entity shall be allowed to transfer state shares and legal person shares to foreign investors until the state promulgates laws allowing this', although the two deals that had already taken place were grandfathered.[8]

---

[7] The GPCL of 1986 was the first national law to confer legal person status on some enterprises.

[8] Guowuyuan Bangongting Guanyu Zhuanfa Guoyuquan Zhengquan Weiyuanhui Guanyu Zanting Jiang Shangshi Gongsi Guojiagu He Farengu Zhuanrang Gei Waishang Qingshi De Tongzhi (Circular of State Council on the

Although FDI is always encouraged, for a long time a foreign-invested enterprise (FIE) was a lifetime business, meaning it could not undergo any fundamental change during its existence. No M&A was allowed between FIEs or between FIEs and domestically invested companies in China. Although occasionally the authorities approved foreign acquisition of Chinese companies or merging and splitting of FIEs on a case-by-case basis, '[a] major factor limiting this [M&A] development was … the lack of a clear statement of policy and of a coherent body of laws and regulations governing cross-border M&A activity'.[9]

WTO accession – and the anticipation of the accession – led to dramatic changes in Chinese regulators' attitudes toward foreign entry into corporate China through M&A. Since the late 1990s, a growing body of regulations on M&A (including cross-border deals) has been issued to fill the legislative gap in this area. In September 1998, the first set of regulations were enacted to legalize the participation of foreign investors in SOE restructuring. In 1999 a body of provisions were released to permit the merger and division of FIEs.[10] The legislative work was accelerated after China joined the WTO in 2001 with the promulgation of a large body of regulations on foreign investment in listed companies, takeover of listed companies, transfer of state and legal person shares to foreign investors, using foreign investment to restructure SOEs, acquisition of domestic enterprises by foreign investors, and foreign investors' strategic investment in Chinese listed companies.[11] The spirit of these new laws was that foreign investors were allowed, subject to certain regulatory restrictions, to acquire both equity interests and assets in domestic Chinese companies (including both listed and non-listed companies). The following Chinese characteristics were embodied in these post-WTO rules:

1. The principle of limited national treatment to foreign investors was established. Foreign investors can buy equity or assets of Chinese companies via various channels. Under certain circumstances, there was no percentage limitation on a foreigner's shareholding in the targeted company. Some of the laws also did not differentiate foreign or domestic M&A in terms of the acquisition procedures

---

Transmission of the Request of the State Council Securities Commission Asking for Suspending the Transfer of State Shares and Legal Person Shares to Foreign Investors), 23 September 1995, Article 1. See also Wang Jiangyu (2004), p. 25.

9 OECD (2006), p. 25.

10 Id, p. 26.

11 For details of these regulations see Wang Jiangyu (2004), p. 26.

and information disclosure requirements. 'Accordingly, a domestic firm acquired by foreign investors is not deemed an FIE and does not enjoy the normal preferential treatment afforded to FIEs under the three major FIE laws.'[12]

2. Foreign investment through M&A was still required to comply with China's state polices regarding the directions for foreign investment in the *Guidelines for Foreign Investment and the Foreign Investment Catalogue*, which, initially imposed on FDI, prohibits or restricts foreign participation in certain sectors.[13]
3. All these laws encouraged foreign investment that intended to stay in China for a long period. Foreign investors, under most circumstances, could only transfer their acquired shareholding after a lock-up period. The purpose of this policy is to 'attract mid- and long-term investment, prevent short-term speculation, and maintain due order in the securities market'.[14]
4. Employees of the target companies shall be taken care of. 'In order for the authorities to approve a deal, a plan for the resettlement of employees of the domestic enterprise subject to the M&A must be submitted as part of the application package.'[15]
5. M&A activity began to be subject to antitrust review under these laws. Most interestingly, China started to assert both domestic and extraterritorial jurisdiction over M&A transactions.[16]

11.4 REGULATION OF FOREIGN ACQUISTIONS OF CHINESE COMPANIES

The main regulations governing foreign acquisition of Chinese domestic companies are the Provisions on Acquisitions of Domestic Enterprises by Foreign Investors (the 'Foreign Acquisition Provisions') jointly issued by the PRC Ministry of Commerce (MOFCOM), CSRC, SAIC and State Taxation Administration, State Administration of Foreign Exchange (SAFE), and SASAC initially in August 2006 and revised in June 2009. The Foreign Acquisition Provisions have replaced the Interim Provisions on Acquisitions of Domestic Enterprises by Foreign Investors ('Foreign Acquisition Interim Provisions') issued in 2003. These provisions apply

---

[12] Wang Jiangyu (2004), p. 27.
[13] Id, p. 28.
[14] Id.
[15] Id, p. 29.
[16] Id.

to foreign acquisition of either equity or assets of Chinese companies. Although these rules offer some guidelines as to how foreigners can buy into once purely domestic Chinese companies, they are more about stipulating the administrative approval procedures and regulatory restrictions on such transactions.

11.4.1 Types of Acquisitions Covered

The acquisition structures in China's M&A market can generally be divided into equity acquisitions (*guquan binggou*) and asset acquisitions (*zichan binggou*). As the names suggest, an equity acquisition involves the purchase of all or part of the equity interest of the domestic Chinese enterprise, and an asset acquisition is the purchase of some or all of the business assets of the Chinese enterprise.

The pros and cons of each type of acquisition are obvious to observe. Equity purchase enables the investor to control another company as a shareholder through a relatively simple and straightforward process that requires less time and fewer procedures. The purchaser will be able to keep some of the tangible and intangible assets, such as government licenses or permits, which are not for sale as assets. Equity acquisition could also be more tax efficient as the parties need only pay stamp duty and possible income tax in connection with any capital gain resulted from the transaction and are not subject to other taxes. The disadvantage is that the buyer will have to assume all the target company's liabilities and, even worse, may be exposed to hidden or contingent liabilities. The employees of the target company will also have to be taken care of under both the relevant M&A regulations and China's labor laws.

In contrast, an asset acquisition allows the purchaser to pick and choose the assets that it deems useful without engaging in restructuring the target company. Especially, the purchaser does not need to bear the liabilities of the target company as well as the burden of handling redundant employees. The purchaser is, of course, also insulated from hidden or contingent liabilities of the target company. Asset deals have, however, a few disadvantages. For instance, the parties may be subject to a variety of taxes such as value-added tax, business tax, land use tax, etc., in addition to possible income tax. Some key assets, such as government licenses, may not be available for sale, for they cannot be legally transferred. Further, the process is more burdensome as different assets may require different procedures and separate government approvals regarding title transfer.

Insofar as the settlement of debts is concerned, Article 13 of the Foreign Acquisition Provisions points out the differences between the two types of acquisitions as follows:

> In the case of an equity acquisition by a foreign investor, the FIE established after the acquisition shall succeed to the claims and debts of the acquired domestic Company.
>
> In the case of an asset acquisition, the domestic enterprise that sold the assets shall bear its existing claims and debts.
>
> The foreign investor, target domestic enterprise, creditors, and other parties concerned may otherwise agree on the settlement of the claims and debts of the target domestic enterprise, provided such agreement does not prejudice the interest of the third parties and the public. The settlement agreement shall also be submitted to the examination and approval authority.
>
> A domestic company that sells its assets shall notify its creditors and make a public announcement in a newspaper of provincial or higher level at least 15 days before the foreign investor submits an application to the examination and approval authority.

The following four scenarios of acquisitions are covered by the Foreign Acquisition Provisions:[17]

- A foreign investor purchases from a shareholder of a non-FIE domestic company the equity interest owned by this shareholder, thereby turning the company into an FIE;
- A foreign investor subscribes to the increase in the registered capital of a non-FIE domestic company, thereby becoming a shareholder of the company and turning it into an FIE;
- A foreign investor incorporates an FIE in China and uses the FIE to purchase assets from a domestic company and operate such assets;
- A foreign investor purchases by agreement the assets of a domestic enterprise and uses such assets as the registered capital to establish an FIE.

Obviously, the first two types are equity acquisitions and the next two are asset acquisitions. It is important to note that the Foreign Acquisition Provisions are concerned only with acquisitions involving new establishment of FIEs. Thus they do not cover M&A deals between FIEs, nor do they govern the acquisition of equity interests or assets from domestic enterprises by foreign investors through FIEs that were established – presumably a long time ago – for purposes other than the acquisition in

[17] Foreign Acquisition Provisions, Article 2.

question.[18] However, acquisitions of domestic enterprises by foreign-funded investment companies in China are also governed by these provisions.[19]

11.4.2 Restrictions in Relation to Foreign Investment Regulation

The use of FIE in the above acquisitions naturally triggers state regulation of foreign investment. As these acquisitions generate new situations that could not be covered by the traditional rules on FDI, the Foreign Acquisition Provisions have organized the following regulatory framework for FIEs established in such acquisitions.

First, all the foreign investment in connection with the acquisitions must comply with Chinese regulations on industries, land use, environmental protection, state-owned assets, foreign exchange control, etc. In particular, they must comply with the general restrictions on the directions of foreign investment:

> An acquisition may not result in a foreign investor owning all of the equity in an enterprise in an industry in which foreign investors are not allowed to establish wholly foreign-owned enterprises (WFOEs) under the Foreign Investment Industrial Guidance Catalogue. The Chinese party shall continue to have a majority controlling interest in the enterprise or a relative controlling interest in the enterprise after the acquisition if the enterprise is in an industry where Chinese controlling interest is required by the Catalogue. A foreign investor may not acquire an enterprise engaged in an industry closed to foreign investors.[20]

Second, the FIE established after the acquisition can be either above or below the minimum 25 percent threshold, which is normally required for foreign shareholding in FIEs.[21] If, after the acquisition, the foreign investor's share in the registered capital of the acquired enterprise exceeds 25 percent, it will be legally treated as an FIE, which entitles it to enjoy all the preferential treatments available for FIEs. In the case where the foreign shareholding in the post-acquisition target is below 25 percent, the FIE incentives will not be available. Implicitly, the target will be regarded as a domestic enterprise in many respects, although the

---

18 Bu Yuanshi (2010), pp. 132–3.
19 Foreign Acquisition Provisions, Article 52.
20 Foreign Acquisition Provisions, Article 4.
21 See Ch. 2 above.

approval and registration authorities will issue it the relevant certificates bearing the note 'Foreign investment less than 25%'.[22]

Aiming to limit the opportunist 'round-trip' investment, the Foreign Acquisition Provisions generally refuse to recognize the 'foreign investor' status of those overseas companies established or controlled by domestic Chinese companies or individuals, especially when they acquire an affiliated domestic Chinese company. Such an affiliated domestic company acquired by an overseas company will not enjoy FIE status, unless the acquisition is in the form of subscribing to the capital increase in the target companies that results in more than a 25 percent of shareholding by such overseas company.[23] In any case, such acquisitions must be submitted to the MOFCOM for approval.[24]

Second, the acquisition must also conform to the statutory ratios between an FIE's registered capital and its total amount of investment. China's FIE regulation has a tradition of imposing such ratios for every FIE, which are not required for domestic Chinese enterprises.[25] For foreign equity acquisitions of Chinese enterprises, the legally prescribed ratios are as follows:[26]

- If the registered capital is less than US$2.1 million, the total amount of investment may not exceed 10/7 of the registered capital;
- If the registered capital is US$2.1 million or more but less than US$5 million, the total amount of investment may not exceed two times the registered capital;
- If the registered capital is US$5 million or more but less than US$12 million, the total amount of investment may not exceed 2.5 times the registered capital;
- If the registered capital is US$12 million or more, the total amount of investment may not exceed three times the registered capital.

---

22 Foreign Acquisition Provisions, Article 9, paras. 1 and 2.

23 Foreign Acquisition Provisions, Article 9, para. 3.

24 Id, Article 11.

25 The original purpose of the requirement of the 'total investment amount' was to determine the total value of tax-exempt imports and total amount of borrowings allowed for FIEs. Loans borrowed by an FIE shall not exceed the difference between the FIE's registered capital and total amount of investment. The total amount of investment is also used to determine the amount of an FIE's registered capital as well as the level of approval authorities in the regulatory bureaucratic system in China. In brief, an FIE's total amount of investment includes its registered capital contributed by its shareholders and funds borrowed from external sources.

26 Foreign Acquisition Provisions, Article 19.

11.4.3 Examination and Approval

All transactions under the Foreign Acquisition Provisions must be approved by competent government agencies. The chief 'examination and approval authority' is the MOFCOM or the provincial counterpart of MOFCOM (the 'provincial commerce department') if necessary.[27] Various other agencies, such as the SASAC, CSRC, and SAFE, will be involved in the approval process for matters falling within their respective jurisdictions.[28]

The foreign investor is tasked to submit acquisition documents to the MOFCOM or the relevant provincial commerce department. For an equity acquisition, the documents should include the following, among others:[29]

1. a unanimous shareholders' resolution in favor of the acquisition if the target company is an LLC or a resolution of the shareholders' general meeting in favor of the acquisition if the target is a JSLC;
2. an application to convert the target company into an FIE, together with the investors' contract for and corporate charter of the post-acquisition FIE;
3. the acquisition agreement (to which the applicable law is Chinese law);
4. a financial audit report for the previous financial year of the target company;
5. plans for the arrangements made for the employees of the target company;
6. plans for the settlement of the target company's claims and debts;
7. an asset appraisal report for the equity interest in question;
8. a statement provided by the parties to the acquisition on whether affiliation relationships exist among the parties.

For an asset acquisition, the foreign investor shall submit the following documents, among others, to the government for approval:[30]

1. the written decision, in favor of the asset sale, adopted by the title owner or the power organ – which refers to the shareholders'

[27] Id, Article 10.
[28] Id, Articles 5, 6, 7, and 8.
[29] Id, Articles 21, 13, 14, and 15.
[30] Id, Articles 23, 13, 14, and 15.

meeting in LLCs and JSLCs – of the enterprise that owns the asset in question;
2. an application to establish an FIE, together with the investors' contract for and corporate charter of the proposed FIE;
3. the acquisition agreement (to which the applicable law is Chinese law);
4. proof of the notices and announcements made for informing the creditors of the target enterprise, as well as a statement on whether the creditors have expressed objections to the acquisition;
5. plans for the arrangements made for the employees of the target company;
6. plans for the settlement of the target company's claims and debts;
7. an asset appraisal report for the asset in question;
8. a statement provided by the parties to the acquisition on whether affiliation relations exist among the parties.

The above documents required by the MOFCOM are worthy of some special attention. Two points are particularly notable. First, the approval of the shareholders' meeting is required for both equity and asset acquisitions. Second, both types of acquisitions require the parties to make arrangements for the employees.

11.4.4 Appraisal, Purchase Price, and Payment

Under Article 14 of the Foreign Acquisition Provisions, the purchase price shall be determined on the basis of the equity to be transferred or the value of the asset to be sold as appraised by an asset appraisal institution. The parties, however, are no longer required to hire a China-incorporated asset appraisal agency, which was initially required in the 2003 Interim Provisions. In any case, the purchase price cannot be decided merely through negotiations between the parties, but should be based on 'asset appraisal conducted in accordance with international accepted ordinary appraisal methods'.[31] Further, 'sending capital overseas in disguise by transferring equity or selling assets at a price markedly lower than the appraisal results is prohibited'. As noted by one commentator, this provision 'must be read against the background of practices in recent years according to which SOE assets were directly or indirectly sold below market price to foreign investors'.[32]

[31] Id, Article 14.
[32] Wolff (2006), p. 80.

The payment of the purchase price can take the form of cash, stock, in kind, intellectual property, or any other form allowed by the law. For cash payment, normally foreign currencies are required, unless the foreign investor is approved by the SAFE to use Chinese Renminbi it lawfully owns to make the payment.[33]

11.4.5 Share Swaps

Part IV of the Foreign Acquisition Provisions is a welcome new addition to the law of cross-border M&A in China. It provides a comprehensive framework for using equity (shares) to pay the purchase price by foreign investors. In the Provisions' own language, 'the use of equity as method of payment in the acquisition of domestic companies by foreign investors' shall mean that 'a shareholder of an overseas company uses the equity it owns in the overseas company, or the overseas company uses the shares purchased from a new offering, as the consideration paid to purchase the equity in a domestic company from its shareholder or shares available in a new share offering by the domestic company'.[34] In summary, a share swap will occur if shares of an overseas company (the foreign investor/acquirer) are used to buy equity interests in a domestic company.

Qualified foreign investors and their shares

The foreign company which wishes to use its shares to purchase an equity interest in a domestic company must meet the following qualifications:[35]

- the company must be legally incorporated in a foreign jurisdiction that has a sound corporate law system;
- the company and its management team have not been subject to regulatory sanctions by the relevant authorities in the past three years; and
- the company should be listed in a place with a sound securities trading system (unless it is an SPV mentioned below).

The shares used by the foreign investors as acquisition consideration shall meet the following requirements:[36]

---

33 Foreign Acquisition Provisions, Article 17.
34 Id, Article 27.
35 Id, Article 28.
36 Id, Article 29.

- they are lawfully held by shareholders and freely transferable;
- they are not under any ownership dispute or constrained by pledge or any third-party rights;
- they are traded on a legally established, public securities market (but not an over-the-counter market); and
- the trading prices of the shares have been stable during the most recent year.

The use of special purpose vehicles for overseas listing

The Foreign Acquisition Provisions set out detailed rules on the use of special purpose vehicles (SPVs, or *teshu mudi gongsi*) in cross-border acquisitions. An SPV is an overseas company controlled, directly or indirectly, by a domestic company or natural person inside China for the purpose of realizing overseas listing of its/his rights and interests in a domestic company. The SPV, like any other foreign investor, could use its own existing shares or shares issued in a subsequent suffering to purchase the existing equity interest or newly offered equity interest of a domestic company.[37] Clearly, the provision of the SPVs indicates the government's willingness to legitimize – and tightly regulate – one of the typical paths for Chinese-owned companies to list shares overseas. These companies are the so-called 'red-chip' companies, as they are legally incorporated in foreign jurisdictions but are controlled by Chinese nationals. In any case, the red-chip companies are also subject to the regulatory authority of the Chinese government according to China's own laws.

The establishment of an SPV in an overseas jurisdiction, as a form of outbound investment, must be approved by the MOFCOM.[38] When the SPV comes back to acquire the domestic company, additional MOFCOM examination and approval are required.[39] Further, both MOFCOM and CSRC will be involved if the SPV is to be turned into a listed company in a foreign stockmarket. For such listing applications, the MOFCOM will review the documents first and render a preliminary decision as to whether it is suitable for overseas listing. With the MOFCOM's preliminary approval, the domestic company shall proceed to seek the CSRC's approval for the SPV's overseas listing. The MOFCOM will allow the acquisition to happen by issuing an FIE certificate only after the CSRC

---

[37] Id, Article 39.
[38] Id, Article 42.
[39] Id, Article 44.

approves the plan for the SPV's listing.[40] It is, however, important to note that the CSRC's approval depends on two conditions on top of the business merits of domestic company and the SPV. First, the stockmarket where the SPV is to be listed has sound legal and regulatory systems. Second, the country or region for such listing has signed a memorandum of understanding on regulatory cooperation with the CSRC.[41]

11.5 FOREIGN ACQUISITIONS IN THE FORM OF STRATEGIC INVESTMENT

11.5.1 Foreign 'Strategic Investment' in Listed Companies

As noted in Chapter 9, foreigners have been allowed, to a limited extent, to purchase shares of listed companies in China. They could buy, by agreement, state and legal person shares, which used to be non-tradable, buy A-shares through Qualified Foreign Institutional Investors (QFIIs), and indirectly buy an equity stake in a listed company in China through offshore transactions.[42]

Another significant channel for foreigners to buy into Chinese listed companies was introduced in 2005 by the Administrative Measures on Strategic Investment in Listed Companies by Foreign Investors.[43] The new regulations have introduced the concept of 'foreign strategic investors' to further liberalize foreign investment in China's stockmarket. In general, foreign strategic investment is defined as 'medium- and long-term merger and acquisition investment of a considerable scale' by foreign investors in buying A-shares of a listed JSLC that has completed its non-tradable share structure reform or a company that was listed on a stock exchange after the completion of the non-tradable share reform programme.[44]

A few general points about the foreign strategic investment are worth noting here. First, this was actually the first law to allow foreign investors to buy A-shares directly in the Chinese equity market. Before this,

---

[40] Id, Article 45.

[41] Id, Article 40.

[42] Bu Yuanshi (2010), pp. 144–5; Wolff (2006), pp. 102–3.

[43] Waiguo Touzizhe Dui Shangshi Gongsi Zhanlue Touzi Guanli Banfa, adopted by the MOFCOM, CSRC, State Taxation Administration, SAIC, and SAFE on 31 December 2005 (hereinafter the Strategic Investment Measures).

[44] Strategic Investment Measures, Article 2. On the non-trade share reform, see Ch. 9 above.

foreigners were only permitted to purchase B-shares directly and A-shares indirectly through QFIIs. Second, the investment has to be a long-term, or at least medium-term, project, meaning that the investment has to last for at least three years.[45] Third, there is no cap on foreign participation through strategic investment. The initial investment from a foreign strategic investor has to reach the minimum threshold of 10 percent of the target company's total outstanding shares, but there is no upper ceiling on foreign shareholding in such a company.[46] Fourth, foreign shareholding in the post-acquisition listed JSLC can be either above or below the traditional 25 percent threshold for FIEs. If, after the strategic acquisition, foreign shareholding reaches 25 percent or more in the JSLC, the company will receive official certificates (including a business license) bearing a note of 'Foreign invested joint stock limited company (acquisition of 25 percent or more of the A-shares)' from the MOFCOM, SAIC, and SAFE.[47]

11.5.2 Qualifications of Foreign Investors

Although not every foreigner is eligible to be a strategic investor, the Strategic Investment Measures are rather friendly in defining the investors.[48] A substantive requirement is that the investor must be a lawfully established foreign legal person with sound financial standing, corporate governance, and internal control.[49] It must own offshore assets of at least US$100 million or manage offshore assets of at least US$500 million.[50] In addition, the investor must not have been subject to any severe punishment imposed by Chinese or overseas regulatory authorities in the past three years.[51] A foreign investor may do strategic investment in China through its wholly owned subsidiary located outside China.[52] In this case, only the parent company needs to comply with the qualification

---

45 Id, Article 5(3), under which the A-shares acquired by foreign strategic investors are subject to a three-year lock-up period.

46 Id, Article 5(2).

47 Id, Articles 17, 18, and 19.

48 Deschandol and Desmeules (2006) (noting that the requirements on strategic investment previously introduced in a government circular 'may have led [one] to think that onerous qualification requirements would be imposed on strategic investors'. On the contrary, the Strategic Investment Measures introduce requirements 'that are surprisingly investor-friendly').

49 Strategic Investment Measures, Article 6(1) and 6(3).

50 Id, Article 6(2).

51 Id, Article 6(4).

52 Id, Article 13.

requirements, but the parent company must commit itself to bearing joint and several liabilities with its subsidiary.

11.5.3 Methods of Investment

The Strategic Investment Provisions provide three methods for foreign investors to acquire A-shares in listed companies: (1) acquisition by a negotiated private transfer agreement between the foreign investor with existing shareholder(s) of the target company; (2) acquisition by a directed placement; (3) acquisition by 'any other methods as allowed by Chinese law'.[53]

An acquisition by agreement (*xieyi zhuanrang*) will lead to a private share transfer to the foreign investor based on the results of negotiations between the investor and the company's existing shareholder(s). It has to comply with the following procedures outlined in the Strategic Investment Provisions:[54]

1. the target company's board of directors adopts a resolution to carry out the strategic investment by a private transfer agreement, followed by the adoption of a resolution of the same nature by the company's shareholders' meeting;
2. the target company signs a share transfer agreement with the foreign investor;
3. the foreign investor submits application documents to the MOFCOM for approval;
4. if approved by the MOFCOM, the foreign investor completes the relevant procedures and formalities with the stock exchange, securities settlement and registration company and the CSRC;
5. upon completion of the negotiated transfer, the post-acquisition listed company collects the FIE approval certificate from the MOFCOM and updates its registration with the company registrar (AIC) concerned.

A directed placement (*dingxiang faxing*), which is essentially a private placement, enables the foreign investor to become a shareholder of the listed company by subscribing to shares directly issued to it in a subsequent offering. Such a transaction is required to follow the following procedures:

---

[53] Id, Article 5(1).

[54] Id, Article 8.

1. the listed company's board of directors adopts resolutions on directed placement of shares to the foreign investor and on a draft of the amendments to the company's charter, followed by the adoption of resolutions of the same nature by the company's shareholders' meeting;
2. the listed company signs an agreement with the foreign investor on the directed placement;
3. the listed company submits application documents to the MOFCOM for FIE approval;
4. with the in-principle approval of the MOFCOM, the listed company should submit application documents to the CSRC for share offering approval;
5. upon completion of the directed placement, the listed company collects the FIE approval certificate from the MOFCOM and updates its registration with the company registrar (AIC) concerned.

11.5.4 Complying with the Takeover Law

An acquisition of shares in a listed company through strategic investment is viewed as a special type of takeover. As such, it should also comply with the information disclosure and reporting obligations for takeover transactions as will be discussed in the next section.[55] It is, however, worth noting here an inconsistency between the Strategic Investment Provisions and the takeover law examined below. Under Article 9 of the Strategic Investment Provisions, the foreign investor has to submit a takeover report to the CSRC to seek a no-objection letter from the CSRC in order to carry out the investment after it acquires 'effective control' of the listed company. However, according to the takeover law below, only a 30 percent shareholding will trigger such obligations. It is thus not clear whether the 'effective control' mentioned in one law is the same as the '30% shareholding' mentioned in another law.

---

[55] Id, Article 10 (providing that strategic investment must comply with the statutory reporting obligations prescribed in the PRC Securities Law and relevant CSRC regulations).

11.6 TAKEOVERS OF LISTED COMPANIES

11.6.1 Regulatory Framework of Takeovers

Takeover of listed companies (*shangshi gongsi shougou*) is regulated by Chapter 4 of the PRC Securities Law as well as by a set of detailed rules contained in the Administrative Measures for the Takeover of Listed Companies issued by the CSRC (hereinafter the 'Takeover Measures').[56] By definition, it is the acquisition of shares by one company (the 'acquirer' or 'bidder') to gain voting control of a listed company (the 'target company'). Under these laws, the acquirer could either become a controlling shareholder by holding shares of the target company or become an actual controlling person through contractual or other arrangements.[57]

The key distinction between takeovers and other types of acquisitions of shares of listed companies is that the former is the sale of corporate control. That is, a takeover must result in the acquirer's actual control of the target company. 'Control' of a listed company is defined as covering any of the following situations:[58]

1. the acquirer is the controlling shareholder who holds 50 percent or more of the company's shares;
2. the acquirer actually controls more than 30 percent of the voting shares of the company;
3. the voting shares actually controlled by the acquirer could determine the election of half or more of the members of the board of directors of the company;
4. the voting shares actually controlled by the acquirer could have material impact on the adoption of resolutions by the shareholders' meeting in the company;
5. other circumstances prescribed by the CSRC.

Under the Securities Law and the Takeover Measures, the takeover of a listed company can be realized through tender offer (*yaoyue shougou*) or private agreement (*xieyi shougou*, or agreed takeover). Each type of takeover is accompanied by a large body of complicated rules and

---

[56] Shangshi Gongsi Shougou Guanli Banfa, adopted by the CSRC on 17 May 2006 and most recently revised on 14 February 2012 (hereinafter the 'Takeover Measures').

[57] Takeover Measures, Article 5.

[58] Id, Article 84.

procedures on information disclosure and government examination and approval. The goal of these rules is twofold. In short, it aims to ensure that sufficient information is provided to shareholders through the imposition of mandatory disclosure requirements, as well as to maintain state control of the market for corporate control through constant regulatory interference during the whole takeover process.[59]

11.6.2 Information Disclosure in Takeovers

Mandatory information disclosure is at the heart of the takeover regulation. The Takeover Measures require the acquirer and members in its buying group, termed the 'investor and persons acting in concert with the investor',[60] to disclose information about their shareholding in a listed company at the following time points.

First, the acquirer and its group members must disclose their foothold position when their share purchases through securities trading on a stock exchange or private transfer agreements reach 5 percent of the company's total outstanding shares. Once the 5 percent threshold is passed, the acquirer and persons acting in concert with it must file disclosure reports with the CSRC and the stock exchange, notify the target company, and make a public announcement within three days. During the three-day window, the acquirer and group members are not allowed to trade shares of the target company.[61] The purpose of the disclosure is to signal to the regulators, the market, the shareholders, and management of the target company that the company may be in play.

After the aforesaid reports and public announcements are made, the acquirer and group members may continue to trade the shares of the target company on the open market or through private agreements. However, the same kind of disclosure should be made whenever there is an increase or decrease by 5 percent of the company's total outstanding shares, no matter if the change is caused by open market trading or

[59] This aim could be easily inferred from Articles 2, 3, 4 and various other articles on the role of the CSRC in the Takeover Measures.

[60] 'Acting in concert' is defined in Article 83 as 'the act or fact of an investor working together other investors through agreements or other arrangements to jointly increase the quantity of voting shares in a listed company under their control'. Article 83 describes 11 situations that will be deemed, prima facie, as acts of acting in concert.

[61] Securities Law, Article 86, para. 1; Takeover Measures, Article 13, para. 1.

private agreements.[62] The acquirer and group members are not allowed to buy or sell the target company's shares during the reporting period and for two days after the disclosure is made.[63]

Second, if the acquirer (and persons acting with it) is the largest shareholder or actual controlling person of the target company, when its shareholding exceeds 5 percent but has not reached 30 percent of the target company's outstanding shares, it (or they) are mandated to disclose the following information by way of a short-form report: (1) names and addresses of the acquirer and group members; (2) purpose of the shareholding and whether they intend to continue to increase their shareholding in the company in the next 12 months; (3) name of the target company as well as the class, quantity, and percentage of shares held by them; (4) when and how the share interests owned by them in the target company reached or exceeded 5 percent of the outstanding shares of the target company and when and how any additional 5 percent increase or decrease occurred; (5) a summary of the purchase and sale of the shares of the target company through securities trading on the stock exchange within the six months prior to the occurrence of the change of interest; (6) the controlling shareholders and actual controlling persons of the acquirer and persons acting in concert with it, as well as the charts illustrating their equity control relationships; (7) the price, amount of required funds and funding sources for acquiring the relevant shares, and other payment arrangements; (8) whether competition and/or affiliated transactions exist between the business of the acquirer and persons acting in concert with the acquirer (and their controlling shareholders and actual controlling persons) and that of the target company; (9) the follow-up plan for adjustments to be made to the assets, business, personnel, organizational structure, and corporate charter of the target company in the next 12 months; and (10) the major transactions between the acquirer (and group members) and the target company in the preceding 24 months.[64] If the acquirer (and group members) are not the largest shareholder or actual controlling person of the company, it only needs to disclose the first five items above.[65]

---

[62] Securities Law, Article 86, para. 1; Takeover Measures, Article 13, para. 2 and Article 14, para. 2.

[63] Takeover Measures, Article 13, para. 2 and Article 14, para. 3.

[64] Takeover Measures, Articles 16 and 17.

[65] Takeover Measures, Article 16.

11.6.3 Tender Offer

In a takeover by tender offer, the acquirer makes a public, open, offer to purchase shares directly from the shareholders of the target company, with a view to acquiring control of the target company. As provided in Article 23 of the Takeover Measures, 'an investor who wishes to acquire shares of a listed company by way of an offer may issue an offer to all shareholders of the target company to acquire all of the shares held by them (a "general offer") or issue an offer to all shareholders of the target company to acquire part of the shares held by them (a "partial offer")'. A partial offer is defined as an offer to buy less than the whole of the target's outstanding shares, which must be at least 5 percent of the target's outstanding shares.

The traditional form of merger, be it merger by absorption or merger by new establishment, has a few disadvantages. The single largest barrier is that a merger requires the consent of both the power organ and the management organ of the target company. In short, it involves the target's board of directors, which should draft the merger plan, and the shareholders' general meeting, which should adopt resolutions to approve the merger plan and amend the corporate charter accordingly. That is, opposition from either the board or the general meeting may kill the merger deal. But even if the plan is endorsed by both the board and the general meeting, the approval process could still be time-consuming and costly. The tender offer is devised as a mechanism to bypass such barriers by allowing the acquirer to make a public offer to shareholders of the target company to buy their shares at a specified price, upon specified terms, and within a fixed period of time. If shareholders holding the majority of the target company's equity interests tender their shares to the acquirer, the acquirer can effectively take control of the target even over the fiercest opposition by the target's management and board. As such, the tender offer is supposed to be used normally in hostile takeovers, which are rather rare in China's stockmarket today.

11.6.4 Mandatory Bid Rule for Tender Offer

The Takeover Measures distinguish between voluntary and mandatory offers. An acquirer can voluntarily choose to make a public offer to acquire the company. Such an offer can be either a general offer or a partial offer.[66] Sometimes the acquirer might be legally 'forced' to issue a

[66] Takeover Measures, Article 23.

tender offer. This is the 'mandatory bid rule' (MBR) introduced by Article 88 of the Securities Law, which reads,

> If, through securities transactions on a stock exchange, an investor holds or jointly holds with others through agreements or other arrangements 30 percent of the outstanding shares of a listed company and wishes to continue to buy up such shares, it should issue an offer of takeover to all the shareholders of the listed company to purchase all or part of the shares of the listed company in accordance with law.

The same rule is also provided in Article 24 of the Takeover Measures, according to which the acquirer has to issue a general or partial tender offer if it plans to buy up more of the target company's shares on the basis of its 30 percent shareholding. In line with the principles of openness, fairness, and impartiality stipulated in the Securities Law,[67] the MBR aims to 'provide a great degree of shareholder protection by ensuring that the control premium is shared amongst all shareholders'.[68]

As will be addressed below, the MRB also applies to takeovers by agreement when the shareholding of the acquirer reaches 30 percent of the target company's total shares. It further governs indirect acquisitions whereby the acquirer, not legally a shareholder, takes control of a company through investment or contractual relations.

11.6.5 Procedure on Tender Offer

Tender offer report

A tender offer begins with the making of a tender offer report (*yaoyue shougou baogao shu*). The acquirer must prepare the report and engage a financial consultant, which is often a securities company, to file the report with the CSRC and the stock exchange concerned, to notify the target company, and to issue a public alert by publishing a summary of the terms of the tender offer. Fifteen days after filing with the CSRC, the acquirer should disclose to the public the tender offer report together with the professional opinion of a financial consultant and the legal opinion of lawyers. However, the disclosure is constrained by the CSRC's veto power, which means the tender offer report may be made public only after the CSRC expresses its 'no-objection' opinion.[69] In addition, the tender offer report has to be made based on the Contents

---

[67] Securities Law, Article 3.

[68] Huang Hui (2008), p. 161. Article 26 of the Takeover Measures require the acquirer to 'treat all of the target company's shareholders equally'.

[69] Takeover Measures, Article 28.

and Formats for Information Disclosure by Companies Offering Shares to the Public Guidelines (No. 17): Takeover-by-offer Report (Rev. 2006), a model tender offer report provided by the CSRC.

Terms of the offer

The Takeover Measures obligate the acquirer to keep the tender offer open for at least 30 days but not more than 60 days.[70] During the tender offer period, the acquirer may not revoke the offer. It also may not change the terms of the offer during the 15 days prior to the expiration of the tender offer period, unless a competing offer emerges. When a competing offer appears, the acquirer must further extend the offer period to make sure that there are at least 15 days available for the target company's shareholders to consider the offers.[71] Between the publication of the tender offer report and the expiration of the tender offer period, the acquirer may neither sell shares of the target company nor purchase shares of the target company in a manner other than that specified in the offer or on terms that surpass those of the tender offer.[72] Further, the terms in the offer must be kept stable and apply to all of the shareholders of the target company. Any proposed change to the offer must be submitted to the CSRC first, and may only be announced to the public after CSRC approval.[73]

Offer pricing is also generally regulated. In short, the offer price for the same class of shares may not be less than the highest price paid by the acquirer for purchasing shares of the same class during the six months prior to the date of the public alert of the offer.[74] This interventionist provision is meant to protect the shareholders to ensure that they receive sufficient consideration for tendering their shares. In addition, if the offer price is less than the arithmetical average of the daily weighted average price for that class of shares within the 30 days prior to the date of the public alert, the financial consultant has a duty to analyze the trading data of the shares in the previous six months and explain whether irregular situations, such as market manipulation, undisclosed persons acting in concert with the acquirer, or other payment arrangements, exist. The financial consultant is obligated to explain to the shareholders whether the offer price is reasonable.[75]

---

70 Id, Article 37.
71 Id, Article 40.
72 Id, Article 38.
73 Id, Article 39.
74 Id, Article 35, para. 1.
75 Id, Article 35, para. 2.

The payment for purchasing the shares in a tender offer transaction can be made in the form of cash, securities, a combination of cash and securities, or other lawful means. For a cash acquisition, 20 percent of the total acquisition amount should be put in an escrow account in a bank designated by the securities registration and clearing company concerned. The securities used for the payment should also be put under the custody of the securities registration and clearing company. If the securities are unlisted shares, the acquirer should provide a cash alternative as an option for the target's shareholders to choose.[76]

The target's shareholders can make 'preliminary acceptance' of the offer, which is legally defined as 'the initial expression of intent by the target company's shareholders to accept the offer which, however, does not constitute a legal undertaking until the acceptance become irrevocable during the tender offer period'.[77] The 'preliminary accepters' could withdraw their acceptance up until three trading days before the tender offer period expires, but no withdrawal is permitted during the three trading days before the expiration of the offer period.[78] This is meant to make it easier for the shareholders to take back their shares from the original acquirer and surrender the shares to a competing acquirer if a competing offer emerges.

After the offer period expires, the acquirer who issued a general offer should buy all the shares tendered by the preliminary accepters according to the specified terms. In the case of a partial offer and if shares under the preliminary acceptance exceed the specified acquisition quantity, the acquirer should purchase the shares on a pro rata basis. A full acquisition of all the shares under the preliminary acceptance should also be made if the purpose of the takeover is to make the company 'go private', i.e. delist it from the stock exchange.

After the takeover, the acquirer can delist the company from the stock exchange where the class of shares in question are listed and traded, provided that the intention of delisting was declared in the tender offer report.[79] The stock exchange may also terminate the trading of the shares of the company if it believes the spread of the share equity of the company – such as the percentage of shares held by public shareholders – no longer meets the exchange's listing conditions.[80] In this regard, a minority shareholder protection is put in the Takeover Measures to ensure

---

76 Id, Article 36.
77 Id, Article 42, para. 2.
78 Id.
79 Id, Article 29.
80 Id, Article 44.

that all the shareholders other than the acquirer (and its group members) have a way to exit. That is, after the tender offer expires but before the takeover is complete, if the acquirer has purchased enough shares – which is usually 75 to 90 percent of the target's outstanding shares – to affect the delisting of the target, the remaining shareholders of the target are entitled to enforce the sale of their shares on the same terms as those in the offer.[81] The purpose of this provision is to ensure that the remaining minority shareholders are protected 'from a freeze-out merger on terms less favorable than those of the offer'.[82]

11.6.6 Target Obligations in Takeovers by Tender Offer

The management team of the target company is under no legal duty to negotiate with the acquirer for obtaining better terms for the shareholders of the company, neither are they obligated to take any defensive measures, as long as the directors, supervisors, and senior management executives of the company act in consistency with their fiduciary duties provided in the Company Law and Takeover Measures.[83] However, the board of directors of the target company is under several due diligence obligations. First, the board should conduct an investigation about the acquirer's qualifications, financial standing, and motives for the tender offer. On this basis, it should analyze the terms of the offer and make recommendations to the shareholders as to whether the offer is acceptable. It should also hire an independent financial consultant to issue a professional opinion about the offer. A 'report of the target company's board of directors on the takeover', together with the financial consultant's professional opinion, should be submitted to the CSRC and made available to the public within 20 days after the public announcement of the acquirer's tender offer report. Any major changes occurring thereafter should also be promptly disclosed to the public.[84]

The Takeover Measures have also imposed a 'business-as-usual' requirement on the target company. After launching an offer and until the takeover is completed, the target company may only continue its normal business activities or implement the resolutions that have already been adopted by the shareholders' meeting. Specifically, the board of directors

---

[81] Id.

[82] Huang Hui (2008), p. 164.

[83] Article 8 of the Takeover Measures provides that 'the directors, supervisors and senior management executives bear duty of loyalty and duty of care to the company'.

[84] Takeover Measures, Article 32.

may not take measures that would have a material impact on the company's assets, liabilities, rights, and benefits, or business results, such as disposing of the company's assets, performing investment, providing loans or guarantees, or changing the company's main business.[85] In addition, directors of the target company may not resign during the tender offer period.[86]

11.6.7 Takeover by Agreement

The takeover of a listed company could also be achieved through private transfer agreement between the acquirer and the shareholders owning controlling blocks of the target company's shares, thus forming an agreed takeover. As one commentator observed, '[t]he highly concentrated ownership structure of Chinese listed companies, in tandem with the trading rules that restricted the free transfer of block shares, has made the takeover via tender offers virtually impossible in the Chinese stock market. Instead, control transactions have been mostly implemented via the private sale of corporate control …'.[87] Although some of the restrictions have been lifted in recent years, it is still rather difficult for a real takeover by tender offer to be launched. Rather, most acquirers would prefer to seek an exemption from the CSRC to waive the obligation for initiating a general offer under the MBR to buy up shares of the target company on top of their 30 percent shareholding.[88] An acquirer could also accumulate shares of the target company via private agreements for up to 30 percent of the company's outstanding shares, provided it complies with the disclosure obligations mentioned above.[89]

For agreed takeover, the acquirer should still prepare a takeover report within the three days after concluding the takeover agreement with the block shareholders of the target company. The takeover report should be submitted to the CSRC by a financial consultant hired by the acquirer, but may be announced to the public only after the CSRC grants an exemption to waive its mandatory offer obligation. This mechanism effectively gives the CSRC the veto power in agreed takeovers of listed companies.

A Chinese acquirer should submit the following documents to the CSRC for approval in agreed takeovers: (1) proof of identification as a

---

85 Id, Article 33.
86 Id, Article 34.
87 Xi (2008), p. 407.
88 Takeover Measures, Article 47.
89 Takeover Measures, Article 47. See also section 11.6.2 above.

Chinese citizen, or proof of registration in China as a legal person or other organization; (2) an explanation of the feasibility of the future development plan for the target company based on the acquirer's own capabilities and experiences in the industry; (3) a statement on the business competition and affiliated transactions between the acquirer (and its related parties) and the target company as well as on how the target's independence can be maintained; (4) a statement that the acquirer's controlling shareholder or actual controlling person has not changed in the past two years; (5) an explanation of the acquirer's core business; (6) the review opinion of the financial consultant on the acquirer's business integrity record in the past three years, the legality of the source of funds for the takeover, and the acquirer's capability to perform their obligations.[90]

Article 47 of the Takeover Measures further provides that, if the acquirer is a foreign legal person or other form of organization, two additional documents are required by the CSRC. First, the financial consultant has to render a review opinion on whether the acquirer satisfies the conditions for making a strategic investment in the target company and whether it has the capability to take over the target company. Second, the acquirer must submit a declaration to accept China's judicial or arbitral jurisdiction.[91] Insofar as foreign investment in takeovers is concerned, two implications could be inferred from this provision. First, foreign investors are permitted to launch takeovers of Chinese listed companies by agreements under the Takeover Measures. Second, foreign investors could only conduct the takeover in the form of foreign strategic investment, which means they also have to comply with the Strategic Investment Measures discussed above.[92]

Like the 'business-as-usual' requirement for the target company in takeovers by tender offer,[93] a similar obligation is imposed by the Takeover Measures on the parties in an agreed takeover with respect to the stability of the target's business and management, especially in the context that a takeover agreement will make the acquirer an influential partner of the target's existing controlling shareholder. The Takeover Measures define the time period between the execution of the takeover agreement and completion of the title transfer of the shares as the 'transition period'. During the transition period, the acquirer is prohibited from electing, through the existing controlling shareholder, a new board

---

90 Takeover Measures, Article 50.
91 Id, Article 47, para. 2.
92 See section 11.5 above.
93 See section 11.6 above.

of directors for the company. If there is indeed a sufficiently strong reason to change the composition of the board, directors from the acquirer may not exceed one-third of the total number of the directors. During the transition period, the target company may not provide guarantees to the acquirer (or its affiliated parties), offer shares to raise capital from the public, carry out a major purchase or sale of assets, make a major investment, or carry out related-party transactions with the acquirer (and its affiliated parties), unless the transaction is done for the purpose of rescuing the company from a crisis or serious financial difficulties.[94]

11.6.8 Management Buyouts through Takeover by Agreements

The Takeover Measures legalize management buyouts (MBOs) for the first time in the form of generally applicable legal rules issued by a central government agency. Now the directors, supervisors, senior management executives, or employees of a listed company (or an entity controlled by the above persons) may take over the listed company in the form of an MBO, but the transaction is subject to rigorous regulatory scrutiny. Basically, the MBO transaction must meet the following conditions:[95]

1. the target company must have sound systems for corporate governance and internal control;
2. at least one-half of the members of the target company's board of directors must be independent directors;
3. the target company should engage a licensed asset appraisal institution to provide an independent appraisal report on the company's assets;
4. the buyout proposal should be approved by a resolution adopted by the non-affiliated directors of the target company's board and consented to by at least two-thirds of the independent directors;
5. after board approval, the buyout proposal should be adopted by the majority of votes of the non-affiliated shareholders present at a shareholders' general meeting; and
6. in the case where the independent directors publicly announce their opinions, they should firstly engage an independent financial consultant to issue a professional opinion on the buyout.

---

[94] Takeover Measures, Article 52.
[95] Takeover Measures, Article 51.

11.6.9 Indirect Takeovers

Normally the acquirer, when launching the takeover by tender offer or by agreement, is already a major shareholder of the target company. A takeover will make the acquirer the controlling shareholder of the target. Under certain circumstances, the obligations in the Takeover Measures will be triggered by an acquirer who is not a shareholder of the target. A non-shareholder acquirer might be able to obtain voting control of a listed company through investment relations, agreements, or other arrangements.[96] For instance, an investor that acquires control of an offshore company who is a controlling shareholder of the Chinese listed company will be deemed to be acquiring the Chinese company. An alternative method is that the offshore company and the acquirer use the offshore company's controlling interest in the Chinese listed company as part of the capital contributions to establish an offshore joint venture in which the acquirer is the controlling shareholder. Either way, the acquirer, as the actual controlling person, has to perform all the relevant disclosure and other obligations prescribed in the Takeover Measures as if it is a shareholder–acquirer.[97]

In indirect takeovers, the actual controlling person of the target company and the shareholder controlled by it are under legal obligations to cooperate with the target company with respect to complying with the disclosure obligations. Failing to cooperate will lead to both civil and administrative liabilities. If the targeted company suffers losses for any administrative or civil liability, it could bring legal actions against the actual controlling person and the shareholder controlled by it for damages. In addition, the CSRC will also impose administrative penalties on those who violate the disclosure rules.[98] Indeed, the target company's board is required by law not to consider any proposals from the shareholder who is controlled by the actual controlling person if the actual controlling person or the said shareholder violate the disclosure obligations and to report the violations to the CSRC; otherwise, the CSRC will disqualify the responsible directors.[99]

---

96 Id, Article 56.
97 Id, Article 57.
98 Id, Articles 58 and 59.
99 Id, Article 60.

11.6.10 Exemptions

Compliance with the complicated tender offer rules, especially the MBR, is a tremendous task. From the acquirer's perspective, the obligations are very demanding, and even draconian, in terms of being both time-consuming and costly. The Takeover Measures provide a back door for the acquirers who do not wish to go through the tender offer process. That is, the acquirers and persons acting in concert with it could seek exemptions from CSRC so that they could avoid launching a tender offer to increase their shareholding or launching a general offer, which is otherwise required under the MBR.[100] In fact, almost all the takeover transactions in China's stockmarket have been carried out under exemptions rather than by standard tender offers.

The acquirer may apply for an exemption under the following circumstances:[101]

1. The acquirer and the seller of shares are able to prove that the transfer will not result in a change in the actual controlling person of the target company;
2. The target company faces serious financial difficulties, the reorganization plan to rescue the company proposed by the acquirer has been approved by the target's shareholders' meeting, and the acquirer undertakes not to transfer its equity interests in the company for a minimum three-year period;
3. The acquirer's shareholding exceeds 30 percent of the target company's outstanding shares through a directed placement offered in accordance with a resolution of the target's shareholders' meeting, provided that the acquirer undertakes not to transfer the new shares for a three-year period and the shareholders' meeting supports the exemption application.

The CSRC is required to render a decision within 20 days after receiving the exemption application. However, an exemption application would not even be necessary if the acquirer in a directed placement were already the controlling shareholder. In such a case, the legality of the acquirer's purchase without launching a tender offer is based directly on the CSRC's approval of the directed placement.

Article 63 of the Takeover Measures offers a fast-track procedure for some transactions. In these circumstances, the acquirer still has to apply

[100] Id, Article 61.
[101] Id, Article 62, para. 1.

to the CSRC for an exemption, but only needs to wait 10 working days; however, the CSRC's silence during the 10 days – meaning it does not raise an express objection – will be deemed an approval where:

1. Due to the gratuitous transfer, change, or merger of state-owned assets approved by the government or the state-owned assets administration department, the acquirer's shareholding in a listed company reaches or exceeds 30 percent of the listed company's outstanding shares;
2. An investor's shareholding exceeds 30 percent of the company's outstanding shares of a listed company due to the company's repurchase of a designated shareholder's shares at a price approved by the shareholders' meeting;
3. Financial institutions such as securities companies and banks hold more than 30 percent of the listed company's outstanding shares as a result of their underwriting or lending business, but the financial institutions have no intention or acts to effectively control the company and have proposed a plan to transfer the shareholding to non-related parties within a reasonable period.

In addition, the acquirer may directly apply to the stock exchange and securities registration and clearing company to carry out the share transfer without applying for an exemption to the CSRC in the following cases:[102]

1. One year after the acquirer's shareholding reaches or exceeds 30 percent of the listed company's outstanding shares, if its subsequent share purchase in every 12 months does not exceed 2 percent of the company's outstanding shares;
2. The acquirer's shareholding in the listed company reaches or exceeds 50 percent of the company's outstanding shares, and continued increase of its interest in the company will not affect the company's listing status;
3. A person's shareholding exceeds 30 percent of the company's outstanding shares as a result of inheritance.

If the acquirer fails to secure an exemption from the CSRC and it still wishes to acquire the target's shares – which rarely happens in practice –

---

102 Id, Article 63, para. 2.

it shall launch a general offer to buy all the shares of all other shareholders. Otherwise, it must reduce its shareholding to 30 percent or less.[103]

11.7 TAKEOVER DEFENSES

11.7.1 Target Management's Duties in Takeover Defenses

A key feature of the takeover, from the acquirer's perspective, is the ability to bypass the target's board of directors and the shareholders' meeting and make an offer to the shareholders directly. If the target management (including the board) does not like this offer, a hostile takeover is likely to take place.

When a tender offer is publicly announced, the target's management must respond. When faced with a hostile offer, it would be only natural if they chose to take defensive measures to repel the bid. As a matter of fact, as previously noted, the target management has to respond anyway under certain circumstances. They may employ a variety of defensive maneuvers or tactics, which may also be called anti-takeover measures, either in the hope of improving the offer or in the hope of defeating the takeover and remaining independent. In this section we will discuss to what extent some of the traditional anti-takeover measures can be applied in China. It is worth noting that there is no systematic anti-takeover legislation in China apart from the various legal rules scattered in different statutes (including not only corporate and securities law but also banking laws). The target management must carefully assess the legality of a particular defensive measure under Chinese law; otherwise, it might risk the measures being disapproved by the regulatory authorities or being sued by the shareholders or acquirers to have the measure revoked or invalidated.

Generally speaking, the management of the target company broadly covers the key players inside the company, which bears the following fiduciary duties in accordance with Article 8 of the Takeover Measures:

> The directors, supervisors and senior management executives of the target company have the duty of loyalty and duty of care to the company, and should treat equally all of the acquirers seeking to take over the company.

---

[103] Id, Article 61, para. 2.

> The decisions and measures taken by the board of directors of the target company with respect to the takeover shall be conducive to safeguarding the interests of the company and its shareholders. The board may not abuse its power to erect inappropriate barriers to the takeover, use company resources to provide financial assistance in any form to the acquirer, or harm in any way the lawful rights and interests of the company and its shareholders.

Management's duties in takeovers are operated within the national framework of fiduciary duties provided in Article 148 of the 2005 Company Law, and thus are enforceable both by the CSRC and by the courts. The duties are meant to address the potential conflict of interest created by the gate-keeping role of the management. As we will see below, adopting takeover defenses is not a difficult issue in many cases, as the usual defensive techniques, such as amending the corporate charter, issuing new shares, selling assets, repurchasing shares, and seeking regulatory or judicial intervention, are all within the management's decisive or coordinating powers. Needless to say, management powers can be exercised in novel ways to erect barriers for stopping takeovers. These powers might also be abused by the management for the insiders' own personal interest, such as keeping their jobs or transferring corporate assets to their own pockets. The fiduciary duties generally mandate that the measures taken by the management shall be for the interest of the company and shareholders. Particularly, the board of directors is prohibited from either using 'inappropriate' anti-takeover measures or assisting the bidder financially. Admittedly, the fiduciary duties framework points in different directions and a reasonable person might be skeptical of its efficacy in resolving the conflict of interest in takeover battles.

11.7.2 Selected Anti-takeover Measures under Chinese Law

Super-majority vote requirements

The target company might provide in its corporate charter that a super-majority (2/3) or even extraordinary majority (3/4) of the company's total voting shares must approve any merger or major sale of assets. There is no problem for implementing a super-majority vote clause in JSLCs in China for it is actually a statutory requirement. Article 104 of the Company Law mandates the consent of a two-thirds majority for matters concerning the amendment of the corporate charter, increase or decrease of the registered capital, or on merger, division, dissolution, or change of the corporate form of the company. A takeover is likely to involve all the aforesaid matters. In addition, it seems to be lawful for the corporate charter to lift the two-thirds majority to a three-quarters majority, thus making the takeover even more difficult.

Restrictions on the voting power of the majority shareholder

Some companies provide in their charter a clause to directly restrict the voting power of the majority shareholder, such as one that limits the voting rights of the majority shareholder to a certain percentage (e.g. one-fifth) of the total voting rights.[104] Cumulative voting, provided (but not made compulsory) in the Company Law,[105] has also been used to limit the voting power of the majority shareholder.

Restrictions on shareholders' nomination power

Some listed companies provide in their charters a nomination clause as a 'shark repellent' to discourage takeovers. The clause would require the nominating shareholders to own a certain percentage of the target's shares for a certain period of time. For instance, the corporate charter of Qionghua Co., Ltd (which was renamed Jiangsu Jincai Technology Co., Ltd on 22 March 2012) required that the candidates for members of the board of directors could only be nominated by the board itself and/or by shareholders who individually or aggregately owned 10 percent of the company's shares. Some corporate charters even stipulate that the candidates for directors can only be nominated by the incumbent board.[106] In these cases, the acquirer's ability to elect a new board would be severely limited.

Staggered board

If a staggered board (or 'classified board') is put in the corporate charter of a listed company, only a minority of the board members will stand for election in any given year. This measure aims to prevent the acquirer from gaining control immediately after it purchases the majority of the target's shares. For instance, if the corporate charter requires that only one-third of the directors may stand for election every year, the acquirer will have to wait two or more years in order to elect his own hand-picked directors to the board.

In theory the staggered board is permitted in China. Article 46, which is applied to JSLCs via Article 109, of the Company Law provides that the term of office of directors is to be stipulated in the corporate charter

---

[104] SSE–SWSC Joint Research Group (2011), p. 65.

[105] Company Law, Article 109.

[106] SSE–SWSC Joint Research Group (2011), pp. 65–6.

as long as each term does not exceed three years. That is, the Company Law neither requires nor prohibits a staggered board for JSLCs. The practice of a staggered board thus seems to be legally permissible in China and has been adopted by many listed companies. However, it is worth noting that it is not entirely clear whether directors can be removed without cause under the Company Law.[107] As noted in Chapter 6, the 2005 Company Law no longer incorporates the provision that 'the shareholders' meeting may not remove a director … without cause', which was contained in the 1993 Company Law. However, listed companies generally still provide in their charters that directors cannot be removed without cause pursuant to Article 95 of the CSRC Model Charter. If directors normally cannot be removed without cause, the acquirer still has to let the incumbent directors finish their term first, and possibly they have to wait for three more years to see the departure of those newly elected directors. Further, one has to keep in mind the 'transition period' provided in the Takeover Measures, during which the acquirer is generally prohibited from electing a new board through the controlling shareholder under the acquirer's control.[108]

New class of stock

The target company can create a second class of shares and require in its charter that the merger of the company be approved by each class. Of course, the new class will be issued to 'friends' of management who will not easily be 'bought' by the acquirer.

It is not clear whether such two-class structures can be established in China. The Company Law does not seem to prohibit the establishment of several classes of shares in a company, but only requires that each share in the same class carry the same rights.[109] However, in the sense that the Company Law authorizes the PRC State Council to enact regulations on the creation of a different class of shares, which the State Council has not done,[110] no company in China has successfully established the two-class structures in the absence of clearly enumerated legal rules.

Private placement to a friend

A useful anti-takeover technique is the target company issuing new shares (of the same common class) to a designated investor who is supposedly a friend of the target management. The new issuance can be

---

[107] See Ch. 6, section 6.3.3 above.
[108] Takeover Measures, Article 52.
[109] Company Law, Article 127.
[110] Id, Article 128.

done in the form of a private placement. If the investor happens to be the 'white knight' sought by the target management, it will launch a competing offer at a price at least as good as the one the hostile acquirer is offering. The new shares could also be sold to the parent company or company employees' shareholding entity that exists in some companies in China.

It is perfectly lawful for a Chinese listed company to carry a private placement of shares, which can now be done under the Administrative Measures on Securities Offering by Listed Companies promulgated by the CSRC in May 2006 (the 'New Offering Measures'). The placement has to be supported by a resolution of the shareholders' meeting, recommended by a licensed sponsor, and approved by the CSRC. The shares can be issued to no more than 10 designated investors. The New Offering Measures do not subject the designated investors to any qualification requirements, except that a placement to a 'foreign strategic investor' must comply with the Strategic Investment Measures examined above.[111]

Finding a 'white knight'

The target management can find a friendly white knight who will acquire the target instead of letting the hostile acquirer take over the company. The Takeover Measures mention the 'competing offer', which might be launched by a white knight, in several places. If a competing offer arises, the first acquirer has to extend the tender offer period to ensure that the shareholders have a full 15 days to consider the offers.

As noted above, a private placement can be performed by the target to issue new shares to the white knight under the New Offering Measures. However, the more traditional 'lock-up' arrangements, in which the white knight acquires by agreement the target's most attractive businesses or assets, cannot be easily made in China. As previously discussed, there is a 'business-as-usual' requirement for the target company pursuant to Article 33 of the Takeover Measures, whereby the target cannot dispose of its major assets without the approval of the shareholders' meeting during the takeover period.

Cross shareholding

It is permissible – at least not prohibited – for friendly or related companies to hold each other's shares under Chinese law, as the

---

[111] New Offering Measures, Chapter 3.

Company Law allows companies to invest in other companies.[112] Cross-shareholding can reduce the number of shares circulated in the public market. Furthermore, when hostile acquisitions occur to one of them, the other might come to the rescue.

Share repurchases

A common defensive tactic in corporate takeovers is share repurchase, through which the company buys back a significant portion of its own shares from the public to both strengthen the controlling position of the insiders and reduce the number of shares available for the hostile acquirer to purchase. Share repurchases are generally prohibited in Chinese law except for purposes of reducing registered capital, merging with another company that holds its shares, awarding the repurchased shares to employees, or buying back the shares of a dissenting shareholder.[113] Share repurchase measures as anti-takeover tactics have to be designed in line with these purposes.

Greenmail

In a greenmail arrangement the target buys back the stake that the acquirer has already built by paying him an above-market price. This is essentially a ransom paid to the acquirer. Greenmail is, however, constrained by the statutory restrictions on share repurchases discussed above.

Pac Man defense

Theoretically there is nothing in Chinese law to prevent the target company from launching a counter-tender for the acquirer. If the target is able to acquire a large amount of the acquirer's shares, it might be able to paralyze the acquirer from within as a large shareholder, and the two companies may end up trading the shares owned by each other. Of course, in practice the target must have enough resources to carry off such a strategy.

Regulatory and judicial intervention

As the acquirer has to comply with a variety of obligations according to the Company Law, Securities Law, and Takeover Measures, the target

---

[112] Article 16 of the Company Law provides that 'a company's investment in another company or provision of security to another company shall be decided by the board of directors or shareholders' meeting in accordance with the corporate charter'.

[113] Company Law, Article 143.

management can conduct an investigation about the background of the acquirer and closely monitor the acquirer's behaviors in the takeover with a view to identifying any violations of the obligations. However, if the acquirer has not violated any legal rules or procedures, the tactic will not work.

In terms of regulatory intervention, the takeover of Yanzhong Industrial Co., Ltd by Bao'an Group in 1994, China's first and most famous hostile acquisition case, is illustrative. The SSE-listed Yanzhong were initially owned mainly by dispersed individual shareholders. In mid-September 1994, Bao'an quietly started to purchase Yanzhong's shares through three of its subsidiaries. On 30 September 1994, Bao'an made a public announcement with respect to the acquisition after it (and the subsidiaries acting in concert with it) built a block of 17.07 percent of Yanzhong's total shares. During this process, Bao'an completely neglected both its reporting obligations and the obligation to stop buying shares after it acquired a 5 percent stake. After the first announcement, Bao'an continued to buy up Yanzhong and accumulated a stake of 19.80 percent by 6 October 1994, which made it Yanzhong's largest shareholder. However, the furious Yanzhong refused to recognize the legitimacy of the Bao'an shareholding beyond the 5 percent stake, and requested the CSRC to stop Bao'an's acquisition activity. After carrying out an investigation, the CSRC levied a Renminbi 1 million fine on Bao'an and requested it to stop purchasing Yanzhong's shares, but decided that Bao'an could legally hold the 19.80 percent stake it had already built. Eventually, a settlement agreement between Bao'an and Yanzhong permitted Bao'an to elect two directors on Yanzhong's board.[114]

A defense technique that is likely to be favored by large target companies is the merger control rules in the PRC Anti-Monopoly Law (AML) that came into effect in August 2008. In particular, mergers that may have the effect of eliminating or restricting competition are prohibited.[115] The acquirer is also required to make a declaration to the state's anti-monopoly authorities if the merger or acquisition will lead to a business scale that reaches the statutory threshold of business concentration in the sector concerned. Without such reporting, the merger or acquisition may not proceed.[116] Further, the AML permits any person to

---

114 See Fu Qilin (2002), pp. 382–4; Green (2003), p. 150.
115 AML, Article 20.
116 Id, Article 21.

report suspicious monopolistic conduct to the anti-monopoly authorities, which may call a stop to any concentrating activities including M&A.[117]

The target might also petition the CSRC to stop the takeover if the acquirer does not meet the qualification requirements stipulated in the Takeover Measures. Specifically, the takeover of a listed company should not even be launched if the acquirer: (1) is encumbered by a relatively large amount of debt that is due and has not been discharged; (2) has committed or is suspected of having committed a major violation of the law in the past three years; or (3) has committed a serious breach of trust in the securities markets in the past three years.[118] If the acquirer is a natural person, he must have the requisite capacities for civil acts and meet the negative qualification requirements concerning personal liabilities in criminal offences, enterprise bankruptcy, or unsettled debts.[119]

In addition to seeking help from regulators, the target company can institute defensive lawsuits before competent courts, alleging that the acquirer has violated its fiduciary or other duties, or is involved in illegal trading activities such as insider trading or market manipulations. Like regulatory interventions, judicial response to hostile takeovers could slow the acquirer down temporarily but is unlikely able to permanently block the tender offer.

Poison pill plans

In theory, a variety of other defensive tactics, including poison pill plans and corporate restructuring, could also be applied in takeovers of listed companies in China. Poison pill plans are widely known shark repellants that aim to ensure that detrimental things will happen to the acquirer if the target is taken over. 'Call plans' give target shareholders the right to buy discounted shares under certain circumstances. In contrast, 'put plans' grant the shareholders the right to sell back their remaining shares in the target at a fair price to the acquirer.

Under relevant Chinese laws, the shareholders can be distributed with warrants that entitle them to buy cheap shares of the surviving company after the takeover, making it possible for call plans to be implemented. Needless to say, the put plans are subject to the share repurchase restrictions provided in the Company Law.

---

117 Id, Articles 38 and 48.
118 Takeover Measures, Article 6.
119 Takeover Measures, Article 6 (4); Company Law, Article 147.

Corporate restructuring

In extreme situations, the target management can take a variety of measures that increase the short-term value to its shareholders, thus burdening the company with heavy liabilities. For instance, the target may borrow heavily from banks and use the bank loans to give shareholders a large one-time dividend of cash, bonds, and/or preference shares. The company might sell the company's major business or assets (the 'crown jewels') for cash that will be distributed to shareholders. The management might even carry out a voluntary liquidation of the company. Some of the measures might lead to 'scorched earth', i.e. self-destruction of the firm.

Whether a specific corporate restructuring measure can be lawfully adopted depends on the nature and extent of the measure. Distributing dividends with borrowed money is completely illegal as companies are only allowed to distribute earned profits.[120] A listed company may sell its major assets, and provide security to others to incur debts, but these powers are constrained by procedural restrictions stipulated in Article 122 of the Company Law which subjects the disposal of major assets or provision of guarantee for third parties to the approval by the majority (2/3) of the total votes presented in the shareholders' voting if the monetary value in question exceeds 30 percent of the company's total assets. Further, Article 33 of the Takeover Measures even prohibits any major change in the target's assets or business operation.

Needless to say, some of the restructuring measures will incur severe damage to the target company and its shareholders. To some extent, the implementation of these measures is like the company committing suicide. In doing this, the target management should keep in mind the aforesaid fiduciary duties imposed on its directors, supervisors, and senior executives.

---

120 See Ch. 10 above.

12. Corporate dissolution, liquidation, and bankruptcy

12.1 TERMINATION OF A COMPANY

The life of a company can be brought to an end by dissolution (*jiesan*) or bankruptcy (*pochan*) under China's corporate law. Bankruptcy occurs when a company is insolvent, namely it no longer has the ability to pay its due debts. Dissolution is the legal termination of a company for other reasons. Dissolution of a company involves three legal steps: (1) a decision adopted by a competent organ to dissolve the company; (2) the liquidation process for winding up of affairs, realization of receivables, payment of debts, and distribution of assets among the shareholders; (3) deregistration of the company to completely end its legal existence. A company is deemed legally dissolved after it is deregistered by the relevant registration authority (AIC) and makes a public announcement of the termination of the company.[1]

The rules governing corporate dissolution are contained in Chapter 10 of the Company Law and the SPC's Company Law Interpretation (II). The procedure for ending a company through the bankruptcy discharge is provided in the PRC Enterprise Bankruptcy Law and will be examined in a later section.

12.2 REASONS FOR DISSOLVING A COMPANY

A company can be terminated by a voluntary dissolution, administrative dissolution, or judicial dissolution. Specifically, the dissolution could occur under any of the following circumstances:[2]

1. Dissolution by expiration of stated duration of operation;
2. Dissolution by the resolution of shareholders;

[1] Company Law, Article 189.
[2] Id, Article 181.

3. Dissolution because of a corporate merger or division;
4. Administrative dissolution;
5. Judicial dissolution.

12.2.1 Voluntary Dissolution

The dissolution by expiration of the stated duration, by the resolution of the shareholders, or by a merger or division of the company can be generally called voluntary dissolution. Such dissolution could either be planned by the shareholders in advance by making provisions in the incorporation agreement or corporate charter, or decided by them at a point of time during the company's operation.

A company may be dissolved upon expiration of a certain period of time or occurrence of a specific event as provided in the corporate charter.[3] The Company Law does not mandate a term of operation for any company, thus leaving this power in the hands of the shareholders. In practice, most companies now provide in their charters that they would exist forever. However, some FIEs are required to stipulate a term of operation in their joint venture agreements or charters.[4] FIE laws have also stipulated events that trigger the dissolution of a company. For example, an EJV might be dissolved if it could not continue its operation due to heavy business losses, the failure of a contracting party to perform its obligations, losses caused by *force majeure*, or frustration of purpose.[5]

Even if its stated duration has expired, a company that still wishes to continue its existence could amend its corporate charter to prolong its life. The charter amendment has to be adopted by a two-thirds majority of the total votes held by all shareholders in an LLC or the same majority of votes cast by shareholders in a general meeting of a JSLC.[6]

A company might also be dissolved by the resolution of the shareholders' meeting.[7] As there are no conditions attached to this power of the shareholders in the Company Law, the shareholders may terminate the company through a resolution at any time. The resolution, which has to be an extraordinary one, must be adopted by an absolute majority

---

[3] Id, Article 181(1).

[4] See e.g. *Zhongwai Hezi Jingying Qiye Heying Qixian Zanxing Guiding* (Interim Provisions on the Term of Operation of Sino-Foreign Equity Joint Ventures), promulgated by the Ministry of Foreign Trade and Economic Co-operation on 22 October 1990.

[5] EJV Implementing Regulations, Article 90.

[6] Company Law, Article 182.

[7] Id, Article 181(2).

accounting for two-thirds or more of the total votes held by all the shareholders in the case of an LLC,[8] or held by the shareholders who are present at the general meeting of a JSLC.[9] The dissolution of a WSOE will have to be decided by its sole shareholder, the state.[10] In companies that do not have shareholders' meetings, such as one-person LLCs or some FIEs, the board of directors can make dissolution decisions in lieu of the shareholders.

Voluntary dissolution might also be caused by the merger or division of a company.[11] A company that is merged into another company or split into two or more companies will have to be dissolved. However, the company does not need to go through the usual liquidation process to pay debts or distribute corporate assets among the shareholders, as its assets and liabilities will be succeeded by the surviving company or companies.

12.2.2 Administrative Dissolution

A company may be dissolved administratively for failure to fulfill certain legal or regulatory requirements. This government-ordered dissolution will be carried out when the government revokes the company's business license, orders the company to be closed down, or cancels its registration.[12] For instance, if a company, without proper justification, fails to commence business within six months after its establishment, or ceases to do business for six consecutive months, its business license may be revoked by the registration authority.[13] A company that refuses to accept annual inspection by the registration authority may also get its business license revoked.[14] Once its business license is taken away by the state, the company has to wind up its business. In addition, a company might be ordered to close down or be deregistered directly by the government for severe violations of laws and regulations.

---

8 Id, Article 44, para. 2.
9 Id, Article 104.
10 Id, Article 67.
11 Id, Article 181(3).
12 Id, Article 181 (4).
13 Company Registration Regulations, Article 72.
14 Id, Article 76.

12.3 CORPORATE DEADLOCK AND JUDICIAL DISSOLUTION OF A COMPANY

12.3.1 Corporate Deadlock

Like any 'family', members in a company might have disagreements over the company's affairs. The major players in a company, including the controlling shareholders, directors, and senior executives, may find themselves at odds with some fundamental corporate matters. When a dispute among them cannot be resolved through internal procedures, the company will get into a 'deadlock' situation in which the company is paralyzed and thus prevented from acting as an independent business entity.

The deadlock may occur at either the shareholder or management level. If the deadlock results in the company's inability to conduct business, judicial interference can be invited to provide involuntary dissolution in a suit by shareholders. Chinese courts used to be indifferent to such deadlock situations, treating them as internal disputes with which the judiciary should not be bothered.[15] The 2005 Company Law has established a framework to make judicial remedies available for certain types of corporate deadlock disputes. Specifically, Article 183 of the Company Law provides,

> Where a company experiences serious difficulties in its business operation or management and its continued existence would cause major losses to the rights and interests of the shareholders, shareholders holding 10 percent or more of the total voting rights of all shareholders of the company, in the absence of any other means to resolve the matter, may request dissolution of the company by a people's court.

Thus, under Article 183, the shareholder may obtain involuntary dissolution in a suit only if the following conditions are met: (1) there are difficulties in the company's business or management, because of which the existence of the company causes losses to the shareholders; (2) the deadlock cannot be resolved through other means such as amending the corporate charter, reappointment of the management, re-election of

---

[15] Before the 2005 Company Law took effect, Chinese courts normally refused to accept dissolution cases. The SPC, in a reply to the Shangdong provincial court issued on 26 August 2002, ordered the lower court not to take a case in which the shareholders asked for involuntary dissolution of a company by the court. See SPC Civil Division II (2008), p. 103.

the board, share transfer or repurchase, etc.; and (3) the suing shareholders hold at least 10 percent of the total voting rights in the company.

12.3.2 'Serious Difficulties' in a Company's Business and Management

Obviously the most difficult part in this framework is how to define the 'serious difficulties' in a company's business and management. The SPC, in its Provisions on Several Issues Concerning the Application of the PRC Company Law (II),[16] provides for involuntary dissolution in a lawsuit by shareholders in any of the following four situations:[17]

1. The company has been unable to convene a shareholders' meeting for at least two consecutive years and serious difficulties have arisen in its business operation and management;
2. Shareholders' voting has not been able to reach the statutory percentage or the percentage specified in the corporate charter, making it impossible for the shareholders' meeting to pass a valid resolution for at least two consecutive years, and serious difficulties have arisen in the company's business operation and management;
3. There has been a long-standing conflict between directors of the company that cannot be resolved by the shareholders' meeting and serious difficulties have arisen in the company's business operation and affairs; or
4. There are other serious difficulties in the business operation and management of the company, because of which the continued existence would cause material losses to the interests of the shareholders.

In other words, the showings are either in the form of shareholder deadlock or director deadlock. The shareholders may be deadlocked in voting power and have failed to pass resolutions and/or elect board members. The directors may be deadlocked in the management of the company's affairs, which cannot be broken by the shareholders' meeting, the company's power organ under Chinese law. However, none of the

---

[16] Zuigao Renmin Fayuan Guanyu Shiyong Zhonghua Renmin Gongheguo Gongsifa Ruogan Wenti De Guiding (II), promulgated by the SPC on 12 May 2008, effective as of 19 May 2008 (hereinafter the Company Law Interpretation (II)).

[17] Id, Article 1, para. 1.

above showings permits the shareholders to petition the courts to dissolve a company in any of the following situations:[18]

1. The shareholders' information rights or rights to dividends have been infringed upon by the company;
2. The company has suffered losses and its assets are insufficient to discharge all of its debts; or
3. A company's business license has been revoked but it has not been liquidated.

The SPC does not exclude other situations, such as oppression of minority shareholders' rights or wastage of corporate assets caused by directors, executives, or controlling shareholders, as long as the company is deadlocked and irreparable injury to the shareholders is suffered or threatened. However, it has been pointed out by the SPC in one of its academic publications that shareholder oppression alone, which is understood as that some shareholders or the actual controller of a company have acted in an oppressive manner to exclude other shareholders from participating in the management of the corporate affairs, cannot serve as a ground for judicial dissolution of the company, as long as the company is still well managed and its business is carried out normally.[19]

12.3.3 Procedural Issues in Judicial Dissolution

The court will not provide judicial dissolution for a company whose business license was revoked simply because judicial dissolution and judicial liquidation are two different types of cases. A company that has lost its license in this way should go directly into the liquidation process.[20]

On procedural matters, the SPC mandates the company to be named as the defendant in a judicial dissolution case. In practice the plaintiff–shareholders tend to bring a legal action jointly against the company and other shareholders, but other shareholders may now only be joined as third parties in the lawsuit.[21] The judgment of the court in a dissolution lawsuit should be binding upon all the shareholders of the company,[22] but

---

[18] Id, Article 1, para. 2.
[19] SPC Civil Division II (2008), p. 117.
[20] Company Law Interpretation (II), Article 2.
[21] Id, Article 4.
[22] Id, Article 6, para. 1.

the court is required to permit other shareholders or interested parties to join the suit either as joint plaintiffs or third parties.[23]

The SPC also encourages lower courts to 'favor' mediation in judicial dissolution cases.[24] In particular, courts are asked to support agreements lawfully reached by the parties to have the company or a shareholder acquire the shares of the plaintiff-shareholders or to have the company's registered capital reduced.[25] Implicitly, they should encourage the parties to reach such agreements through consultations.

12.4 CORPORATE LIQUIDATION PROCEDURE

12.4.1 Establishment of the Liquidation Group

After a company is declared to have been dissolved, either voluntarily or involuntarily, the next stage of its life is liquidation, or winding up, through which it will cease to exist by being liquidated and struck off the register of companies by the relevant AIC. The company could be liquidated voluntarily by its own members. The company then shall establish a liquidation group (*qingsuan zu*) within 15 days after the occurrence of the dissolution event. The liquidation group shall comprise the shareholders in an LLC. For a JSLC, members of the liquidation group shall be composed of the directors or persons appointed by the shareholders' general meeting.[26]

The judiciary will step in to organize court-sponsored liquidation if members of the company do not act to wind up the corporate affairs in time. A people's court will, upon the request of the creditors, organize a liquidation group to carry out the winding up.[27] Specifically, the court may act in the following circumstances: (1) the company does not establish a liquidation group to carry out the winding up within the statutory limit; (2) the liquidation group has been established but is deliberately holding up the liquidation; or (3) the liquidation is illegal

---

[23] Id, Article 4, para. 3.

[24] Id, Article 5.

[25] Id. Shareholdings acquired by the company from the plaintiff-shareholder shall be cancelled within six months from the date on which the mediated settlement agreement entered into effect.

[26] Company Law, Article 184.

[27] Id.

and could materially harm the interests of the creditors and shareholders.[28] Further, in the second circumstance above, the shareholders can petition the court to appoint a different liquidation group if the creditors don't act.[29] Members of a court-appointed liquidation group can be chosen by the court from the following persons: (1) the company's shareholders, directors, supervisors, or senior management executives; (2) intermediaries such as law firms, accounting firms, or bankruptcy liquidation firms; or (3) licensed individual professionals in the aforesaid intermediaries.[30]

12.4.2 Powers of the Liquidation Group

In general, the liquidation group serves as both the power organ and the management team of the company. It has the following statutory powers as provided in the Company Law:[31]

1. Examining the assets of the company and preparing a balance sheet and a schedule of assets;
2. Notifying the creditors by individual notices or public announcements;
3. Handling the outstanding business of the company that is related to the liquidation;
4. Paying all outstanding taxes;
5. Making settlement for all claims and debts;
6. Disposing of assets remaining after settlement of the company's debts;
7. Representing the company in civil litigation.

In short, during the liquidation process, the company continues to exist as a legal entity, and the liquidation group serves as its 'head'. With the commencement of the liquidation, the board of directors and the management executives cease to control the company and the liquidation group manages the company with a view to winding up all of its affairs. The liquidation group itself is not an independent legal entity. In judicial practice, some courts used to treat the liquidation group as an independent legal person and asked it to participate in civil litigation in its own

28 Company Law Interpretation (II), Article 7, para. 2.
29 Id, Article 7, para. 3.
30 Id, Article 8.
31 Company Law, Article 185.

name.[32] The SPC has recently clarified this conceptual confusion, mandating that all the civil lawsuits involving a company under liquidation should be participated in by the liquidation group in the name of the company, and that the head of the liquidation group be treated as the legal representative of the company.[33]

12.4.3 Liquidation Process

The liquidation group, on behalf of the company, should only carry on the business of the company that is related to the liquidation. It should also pursue the company's claims against third parties and collect the monies owed to the company by others.

The liquidation group is also required to notify the creditors of the company within 10 days from the date of its establishment and, within 60 days, make newspaper announcement of the liquidation. The creditors then have 30 days after receiving the notification to declare the claims to the liquidation group, and those creditors who did not receive the notification have 45 days to declare their claims after the newspaper announcement of the liquidation.[34]

After examining the company's property and preparing a balance sheet and a schedule of assets, the liquidation group will formulate a liquidation plan that shall be submitted to the shareholders' meeting – or the court if the liquidation group was appointed by the court – for approval. The major part of the plan normally concerns the distribution of the company's available remaining assets. In general, the assets are applied in the following order:[35]

1. The proper expenses of the liquidation;
2. Employees' wages;
3. Social security premiums;
4. Statutory compensation of staff and workers;
5. Outstanding taxes;
6. Payment of creditors;
7. Distribution to shareholders.

After examining the company's total assets, if the liquidation group forms the opinion that the company's total assets are insufficient to pay

[32] Liu Junhai (2011), p. 935.
[33] Company Law Interpretation (II), Article 10.
[34] Company Law, Article 186.
[35] Company Law, Article 187, para. 2.

its debts, it shall stop the liquidation and apply to a people's court for a declaration of bankruptcy.[36] The bankruptcy of a company will be examined in the next section.

Following the completion of the liquidation, the liquidation group should prepare and submit a liquidation report to the shareholders' meeting or the court for confirmation, and send the report also to the relevant company registration authority (AIC) to apply to strike off the company from the register of companies. Following the de-registration, a public announcement of the termination of the company shall be made, marking the official death of the company.[37]

12.4.4 Statutory Duties of the Liquidators

Since the liquidation group controls the company's assets and business, its members are viewed as having the status of an ordinary company's directors, supervisors, and senior management executives.[38] In other words, as fiduciary officers, members of the liquidation group owe duties not only to the company and its shareholders, but also to the creditors of the company. The duties are embodied in Article 190 of the Company Law, which reads:

> Members of a liquidation group shall be faithful in discharging their duties and the liquidation obligations according to law. [They] may not abuse their powers and duties to accept bribes or other illegal income and shall not misappropriate corporate property. [They] shall be liable for compensation if they willfully or, through gross negligence, cause losses to the company and its creditors.[39]

The SPC has made it clear that now both the company and the creditors of the company could sue the members of the liquidation group for damage if they violate laws, administrative regulations, or the corporate charter so as to cause losses to the company or its creditors. In addition, the shareholders of the company may launch a derivative action against the members of the liquidation group under Article 152 of the Company Law. These lawsuits can be instituted against those members even after the company has already been liquidated and de-registered.[40]

---

36 Id, Article 188.
37 Id, Article 189.
38 Liu Junhai (2011), p. 938.
39 Company Law, Article 190 (paragraphs reorganized).
40 Company Law Interpretation (II), Article 23.

12.5 CORPORATE BANKRUPTCY

12.5.1 Grounds for Initiating Bankruptcy Proceedings

Bankruptcy is not the only reason for the life of a company to be terminated, but it is probably the most common ground. As noted above, either in voluntary or involuntary dissolution of a company, when the liquidation group figures out that the assets of the company are not sufficient to meet all the claims, it shall transfer the case to the court to apply the bankruptcy proceeding to the company. Corporate bankruptcy is now governed by the PRC Enterprise Bankruptcy Law, which was adopted by the NPC on 27 August 2006 (hereafter the EBL).

Under the EBL, a company, which is the insolvent debtor, may file for reorganization, conciliation, or bankruptcy liquidation if either of the two statutory criteria is met: (1) the company fails to discharge its debts as they fall due and its assets are insufficient for the settlement of all debts; or (2) the company fails to discharge its debts as they fall due and it obviously lacks the ability to discharge its debts.[41] Further, a lower threshold applies to the creditors' initiation of the bankruptcy proceeding: the creditors may petition a people's court for reorganization or bankruptcy liquidation of the debtor company simply because the company fails to discharge its debts as they become due.[42]

12.5.2 Administrator

When a court accepts a bankruptcy application, it shall appoint an administrator for the debtor. The administrator could be the liquidation group of the company, an intermediary such as a law firm, accounting firm, or bankruptcy liquidation firm, or a licensed individual professional of such an intermediary.[43] The administrator reports to the court, but should accept the supervision by the creditors' meeting and the creditors' committee. It functions as the manager of the company and has the powers ranging from taking possession and disposing of assets of the debtor to determining its internal management affairs. In addition, it has the power to decide whether to continue the debtor's business before the

---

[41] EBL, Articles 2 and 7.
[42] EBL, Article 7, para. 2.
[43] EBL, Article 24.

creditors' first meeting is convened, and to represent the debtor in any legal proceedings.[44]

12.5.3 Creditors' Meeting

The creditors' meeting in bankruptcy proceedings is the functional equivalent of the shareholders' meeting of a normal company, for creditors are actually the owners of the assets of the debtor company in the case of bankruptcy. All the creditors who have declared their claims are allowed to participate and vote in the creditors' meeting. The meeting has the power to supervise the administrator, to request the court to replace the administrator, to decide on whether the debtor should continue or suspend its business operation, and to adopt the reorganization plan, the conciliation agreement, the plan for the management of the debtor's property, the plan for the realization of the bankruptcy property, and the plan for the distribution of the bankruptcy property.[45] The creditors' meeting may elect a creditors' committee to exercise some powers of the creditors' meeting.

12.5.4 Reorganization (*chongzheng*) and Conciliation (*hejie*)

The idea behind the introduction of the reorganization procedure is to provide a period of calm for the debtor company within which measures can be taken for restructuring the business, ownership, and liabilities of the debtor. The debtor or its creditors may apply directly to a people's court for reorganization of the debtor. If the debtor is already in the bankruptcy process – namely the application for its bankruptcy has already been accepted by the court – the creditors or shareholders whose capital contributions represent one-tenth or more of the registered capital of the debtor may also apply to the court for the company's reorganization.[46] The debtor will enter into the reorganization stage when the court makes and publicly announces a ruling on the reorganization.[47]

During the reorganization period, certain proceedings and claims against the debtor are frozen to allow the debtor to restructure its corporate affairs with a view to bringing it back to solvency. In particular, the secured creditors' rights to enforce the security collaterals are

44 EBL, Article 35.
45 EBL, Article 61.
46 EBL, Article 70.
47 EBL, Articles 71 and 72.

suspended.[48] In addition, a third party whose property is lawfully possessed by the debtor is only entitled to take back the property under previously agreed terms.[49] The distribution of dividends to shareholders and transfer of shares to third parties by the debtor's directors, supervisors, and senior executives are all frozen.[50]

The reorganization plan, if approved by the court, binds the debtor and all the creditors. If the reorganization is successful, the company may be restored to a profitable position and repay the debts – or at least part of them – it owes to the creditors. If the reorganization fails, the court will issue a ruling to terminate the implementation of the plan and declare the debtor bankrupt.[51]

Apart from reorganization, the debtor may also present a draft conciliation agreement to the court and apply for court-sponsored conciliation.[52] If the court considers the application compliant with the EBL, it will convene a creditors' meeting to discuss it. A conciliation agreement adopted by the creditors' meeting and approved by the court will be binding upon the debtor and all unsecured creditors.[53]

12.5.5 Bankruptcy Liquidation

The court may declare a company bankrupt either at the request of the parties or on its own initiative. Once the declaration is made, the company has to be liquidated in accordance with the bankruptcy liquidation procedure in the EBL. In this process, the administrator shall submit a bankruptcy property realization plan to the creditors' meeting and realize and sell the debtor's remaining assets according to the decisions of the creditors' meeting.

An important question here is whether secured creditors have the right of priority to be paid. The EBL distinguishes between preferential claims and ordinary claims. The claim of a holder of a security right over a specific property of the debtor is therefore considered a preferential claim, and this secured creditor has the right of priority of payment against such specific property.[54] Unsecured claims are ordinary claims. If

---

48 EBL, Article 76.
49 EBL, Article 76.
50 EBL, Article 77.
51 EBL, Article 93.
52 EBL, Article 95.
53 EBL, Article 100.
54 EBL, Article 109.

the secured creditor still cannot be fully repaid by exercising the right of priority, its unpaid claims will be considered as ordinary claims.[55]

The bankruptcy property will be distributed in the following order after payment of bankruptcy expenses and debts for common benefits:[56]

1. The wages, medical allowance, disability assistance, and compassionate payment owed by the debtor to the employees, as well as any compensation payable to the employees as required by laws and administrative regulations;
2. Unpaid social insurance premiums and taxes;
3. All ordinary bankruptcy claims.

12.5.6 Dissolution

The administrator, after distribution of the available remaining assets or in the case where there are no assets to distribute, should request the court to issue a ruling on the termination of the bankruptcy proceedings. Within 10 days of the court ruling, the administrator should apply to the relevant AIC to cancel the registration of the debtor. The debtor company will completely cease to exist upon the de-registration, although the creditors have two more years to request the court to make additional distributions if other assets owned by the debtor are found.[57]

12.6 UNPAID CAPITAL CONTRIBUTIONS IN CORPORATE LIQUIDATION AND BANKRUPTY

The last part of this book deals with an issue that has emerged as a source of disputes in corporate liquidation and bankruptcy cases in recent years. It happens when a person is both a shareholder and a creditor. In theory, this person should first join the group of creditors and participate in the pro rata distribution of the debtor company's assets, and participate again in the pro rata distribution to shareholders if there are any remaining assets available after fulfilling the claims of the creditors. A controversial question would arise if the shareholder has not made or fully made his contribution to the registered capital of the company. When the company gets to the stage of liquidation or bankruptcy, the

[55] EBL, Article 110.
[56] EBL, Article 113.
[57] EBL, Articles 121, 122, and 123.

shareholder–creditor may wish to set off the unpaid capital contribution against the debt the company owes to him.

As noted in Chapter 4, PRC laws on incorporation follow strictly the principle of legally mandated capital. A shareholder has the legal obligation to make capital contributions it has subscribed as specified in the relevant documents of the company, on time and in full. Should a shareholder fail to make adequate contributions, it shall first of all make capital contributions in full to the company and may be liable to others concerned for damages and to the state for violations of mandatory legal provisions. This principle applies to the establishment of all companies in China.[58]

It has been especially pointed out by the SPC that unpaid capital contributions by the shareholders shall be treated as part of the assets under liquidation.[59] That is to say, the unpaid capital contributions shall be collected by the liquidation group and distributed as part of the total assets of the company in accordance with the statutory order of payment of debts provided in Article 187 of the Company Law. Thus if the shareholder concerned is also a creditor of the company, it will not be allowed to set off its claims against its unpaid capital contribution. It must fulfill its obligation of making the capital contribution first, and then wait for the liquidation group to distribute to it assets in proportion to its share of the company's registered capital. If the assets of the company are insufficient to discharge its debts, the creditors of the company may, through a lawsuit, hold the shareholders who have not made full payment of their capital contributions jointly and severally liable for the company's debts to the extent of their unpaid capital contributions.[60]

For a company under bankruptcy administration, after a people's court accepts a bankruptcy application, if it is found that there are unpaid capital contributions by an investor, the bankruptcy administrator shall request the investor to make full contribution of the capital it subscribed.[61]

On the right to set off, the EBL permits a creditor of the bankrupt to set off debts it owes to the bankrupt against debts owed by the bankrupt to the creditor.[62] This principle, however, does not apply to unpaid capital contributions. This is because the obligation to make capital contributions

---

58 Company Law, Article 28.
59 Company Law Interpretation (II), Article 22, para. 1.
60 Id, Article 22, para. 2.
61 EBL, Article 35.
62 EBL, Article 40.

is not treated as 'debts' in China. In China's civil law system, debts, arising out of contracts, tortious acts, unjust enrichment, or management without mandate, could be mutually cancelled. Making capital contributions is, however, a mandatory legal obligation in and after the incorporation process and hence does not belong to the arena of debts covered in China's traditional civil law system.

As noted above, a shareholder has a legal obligation to make the capital contributions it subscribes. The strict principle of legally mandated capital sets out an absolute obligation to make capital contributions in full and on time. In the case of enterprise bankruptcy, this principle is further strengthened by Article 35 of the EBL, which requires the bankruptcy administrator to request the shareholder to make payment in full of its unpaid capital contributions.

Finally, the SPC prohibited such a kind of set-off in a previous case in 1995 through a Judicial Interpretation. In the Reply to the Higher People's Court of Hubei Province on Whether Debt Claims Can Be Offset against Unpaid Capital Contributions, the SPC ruled that, after an application for bankruptcy for a company is filed, all the creditors should have equal rights with respect to the satisfaction of their claims. In order to protect the lawful interest of other creditors, the court should not allow the set-off of debts owed to one creditor/shareholder against the unpaid capital contributions by that creditor/shareholder. This Reply, since it was issued in the form of the Judicial Interpretation that is a formal source of law in China, is currently good and enforceable law and should be applied to the bankruptcy cases concerning the set-off of unpaid capital contributions against debts, because it has never been explicitly or implicitly abolished by the SPC. The promulgation of the EBL does not have any negative effect on the validity of this Reply because none of the provisions of the EBL is contradictory to the Reply.

Bibliography

REFERENCES IN ENGLISH

Albert, David M. (2002). 'Addressing Abuse of the Corporate Entity in the People's Republic of China: New Thoughts on China's Need for a Defined Veil Piercing Doctrine', 23 *University of Pennsylvania Journal of International Economic Law* 873–97.

Allen, Franklin, Jun Qian, and Meijun Qian (2005). 'Law, Finance, and Economic Growth in China', 77 *Journal of Financial Economics* 57–116.

Anderson, Braig and Bingna Guo (2006a). 'Corporate Governance under the New Company Law (Part 1): Fiduciary Duties and Minority Shareholder Protection', 4 *China Law & Practice*, available at http://www.chinalawandpractice.com.

Anderson, Braig and Bingna Guo (2006b). 'Corporate Governance under the New Company Law (Part 2): Shareholder Lawsuits and Enforcement', *China Law & Practice*, available at http://www.chinalawandpractice.com.

Armstrong, Rachel (2011). 'China Accounting Scandals Put Big Four Auditors on Red Alert', *Reuters*, 24 June 2011, available at http://www.reuters.com.

Art, Robert C. and Minkang Gu (1995). 'China Incorporated: The First Corporation Law of the People's Republic of China', 20 *Yale Journal of International Law* 273–308.

Bainbridge, Stephen M. (2008). *The New Corporate Governance in Theory and Practice*. Oxford: Oxford University Press.

Bainbridge, Stephen M. (2009). *Corporate Law* (2nd ed.). New York: Thomson Reuters/Foundation Press.

Bath, Vivienne (2007). 'The Company Law and Foreign Investment Enterprises in the PRC – Parallel Systems of Chinese–Foreign Regulation', 30.3 *UNSW Law Journal* 774–85.

Baysinger, Barry D. and Henry N. Butler (1984). 'Revolution Versus Evolution in Corporation Law: The ALI's Project and the Independent Director', 52 *George Washington Law Review* 560–81.

Becht, Marco, Patrick Bolton, and Ailsa Roell (2003), 'Chapter 1: Corporate Governance and Control', in G.M. Constantinides, M. Harris and R. Stulz (eds.), *Handbook of the Economics of Finance*. Amsterdam: Elsevier B.V.

Beijing Modern Business Daily (2004). 'Yinian Ban 10 Ren Juanzou Shangshi Gongsi Baiyi. Gaoguan Waitao Qian Zhengzhao' [10 Billion of Yuan Embezzlement out [China's] Listed Companies. The Signs before the Impending Escape of Senior Managers from the Companies]. Beijing Xiandai Shangbao [*Beijing Modern Business Daily*], 23 June 2004, available at http://news.xinhuanet.com/stock/2004-06/23/content_1541441.htm.

Berlin Initiative Group, 'German Code of Corporate Governance', available at http://www.ecgi.org.

Bersani, Matthew D. (1993). 'Privatization and the Creation of Stock Companies in China', 3 *Columbia Business Law Review* 301–28.

Bhagat, S. and B. Black (1998). 'The Relationship between Board Composition and Firm Performance', in K.J. Hopt and S. Prigge (eds.), *Comparative Corporate Governance: The State of the Art and Emerging Research*. Oxford: Oxford University Press pp. 281–306.

Bu, Yuanshi (2010). *Chinese Business Law*. Munich: Verlag C.H. Beck oHG.

Cahn, Andreas and David C. Donald (2010). *Comparative Company Law: Text and Cases on the Laws Governing Corporations in German, the UK and the USA*. Cambridge: Cambridge University Press.

CCH (2005). *China Company Law Guide*. The Hague: Kluwer Law International.

CCH (2006), *Hong Kong Company Law and Practice Commentary*. Hong Kong: CCH Asia.

Cha, Laura M. (2001). 'The Future of China's Capital Markets and the Role of Corporate Governance', Luncheon Speech at China Business Summit by Laura M. Cha, Vice Chairman of the China Securities Regulatory Commission, 18 April 2001, available at http://www.csrc.gov.cn/en/jsp/detail.jsp?infoid=1061948105100&type=CMS.STD.

Chan, Gordon Y.M. (2009). 'Why Does China Not Abolish the Minimum Capital Requirement for Limited Liability Companies?', 30.10 *Company Lawyer* 306–11.

Chan, Gordon Y.M. (2009a). 'Company Promoters under the Chinese Company Law – A Comparative Analysis', 39 *Hong Kong Law Journal* 223–44.

Chang, Eric C. and Sonia M.L. Wong (2004). 'Political Control and Performance in China's Listed Companies', 32 *Journal of Comparative Economics* 617–36.

Chen, A.H.Y. (2000). 'Socialist Law, Civil Law, Common Law, and the Classification of Contemporary Chinese Law', in J.M. Otto, M.V.

Polak, J. Chen and Y. Li (eds.), *Law-Making in the People's Republic of China*. The Hague: Kluwer Law International pp. 55–74.
Chen, A.H.Y. (2004). *An Introduction to the Legal System of the People's Republic of China*. Hong Kong: LexisNexis.
Chen, Jianfu (1999). *Chinese Law: Towards an Understanding of Chinese Law, its Nature and Development.* The Hague: Kluwer Law International.
Chen, Jianfu (2008). *Chinese Law: Context and Transformation*. Leiden: Martinus Nijhoff Publishers.
Chen, Zhiwu (2003). 'Capital Markets and Legal Development: The China Case', 14.4 *China Economic Review* 451–72.
China Securities Daily (2005). 'Zhongguo Dudong Diaocha Ji Zhidu Fansi' [Survey on China's Independent Directors and Reflections on the Institutions]. Zhongguo Zhengquan Bao [*China Securities Daily*], 28 July 2005, available at http://www.cs.com.cn/sylm/04/t20050728_723933.htm.
China Securities Regulatory Commission (CSRC) (2006). *China's Securities and Futures Markets*. Beijing: CSRC.
China Securities Regulatory Commission (CSRC) (2008). *China Capital Markets Development Report.* Beijing: China Financial Publishing House.
China Securities Regulatory Commission (CSRC) (2011). *Corporate Governance of Listed Companies in China: Self-Assessment by the China Securities Regulatory Commission.* Paris: OECD.
Choper, Jesse H., John C. Coffee, Jr., and Ronald J. Gilson (2004). *Cases and Materials on Corporations*. New York: Aspen Publishers.
Clark, Robert Charles (1986). *Corporate Law*. Boston and Toronto: Little, Brown and Company.
Clarke, Donald C. (2003). 'Corporate Governance in China: An Overview', 14 *China Economic Review* 494–507.
Clarke, Donald C. (2003a), 'Corporatisation, not Privatisation', 7:3 *China Economic Quarterly* 27–30.
Clarke, Donald C. (2005). 'How Do We Know when an Enterprise Exists? Unanswerable Questions and Legal Polycentricity in China', 19:1 *Columbia Journal of Asian Law* 50–71.
Clarke, Donald C. (2006). 'The Independent Director in Chinese Corporate Governance', 31 *Delaware Journal of Corporate Law* 125–8.
Cohen, Jerome A. and Johan E. Lange (1997). 'The Chinese Legal System: A Primer for Investors', 17 *New York Law School Journal of International and Comparative Law* 345–77.
Cox, James D. and Thomas Lee Hazen (2003). *Corporations* (2nd ed.). New York: Aspen Publishers.

CVCRI (China Venture Capital Research Institute) (2009). *China Venture Capital Yearbook 2009*. Beijing: Minzhu yu Jianshe Chubanshe.

Dahya, Jay *et al.* (2003). 'The Usefulness of the Supervisory Board Report in China', 11:4 *Corporate Governance* 308–21.

David, Rene and John E.C. Brierley (1985). *Major Legal Systems in the World Today* (3rd ed.). London: Stevens & Sons.

Davies, Paul L. (2003). *Gower and Davies' Principles of Modern Company Law* (7th ed.). London: Sweet & Maxwell.

Davies, Paul L. (2008). *Gower and Davies' Principles of Modern Company Law* (8th ed.). London: Sweet & Maxwell.

Deschandol, Jean-Marc and Charles Desmeules (2006). 'New Rules on Strategic Investment by Foreign Investors in Listed Companies', 2 *China Law & Practice*.

Dickinson, Steven M. (2007), 'Introduction to the New Company Law of the People's Republic of China', 16:1 *Pacific Rim Law & Policy Journal* 1–11.

Djankov, Simeon, Rafael La Porta, Florencio Lopez-de-Silanes, and Andrei Shleifer (2002). 'The Regulation of Entry', CXVII.1 *The Quarterly Journal of Economics* 1–37.

du Plessis, Jean Jacques *et al.* (2005). *Principles of Contemporary Corporate Governance*. Cambridge: Cambridge University Press.

Economist Intelligence Unit (EIU) (2007), *China Hand: The Complete Guide to Doing Business in China*, Chapter 4: Investing. London: The Economist Intelligence Unit.

Emanuel, Steven L. (1997). *Corporations*. New York: Emanuel Publishing Corp.

Emanuel, Steven L. (2009). *Corporations*. New York: Aspen Publishers.

Fairbank, John King, and Merle Goldman (2006). *China: A New History*. (2nd enlarged ed.). Cambridge, MA: The Belknap Press Harvard University Press.

Fang, Liufang (1995). 'China's Corporatization Experiment', 5 *Duke Journal of Comparative & International Law* 149–270.

Fewsmith, Joseph (2004). 'Promoting the Scientific Development Concept', 11 *China Leadership Monitor*, available at http://www.hoover.org.

Foster, Nicholas H.D. (2000). 'Company Law Theory in Comparative Perspective: England and France', 48 *American Journal of Comparative Law* 573–621.

Fu, Jane (2010). *Corporate Disclosure and Corporate Governance in China*. The Netherlands: Kluwer Law International.

Fu, Jian, and Jie Yuan (2006). *PRC Company Law and Securities Law – A Practical Guide*. Hong Kong: CCH Asia.

Fu, Yulin and Randall Peerenboom (2010). 'A New Analytic Framework for Understanding and Promoting Judicial Independence in China', in Randall Peerenboom (ed.), *Judicial Independence in China: Lessons for Global Rule of Law Promotion*. Cambridge: Cambridge University Press, pp. 95–133.

Gaughan, Patrick A. (2007). *Mergers, Acquisitions, and Corporate Restructuring* (4th ed.). New Jersey: John, Wiley & Sons.

Ginsburg, Tom (2010). 'Judicial Independence in East Asia: Lessons for China', in Randall Peerenboom (ed.), *Judicial Independence in China: Lessons for Global Rule of Law Promotion*. Cambridge: Cambridge University Press, pp. 247–59.

Green, Stephen (2003). *China's Stockmarket: A Guide to Its Progress, Players and Prospects*. London: The Economist.

Green, Stephen (2004). *The Development of China's Stock Market, 1984–2002: Equity Politics and Market Institutions*. London and New York: RoutledgeCurzon.

Gu, Minkang (2003). 'Will an Independent Director Perform Better than a Supervisory?', 6 *Journal of Chinese and Comparative Law* 59–76.

Gu, Minkang (2010). *Understanding Chinese Company Law* (2nd ed.). Hong Kong University Press.

Hamilton, Gary G. (2006). *Commerce and Capitalism in Chinese Societies*. London and New York: Routledge.

Halsbury's Laws of Hong Kong (2005). Volume 6(1), 'Companies and Corporations', Hong Kong: LexisNexis Butterworth.

Hansmann, Henry and Reinier Kraakman (2001). 'The End of History for Corporate Law', 89 *Georgetown Law Journal* 439–68.

Hansmann, Henry and Reinier Kraakman (2004). 'What is Corporate Law?' in Reinier Kraakman *et al.*, *The Anatomy of Corporate Law*. Oxford: Oxford University Press, pp. 1–19, available at http://ssrn.com/abstract=568623.

Hawes, Colin (2007). 'Interpreting the PRC Company Law through the Lens of Chinese Political and Corporate Culture', 30 *UNSW Law Journal* 813–23.

Horn, Norbert, Hein Kotz, and Hans G. Leser (1982). *German Private and Commercial Law: An Introduction* (translated by Tony Weir). Oxford: Clarendon Press.

Howson, Nicholas C. (1997). 'China's Company Law: One Step Forward, Two Steps Back? A Modest Complaint', 11 *Columbia Journal of Asian Law* 127–72.

Howson, Nicholas C. (2008). 'The Doctrine that Dared Not Speak its Name: Anglo-American Fiduciary Duties in China's 2005 Company Law and Case Intimations of Prior Convergence', in Hideki Kanda,

Kon-Sik Kim and Curtis J. Milhaupt (eds.), *Transforming Corporate Governance in East Asia*. London and New York: Routledge, pp. 193–254.

Howson, Nicholas C. (2010). 'Corporate Law in the Shanghai People's Courts, 1992–2008: Judicial Autonomy in a Contemporary Authoritarian State', 5 *East Asia Law Review* 303–442.

Howson, Nicholas C. (2010a). 'Judicial Independence and the Company Law in Shanghai Courts', in Randall Peerenboom (ed.), *Judicial Independence in China: Lessons for Global Rule of Law Promotion*. Cambridge: Cambridge University Press, pp. 134–53.

Hui, Huang (2007). 'The Statutory Derivative Action in China: Critical Analysis and Recommendations for Reform', 4:2 *Berkeley Business Law Journal* 227–50.

Hui, Huang (2008). 'The New Takeover Regulation in China: Evolution and Enhancement', 42:1 *The International Lawyer* 153–75.

Jensen, Mads Holst (2006). 'Serve the People! Corporate Social Responsibility (CSR) in China', Discussion Papers 2006-6, Asia Research Centre, CBS, Copenhagen.

Keller, Perry (1994). 'Sources of Order in Chinese Law', 42 *American Journal of Comparative Law* 711–59.

Kirby, William C. (1995). 'China Unincorporated: Company Law and Business Enterprises in Twentieth-Century China', 54:1 *The Journal of Asian Studies* 43–63.

Koh, Pcter S.K. (2010). *Major Issues in Company Law (with PRC and English Comparative Law Notes)*. Singapore: Sweet & Maxwell.

Kraakman, Reinier *et al.* (2004). *The Anatomy of Corporate Law*. Oxford: Oxford University Press.

Kraakman, Reinier *et al.* (2009). *The Anatomy of Corporate Law: A Comparative and Functional Approach* (2nd ed.) Oxford: Oxford University Press.

La Porta, Rafael, Florencio Lopez-de-Silanes, Andrei Shleifer and Rovert W. Vinhny (1998). 'Law and Finance', 106:6 *The Journal of Political Economy* 1113–55.

La Porta, Rafael, Florencio Lopez-de-Silanes, and Andrei Shleifer (2006). 'What Works in Securities Laws?', LXI:1 *Journal of Finance* 1–32.

Lau, K.L. Alex (2007). 'Why Are the Initial Paid-up Capital of Private Limited Companies in China 2,000 Times Bigger than Those in the United Kingdom?', 28:8 *Company Lawyer* 248–52.

Law Commission UK (2003). 'Partnership Law – Report on a Reference under Section 3(1)(e) of the Law Commissions Act 1965', LAW COM No. 283 (London: The Law Commission), available at http://www.lawcom.gov.uk.

Lee, Junyeop (2009). 'State Owned Enterprises in China: Reviewing the Evidence', OECD Occasional Paper. Paris: OECD.

Lee, Rebecca (2007). 'Fiduciary Duty without Equity: 'Fiduciary Duties' of Directors under the Revised Company Law of the PRC', 47 *Virginia Journal of International Law* 897–926.

Lin, Li-Wen and Curtis J. Milhaupt (2013). 'We are the (National) Champions: Understanding the Mechanisms of State Capitalism in China', 65 *Stanford Law Review* 697–759.

Li, Xiaoning (2007). *A Comparative Study of Shareholders' Derivative Action*. The Netherlands: Kluwer.

Ling, Bing (2002). *Contract Law in China.* Hong Kong: Sweet & Maxwell Asia.

Liu, Lawrence S. (2008). 'The Politics of Corporate Governance in Taiwan', in Hideki Kanda, Kon-Sik Kim and Curtis J. Milhaupt, *Transforming Corporate Governance in East Asia*. London and New York: Routledge, pp. 255–77.

Liu, Qiao (2006). 'Corporate Governance in China: Current Practices, Economic Effects and Institutional Determinants', 52:2 *CESifo Economic Studies* 415–53.

Loss, Louis and Joel Seligman (1995). *Fundamentals of Securities Regulation*. U.S.: Aspen Law & Business.

Lowry, John, and Alan Dignam (2006). *Company Law*. Oxford: Oxford University Press.

Luo, Yadong (2007). *Guanxi and Business* (2nd ed.). Singapore: World Scientific.

Manne, Henry G. (2006). 'Milton Friedman Was Right: 'Corporate social responsibility' is bunk', *The Wall Street Journal*, 24 November 2006.

Mayson, Stephen, Derek French, and Christopher Ryan (2006). *Company Law* (23rd ed.). Oxford: Oxford University Press.

McGregor, Richard (2009). 'The Party Organizer', *Financial Times*, 30 September 2009, available at http://www.ft.com.

McGregor, Richard (2010). *The Party: The Secret World of China's Communist Rulers.* New York: HarperCollins Publishers.

Miller, Alice (2006). 'Hu Jintao and the Sixth Plenum', 20 *China Leadership Monitor*, available at http://www.hoover.org.

Monks, Robert A.G. and Nell Minow (2004). *Corporate Governance* (3rd ed.). Oxford: Blackwell Publishing.

Naughton, Barry (2007). *The Chinese Economy: Transition and Growth.* Cambridge, MA: MIT Press.

Nestor, Stilpon and John K. Thompson (1999). 'Corporate Governance Patterns in OECD Economies: Is Convergence Under Way?', Paris: OECD.

Neumann, Peter A. (2006). 'China's Foreign-invested Companies: A Standardization of Practices', 7 *China Law & Practice*, available at http://www.chinalawandpractice.com.

Neumann, Peter A. and Tony Zhang (2006). 'China's New Foreign-funded M&A Provisions: Greater Legal Protection or Legalized Protectionism?', 10 *China Law & Practice*, available at http://www.chinalawandpractice.com.

NPCLCA (The Legislative Affairs Commission of the National People's Congress Standing Committee) (2006). *Explanations of the PRC Partnership Enterprise Law*. Beijing: Falu Chubanshe (Law Press China).

OECD (2000). *Reforming China's Enterprises*. Paris: Organisation for Economic Co-operation and Development (OECD) Publishing.

OECD (2002). *China in the World Economy: The Domestic Policy Challenges*. Paris: OECD Publishing.

OECD (2003). *OECD Investment Policy Review of China 2003*: *Progress and Reform Challenges*. Paris: OECD Publishing.

OECD (2004). *Principles of Corporate Governance* (Revised Version). Paris: OECD Publishing.

OECD (2005). *Economic Surveys: China*. Paris: OECD Publishing.

OECD (2006), *OECD Investment Policy Review of China 2006: Open Policies Towards Mergers and Acquisitions*. Paris: OECD Publishing.

OECD (2006a). 'Recent Developments in China's Policies Towards Cross-Border Mergers and Acquisitions', December 2006. Paris: OECD Publishing.

OECD (2010). *OECD Economic Surveys: China*. Paris: OECD Publishing.

Palmiter, Alan R. (2008). *Securities Regulation: Examples and Explanations*. New York: Aspen Publishers.

Peerenboom, Randall (2006). 'Courts as Legislators', The Rule of Law in China: Policy Brief 1. Oxford: The Foundation for Law, Justice and Society.

Peerenboom, Randall (2010a). 'Introduction', in Randall Peerenboom (ed.), *Judicial Independence in China: Lessons for Global Rule of Law Promotion*. Cambridge: Cambridge University Press, pp. 1–22.

Peerenboom, Randall (2010b). 'A New Analytic Framework for Undertaking and Promoting Judicial Independence in China', in Randall Peerenboom (ed.), *Judicial Independence in China: Lessons for Global Rule of Law Promotion*. Cambridge: Cambridge University Press, pp. 95–133.

Peng, Mike W. (2004). 'Outside Directors and Firm Performance during Institutional Transitions', 25 *Strategic Management Journal* 453–71.

Pettet, Ben (2005). *Company Law* (2nd ed.). Edinburgh: Pearson Longman.

Pistor, Katharina *et al.* (2003). 'Evolution of Corporate Law and the Transplant Effect: Lessons from Six Countries', 18:1 *The World Bank Research Observer* 89–112.

Pistor, Katharina, and Chenggang Xu (2003). 'Fiduciary Duty in Transitional Civil Law Jurisdictions: Lessons from the Incomplete Law Theory', in Curtis J. Milhaupt, *Global Markets, Domestic Institutions: Corporate Law and Governance in a New Era of Cross-Border Deals*. New York: Columbia University Press, pp. 77–106.

Porter, Michael E. and Mark R. Kramer (2006). 'The Link between Competitive Advantage and Corporate Social Responsibility', 12 *Harvard Business Review* 1–13.

Qu, Charles Zhen (2008). 'Pre-incorporation Contracts in China: A Proposal for Optimal Rules', 38:3 *Hong Kong Law Journal* 793–830.

Qu, Charles Zhen (2008a). 'The Representative Power of Shareholders' General Meeting under Chinese Law', 17 *Pacific Rim Law and Policy Journal* 295–323.

Reisberg, Arad (2007). *Derivative Actions and Corporate Governance: Theory and Operation.* Oxford: Oxford University Press.

Ruskola, Teemu (2000). 'Conceptualizing Corporations and Kinship: Comparative Law and Development Theory in a Chinese Perspective', 52 *Stanford Law Review* 1599–1729.

Sadowsky, James, S.J. (1966). 'Private and Collective Ownership', *Left and Right*, available at http://www.quebecoislibre.org/030607-3.htm.

Schneider, Hannes and Heidenhain, Martin (1996). *The German Stock Corporation Act*. The Hague: Kluwer Law International.

SEC (U.S. Securities and Exchange Commission) (2012). 'The Investor's Advocate: How the SEC Protects Investors, Maintains Market Integrity, and Facilitates Capital Formation', Washington D.C.: US Securities and Exchange Commission, available at http://www.sec.gov.

Securities Times (2003). 'Xianzhuang Diaocha: Duli Dongshi Zenmeyang Le?' [A Survey of the Current Situation: What Happens to Independent Directors?] 7 August 2003, Zhengquan Shibao [*Securities Times*], available at http://business.sohu.com/37/91/news211889137.shtml.

Semler, Johannes (1998). 'The Practice of the German Aufsichtsrat', in K.J. Hopt, H. Kanda, M.J. Roe, E. Wymeersch and S. Prigge (eds.), *Comparative Corporate Governance: The State of the Art and Emerging Research*. Oxford: Oxford University Press, pp. 267–280.

Shanghai Securities News (2004). 'Zhongguo Dudong Diaocha: Zhongguo Dudong Shengcun Xianzhuang Diaochao' [Survey of China's Independent Directors: The State of Living of China's Independent

Directors], Shanghai Zhengquan Bao [*Shanghai Securities News*], 27 May 2004, available at http://paper.cnstock.com/ssnews/2004-5-27/liuban/t20040527_571548.htm.

Shanghai Securities News (2004a). 'Zhongguo Dudong Diaocha: Wo De Dudong Shengya' [Survey of China's Independent Directors: My Career as an Independent Director], Shanghai Zhengquan Bao [*Shanghai Securities News*], 27 May 2004, available at http://paper.cnstock.com/ssnews/2004-5-27/qiban/t20040527_571546.htm.

Sherman, Andrew J. and Milledge A. Hart (2006). *Mergers and Acquisitions from A to Z*. New York: American Management Association.

Siems, Mathias (2008). *Convergence in Shareholder Law*. Cambridge: Cambridge University Press.

Simon, William H. (1996). 'The Legal Structure of the Chinese "Socialist Market" Enterprises', 21 *Journal of Corporate Law* 267–306.

Soderquist, Larry D. and Theresa A. Gabaldon (2004). *Securities Law* (2nd ed.). New York: Foundation Press.

Soderquist, Larry D., *et al.* (1999). *Corporate Law and Practice*. New York: Practicing Law Institute.

Solomon, Lewis D. and Alan R. Palmiter (2004). *Corporations: Examples and Explanations* (3rd ed.). Published by Aspen Law & Business (New York) and republished by China Fangzheng Press (Beijing).

Spence, Jonathan D. (1999). *The Search for Modern China* (2nd ed.). New York: W.W. Norton & Company.

SSE (Shanghai Stock Exchange Research Center) (2003). *Zhongguo Gongsi Zhili Baogao (2003 nian)* [*China Corporate Governance Report 2003*]. Shanghai: Fudan University Press.

SSE (Shanghai Stock Exchange Research Center) (2004). *Zhongguo Gongsi Zhili Baogao (2004 nian)* [*China Corporate Governance Report 2004*]. Shanghai: Fudan University Press.

Standard & Poor's (2003). 'Corporate Governance in China', November, 2003.

Stott, Vanessa (2005). *Hong Kong Company Law* (11th ed.). Hong Kong: Longman Hong Kong Education.

Stout, Lynn A. (2003). 'On the Export of U.S.-Style Corporate Fiduciary Duties to Other Cultures: Can a Transplant Take?', in Curtis J. Milhaupt (ed.), *Global Markets, Domestic Institutions: Corporate Law and Governance in a New Era of Cross-Border Deals*. New York: Columbia University Press, pp. 46–76.

Sui, Hui (2011). 'Problems Existing in Dividends Policies in China Listed Companies and Countermeasures', 7:10 *Asian Social Sciences* 213–15.

Tan, Cheng Han (2003). 'Corporate Governance and Independent Directors', 15 *Singapore Academy of Law Review* 355–91.

Tan, Lay-Hong and Wang, Jiangyu (2007). 'Modelling an Effective Corporate Governance System for China's Listed State-owned Enterprises: Issues and Challenges in a Transitional Economy', 7:1 *Journal of Corporate Law Studies* 143–183.

Tang, Xin (2008). 'Protecting Minority Shareholders in China: A Task for Both Legislation and Enforcement', in Hideki Kanda, Kon-Sik Kim and Curtis J. Milhaupt (eds.), *Transforming Corporate Governance in East Asia*. London and New York: Routledge, pp. 141–67.

Tenev, Stoyan and Chunlin Zhang (with Loup Brefort) (2002). *Corporate Governance and Enterprise Reform in China: Building the Institutions of Modern Markets*. Washington D.C.: World Bank and the International Finance Corporation.

Tomasic, Roman, and Jian Fu (1999). 'Company Law in China', in Roman Tomasic (ed.), *Company Law in East Asia*. Aldershot, UK: Ashgate Publishing Limited, pp. 135–182.

Trifiro, Noelle (2007). 'China's Financial Reporting Standards: Will Corporate Governance Induce Compliance in Listed Companies?', 16 *Tulane Journal of International and Comparative Law* 271–93.

USCC (U.S.–China Economic and Security Review Commission) (2004). *China's Presence in the Global Capital Markets*. Hearing before the U.S.–China Economic and Security Review Commission, One Hundred and Eighth Congress, Second Session, 16 April 2004, available at http://www.uscc.gov.

Walter, Carl E. and Fraser J.T. Howie (2003). *Privatizing China: The Stock Markets and their Role in Corporate Reform*. Singapore: John Wiley & Sons (Asia).

Wang, Baoshu and Hui Huang (2006). 'China's New Company Law and Securities Law: An Overview and Assessment', 19 *Australian Journal of Corporate Law* 1–14.

Wang, Guiguo (2003). *Wang's Business Law of China*. Hong Kong: LexisNexis (Asia).

Wang, Jiangyu (2004). 'Dancing with Wolves: Regulation and Deregulation of Foreign Investment in China's Stock Market', 5 *Asian-Pacific Law and Policy Journal* 1–61.

Wang, Jiangyu (2004a). 'The Rule of Law in China: A Realistic View of the Jurisprudence, the Impact of the WTO, and the Prospects for Future Development', (2004) *Singapore Journal of Legal Studies* 347–89.

Wang, Jiangyu (2007). 'Rule of Law and Rule of Officials: Shareholder Litigation and Anti-Dumping Investigation in China', Paper No. 4 in the 'Rule of Law in China: Chinese Law and Business' Series. Oxford: The Foundation for Law, Justice and Society.

Wang, Jiangyu (2009). 'Regulatory Competition and Cooperation between Securities Markets in Hong Kong and Mainland China', 4:3 *Capital Markets Law Journal* 1–22.

Wang, Wallace Wen-Yeu and Jian-Lin Chen (2006). 'Bargaining for Compensation in the Shadow of Regulatory Giving: The Case of Stock Trading Rights Reform in China', 20 *Columbia Journal of Asian Law* 298–356.

Wei, Yuwa (2006). 'Directors' Duties under Chinese Law: A Comparative Review', 3 *University of New England Law Journal (UNELJ)* 31–56.

Weston, J. Fred, Mark L. Mitchell and J. Harold Mulherin (2006). *Takeovers, Restructuring, and Corporate Governance* (China edition). Beijing: Peking University Press.

Wolff, Lutz-Christian (2006). *Mergers and Acquisitions in China: Law and Practice*. Hong Kong: CCH Hong Kong Limited.

World Bank (2004). *Doing Business 2004: Understanding Regulation*. Washington D.C.: The International Bank for Reconstruction and Development/The World Bank.

World Bank (2005). *Doing Business 2005: Removing Obstacles to Growth.* Washington D.C.: The International Bank for Reconstruction and Development/The World Bank.

World Bank (2005a). *China – Deepening Public Services Unit Reform to Improve Service Delivery*, Report No. 32341-CHA, July 2005. Washington D.C.: The International Bank for Reconstruction and Development/The World Bank.

World Bank (2006). *Doing Business 2006: Creating Jobs.* Washington D.C.: The International Bank for Reconstruction and Development/The World Bank.

World Bank (2007). *Doing Business 2007: How to Reform.* Washington D.C.: The International Bank for Reconstruction and Development/The World Bank.

World Bank (2008). *Doing Business 2008.* Washington D.C.: The International Bank for Reconstruction and Development/The World Bank.

World Bank (2008a). *Doing Business in China 2008*. Washington D.C.: The International Bank for Reconstruction and Development/The World Bank.

World Bank (2010). *Doing Business 2010: China*. Washington D.C.: The International Bank for Reconstruction and Development/The World Bank.

Wu, Jinglian (2005). *Understanding and Interpreting Chinese Economic Reform*. Mason: Thomson Higher Education.

Wu, Mark (2007–2008), 'Piercing China's Corporate Veil: Open Questions from the New Company Law', 117 *Yale Law Journal* 329–38.

Xi, Chao (2006a). 'In Search of an Effective Monitoring Board Model: Board Reforms and the Political Economy of Corporate Law in China', 22:1 *Connecticut Journal of International Law* 1–46.

Xi, Chao (2006b). 'Case Note: Private Enforcement of Securities Law in China: *Daqing Lianyi Co v ZHONG Weida and Others* (2004) Heilongjiang High Court', 1:2 *Journal of Comparative Law* 492–6.

Xi, Chao (2008). 'Foreign Solutions for Local Problems? The Use of US-Style Fiduciary Duties to Regulate Agreed Takeovers in China', 6:4 *Journal of Chinese Economic and Business Studies* 407–20.

Xu, Xiaonian and Yan Wang (1997). 'Ownership Structure, Corporate Governance, and Firm's Performance: The Case of Chinese Stock Companies', World Bank Policy Research Working Paper No. 1794.

Yang, Chao and Fan, Qinghua (2004). 'Independent Directors: The Vase was Broken', 9 *Zhongwai Guanli* [Sino-Foreign Management], available at http://www.zwgl.com.cn/doc/Article/2004831183336-1.shtml (in Chinese).

Yang, Hua (2005). 'Overview of Governance of State-owned Listed Companies in China', OECD, Proceedings of the Second Policy Dialogue on Corporate Governance in China, Beijing 19 May 2005, available at http://www.oecd.org/dataoecd/14/6/34974067.pdf (conference materials website: http://www.oecd.org/document/45/0,2340,en_2649_201185_34965229_1_1_1_1,00.html).

Yusuf, Shahid, Kaoru Nabeshima, and Dwight H. Perkins (2006). *Under New Ownership: Privatizing China's State-owned Enterprises*. Stanford and Washington D.C.: Stanford University Press and The World Bank.

REFERENCES IN CHINESE

An, Jian (ed.) (2005). *Zhonghua Renmin Gongheguo Gongsifa Shiyi* [*Annotations to the Company Law of the People's Republic of China*]. Beijing: Law Press China.

Beijing Modern Business Daily (2004). 'Yinian Ban 10 Ren Juanzou Shangshi Gongsi Baiyi. Gaoguan Waitao Qian Zhengzhao' [10 Billion of Yuan Embezzlement out [China's] Listed Companies. The Signs before the Impending Escape of Senior Managers from the Companies]. Beijing Xiandai Shangbao [*Beijing Modern Business Daily*], 23 June 2004, available at http://news.xinhuanet.com/stock/2004-06/23/content_1541441.htm.

Chen, Hua (2005). '1 Ge Yue 12 Wei Gaoguan Luoma. Shangshi Gongsi Neibu Jianguan Lingren Danyou' [The Fall of 12 Senior Managers in One Month. Insider Supervision of Listed Companies is Worrisome].

Caijing Shibao [*Caijing Daily*], 5 February 2005, available at http://finance.sina.com.cn/stock/stocktalk/20050205/10191351494.shtml.

Cheng, Weibing (2006). 'Gongsi Liyi yu Gudong Zhiqingquan de Pingheng' [Balance between the Company's Interests and the Shareholders' Informational Rights] 2 *Guangdong Lawyer*, available at http://www.legalinfo.gov.cn.

China Securities Daily (2005). 'Zhongguo Dudong Diaocha Ji Zhidu Fansi' [Survey on China's Independent Directors and Reflections on the Institutions]. Zhongguo Zhengquan Bao [*China Securities Daily*], 28 July 2005, available at http://www.cs.com.cn/sylm/04/t20050728_723933.htm.

Dong, Furen (2001). *Zhonghua Renmin Gongheguo Jijishi* [*The Economic History of the People's Republic of China*], Vol. 1. Hong Kong: Joint Publishing (H.K.) Co., Ltd.

Fan, Jian and Jiang Daxing (1998), 'Jingliquan Falu Wenti Bijiao Yanjiu' [A Comparative Study on the Authority of the Company Manager], in *Nanjing Daxue Xuebao* (Zhexue, Renwen Kexue, Shehui Kexue Ban) 3 [*Journal of Nanjing University (Philosophy, Humanities and Social Sciences)* Issue No. 3 of 1998] 135–143.

Fang, Liufang (1999). 'Guoqi Fading Daibiaoren de Falu Diwei, Quanli he Liyi Chongtu' [The Legal Status, Power and Conflict of Interest of the Legal Representatives of State Owned Enterprises], in *Bijiaofa Yanjiu* [*Comparative Law Study*], No. 3, available at http://www.civillaw.com.cn/article/default.asp?id=9199 (accessed 30 March 2012).

Fang, Liufang (2002). 'Shijie Xie Fucheng he Kebi de Zhongguo Gongzi Zhimi' [Trying to Understand the China Corporation Puzzle of Xue Fucheng and Kirby], in Liang Zhiping (ed), *Fazhi zai Zhongguo: Zhidu, Huayu yu Shijian* [Rule of Law in China: Institutions, Discourses and Practices]. Beijing: China University of Political Science and Law Press, pp. 280–326.

Fu, Qilin (2002). *Zhongguo Zhengquan Shichang Shinian Zhuming Anli Pingxi* [*Comments and Analysis on the Famous Cases in China's Securities Markets of the Past Ten Years*]. Beijing: China University of Political Science and Law Press.

Gan, Peizhong (2007). *Qiye yu Gongsi Faxue* [*Enterprise and Company Law*]. Beijing: Peking University Press.

Guo, Mingrui (eds.) (2007). *Minfa* [*Civil Law*]. Beijing: Higher Education Press.

Hao, Lei (2008). 'Woguo Gongsi Zhuantouzi Zhidu de Zai Tantao' [Revisiting the Corporate Reinvestment Regime in Our Country], in *Zhongguo Shangfa Niankan (2008)* [*China Year Book of Commercial Law (2008)*].

Huai, Xiaofeng (2007). *Zhongguo Zuixin Gongsifa: Dianxing Anli Pingxi* [*Latest PRC Company Law: Cases and Commentaries*]. Beijing: Law Press China.

Jiang, Ping (2006). '*Qiye Fading Zhuyi De Ruogan Wenti*' [Several Questions Concerning *nullem crimen sine lege*], *Fazhi Ribao* [*Legal Daily China*], 31 October 2006.

Jiang, Ping (2007). 'Xiuding Gongsi Fa Cong Wuge Fangmian Gei Qiye Dailai Yixiang' [Revision of the Company Law Brings Five Impacts on Enterprises], in She Sibao (ed.), *Zhongguo Touzi Falu Zhinan* [*Legal Aspects of Doing Business in China (II)*]. Beijing: University of International Business and Economics Press.

Li, Guoguang and Wang Chuang (2005). 'Shenqi Gongsi Susong Ruogan Wenti (I)' [Several Questions on the Courts' Adjudication of Corporate Disputes (Part I)], *People's Court Daily*, 29 November 2005, available at http://old.chinacourt.org/public/detail.php?id=187288 (accessed 30 March 2012).

Li, Honggu (2004). 'Deng Xiaoping De 1979: Heping Jueqi Yuannian' [Deng Xiaoping's 1979: Peaceful Rise Year One]. *Sanlian Shenghuo Zhoukan* [*Sanlian Life Weekly*], 12 August 2004.

Li, Hua (2008). 'Gongsifa Renge Fouren Falu Wenti Yanjiu' [A Research on the Doctrine of Disregarding Corporate Legal Personality under the Company Law], available at http://www.chinacourt.org.

Li, Weian *et al.* (2004). 'Calculating the Value of the Independent Directors System Three Years after its Adoption' [Nankai Pandian Sannian Dudong Zhidu De Gongsi Zhili Jiazhi] 9 *Zhongwai Guanli* [Sino-Foreign Management].

Liang, Huixing (2004). *Minfa* (Di Er Ban) [*General Introduction to Civil Law* (2nd ed.)]. Beijing: Law Press.

Liu, Junhai (2005). 'Xin Gongsifa de Zhidu Chuangxin' [Institutional Innovations in the New Company Law]. *Fazhi Ribao* [*Legal Daily China*], 1 November 2005.

Liu, Junhai (2006). *Xin Gongsifa de Zhidu Chuangxin: Lifa Zhengdian yu Jieshi Nandian* [*Institutional Innovations in the New Company Law: Legislative Controversies and Interpretational Difficulties*]. Beijing: Law Press China.

Liu, Junhai (2008). *Xiandai Gongsi Fa* [*Modern Corporation Law*]. Beijing: Law

Liu, Junhai (2011). *Xiandai Gongsi Fa* (Di Er Ban) [*Modern Corporation Law* (2nd ed.)]. Beijing: Law Press China.

Liu, Kaixiang (ed.) (2003). *Minfaxue* [*Science of Civil Law*]. Beijing: China Legal Publishing House.

Liu, Lanfang (ed.) (2009). *Xin Gongsifa Yinan Anli Panjie* [*Understanding the Difficult Cases under the New Company Law*]. Beijing: Falv Chubanshe [Law Press China].

Lu, Yi (2011). 'Wuzhi Jiaoyi Zhongguo Houlaijushang' [China caught up from behind by being the first country to adopt paperless transactions], *FT Chinese*, 6 September 2011, available at http://www.ftchinese.com/story/001040527.

Ma, Baihua (2009). 'Chuyi Faren Renge Fouding Zhidu de Wanshan' [A Meager Opinion on Perfecting the Doctrine of Disregarding Legal Personality], available at http://www.chinacourt.org.

NBSC (National Bureau of Statistics of China) (2009). 'Report on the Major Statistics Resulting from the Second National Economic Survey (No. 1)', 25 December 2009, available at http://www.gov.cn/gzdt/2009-12/25/content_1496439.htm#.

NPC Working Group (Quanguo Renda Zhengquanfa Xiugai Qicao Gongzuo Xiaozu [The Working Group of the National People's Congress for Revising the Securities Law]) (2006). *Annotations to the PRC Securities Law.* Beijing: China Financial Publishing House.

Peng, Bing (2005). *Zhongguo Zhengquan Faxue* [*Study of Chinese Securities Law*]. Beijing: Higher Education Press.

People's Bank of China (PBC) (2006). Monetary Policy Implementation Report (The Fourth Quarter of 2005). Beijing: The People's Bank of China, 21 February 2006.

People's Bank of China (PBC) (2006a). Monetary Policy Implementation Report (The Third Quarter of 2006). Beijing: The People's Bank of China, 21 February 2006.

Shi, Tiantao (2006). *Gongsifa Lun (Di'er Ban)* [*Corporation Law* (2nd ed.)]. Beijing: Law Press China.

Shi, Tiantao (2006a). 'Xin Gongsifa Shifei Pingshuo: Ba, Er Fen Gongguo' [Right or Wrong about the New Company Law: 80 Percent Success, 20 Percent Failure]. Beijing: Law Press China.

SSE–SWSC Joint Research Group (2011). 'Woguo Shangshi Gongsi Binggou Chongzu Falu Zhidu Yanjiu' [A Research Report on How to Improve the Legal Institutions on Takeover and Reorganization of Listed Companies in China]. Shanghai: Shanghai Stock Exchange.

SPC Civil Division II (Civil Division II of the Supreme Peoples' Court) (2006). *Zuigao Renmin Fayuan MinShang Shenpan Yao'an Jingxi* [*Supreme People's Court Analysis of Certain Important Civil and Commercial Cases*.] Beijing: The People's Court Press.

SPC Civil Division II (Civil Division II of the Supreme Peoples' Court) (2008). *Zuigao Renmin Fayuan Guanyu Gongsifa Sifa Jieshi I, II Lijie yu Shiyong* [*Understanding and Applying the Judicial Interpretations I and II of the Company Law by the Supreme People's Court*]. Beijing: The People's Court Press.

SPC Civil Division II (Civil Division II of the Supreme Peoples' Court) (2011). *Zuigao Renmin Fayuan Guanyu Gongsifa Jieshi III, Qingsuan Jiyao Lijie yu Shiyong* [*Understanding and Applying the Judicial Interpretation III of the Company Law and the Conference Minutes on Company Liquidation*]. Beijing: The People's Court Press.

SPC Civil Division II (Civil Division II of the Supreme Peoples' Court) (2011a). *Zuigao Renmin Fayuan Shangshi Shenpan Zhidao Anli: Gongsi Juan* [*Supreme People's Court Guiding Cases: Corporations*]. Beijing: China Legal Publishing House.

United Securities and Fudan University Task Force (2004). 'Woguo Shangshi Gongsi IPO Zhidu Chuangxin Yanjiu' [Innovations in the IPO System in China]. Report No. 11, Shanghai Stock Exchange United Research Project, July 2004, available at http://www.sse.com.cn.

Wang, Baoshu (2007), 'Xiuding Gongsifa, Xiang Xiandai Gongsifa Maijin' [Chinese Company Law Heads for Modernization in the Course of Reform], in She Sibao (ed.), *Zhongguo Touzi Falu Zhinan* [*Legal Aspects of Doing Business in China (II)*]. Beijing: University of International Business and Economics Press.

Wang, Jun (2011). 'Gongsi Jingyingzhe Zhongshi he Qinmian Yiwu Susong Yanjiu – Yi 14 Sheng, Zhixiashi de 137 Jian Panjueshu Wei Yangben' [Empirical Research on the Lawsuits on Corporate Fiduciary Duties – Based on 137 Court Decisions in 14 Provinces and Municipalities], 5:4 *Beifang Faxue* [*Northern Law Review*] 24–38.

Wang, Liming (ed.) (2004). *Minfa Xue* [The Science of Civil Law]. Shanghai: Fudan University Press.

Wang, Liming (ed.) (2010). *Minfa* (Di Wu Ban) [*Civil Law* (5th ed)]. Beijing: Renmin University Press.

Wang Wenjie (ed.) (2006). *Yuedan Minshangfa Yanjiu: Zuixin Liang'an Gongsifa Yu Zhengquanfa Pingxi* [*Yuedan Research on Civil and Commercial Law: Analyses of the Corporate and Securities Laws in Taiwan and Mainland China*]. Beijing: Tsinghua University Press.

Wang, Xinxin (2008). *Gongsifa* [*Company Law*]. Beijing: Renmin University Press.

Wang, Xinxin (2011). *Pochan Fa* (Di San Ban) [*Bankruptcy Law* (3rd ed.)]. Beijing: Renmin University Press.

Wang, Yong *et al.* (2005). 'Gongsifa Xiugai Sanren Tan' [Three Persons' Dialogue on the Company Law's Revision], in Zhao Xudong (ed.) (2005), 3 *Gongsifa Pinglun* [*Corporation Law Review*] 163–95.

Wang, Zhenmin and Wu Ge (eds.) (2011). *Gongsi Guquan: Zhidao Anli yu Shenpan Yiju* [*Corporate Equity Interests: Guiding Cases and Trial Criteria*]. Beijing: Law Press China.

Wen, Yan (2005). 'Zhongguo Gongsi Fa Bainian' [A Hundred Years' History of China's Company Law], in Zhao Xudong (ed.), 4 *Gongsi Fa Pinglun* [*Corporation Law Review*] 119–129.

Wu, Qingbao (2010). *QuanWei Dianping Zuigao Fayuan Gongsifa Zhidao Anli* [*Authoritative Commentaries on the Guiding Corporate Law Cases by the Supreme People's Court*]. Beijing: China Legal Publishing House.

Xi, Xiaoming and Jin Jianfeng (2008). *Gongsi Susong: Lilun yu Shiwu Wenti Yanjiu* [*Corporate Litigation: Theory and Practices*]. Beijing: People's Court Press.

Xie, Chaobin (2004). *Duli Dongshi Falv Zhidu Yanjiu* [A Study of the Independent Director System]. Beijing: Law Press China.

Xing, Haibao (2010). *Zhengquan Faxue Yuanli Yu Anli JiaoCheng* [*Teaching Book for Securities Law Theory and Cases*]. Beijing: Renmin University Press.

Yang, Chao and Fan, Qinghua (2004). 'Duli Dongshi: Huaping Suile' [Independent Directors: The Vase was Broken] 9 *Zhongwai Guanli* [*Sino-Foreign Management*] 16–18.

Yao, Hong (2007). *Zhonghua Renmin Gongheguo Minshi Susongfa Shiyi* [*Annotations to the Civil Procedure Law of the People's Republic of China*]. Beijing: Law Press China.

Zhang, Minan (2003), 'Gongsi Sheli Zhidu Yanjiu' [A Study on the System of Company Formation], 1 *Jilin University Journal of Social Science Edition* 58–64.

Zhao, Xudong (2005). *Xin Gongsi Fa Anli Jiedu* [*Understanding the New Company Law through Cases*]. Beijing: People's Court Press.

Zhao, Xudong (2006). *Gongsi Faxue* (Di Er Ban) [*Corporate Law Study* (2nd ed.)]. Beijing: Higher Education Press.

Zhang, Xuebing (2004). *Gongsifa Anli Xueli Jingjie* [Company Law: Cases and Jurisprudential Interpretations]. Beijing: China Economic Publishing House.

Zhou, Yousu (2006). *Xin Gongsi Fa Lun* [*New Survey on Corporation Law*]. Beijing: Law Press China.

Zhu, Ciyun (1998). *Gongsifa Renge Fouren Fali Yanjiu* [*A Study on the Disregard of Personality in Corporate Law*]. Beijing: Law Press China.

Index